Readings in Juvenile Justice Administration

READINGS IN CRIME AND PUNISHMENT
Michael Tonry, *General Editor*

What Works in Policing
David H. Bayley

Criminology at the Crossroads:
Feminist Readings in Crime and Justice
Kathleen Daly and Lisa Maher

Community Corrections:
Probation, Parole, and Intermediate Sanctions
Joan Petersilia

Incarcerating Criminals:
Prisons and Jails in Social and Organizational Context
Timothy J. Flanagan, James W. Marquart, and Kenneth G. Adams

Readings in Juvenile Justice Administration
Barry C. Feld

Readings in Juvenile Justice Administration

Edited by
Barry C. Feld
University of Minnesota

New York   Oxford
OXFORD UNIVERSITY PRESS

Oxford University Press

Oxford   New York
Athens   Auckland   Bangkok   Bogotá   Buenos Aires   Calcutta
Cape Town   Chennai   Dar es Salaam   Delhi   Florence   Hong Kong   Istanbul
Karachi   Kuala Lumpur   Madrid   Melbourne   Mexico City   Mumbai
Nairobi   Paris   São Paulo   Singapore   Taipei   Tokyo   Toronto   Warsaw

and associated companies in
Berlin   Ibadan

Copyright © 1999 by Oxford University Press, Inc.

Published by Oxford University Press, Inc.,
198 Madison Avenue, New York, New York 10016
http://www.oup-usa.org

Oxford is a registered trademark of Oxford University Press

Library of Congress Cataloging-in-Publication Data

Readings in juvenile justice administration / Barry C. Feld, [editor].
    p.   cm. — (Readings in crime and punishment)

ISBN 978-0-19-510405-9

    1. Juvenile justice, Administration of—United States.
    2. Juvenile courts—United States.   I. Feld, Barry C.   II. Series.
KF9779.A2R43   1999
345.73′05—DC21   98-21053
                                                                  CIP

Printed in the United States of America
on acid-free paper

Contents

Readings in Juvenile Justice Administration

Introduction

This reader examines the juvenile justice system. It focuses on the judicial, administrative, and correctional agencies used to control delinquent offenders, that is, youths charged with offenses that would be crimes if committed by adults. The various legal, criminological, and sociological articles focus primarily on juvenile justice administration and the processing of young offenders through the justice system, rather than juvenile delinquency. They provide information about youth crime and the various agencies to control young offenders. The readings address a broad range of policy issues concerning the juvenile justice system's responses to youth crime.

Although juvenile courts constitute a fixture of the justice system today, the idea of a separate justice system only for youths emerged about a century ago. Ideological changes in the cultural conception of children and in strategies of social control during the nineteenth century led progressive reformers to create the first juvenile court in Cook County, Illinois, in 1899. Throughout most of human history, people regarded children as miniature adults, smaller versions of their parents, and age provided neither a basis for a separate legal status nor for social segregation. By the end of the nineteenth century, however, adults increasingly viewed children as vulnerable, innocent, passive, and dependent beings who needed extended preparation for life. Similarly, changes in ideological assumptions about the causes of crime inspired many Progressive criminal justice reforms. Although classical criminal law attributed crime to free-willed actors, positivist criminology regarded crime as determined rather than chosen. Criminology's attempt to identify the antecedent causes of criminal behavior reduced the actors' moral responsibility and focused on reforming offenders rather than punishing them for their offenses. Applying medical analogies to the treatment of offenders, a growing class of social science professionals fostered the "reha-

1

bilitative ideal." At the dawn of the twentieth century, Progressive reformers applied the new theories of social control to the new ideas about childhood and created a social welfare alternative to criminal courts to treat criminal and noncriminal misconduct by youths.

The Progressives situated the juvenile court on a number of cultural and criminological fault-lines and institutionalized several binary conceptions for the respective justice systems: either child or adult, either determinism or free will, either treatment or punishment, either procedural informality or formality, either discretion or the rule of law. Many of the recent changes in juvenile courts' procedures and sentencing practices represent efforts to modify the Progressives' bifurcation between these competing conceptions of children and crime control.

The Supreme Court's decision *In re Gault* in 1967, began to transform the juvenile court into a very different institution than the Progressives contemplated. Progressives envisioned an informal court whose dispositions reflected the "best interests" of the child. In *Gault*, the Supreme Court engrafted formal trial procedures onto the juvenile court's individualized treatment sentencing scheme. *Gault* provided unintended impetus to convert the juvenile court from an informal welfare agency into a scaled-down criminal court for young offenders. Although the Court did not intend to alter the juvenile court's therapeutic mission, in the past three decades, legislative, judicial, and administrative responses to *Gault* have modified the court's jurisdiction, purpose, and procedures. As a result, today juvenile courts increasingly converge procedurally and substantively with adult criminal courts.

The articles reflect the historical origins and more recent transformation of the juvenile justice system. Chapter 1 includes articles on the origins of the juvenile court. Chapter 2 includes articles on the overall structure of the juvenile justice process and the screening and selection of youths for formal or informal processing in the juvenile justice system. These selections illustrate the variability of juvenile courts, "justice by geography," and the impact of social context on juvenile justice administration.

Chapter 3 examines the procedural formalization of juvenile courts and the quality of justice available to youths in the aftermath of *Gault*. Theoretically, juvenile courts' procedural safeguards closely resemble those of criminal courts; the Constitution and states' laws entitle delinquents to formal trials and the assistance of counsel. In actuality, the quality of procedural justice young people receive may be far different. The articles in this section compare and contrast the "law on the books" and the "law in action." Although in principle juvenile courts' procedural safeguards closely resemble those of criminal courts, in practice, the procedural justice routinely afforded juveniles may be far less than the minimum insisted upon for adults.

Ironically, within the past three decades the increased procedural formality mandated by *Gault* also served to legitimate the imposition of more punitive sanctions in juvenile courts. The articles in Chapters 4 and 5 analyze jurisdictional and jurisprudential reforms in the contemporary juvenile justice system in the wake of the "constitutional domestication" of the juvenile court. Chapter 4 examines jurisdictional changes at the "hard-end" of juvenile courts' clientele and the criminalizing of serious juvenile offenders. Transfer or waiver of juvenile court jurisdiction defines the boundary between delinquents and criminals, between children and adults, between treatment and punishment. In the wake of recent increases in some serious youth crime, courts and legislatures increasingly transfer some youths from juvenile courts to criminal courts for prosecution as adults. The various articles examine the processes by which legislators, prosecutors, and judges decide whether to process a youth as a delinquent or a criminal.

The articles in Chapter 5 analyze various aspects of the sentencing of delinquents charged with crimes. As juvenile courts' jurisdiction contracts with the waiver of serious offenders and removal of noncriminal status offenders, the sentences that delinquents receive increasingly reflect the idea of just deserts rather than the child's "real needs." Proportional and determinate sentences based on the present offense and prior record, rather than the "best interests" of the child, dictate the length, location, and intensity of intervention. Because the idea of "rehabilitation" provides a primary rationale for a separate juvenile justice system, the articles focus on the meaning and effectiveness of intervention.

These jurisdictional and jurisprudential changes—"decriminalization" of status offenders, waiver of serious offenders for adult prosecution, and increased punishment of delinquents—constitute a form of criminological "triage" in juvenile justice administration. As juvenile courts converge procedurally and substantively with criminal courts, does any reason remain to maintain a separate justice system whose only distinctions are procedures under which no adult would agree to be tried? Chapter 6 contains excerpts from the current policy debate about the future of the juvenile court as an institution. If juvenile courts constitute little more than scaled-down second-class criminal courts for young offenders, should they be retained? If so, then how should they be reformed? How should a system of social control for young people differ from that for adult offenders? If the dilemma of juvenile justice is the conundrum posed because the child is a criminal and the criminal is a child, can the legal system resolve it?

Three overarching themes emerge in our analyses of the systems of social control for youths. The first concerns the procedural and substantive implications of a justice system that nominally "treats" and "rehabilitates" rather than "punishes" or "incapacitates" young offenders. What are the theoretical and practical differences between helping and hurting, and how are these differences reflected in the operation and administration of the legal process? The second theme explores the consequences of regulating children rather than adults. To what extent do physical, psychological, or socioeconomic characteristics of young people require modifications of legal doctrines originally developed in the criminal law for presumptively competent adult actors? How should the legal process resolve the tension posed when the child is a criminal and the criminal is a child? The third theme contrasts the treatment of children with the punishment of adults, and the resulting tensions between a system that emphasizes discretion and one predicated on the rule of law. The issue of racial disparities in juvenile justice administration serves to highlight linkages between an individualized treatment ideology, discretionary decision making, and disparate racial outcomes. Can a juvenile court be a "real" court? And if it becomes a "real" criminal court, can it retain the unique features, flexibility, and informality that historically characterized it?

I have selected articles that illuminate the substantive policy debate, represent competing resolutions to the problems posed by young offenders, and provide examples of methodological or empirical strategies to advance the policy debates. In the interests of space-economy and readability, I have edited many of the articles extensively, deleted all citations, references, and footnotes, and eliminated most statistical tables as well. I hope that the reader will come away from these excerpts with an appreciation of the complexity and diversity of youth crime, emerging trends and issues in juvenile justice administration, and the breadth of the debate about juvenile justice and public policies.

CHAPTER 1

Origins of the Juvenile Court

By the end of the nineteenth century, America changed from a rural, agrarian society into an urban, industrial one. Between 1870 and World War I, railroads fostered economic growth, changed the processes of manufacturing, and ushered in a period of rapid social and economic modernization. Traditional social patterns faced new challenges as immigrants, primarily from southern and eastern Europe, and rural America, flooded into the burgeoning cities to take advantage of new economic opportunities. The "new" European immigrants differed in language, religion, political heritage, and culture from the dominant Anglo-Protestant Americans who had preceded them.

Economic modernization during the nineteenth century brought with it changes in family structure, altered the function of the family in society, and fostered a new cultural conception of childhood. Families became more private, women's roles more domestic, and childhood and adolescence emerged as distinct developmental stages. Especially within the upper and middle classes, a more modern conception of childhood appeared which conceived of children as corruptible innocents whose upbringing required greater physical, social, and moral structure than had previously been regarded as prerequisite to adulthood.

The social and economic changes associated with modernization and industrialization sparked the Progressive Movement. Progressivism encompassed a host of ideologies and addressed issues ranging from economic regulation to criminal justice and social and political reform. Progressives believed that benevolent state action guided by experts could alleviate social ills; they created a variety of state agencies to inculcate their middle-class values and to assimilate and "Americanize" immigrants and the poor to become virtuous citizens like themselves. The Progressives' trust of state power coupled with the changing cultural conception of children and child rearing led them into the realm of "child saving"; many Progressive programs shared a child-centered theme. Progressives' policies, embodied in juvenile court legislation, child labor laws, child welfare laws, and compulsory school attendance laws, both reflected and advanced the changing cultural conception of childhood.

Changes in ideological assumptions about human behavior and the causes of crime and deviance led Progressives to new views on criminal justice and social control policies. Positivism—the effort to identify the various factors that cause crime and deviance—challenged the classic formulations of crime as the product of conscious free-will choices. Positive criminology, as distinguished from "free will," asserted a scientific determinism of deviance, sought to identify the causal variables producing crime and delinquency, and informed many Progressive criminal justice reforms. By attributing criminal behavior to external forces rather than to a deliberate "evil" choice, Progressives reduced an actor's moral responsibility for crime and focused on efforts to reform rather than punish the offender. The Progressives introduced a variety of criminal justice reforms at the turn of the century—probation, parole, indeterminate sentences, and the juvenile court—all of which emphasized open-ended, informal, and highly flexible policies to rehabilitate deviants.

Progressive reformers combined the new strategies of social control with the new social construction of childhood to create a social welfare alternative to criminal courts to control the criminal and noncriminal misconduct of youth. The juvenile court movement attempted to remove children from the adult criminal justice and corrections systems, and provide them with individualized treatment in a separate system. The legal doctrine of *parens patriae*, the state as parent, legitimated governmental intervention, and juvenile courts emphasized treatment, supervision, and control rather than punishment. The *parens patriae* doctrine drew no distinction between criminal and noncriminal conduct, supported the Progressive position that juvenile court proceedings were civil rather than criminal in nature, and allowed the State wider discretion to intervene in the lives of young offenders. Because the reformers eschewed punishment, through the juvenile court's "status jurisdiction," they could respond to noncriminal misbehavior such as smoking, sexual activity, truancy, immorality, or living a wayward, idle, and dissolute life—activities that previously might have been ignored but that the Progressives wished to end because such activities betokened premature adulthood.

In separating child from adult offenders, the juvenile court system also rejected the jurisprudence and procedure of adult criminal prosecutions. Reformers modified courtroom procedures to eliminate any implication of a criminal proceeding, introduced a euphemistic vocabulary, and employed a physically separate court building to avoid the stigma of adult prosecutions. Juvenile courts conducted confidential hearings, limited access to court records, and found children to be delinquent rather than guilty of committing a crime. Juvenile court proceedings concentrated on the child's background and welfare rather than the details surrounding the commission of a specific crime. Because the important issues involved the child's "real needs" and "best interests" rather than the commission of a specific crime, courts dispensed with juries, lawyers, rules of evidence, and formal procedures.

The "rehabilitative ideal," as implemented in the juvenile court, envisioned a specialized judge trained in social sciences and child development whose empathic qualities and insights would aid in making individualized dispositions. Reformers anticipated that juvenile court judges, assisted by social workers and probation officers, would investigate the problematic child's background, identify the sources of the misconduct at issue, and develop a treatment plan to meet the child's needs. Juvenile court personnel enjoyed enormous discretion to make dispositions in the child's "best interests." The overall inquiry about "real needs" accorded relatively minor significance to the offense the child committed; rather the court directed its attention first and foremost to the child's character and lifestyle. Indeterminate and nonproportional dispositions could continue for the duration of minority. The events that brought the child before the court affected neither the degree nor the duration of intervention, because each child's needs differed and no limits could be defined in advance.

The articles selected for this introductory section provide various pieces of the puzzle of the origins of the juvenile court. Janet Ainsworth's "Reimagining Childhood" introduces the important idea of "childhood" as a "social construct" rather than an invariant attribute of young people. She analyzes the relationship between the Progressives' conception of childhood and the characteristics of the juvenile court. Judge Julian Mack, one of the original architects of the juvenile court, portrayed the juvenile court as an important legal innovation to meet the need of young people. His essay, "The Juvenile Court," written in 1909, provides one of the most systematic analyses of the juvenile court as seen by those Progressive reformers who helped to create it. Anthony Platt's seminal study of the origins of the Cook County, Illinois, juvenile court in *The Childsavers: The Invention of Delinquency* (1969), challenged the Progressives' contention that juvenile courts constituted humanitarian attempts to save poor and immigrant children. Rather, he presented the revisionist thesis that juvenile courts reflected the efforts of the nativist elites to expand state social control over threatening lower-class and immigrant youths. In "The Triumph of Benevolence," he further elaborates that the social control of youth constituted part of a larger strategy of elite and corporate interests to rationalize the economy, preserve existing power and privilege, and maintain social order. These excerpts raise the issues of the differences between children and adults, between a justice system that emphasizes treatment rather than punishment, and between a legal process in which "benevolent discretion" and the rule of law prevail.

Re-imagining Childhood and Reconstructing the Legal Order: The Case for Abolishing the Juvenile Court

JANET E. AINSWORTH

Juvenile courts exist in all fifty states of the United States and the District of Columbia, as well as in virtually all of the industrialized nations of the world. So ubiquitous is the institution of the juvenile court in the contemporary world that one easily might forget that it did not always exist. In fact, the juvenile court is a relatively recent invention. . . .

II. THE INVENTION OF CHILDHOOD

The choice of the word "invention" for this subheading is meant to be subtly jarring. After all, it is human creations which ordinarily are said to be "invented," whereas aspects of the natural world are said to be "discovered." By calling childhood an invention, I am suggesting that childhood is better seen as a social fact than as a biological one. . . .

B. The Social Construction of Childhood and Adolescence

It is one thing to recognize that aspects of society such as parliamentary democracy, the exclusionary rule, and rugged individualism are socially contingent artifacts, but perhaps harder to accept that the life-stage we call "childhood" is likewise a culturally and historically situated social construction. Of course, infants and young children are physiologically and psychologically different from older youths and adults; these differences undoubtedly persist across time and place. As anthropologist Ruth Benedict once observed, however, "The facts of nature are 'doctored' in different ways by different cultures." Human biology may set the outside limits on our social definition of ourselves, but, since biological constructs are themselves human artifacts, social reality constrains what we imagine to be biological necessity as well.

Social definitions of reality determine which biological attributes will be considered authentic, meaningful, and constituent of identity, and which will be trivialized, ignored, suppressed, or even explicitly denied. For example, the biological differences between human males and females might seem to be an obvious instance where immutable biology invariably overrides any of

Excerpted from *North Carolina Law Review*, vol. 69, pp. 1083–1100. © 1991 North Carolina Law Review Association.

society's attempts to deny or evade its constraints. No human society, one might think, could define males as the producers of young in light of the inescapable biological fact that males cannot give birth. Yet for many years, Western natural science actually did credit males with creating the fetus without any contribution from the female; scientists even "observed" tiny homunculi when they examined sperm under primitive microscopes. More generally, much research in psychology, sociology, and anthropology, as well as feminist theory, confirms the socially constructed nature of gender identity and much of what are often assumed to be natural gender characteristics.

Similarly, the socially constructed aspects of human life-stages such as childhood and adolescence far outweigh their invariant biological attributes. The number of stages into which an individual's life is divided and the essential qualities deemed characteristic of each stage in the life-cycle have varied over time and across cultures. Indeed, the very concept that human lives pass through life-stages with distinct characteristics has not always held the social and legal significance that it does in the contemporary West.

The definition of childhood—who is classified as a child, and what emotional, intellectual, and moral properties children are assumed to possess— has changed over time in response to changes in other facets of society. Historian Philippe Aries first pointed out the dramatic contrast between the modern Western conception of childhood and the conception held in the medieval European world. As he observed, "In medieval society, the idea of childhood did not exist. . . . [The] awareness of the particular nature of childhood . . . which distinguishes the child from the adult . . . was lacking." At that time, the primary age-based boundary was drawn between infancy, a time of physical dependence ending roughly at age seven, and full personhood. Those persons older than seven, especially those in the lower social classes, participated in the normal range of adult activities: they were apprenticed to begin their working lives, drank in taverns, shared the same games and amusements as adults, gambled, and were exposed to sexual behavior and jokes. Wearing the same kind of clothing, these young people even looked like adults. Not surprisingly, then, medieval art depicted them as miniature adults. In short, within the medieval world, the young were fully integrated members of the community. No one believed that young people were innocent beings who needed to be quarantined from a harsh adult world.

In later centuries, the period between the end of infancy and sexual maturity was redefined as a discrete stage in human development. Two seemingly contradictory strands of Western thought gave rise to this refiguration of childhood. On the one hand, the Calvinist doctrine of infant depravity characterized the young as inherently sinful and doomed to spiritual death absent coercive discipline by adults. In contrast, Enlightenment philosophy and the later romanticism of Rousseau saw children as innately innocent beings whose potential should be nurtured by parents without corrupting their natural goodness. What both of these conceptions of childhood shared, however, in contrast to the earlier medieval construction, was the belief that children are essentially *different* from adults and that one aspect of that difference is their intrinsic malleability.

The late nineteenth and early twentieth centuries saw an extension of this dramatic reconstruction of childhood. In the academy, experts dedicating their scholarship to the study of the child placed great emphasis on how inherently and essentially different children are from adults. The so-called "child-study" movement was predicated on the belief that childhood is composed of stages, each with characteristic emotions, capacities and needs. Appropriating from the theory of evolution the slogan "ontogeny recapitulates phylogeny," proponents of child study now had a model justifying scholarly focus on childhood. Because they believed that the chronological development of the individual human echoes the historical development of human civilization, studying childhood was thought to provide a window on the otherwise unknowable human past. By the same token, child study proponents reasoned, what society knew of the past would teach it how best to socialize the young.

As this "child-study" movement gained momentum, prominent universities such as Harvard, Yale and Princeton rushed to set up departments of child development. In medicine, the perception of the uniqueness of childhood led to the birth of pediatrics and the founding of specialized children's hospitals. On the political front, Congress, in 1912, passed a federal bill to establish a special Children's Bureau within the Cabinet Department of Commerce and Labor.

At the same time that academic and governmental attention was focusing on childhood, the temporal contours of childhood were extended through the creation of a new stage of preadulthood—adolescence. Although the word "adolescence" was not actually invented during this period, the term rarely was used prior to the late nineteenth century, and little or no attention paid to any special characteristics that teenagers might have. By the turn of the century, the attributes of childhood were being applied to teenagers, who only a generation earlier would not have been distinguished from older adults. Since as children they were assumed to be vulnerable, malleable, and in need of adult guidance, training, and control before they could graduate to full personhood, adolescents now became targets of paternal adult attention. Compulsory school attendance laws, which earlier had been ignored in those few jurisdictions that enacted them, were passed in state legislatures and were increasingly enforced. Between 1900 and 1930, the number of high school graduates increased 600 percent. At the same time, legislatures promulgated child labor laws establishing a minimum age for workers, limiting the hours that could be worked, and regulating the conditions of employment. As a result, the number of people between the ages of ten and fifteen who were gainfully employed declined seventy-five percent from 1910 to 1930. The minimum age for marriage was raised to discourage early marrying. The consequences of this spate of law reform prolonged the economic dependence of adolescents, increased the amount of age stratification in society, and established a greater degree of formal social control over the young than had existed previously.

III. THE INVENTION OF ADOLESCENCE AND THE IDEOLOGY OF JUVENILE COURT

Among all of the law reforms adopted during the Progressive Era to accommodate the new perception of the adolescent's nature and needs, the creation of the juvenile court undoubtedly ranks as the most far-reaching achievement. The rapidity with which the concept spread is striking. In 1899, Illinois passed the Juvenile Court Act, founding a juvenile system widely acknowledged at the time as the model for other states to follow. And follow they did; within twenty years all but three states had similar juvenile justice systems in place.

The desirability, even necessity, for a separate court system to address the problems of young people appeared obvious, given the newly emerging view of the adolescent as an immature creature in need of adult control. When parental control failed, the benevolent, if coercive, hand of the state could provide the corrective molding needed by the errant youth. By categorizing the adolescent as a sub-class of the child rather than as a type of adult, the Progressives fashioned a discrete juvenile justice system premised upon the belief that, like other children, adolescents are not morally accountable for their behavior. Thus, ordinary retributive punishment for the adolescent would be inappropriate. The Progressives treated lawbreaking by juveniles as a symptom justifying, in fact humanely requiring, state intervention to save them from a life of crime that might otherwise be their fate.

The allusion to medical treatment suggested by the word "symptom" is not accidental; the Progressives frequently compared social deviance to physical disease. Although Progressive ideology entertained an eclectic set of conflicting notions about the causes of deviant behavior, including physiological, genetic, and environmental theories, the belief that criminal behavior was caused by unwholesome environment, especially the baneful influence of squalid urban life, came to dominate correctional thinking. Juvenile misbehavior was seen as merely the overt manifestation of underlying social pathology. Like physical pathology, social pathology could not be ignored or the "disease" might progressively worsen. With proper diagnosis and treatment, however, social pathology was considered as susceptible to cure as physical ailments. Particularly in light of the supposedly malleable nature of juveniles, the Progressives exuded confidence in their ability to cure juvenile delinquency.

The juvenile court movement gained momentum from the proselytizing efforts of some of its early judges. In stump speeches to civic groups, in editorials in the popular press, and in articles in professional journals, these advocates of the new juvenile court system tirelessly promoted the redemptive message embodied in juvenile court ideology. One such advocate, Judge Julian Mack, attributed the necessity for a separate juvenile court system to its exclusive concern for the social rehabilitation of needy youths. In contrast, criminal courts focused on the judgment of whether the accused had violated the law and if so, what penalty was warranted. He wrote, "The problem for determination by the judge is not, Has this boy or girl committed a specific wrong, but What is he, how has he become what he is, and what had best be done in his interest and in the interest of the state to save him from a downward career." To the advocates of the juvenile court, the essential difference between the moral and cognitive capacities of the juvenile and those of the adult did not serve merely to mitigate juvenile culpability for breaking the law, but to absolve the juvenile completely from criminal liability.

Juvenile court philosophy made no distinction between criminal and noncriminal behavior, as long as the behavior was considered deviant or inappropriate to the age of the juvenile. Behavior such as smoking, sexual activity, stubbornness, running away from home, swearing, and truancy could trigger juvenile court jurisdiction as validly as could breaking a criminal law. Because the child was not being punished, but rather protected by the state, juvenile court had a mandate to assume liberal jurisdiction over the wayward young, much as it might over other helpless and needy members of society. The idea that the peculiar vulnerability of children justified state control over them was analogized to the well-established chancery court principle, *parens patriae*, which gave the state authority over parentless children. Invoking a chancery court pedigree for juvenile court jurisdiction, the *parens patriae* doctrine lent legitimacy to the new court system while it obscured the extent to which juvenile court marked an unprecedented expansion of state social control over adolescents.

Every aspect of the *parens patriae* juvenile court was designed to mold wayward youths into good citizens. The hallmark of the system was its disposition, individually tailored to address the needs and abilities of the juvenile in question. To that end, judges were given almost limitless discretion in crafting the disposition to facilitate whatever the judge thought would "cure" the youth. Juveniles could be put on probation until their majority, giving the juvenile court total control over every aspect of the probationer's life. If the juvenile was incarcerated in a juvenile detention facility, the commitment would be for an indeterminate period, because the judge could not perfectly predict in advance the amenability of the youth to rehabilitative treatment. Once rehabilitated, the youth would be released from further court control, regardless of the seriousness of the offense that gave rise to juvenile court jurisdiction, because the court's basis for its disposition was treatment, not punitive sanction. Indeed, the juvenile court judge could, at least in theory, discharge the juvenile offender immediately after the dispositional hearing if the judge believed that the youth had no need for court-monitored treatment or services, even if the juvenile had committed a serious offense.

Some states deliberately eliminated the usual procedural formalities of criminal adjudication from juvenile court. These formalities were considered both unnecessary and undesirable: unnecessary because the role of the court was not to adjudicate guilt and punish, but to prescribe treatment; undesirable because informality itself was deemed a part of the rehabilitative process. For this reason, trial by jury was eliminated in most juvenile courts as irrelevant to the proper determination before the court, because the court was less concerned with factually determining whether the child had broken the law than with sensitively diagnosing and treating the child's social pathology. As the Pennsylvania Supreme Court observed, "Whether the child deserves to be saved by the state is no more a question for a jury than whether the father, if able to save it, ought to save it."

The object of what Judge Mack termed "not so much the power, as the friendly interest of the state" was invariably referred to as "the child," the "boy or girl" or "the lad." Calling teenaged lawbreakers "children" was not disingenuous rhetoric. Rather, it demonstrates that the social construction of adolescence as a species of childhood powerfully informed the ideology and practice of the *parens patriae* juvenile court. . . .

The Juvenile Court

JULIAN W. MACK

The past decade marks a revolution in the attitude of the state toward its offending children. . . . The problem of the delinquent child, though juristically comparatively simple, is, in its social significance, of the greatest importance, for upon its wise solution depends the future of many of the rising generation. The legal questions, while not complicated, have, nevertheless, given rise to some discussion and to some slight dissent from the standpoint of constitutional law.

The first thought which suggests itself in connection with the juvenile court is, What is there distinctively new about it? We are familiar with the conception that the state is the higher or the ultimate parent of all of the dependents within its borders. We know that, whatever may have been the historical origin of the practice, for over two centuries, as evidenced by judg-

Excerpted from 23 *Harvard Law Review* 104–122. Copyright © 1909 by The Harvard Law Review Association.

ments both of the House of Lords and of the Chancellors, the courts of chancery in England have exercised jurisdiction for the protection of the unfortunate child. . . .

Our common criminal law did not differentiate between the adult and the minor who had reached the age of criminal responsibility, seven at common law and in some of our states, ten in others, with a chance of escape up to twelve, if lacking in mental and moral maturity. The majesty and dignity of the state demanded vindication for infractions from both alike. The fundamental thought in our criminal jurisprudence was not, and in most jurisdictions is not, reformation of the criminal, but punishment; punishment as expiation for the wrong, punishment as a warning to other possible wrongdoers. The child was arrested, put into prison, indicted by the grand jury, tried by a petit jury, under all the forms and technicalities of our criminal law, with the aim of ascertaining whether it had done the specific act—nothing else—and if it had, then of visiting the punishment of the state upon it.

It is true that during the last century ameliorating influences mitigated the severity of the old regime; in the last fifty years our reformatories have played a great and very beneficent part in dealing with juvenile offenders. They supplanted the penitentiary. In them the endeavor was made, while punishing, to reform, to build up, to educate the prisoner so that when his time should have expired he could go out into the world capable at least of making an honest living. And in course of time, in some jurisdictions, the youths were separated from the older offenders even in stations, jails, and workhouses; but, nevertheless, generally in this country, the two classes were huddled together. The result of it all was that instead of the state's training its bad boys so as to make of them decent citizens, it permitted them to become the outlaws and outcasts of society; it criminalized them by the very methods that it used in dealing with them. It did not aim to find out what the accused's history was, what his heredity, his environments, his associations; it did not ask how he had come to do the particular act which had brought him before the court. It put but one question, "Has he committed this crime?" It did not inquire, "What is the best thing to do for this lad?" It did not even punish him in a manner that would tend to improve him; the punishment was visited in proportion to the degree of wrongdoing evidenced by the single act; not by the needs of the boy, not by the needs of the state.

To-day, however, the thinking public is putting another sort of question. Why is it not just and proper to treat these juvenile offenders, as we deal with the neglected children, as a wise and merciful father handles his own child whose errors are not discovered by the authorities? Why is it not the duty of the state, instead of asking merely whether a boy or a girl has committed a specific offense, to find out what he is, physically, mentally, morally, and then if it learns that he is treading the path that leads to criminality, to take him in charge, not so much to punish as to reform, not to degrade but to uplift, not to crush but to develop, not to make him a criminal but a worthy citizen.

And it is this thought—the thought that the child who has begun to go wrong, who is incorrigible, who has broken a law or an ordinance, is to be taken in hand by the state, not as an enemy but as a protector, as the ultimate guardian, because either the unwillingness or inability of the natural parents to guide it toward good citizenship has compelled the intervention of the public authorities; it is this principle, which . . . was first fully and clearly declared, in the Act under which the Juvenile Court of Cook County, Illinois, was opened in Chicago, on July 1, 1899, the Hon. R. S. Tuthill presiding. Colorado followed soon after, and since that time similar legislation has been adopted in over thirty American jurisdictions . . . .

But in Illinois, and following the lead of Illinois, in most jurisdictions, the form of procedure is totally different and wisely so. It would seem to be obvious that, if the common law could fix the age of criminal responsibility at seven, and if the legislature could advance that age to ten or twelve, it can also raise it to sixteen or seventeen or eighteen, and that is what, in some measure, has been done. Under most of the juvenile-court laws a child under the designated age is to be proceeded against as a criminal only when in the judgment of the judge of the juvenile court, either as to any child, or in some states as to one over fourteen or over sixteen years of age, the interests of the state and of the child require that this be done. . . .

To get away from the notion that the child is to be dealt with as a criminal; to save it from the brand of criminality, the brand that sticks to it for life; to take it in hand and instead of first stigmatizing and then reforming it, to protect it from the stigma,—this is the work which is now being accomplished by dealing even with most of the delinquent children through the court that represents the *parens patriae* power of the state, the court of chancery. Proceedings are brought to have a guardian or representative of the state appointed to look after the child, to have the state intervene between the natural parent and the child because the child needs it, as evidenced by some of its acts, and because the parent is either unwilling or unable to train the child properly.

Objection has been made from time to time that this is nevertheless a criminal proceeding, and that therefore the child is entitled to a trial by jury and to all the constitutional rights that hedge about the criminal.

The Supreme Courts of several states have well answered this objection. In *Commonwealth v. Fisher* the court says:

"To save a child from becoming a criminal, or from continuing in a career of crime, to end in maturer years in public punishment and disgrace, the legislature surely may provide for the salvation of such a child, if its parents or guardian be unable or unwilling to do so, by bringing it into one of the courts of the state without any process at all, for the purpose of subjecting it to the state's guardianship and protection.

"The action is not for the trial of a child charged with a crime, but is mercifully to save it from such an ordeal, with the prison or penitentiary in its wake, if the child's own good and the best interests of the state justify such salvation. Whether the child deserves to be saved by the state is no more a question for a jury than whether the father, if able to save it, ought to save it. The act is but an exercise by the state of its supreme power over the welfare of its children, a power under which it can take a child from its father, and let it go where it will, without committing it to any guardianship or any institution, if the welfare of the child, taking its age into consideration, can be thus best promoted.

"The design is not punishment, nor the restraint imprisonment, any more than is the wholesome restraint which a parent exercises over his child. The severity in either case must necessarily be tempered to meet the necessities of the particular situation. There is no probability, in the proper administration of the law, of the child's liberty being unduly invaded. Every statute which is designed to give protection, care, and training to children, as a needed substitute for parental authority, and performance of parental duty, is but a recognition of the duty of the state, as the legitimate guardian and protector of children where other guardianship fails. No constitutional right is violated." . . .

Years ago, in [*Ex parte* Crouse] considering the power of the court to send a child to the House of Refuge, Chief Justice Gibson said:

"May not the natural parents, when unequal to the task of education, or unworthy of it, be superseded by the *parens patriae*, or common guardian of the community? It is to be remembered that the public has a paramount interest in the virtue and knowledge of its members, and that of strict right the business of education belongs to it. That parents are ordinarily entrusted with it, is because it can seldom be put in better hands; but where they are incompetent or corrupt, what is there to prevent the public from withdrawing their faculties, held as they obviously are, at its sufferance? The right of parental control is a natural, but not an inalienable one. It is not excepted by the declaration of rights out of the subject of ordinary legislation."

Care must, however, be taken not to provide for dealing with the child as a criminal. . . .

It is, therefore, important to provide, as has been done in the most recent statutes, but as was not done in the earlier acts, that the parents be made parties to the proceedings, and that they be given an opportunity to be heard therein in defense of their parental rights. . . .

One more legal question remains. . . . [T]the Supreme Court of Illinois, in *People ex rel. v. Turner*, released a child from the reformatory on the ground that the reformatory was a prison; that incarceration therein was necessarily punishment for a crime, and that such a punishment could be inflicted only after criminal proceedings conducted with due regard to the constitutional rights of the defendant. Whether the criticism be just or not, the case suggests a real truth, and one which, in the enthusiastic progress of the juvenile-court movement, is in danger of being overlooked. If a child must be taken away from its home, if for the natural parental care that of the state is to be substituted, a real school, not a prison in disguise, must be provided. Whether the institutional life be only temporary until a foster home can be found, or for a longer period until the child can be restored to its own home or be given its complete freedom, the state must, both to avoid the constitutional objections suggested by the Turner case, and in fulfillment of its moral obligation to the child, furnish the proper care. This cannot be done in one great building, with a single dormitory for all of the two or three or four hundred or more children, in which there will be no possibility of classification along the lines of age or degrees of delinquency, in which there will be no individualized attention. What is needed is a large area, preferably in the country,—because these children require the fresh air and contact with the soil even more than does the normal child,—laid out on the cottage plan, giving opportunity for family life, and in each cottage some good man and woman who will live with and for the children. Locks and bars and other indicia of prisons must be avoided; human love, supplemented by human interest and vigilance, must replace them. In such schools there must be opportunity for agricultural and industrial training, so that when the boys and girls come out, they will be fitted to do a man's or woman's work in the world, and not be merely a helpless lot, drifting aimlessly about.

Some states have begun to supply this need. But despite the great ultimate financial saving to the state through this method of dealing with children, a saving represented by the value of a decent citizen as against a criminal, the public authorities are nowhere fully alive to the new obligations that the spirit as well as the letter of this legislation imposes upon them. . . .

Private philanthropy has supplemented, and doubtless in the future will supplement the work of the state in providing for the delinquents. To a large extent it is denominational, though many organizations are non-sectarian. None have accomplished more good or give promise of greater continued usefulness than the George Junior Republics and similar organizations that stand for self-government, self-reliance, and redemption through honest labor. . . .

To these, however, should be added, as the fourth principle, that taking a child away from its parents and sending it even to, an industrial school is, as far as possible, to be avoided; and . . . when it is allowed to return home, it must be under probation, subject to the guidance and friendly interest of the probation officer, the representative of the court. To raise the age of criminal responsibility from seven or ten to sixteen or eighteen, without providing for an efficient system of probation, would indeed be disastrous. Probation is, in fact, the keynote of juvenile-court legislation.

But even in this there is nothing radically new. Massachusetts has had probation, not only in the case of minors, but even in the case of adults, for nearly forty years, and several other states now have provisions for the suspension of a criminal sentence in the case of adults, permitting the defendant to go free, but subject to the control of a probation officer. Wherever juvenile courts have been established, a system of probation has been provided for, and even where as yet the juvenile-court system has not been fully developed, some steps have been taken to substitute probation for imprisonment of juvenile offenders.

Most of the children who come before the court are, naturally, the children of the poor. In many cases the parents are foreigners, frequently unable to speak English, and without an understanding of American methods and views. What they need, more than anything else, is kindly assistance; and the aim of the court, in appointing a probation officer for the child, is to have the child and the parents feel, not so much the power, as the friendly interest of the state; to show them that the object of the court is to help them to train the child right; and therefore the probation officers must be men and women fitted for these tasks.

Their duties are oftentimes of the most delicate nature. Tact, forbearance, and sympathy with the child, as well as a full appreciation of the difficulties that the poorer classes, and especially the immigrants, are confronted with in our large cities, are indispensable. . . .

The procedure and practice of the juvenile court is simple. In the first place the number of arrests is greatly decreased. The child and the parents are notified to appear in court, and unless the danger of escape is great, or the offense very serious, or the home totally unfit for the child, detention before hearing is unnecessary. Children are permitted to go on their own recognizance or that of their parents, or on giving bail. Probation officers should be and often are authorized to act in this respect. If, however, it becomes necessary to detain the children either before a hearing or pending a continuance, or even after the adjudication, before they can be admitted into the home or institution to which they are to be sent, they are no longer kept in prisons or jails, but in detention homes. In some states, the laws are mandatory that the local authorities provide such homes managed in accordance with the spirit of this legislation. These are feasible even in the smallest communities, inasmuch as the simplest kind of a building best meets the need.

The jurisdiction to hear the cases is generally granted to an existing court having full equity powers. In some cities, however, special courts have been provided, with judges devoting their entire time to this work. If these special courts can constitutionally be vested with full and complete chancery and criminal jurisdiction, much is to be said in favor of their establishment. In the large cities particularly the entire time of one judge may well be needed. It has been suggested from time to time that all of the judges of the municipal or special sessions courts be empowered to act in these cases, but while it would be valuable in metropolitan communities to have more than one detention home and court house, nevertheless it would seem to be even more important to have a single juvenile court judge. . . .

The personality of the judge is an all-important matter. . . . Because of the extent of his jurisdiction and the tremendous responsibility that it entails, it is . . . absolutely essential that he be a trained lawyer thoroughly imbued with the doctrine that ours is a "government of laws and not of men."

He must, however, be more than this. He must be a student of and deeply interested in the problems of philanthropy and child life, as well as a lover of children. He must be able to understand the boys' point of view and ideas of justice; he must be willing and patient enough to search out the underlying causes of the trouble and to formulate the plan by which, through the cooperation, ofttimes, of many agencies, the cure may be effected.

In some very important jurisdictions the vicious practice is indulged in of assigning a different judge to the juvenile-court work every month or every three months. It is impossible for these judges to gain the necessary experience or to devote the necessary time to the study of new problems. The service should under no circumstances be for less than one year, and preferably for a longer period. In some of our cities, notably in Denver, the judge has discharged not only the judicial functions, but also those of the most efficient probation officer. Judge Lindsey's love for the work and his personality has enabled him to exert a powerful influence on the boys and girls that are brought before him. While doubtless the best results can be obtained in such a court, lack of time would prevent a judge in the largest cities from adding this work to his strictly judicial duties, even were it not extremely difficult to find the necessary combination of elements in one man.

The problem for determination by the judge is not, Has this boy or girl committed a specific wrong, but What is he, how has he become what he is, and what had best be done in his interest and in the interest of the state to save him from a downward career. It is apparent at once that the ordinary legal evidence in a criminal court is not the sort of evidence to be heard in such a proceeding. A thorough investigation, usually made by the probation officer, will give the court much information bearing on the heredity and environment of the child. This, of course, will be supplemented in every possible way; but this alone is not enough. The physical and mental condition of the child must be known, for the relation between physical defects and criminality is very close. It is, therefore, of the utmost importance that there be attached to the court, as has been done in a few cities, a child study department, where every child, before hearing, shall be subjected to a thorough psycho-physical examination. In hundreds of cases the discovery and remedy of defective eyesight or hearing or some slight surgical operation will effectuate a complete change in the character of the lad.

The child who must be brought into court should, of course, be made to know that he is face to face with the power of the state, but he should at the same time, and more emphatically, be made to feel that he is the object of its care and solicitude. The ordinary trappings of the court-room are out of place in such hearings. The judge on a bench, looking down upon the boy standing at the bar, can never evoke a proper sympathetic spirit. Seated at a desk, with the child at his side, where he can on occasion put his arm around his shoulder and draw the lad to him, the judge, while losing none of his judicial dignity, will gain immensely in the effectiveness of his work.

The object of the juvenile court and of the intervention of the state is, of course, in no case to lessen or to weaken the sense of responsibility either of the child or of the parent. On the contrary, the aim is to develop and to enforce it. Therefore it is wisely provided in most of the recent acts that the child may be compelled when on probation, if of working age, to make restitution for any damage done by it. Moreover, the parents may not only be compelled to contribute to the support even of the children who are taken away from them and sent to institutions, but following Colorado, in many states, they, as well as any other adults, may be made criminally liable for their acts or neglect contributing to a child's dependency or delinquency. In most of the jurisdictions which have established separate juvenile courts, as well as in some of the others, all criminal cases affecting children are tried by the juvenile-court judge. . . .

Valuable, however, as is the introduction of the juvenile court into our system of jurisprudence, valuable both in its effect upon the child, the parents, and the community at large, and in the great material saving to the state which the substitution of probation for imprisonment has brought about, nevertheless it is in no sense a cure-all. . . .

But more than this, the work of the juvenile court is, at the best, palliative, curative. The more important, indeed the vital thing, is to prevent the children from reaching that condition in which they have to be dealt with in any court, and we are not doing our duty to the children of today, the men and women of tomorrow, when we neglect to destroy the evils that are leading them into careers of delinquency, when we fail not merely to uproot the wrong, but to implant in place of it the positive good. It is to a study of the underlying causes of juvenile delinquency and to a realization of these preventive and positive measures that the trained professional men of the United States, following the splendid lead of many of their European brethren, should give some thought and some care. The work demands the united and aroused efforts of the whole community, bent on keeping children from becoming criminals, determined that those who are treading the downward path shall be halted and led back. . . .

The Triumph of Benevolence: The Origins of the Juvenile Justice System in the United States

Anthony Platt

TRADITIONAL PERSPECTIVES ON JUVENILE JUSTICE

The creation of the juvenile court and its accompanying services is generally regarded by scholars as one of the most innovative and idealistic products of the age of reform. It typified the "spirit of social justice," and, ac-

Excerpted from Richard Quinney, ed., *Criminal Justice in America* pp. 362–389, © 1974 Little, Brown and Company, assigned to Aspen Law & Business, a division of Aspen Publishers, Inc.

cording to the National Crime Commission, represented a progressive effort by concerned reformers to alleviate the miseries of urban life and to solve social problems by rational, enlightened and scientific methods. The juvenile justice system was widely heralded as "one of the greatest advances in child welfare that has ever occurred" and "an integral part of total welfare planning." ... Scholars from a variety of disciplines, such as the American sociologist George Herbert Mead and the German psychiatrist August Aichhorn, agreed that the juvenile court system represented a triumph of progressive liberalism over the forces of reaction and ignorance. More recently, the juvenile court and related reforms have been characterized as a "reflection of the humanitarianism that flowered in the last decades of the 19th century" and an indication of "America's great sense of philanthropy and private concern about the common weal."

Histories and accounts of the child-saving movement tend either to represent an "official" perspective or to imply a gradualist view of social progress. This latter view is typified in Robert Pickett's study of the House of Refuge movement in New York in the middle of the last century:

> In the earlier era, it had taken a band of largely religiously motivated humanitarians to see a need and move to meet that need. Although much of their vision eventually would be supplanted by more enlightened policies and techniques and far more elaborate support mechanisms, the main outlines of their program, which included mild discipline, academic and moral education, vocational training, the utilization of surrogate parents, and probationary surveillance, have stood the test of time. The survival of many of the notions of the founders of the House of Refuge testifies, at least in part, to their creative genius in meeting human needs. Their motivations may have been mixed and their oversights many, but their efforts contributed to a considerable advance in the care and treatment of wayward youth.

This view of the nineteenth century reform movement as fundamentally benevolent, humanitarian and gradualist is shared by most historians and criminologists who have written about the Progressive era. They argue that this reform impulse has its roots in the earliest ideals of modern liberalism and that it is part of a continuing struggle to overcome injustice and fulfill the promise of American life. At the same time, these writers recognize that reform movements often degenerate into crusades and suffer from excessive idealism and moral absolutism. The faults and limitations of the child-saving movement, for example, are generally explained in terms of the psychological tendency of its leaders to adopt attitudes of rigidity and moral righteousness. But this form of criticism is misleading because it overlooks larger political issues and depends too much on a subjective critique.

Although the Progressive era was a period of considerable change and reform in all areas of social, legal, political and economic life, its history has been garnished with various myths. Conventional historical analysis, typified by the work of American historians in the 1940s and 1950s, promoted the view that American history consisted of regular confrontations between vested economic interests and various popular reform movements. . . .

Conventional histories of progressivism argue that the reformers, who were for the most part drawn from the urban middle classes, were opposed to big business and felt victimized by the rapid changes in the economy, especially the emergence of the corporation as the dominant form of financial enterprise. Their reform efforts were aimed at curbing the power of big business, eliminating corruption from the urban political machines, and extending the powers of the state through federal regulation of the economy and the development of a vision of "social responsibility" in local government. They were joined in this mission by sectors of the working class who shared their alienation and many of their grievances. For liberal historians like Richard Hofstadter, this alliance represented part of a continuing theme in American politics:

> It has been the function of the liberal tradition in American politics, from the time of Jeffersonian democracy down through Populism, Progressivism, and the New Deal, at first to broaden the numbers of those who could benefit from the great American bonanza and then to humanize its workings and help heal its casualties. Without this sustained tradition of opposition and protest, and reform, the American system would have been, as in times and places it was, nothing but a jungle, and would probably have failed to develop into the remarkable system for production and distribution that it is.

The political and racial crises of the 1960s, however, provoked a reevaluation of this earlier view of the liberal tradition in American politics, a tradition which appeared bankrupt in the face of rising crime rates, ghetto rebellions, and widespread protests against the state and its agencies of criminal justice. In the field of criminology, this reevaluation took place in national commissions such as the Kerner Commission and President Johnson's Commission on Law Enforcement and the Administration of Justice. Johnson's Crime Commission, as it is known, included a lengthy and detailed analysis of the juvenile justice system and its ineffectiveness in dealing with juvenile delinquency.

The Crime Commission's view of the juvenile justice system is cautious and pragmatic, designed to "shore up" institutional deficiencies and modernize the system's efficiency and accountability. Noting the rising rate of juvenile delinquency, increasing disrespect for constituted authority and the failure of reformatories to rehabilitate offenders, the Commission attributes the failures of the juvenile justice system to the "grossly over optimistic" expectations of nineteenth century reformers and the "community's continuing unwillingness to provide the resources—the people and facilities and concern—necessary to permit [the juvenile courts] to realize their potential. . . ."

In the following pages we will argue that the above views and interpretations of juvenile justice are factually inaccurate and suffer from a serious misconception about the functions of modern liberalism. The prevailing myths about the juvenile justice system can be summarized as follows: (1) The child-saving movement in the late nineteenth century was successful in humanizing the criminal justice system, rescuing children from jails and prisons, developing humanitarian judicial and penal institutions for juveniles, and defending the poor against economic and political exploitation. (2) The child-savers were "disinterested" reformers, representing an enlightened and socially responsible urban middle class, and opposed to big business. (3) The failures of the juvenile justice system are attributable partly to the overoptimism and moral absolutism of earlier reformers and partly to bureaucratic inefficiency and a lack of fiscal resources and trained personnel.

These myths are grounded in a liberal conception of American history which characterizes the child-savers as part of a much larger reform movement directed at restraining the power of political and business elites. In contrast, we will offer evidence that the child-saving movement was a coercive and conservatizing influence, that liberalism in the Progressive era was the conscious product of policies initiated or supported by leaders of major corporations and financial institutions, and that many social reformers wanted to secure existing political and economic arrangements, albeit in an ameliorated and regulated form.

THE CHILD-SAVING MOVEMENT

Although the modern juvenile justice system can be traced in part to the development of various charitable and institutional programs in the early nineteenth century, it was not until the close of the century that the modern system was systematically organized to include juvenile courts, probation, child guidance clinics, truant officers, and reformatories. The child-saving movement—an amalgam of philanthropists, middle-class reformers and professionals—was responsible for the consolidation of these reforms.

The 1890s represented for many middle-class intellectuals and professionals a period of discovery of "dim attics and damp cellars in poverty-stricken sections of populous towns" and "innumerable haunts of misery throughout the land." The city was suddenly discovered to be a place of scarcity, disease, neglect, ignorance, and "dangerous influences." Its slums were the "last resorts of the penniless and the criminal"; here humanity reached the lowest level of degradation and despair. These conditions were not new to American urban life and the working class had been suffering such hardships for many years. . . .

What distinguished the late 1890s from earlier periods was the recognition by some sectors of the privileged classes that far-reaching economic, political and social reforms were desperately needed to restore order and stability. In the economy, these reforms were achieved through the corporation which extended its influence into all aspects of domestic and foreign policies so that by the 1940s some 139 corporations owned 45 percent of all the manufacturing assets in the country. It was the aim of corporate capitalists to limit traditional laissez-faire business competition and to transform the economy into a rational and interrelated system, characterized by extensive long-range planning and bureaucratic routine. In politics, these reforms were achieved nationally by extending the regulatory powers of the federal government and locally by the development of commission and city manager forms of government as an antidote to corrupt machine politics. In social life, economic and political reforms were paralleled by the construction of new social service bureaucracies which regulated crime, education, health, labor and welfare.

The child-saving movement tried to do for the criminal justice system what industrialists and corporate leaders were trying to do for the economy—that is, achieve order, stability and control while preserving the existing class system and distribution of wealth. While the child-saving movement, like most Progressive reforms, drew its most active and visible supporters from the middle class and professions, it would not have been capable of achieving significant reforms without the financial and political support of the wealthy and powerful. Such support was not without precedent in various philanthropic movements preceding the child-savers. . . .

The child-saving movement similarly enjoyed the support of propertied and powerful individuals. In Chicago, for example, where the movement had some of its most notable successes, the child-savers included Louise Bowen and Ellen Henrotin who were both married to bankers; Mrs. Potter Palmer, whose husband owned vast amounts of land and property, was an ardent child-saver when not involved in the exclusive Fortnightly Club, the elite Chicago Woman's Club or the Board of Lady Managers of the World's Fair; another child-saver in Chicago, Mrs. Perry Smith, was married to the vice-president of the Chicago and Northwestern Railroad. Even the more radically-minded child-savers came from upper-class backgrounds. The fathers of Jane Addams and Julia Lathrop, for example, were both lawyers and Republican senators in the Illinois legislature. Jane Addams' father was one of the richest men in northern Illinois, and her stepbrother, Harry Haldeman, was a socialite from Baltimore who later amassed a large fortune in Kansas City.

The child-saving movement was not simply a humanistic enterprise on behalf of the lower classes against the established order. On the contrary, its impetus came primarily from the middle and upper classes who were instrumental in devising new forms of social control to protect their privileged positions in American society. The child-saving movement was not an isolated phenomenon but rather reflected massive changes in productive relationships, from laissez-faire to monopoly capitalism, and in strategies of social control, from inefficient repression to welfare state benevolence. This reconstruction of economic and social institutions, which was not achieved without conflict within the ruling class, represented a victory for the more "enlightened" wing of corporate leaders who advocated strategic alliances with urban reformers and support of liberal reforms.

Many large corporations and business leaders, for example, supported federal regulation of the economy in order to protect their own investments and stabilize the marketplace. Business leaders and political spokesmen were often in basic agreement about fundamental economic issues. . . .

Progressivism was in part a businessmen's movement and big business played a central role in the Progressive coalition's support of welfare reforms. Child labor legislation in New York, for example, was supported by several groups, including upper-class industrialists who did not depend on cheap child labor. According to Jeremy Felt's history of that movement, "the abolition of child labor could be viewed as a means of driving out marginal manufacturers and tenement operators, hence increasing the consolidation and efficiency of business." The rise of compulsory education, another welfare state reform, was also closely tied to the changing forms of industrial production and social control. Charles Loring Brace, writing in the mid-nineteenth century, anticipated the use of education as preparation for industrial discipline when, "in the interests of public order, of liberty, of property, for the sake of our own safety and the endurance of free institutions here," he advocated "a strict and careful law, which shall compel every minor to learn and read and write, under severe penalties in case of disobedience." By the end of the century, the working class had imposed upon them a sterile and authoritarian educational system which mirrored the ethos of the corporate workplace and was designed to provide "an increasingly refined training and selection mechanism for the labor force.

While the child-saving movement was supported and financed by corporate liberals, the day-to-day work of lobbying, public education and organizing was undertaken by middle-class urban reformers, professionals and special interest groups. The more moderate and conservative sectors of the feminist movement were especially active in anti-delinquency reforms. Their successful participation derived in part from public stereotypes of women as the "natural caretakers" of "wayward children." Women's claim to the public care of children had precedent during the nineteenth century and their role in child rearing was paramount. Women, generally regarded as better teachers than men, were more influential in child-training and discipline at home. The fact that public education also came more under the direction of women teachers in the schools served to legitimize the predominance of women in other areas of "child-saving."

The child-saving movement attracted women from a variety of political and class backgrounds, though it was dominated by the daughters of the old landed gentry and wives of the upper-class nouveau riche. Career women and society philanthropists, elite women's clubs and settlement houses, and political and civic organizations worked together on the problems of child care, education and juvenile delinquency. Professional and political women's groups regarded childsaving as a problem of women's rights, whereas their opponents seized upon it as an opportunity to keep women in their "proper place." Child-saving became a reputable task for any woman who wanted to extend her "housekeeping" functions into the community without denying anti-feminist stereotypes of woman's nature and place.

For traditionally educated women and daughters of the landed and industrial gentry, the child-saving movement presented an opportunity for pursuing socially acceptable public roles and for restoring some of the authority and spiritual influence which many women felt they had lost through the urbanization of family life. Their traditional functions were dramatically threatened by the weakening of domestic roles and the specialized rearrangement of the family. The child-savers were aware that their championship of social outsiders such as immigrants, the poor and children, was not wholly motivated by disinterested ideals of justice and equality. Philanthropic work filled a void in their own lives, a void which was created in part by the decline of traditional religion, increased leisure and boredom, the rise of public education, and the breakdown of communal life in large, crowded cities. . . . Women were exhorted to make their lives useful by participating in welfare programs, by volunteering their time and services, and by getting acquainted with less privileged groups. . . .

While the child-saving movement can be partly understood as a "symbolic crusade" which served ceremonial and status functions for many women, it was by no means a reactionary and romantic movement, nor was it supported only by women and members of the old gentry. Child-saving also had considerable instrumental significance for legitimizing new career openings for women. The new role of social worker combined elements of an old and partly fictitious role—defender of family life—and elements of a new role—social servant. Social work and professional child-saving provided new opportunities for career-minded women who found the traditional professions dominated and controlled by men. These child-savers were members of the emerging bourgeoisie created by the new industrial order.

It is not surprising that the professions also supported the child-saving movement, for they were capable of reaping enormous economic and status rewards from the changes taking place. The clergy had nothing to lose (but more of their rapidly declining constituency) and everything to gain by incorporating social services into traditional religion. Lawyers were needed for their technical expertise, and to administer new institutions. And academics discovered a new market which paid them as consultants, elevated them to positions of national prestige and furnished endless materials for books, articles and conferences. . . .

While the rank and file reformers in the child-saving movement worked closely with corporate liberals, it would be inaccurate to simply characterize them as lackeys of big business. Many were principled and genuinely concerned about alleviating human misery and improving the lives of the poor. Moreover, many women who participated in the movement were able to free themselves from male domination and participate more fully in society. But for the most part, the child-savers and other Progressive reformers defended capitalism and rejected socialist alternatives. Most reformers accepted the structure of the new industrial order and sought to moderate its cruder inequities and reduce inharmonies in the existing system. Though many child-savers were "socialists of the heart" and ardent critics of society, their programs were typically reformist and did not alter basic economic inequalities. Rhetoric and righteous indignation were more prevalent than programs of radical action.

The intellectual and professional communities did little to criticize Progressive reforms, partly because so many benefited from their new role as government consultants and experts, and partly because their conception of social change was limited and elitist. As Jackson Wilson observed, many intellectuals in the Progressive movement were "interested in creating a system of government which would allow the people to rule only at a carefully kept distance and at infrequent intervals' reserving most real power and planning to a corps of experts and professionals." Those few reformers who had a genuine concern for liberating the lives of the poor by considering socialist alternatives were either coopted by their allies, betrayed by their own class interests, or became the prisoners of social and economic forces beyond their control.

IMAGES OF CRIME AND DELINQUENCY

The child-saving reformers were part of a much larger movement to readjust institutions to conform to the requirements of corporate capitalism and the modern welfare state. As the country emerged from the depressions and industrial violence of the late nineteenth century, efforts were made to rescue and regulate capitalism through developing a new political economy, designed to stabilize production and profits. The stability and smooth functioning of this new order depended heavily on the capacity of welfare state institutions, especially the schools, to achieve cultural hegemony and guarantee loyalty to the State. . . . In order to develop support for and legitimize the corporate liberal State, a new ideology was promoted in which chaos was equated with crime and violence, and salvation was to be found in the development of new and more extensive forms of social control.

The child-savers viewed the "criminal classes" with a mixture of contempt and benevolence. Crime was portrayed as rising from the "lowest orders" and threatening to engulf "respectable" society like a virulent disease. Charles Loring Brace, a leading child-saver, typified popular and professional views about crime and delinquency:

> As Christian men, we cannot look upon this great multitude of unhappy, deserted, and degraded boys and girls without feeling our responsibility to God for them. The class increases: immigration is pouring in its multitudes of poor foreigners who leave these young outcasts everywhere in our midst.

> These boys and girls ... will soon form the great lower class of our city.
> They will influence elections; they may shape the policy of the city; they
> will assuredly, if unreclaimed, poison society all around them. They will help
> to form the great multitude of robbers, thieves, and vagrants, who are now
> such a burden upon the law-respecting community. . . .

This attitude of contempt derived from a view of criminals as less-than-
human, a perspective which was strongly influenced and aggravated by nativist and racist ideologies. The "criminal class" was variously described as
"creatures" living in "burrows," "dens," and "slime"; as "little Arabs" and
"foreign childhood that floats along the streets and docks of the city—
vagabondish, thievish, familiar with the vicious ways and places of the town";
and as "ignorant," "shiftless," "indolent," and "dissipated."

The child-savers were alarmed and frightened by the "dangerous
classes" whose "very number makes one stand aghast," noted the urban reformer Jacob Riis. Law and order were widely demanded:

> The "dangerous classes" of New York are mainly American-born, but the
> children of Irish and German immigrants. They are as ignorant as London
> flashmen or costermongers. They are far more brutal than the peasantry
> from whom they descend, and they are much banded together, in associa-
> tions, such as "Dead Rabbit," "Plug-ugly," and various target companies.
> They are our *enfant perdus*, grown up to young manhood. . . . They are ready
> for any offense or crime, however degraded or bloody. . . . Let but Law lift
> its hand from them for a season, or let the civilizing influences of American
> life fail to reach them, and, if the opportunity offered, we should see an ex-
> plosion from this class which might leave this city in ashes and blood.

These views derived considerable legitimacy from prevailing theories of social and reform Darwinism which, *inter alia*, proposed that criminals were
a dangerous and atavistic class, standing outside the boundaries of morally
regulated relationships. Herbert Spencer's writings had a major impact on
American intellectuals and Cesare Lombroso, perhaps the most significant
figure in nineteenth century criminology, looked for recognition in the
United States when he felt that his experiments on the "criminal type" had
been neglected in Europe.

Although Lombroso's theoretical and experimental studies were not
translated into English until 1911, his findings were known by American academics in the early 1890s, and their popularity, like that of Spencer's works,
was based on the fact that they confirmed widely-held stereotypes about the
biological basis and inferior character of a "criminal class." . . .

Literature on "social degradation" was extremely popular during the
1870s and 1880s, though most such "studies" were little more than crude and
racist polemics, padded with moralistic epithets and preconceived value
judgments. Richard Dugdale's series of papers on the Jukes family, which
became a model for the case-study approach to social problems, was dis-
torted almost beyond recognition by anti-intellectual supporters of hereditary theories of crime. Confronted by the evidence of Darwin, Galton, Dug-

dale, Caldwell and many other disciples of the biological image of behavior, many child-savers were compelled to admit that "a large proportion of the unfortunate children that go to make up the great army of criminals are not born right." Reformers adopted and modified the rhetoric of social Darwinism in order to emphasize the urgent need for confronting the "crime problem" before it got completely out of hand. A popular proposal, for example, was the "methodized registration and training" of potential criminals, "or these failing, their early and entire withdrawal from the community."

Although some child-savers advocated drastic methods of crime control—including birth control through sterilization, cruel punishments, and life-long incarceration—more moderate views prevailed. This victory for moderation was related to the recognition by many Progressive reformers that short-range repression was counter-productive as well as cruel and that long-range planning and amelioration were required to achieve economic and political stability. The rise of more benevolent strategies of social control occurred at about the same time that influential capitalists were realizing that existing economic arrangements could not be successfully maintained only through the use of private police and government troops. While the child-savers justified their reforms as humanitarian, it is clear that this humanitarianism reflected their class background and elitist conceptions of human potentiality. The child-savers shared the view of more conservative professionals that "criminals" were a distinct and dangerous class, indigenous to working-class culture, and a threat to "civilized" society. They differed mainly in the procedures by which the "criminal class" should be controlled or neutralized.

Gradually, a more "enlightened" view about strategies of control prevailed among the leading representatives of professional associations. Correctional workers, for example, did not want to think of themselves merely as the custodians of a pariah class. The self-image of penal reformers as "doctors" rather than "guards," and the medical domination of criminological research in the United States at that time facilitated the acceptance of "therapeutic" strategies in prisons and reformatories. Physicians gradually provided the official rhetoric of penal reform, replacing cruder concepts of social Darwinism with a new optimism. Admittedly, the criminal was "pathological" and "diseased," but medical science offered the possibility of miraculous cures. Although there was a popular belief in the existence of a "criminal class" separated from the rest of humanity by a "vague boundary line," there was no good reason why this class could not be identified, diagnosed, segregated, changed and incorporated back into society.

By the late 1890s, most child-savers agreed that hereditary theories of crime were overfatalistic. . . . Although there was a wide difference of opinion among experts as to the precipitating causes of crime, it was generally agreed that criminals were abnormally conditioned by a multitude of biological and environmental forces, some of which were permanent and irreversible. Strictly biological theories of crime were modified to incorporate a developmental view of human behavior. If, as it was believed, criminals are conditioned by biological heritage and brutish living conditions, then prophylactic measures must be taken early in life. "We must get hold of the little waifs that grow up to form the criminal element just as early in life as possible," exhorted an influential child-saver. "Hunt up the children of poverty, of crime, and of brutality, just as soon as they can be reached." Efforts were needed to reach the criminals of future generations. "They are born to crime," wrote the penologist Enoch Wines, "brought up for it. They must be saved." New institutions and new programs were required to meet this challenge.

JUVENILE COURT AND THE REFORMATORY SYSTEM

The essential preoccupation of the child-saving movement was the recognition and control of youthful deviance. It brought attention to, and thus "invented" new categories of youthful misbehavior which had been hitherto unappreciated. The efforts of the child-savers were institutionally expressed in the juvenile court which, despite recent legislative and constitutional reforms, is generally acknowledged as their most significant contribution to progressive penology. There is some dispute about which state first created a special tribunal for children. Massachusetts and New York passed laws, in 1874 and 1892 respectively, providing for the trials of minors apart from adults charged with crimes. Ben Lindsey, a renowned judge and reformer, also claimed this distinction for Colorado where a juvenile court was, in effect, established through an educational law of 1899. However, most authorities agree that the Juvenile Court Act, passed by the Illinois legislature in the same year, was the first official enactment to be recognized as a model statute by other states and countries. By 1917, juvenile court legislation had been passed in all but three states and by 1932 there were over 600 independent juvenile courts throughout the United States.

The juvenile court system was part of a general movement directed towards developing a specialized labor market and industrial discipline under corporate capitalism by creating new programs of adjudication and control for "delinquent," "dependent" and "neglected" youth. This in turn was related to augmenting the family and enforcing compulsory education in order to guarantee the proper reproduction of the labor force. For example, underlying the juvenile court system was the concept of *parens patriae* by which the courts were authorized to handle with wide discretion the problems of "its least fortunate junior citizens." The administration of juvenile justice, which differed in many important respects from the criminal court system, was delegated extensive powers of control over youth. A child was not accused of a crime but offered assistance and guidance; intervention in the lives of "delinquents" was not supposed to carry the stigma of criminal guilt. Judicial records were not generally available to the press or public, and juvenile hearings were typically conducted in private. Court procedures were informal and inquisitorial, not requiring the presence of a defense attorney. Specific criminal safeguards of due process were not applicable because juvenile proceedings were defined by statute as civil in character.

The judges of the new court were empowered to investigate the character and social background of "predelinquent" as well as delinquent children; they concerned themselves with motivation rather than intent, seeking to identify the moral reputation of problematic children. The requirements of preventive penology and child-saving further justified the court's intervention in cases where no offense had actually been committed, but where, for example, a child was posing problems for some person in authority, such as a parent or teacher or social worker.

The role model for juvenile court judges was doctor-counselor rather than lawyer. "Judicial therapists" were expected to establish a one-to-one relationship with "delinquents" in the same way that a country doctor might give his time and attention to a favorite patient. Juvenile courtrooms were often arranged like a clinic and the vocabulary of its participants was largely composed of medical metaphors. . . .

The unique character of the child-saving movement was its concerns for predelinquent offenders—"children who occupy the debatable ground between criminality and innocence"—and its claim that it could transform potential criminals into respectable citizens by training them in "habits of industry, self-control and obedience to law." This policy justified the diminishing of traditional procedures and allowed police, judges, probation officers and truant officers to work together without legal hindrance. If children were to be rescued, it was important that the rescuers be free to pursue their mission without the interference of defense lawyers and due process. Delinquents had to be saved, transformed and reconstituted. "There is no essential difference," noted a prominent child-saver, "between a criminal and any other sinner. The means and methods of restoration are the same for both."

The juvenile court legislation enabled the state to investigate and control a wide variety of behaviors. As Joel Handler has observed, "the critical philosophical position of the reform movement was that no formal, legal distinctions should be made between the delinquent and the dependent or neglected." Statutory definitions of "delinquency" encompassed (1) acts that would be criminal if committed by adults; (2) acts that violated county, town, or municipal ordinances; and (3) violations of vaguely worded catch-alls—such as "vicious or immoral behavior," "incorrigibility," and "truancy"—which "seem to express the notion that the adolescent, if allowed to continue, will engage in more serious conduct. "

The juvenile court movement went far beyond a concern for special treatment of adolescent offenders. It brought within the ambit of governmental control a set of youthful activities that had been previously ignored or dealt with on an informal basis. It was not by accident that the behavior subject to penalties—drinking, sexual "license," roaming the streets, begging, frequenting dance halls and movies, fighting, and being seen in public late at night—was especially characteristic of the children of working-class and immigrant families. Once arrested and adjudicated, these "delinquents" became wards of the court and eligible for salvation.

It was through the reformatory system that the child-savers hoped to demonstrate that delinquents were capable of being converted into law-abiding citizens. . . . [T]he reformatory was initially developed in the United States during the middle of the nineteenth century as a special form of prison discipline for adolescents and young adults. . . .

The reformatory was distinguished from the traditional penitentiary in several ways: it adopted a policy of indeterminate sentencing; it emphasized the importance of a countryside location; and it typically was organized on the "cottage" plan as opposed to the traditional congregate housing found in penitentiaries. The ultimate aim of the reformatory was reformation of the criminal, which could only be achieved "by placing the prisoner's fate, as far as possible, in his own hand, by enabling him through industry and good conduct to raise himself, step by step, to a position of less restraint. . . ."

Based on a crude theory of rewards and punishments, the "new penology" set itself the task of re-socializing the "dangerous classes." The typical resident of a reformatory, according to one child-saver, had been "cradled in infamy, imbibing with its earliest natural nourishment the germs of a depraved appetite, and reared in the midst of people whose lives are an atrocious crime against natural and divine law and the rights of society." In order to correct and reform such a person, the reformatory plan was designed to teach the value of adjustment, private enterprise, thrift and self-reliance. "To make a good boy out of this bundle of perversities, his entire being must be revolutionized. He must be taught self-control, industry, respect for himself and the rights of others." The real test of reformation in a delinquent, as William Letchworth told the National Conference of Charities and Correction in 1886, was his uncomplaining adjustment to his former environment. "If he is truly reformed in the midst of adverse influences," said Letchworth, "he gains that moral strength which makes his reform permanent." . . .

Reformation of delinquents was to be achieved in a number of different ways. The trend from congregate housing to group living represented a significant change in the organization of penal institutions. The "cottage" plan was designed to provide more intensive supervision and to reproduce, symbolically at least, an atmosphere of family life conducive to the re-socialization of youth. The "new penology" also urged the benefits of a rural location, partly in order to teach agricultural skills, but mainly in order to guarantee a totally controlled environment. This was justified by appealing to the romantic theory that corrupt delinquents would be spiritually regenerated by their contact with unspoiled nature.

Education was stressed as the main form of industrial and moral training in reformatories. According to Michael Katz, in his study on nineteenth-century education, the reformatory provided "the first form of compulsory schooling in the United States." The prominence of education as a technique of reform reflected the widespread emphasis on socialization and assimilation instead of cruder methods of social control. But as Georg Rusche and Otto Kirchheimer observed in their study of the relationship between economic and penal policies, the rise of "rehabilitative" and educational programs was "largely the result of opposition on the part of free workers," for "wherever working-class organizations were powerful enough to influence state politics, they succeeded in obtaining complete abolition of all forms of prison labor (Pennsylvania in 1897, for example), causing much suffering to the prisoners, or at least in obtaining very considerable limitations, such as work without modern machinery, conventional rather than modern types of prison industry, or work for the government instead of for the free market."

Although the reformatory system, as envisioned by urban reformers, suffered in practice from overcrowding, mismanagement, inadequate financing and staff hiring problems, its basic ideology was still tough-minded and uncompromising. . . . The child-savers were not averse to using corporal punishment and other severe disciplinary measures when inmates were recalcitrant. . . . Child-saving was a job for resolute professionals who realized that "sickly sentimentalism" had no place in their work.

"Criminals shall either be cured," Brockway told the National Prison Congress in 1870, "or kept under such continued restraint as gives guarantee of safety from further depredations." Restraint and discipline were an integral part of the "treatment" program and not merely expediencies of administration. Military drill, "training of the will," and long hours of tedious labor were the essence of the reformatory system and the indeterminate sentencing policy guaranteed its smooth operation. "Nothing can tend more certainly to secure the most hardened and desperate criminals than the present system of short sentences," wrote the reformer Bradford Kinney Peirce in 1869. Several years later, Enoch Wines was able to report that "the sentences of young offenders are wisely regulated for their amendment; they are not absurdly shortened as if they signified only so much endurance of vindictive suffering."

Since the child-savers professed to be seeking the "best interests" of their "wards" on the basis of corporate liberal values, there was no need to formulate legal regulation of the right and duty to "treat" in the same way that the right and duty to punish had been previously regulated. The adversary system, therefore, ceased to exist for youth, even as a legal fiction. The myth of the child-saving movement as a humanitarian enterprise is based partly on a superficial interpretation of the child-savers' rhetoric of rehabilitation and partly on a misconception of how the child-savers viewed punishment. While it is true that the child-savers advocated minimal use of corporal punishment, considerable evidence suggests that this recommendation was based on managerial rather than moral considerations. . . .

The decline in the use of corporal punishment was due to the fact that indeterminate sentencing, the "mark" or "stage" system of rewards and punishments, and other techniques of "organized persuasion" were far more effective in maintaining order and compliance than cruder methods of control. The chief virtue of the "stage" system, a graduated system of punishments and privileges, was its capacity to keep prisoners disciplined and submissive. The child-savers had learned from industrialists that persuasive benevolence backed up by force was a far more effective device of social control than arbitrary displays of terrorism. Like an earlier generation of penal reformers in France and Italy, the child-savers stressed the efficacy of new and indirect forms of social control as a "practical measure of defense against social revolution as well as against individual acts.

Although the child-saving movement had far-reaching consequences for the organization and administration of the juvenile justice system, its overall impact was conservative in both spirit and achievement. The child-savers' reforms were generally aimed at imposing sanctions on conduct unbecoming "youth" and disqualifying youth from the benefit of adult privileges. The child-savers were prohibitionists, in a general sense, who believed that social progress depended on efficient law enforcement, strict supervision of children's leisure and recreation, and enforced education. They were primarily concerned with regulating social behavior, eliminating "foreign" and radical ideologies, and preparing youth as a disciplined and devoted work force. The austerity of the criminal law and penal institutions was only of incidental concern; their central interest was in the normative outlook of youth and they were most successful in their efforts to extend governmental control over a whole range of youthful activities which had previously been handled locally and informally. In this sense, their reforms were aimed at defining, rationalizing and regulating the dependent status of youth. Although the child-savers' attitudes to youth were often paternalistic and romantic, their commands were backed up by force and an abiding faith in the benevolence of government.

The child-saving movement had its most direct impact on the children of the urban poor. The fact that "troublesome" adolescents were depicted as "sick" or "pathological," imprisoned "for their own good," addressed in paternalistic vocabulary, and exempted from criminal law processes, did not alter the subjective experiences of control, restraint and punishment. It is ironic, as Philippe Aries observed in his historical study of European family life, that the obsessive solicitude of family, church, moralists and administrators for child welfare served to deprive children of the freedoms which they had previously shared with adults and to deny their capacity for initiative, responsibility and autonomy.

The child-savers' rhetoric of benevolence should not be mistaken for popular, democratic programs. Paternalism was a typical ingredient of most reforms in the Progressive era, legitimizing imperialism in foreign policy and extensive state control at home. Even the corporate rich, according to William Appleman Williams, "revealed a strikingly firm conception of a benevolent feudal approach to the firm and its workers" and "were willing to extend—to provide in the manner of traditional beneficence—such things as new housing, old age pensions, death payments, wage and job schedules, and bureaus charged with responsibility for welfare, safety, and sanitation." But when benevolence failed—in domestic institutions such as schools and courts or in economic policies abroad—government officials and industrial leaders were quick to resort to massive and overwhelming force.

This is not to suggest that the child-savers and other Progressive movements did not achieve significant reforms. They did in fact create major changes. In the arena of criminal justice they were responsible for developing important new institutions which transformed the character of the administration of juvenile justice. . . . [T]he child-saving movement was a "reformist reform." It was not controlled by those whom it was supposed to benefit; it did not create new centers of democratic power; it extended and consolidated the powers of the state; and it helped to preserve existing economic and political relationships.

CHAPTER 2

Gateway to the Juvenile Justice Process: Varieties of Juvenile Courts

A number of individuals in the juvenile justice system make decisions that affect the welfare and processing of youth engaged in criminal misconduct. Police officers who encounter youths may adjust a case informally on the street or at the station house, divert it to a diversion program, or refer the youth to juvenile court intake for formal processing. Police also may make the initial decision whether to place a youth in a pretrial detention facility pending further review by a prosecutor or juvenile court judge. Probation officers at a juvenile court's intake may refer a youth to the juvenile court for formal adjudication or dispose of the case through informal supervision or diversion to a program run by the juvenile court or another agency. Juvenile court intake workers and the juvenile court also review the case of any youth held in pretrial detention. Finally, even after formal adjudication, the juvenile court judge may choose from a wide array of dispositional alternatives ranging from continuing a case without a finding of delinquency, informal or formal probation, out-of-home placement, or commitment to a state training school.

Recent research, some of which is included in Chapter 5, indicates that the juvenile justice dispositional decision-making process is a cumulative one; decisions made by the initial participants, for example, the police or court intake, affect the decisions made by subsequent participants, for example, juvenile court judges. Thus, assessing juvenile court sentencing practices and judicial decision making requires familiarity with decisions made by other juvenile justice actors at other stages of the process.

Several studies evaluate dispositional decision making by police officers in their initial encounters with juveniles and suggest that a youth's demeanor, her "impression management," as well as her offense affect police officers' exercises of discretion. If the police refer a case to juvenile court, typically an intake probation officer will screen it to decide whether to process the case formally or informally. Probation officers close or informally adjust about half of the cases referred to juvenile court intake. Over the past three decades, for example, the percentage of delinquency referrals resulting in the filing of formal delinquency petitions has ranged between about 41% and 55%. In 1994, 55% of referrals resulted in the filing of formal petitions, the highest rate in a decades. [See e.g., Jeffrey Butts, Howard Snyder, Terrence Finnegan, Anne Aughenbaugh, and Rowen Poole, *Juvenile Court Statistics 1994* 9 (1996)]. Several studies suggest that a child's social characteristics, family status, demeanor, or race, rather than the referral offenses, influence intake decision making, and may amplify racial and class disparities in processing youths referred to juvenile court. Racial disparities in the processing of youths at each decisional point now emerge as one of the central juvenile justice policy issues.

Following referral to juvenile court, either the local prosecuting authority or the juvenile court's probation or intake department make a screening decision whether to process a case formally or informally. These "gatekeepers" close many referrals at intake with some type of *informal disposition*: dismissal, counseling, warning, referral to another agency, community service, or informal probation. In about half of the cases, the prosecuting authority or a probation officer files a petition, a charging document, to formally initiate the juvenile court process. A petition compares legally with a prosecutor's filing of a complaint or information, or a grand jury's indictment in the adult criminal process. The relationship between the screening functions of a juvenile court's intake staff and the charging functions in the prosecuting attorney's office vary from state to state and county to county within a state.

Once a prosecutor or probation officer files a formal delinquency petition, the juvenile court arraigns the juvenile offender on the petition. Because the right to counsel attaches in juvenile court only after the petition is filed, a juvenile court judge typically appoints counsel to represent the juvenile beginning at this stage, if at all. For youths held in pretrial detention, the juvenile court also conducts a detention hearing to determine the youths' residential status pending further court processing. At the arraignment, a juvenile may admit or deny the allegations in the petition. For those youths held in detention, the court also makes a pretrial custody decision. As will appear in Chapters 3 and 5, for many youths, the detention hearing represents one of the most significant decisions that juvenile court judges make, because the initial decision to detain also may affect the subsequent sentence.

In many cases, juveniles admit the allegations of the petition at the arraignment and the court quickly disposes of their cases, often without the appointment of a defense attorney. In other cases, the juvenile court appoints a public defender or court-appointed lawyer who confers briefly with the juvenile before the youth admits or denies the allegations in the petition. Only a very small fraction of cases actually result in formal, contested hearings or trials. As Chapter 3 reports, the procedural safeguards available to delinquents charged with criminal offenses differ in some important ways from those available to adult criminal defendants. Following a delinquency adjudication, the juvenile court judge possesses enormous discretion within which to impose a disposition. Chapter 5 describes aspects of the juvenile court sentencing process, judicial decision making, and the various dispositional options available to the court.

The materials included in Chapter 2, "Varieties of Juvenile Courts," illustrate the variability of juvenile courts and justice administration. Howard Snyder and Melissa Sickmund's excerpt, "Juvenile Courts and Juvenile Crime," provides a comprehensive overview of the juvenile justice process, with information and data on the flow of cases, the volume and characteristics of delinquent offenders, and comparisons of recent changes in juvenile courts' caseloads. They also introduce the role that formal and informal processing, and organizational variation play in juvenile justice administration. Barry Feld, "Justice by Geography," illustrates that juvenile courts and juvenile justice administration vary considerably with social context. Even within the same state, social structural context and geographic variability affect the types of youth crime problems that juvenile courts confront, the types of justice systems they administer, and the consequences for youths. Finally, Robert Sampson and John Laub, "Structural Variations in Juvenile Court Processing," further refine the relationship between social structure and juvenile justice administration. Even among urban juvenile courts, racial and structural inequalities affect juvenile justice administration and begin to explain some of the racial disparities in case processing. Taken together, these articles illustrate the complexity and diversity of juvenile courts and the difficulties of generalizing about the juvenile justice system.

Juvenile Courts and Juvenile Crime

HOWARD SNYDER AND MELISSA SICKMUND

Nearly two-thirds of all youth arrested are referred to a court with juvenile jurisdiction for further processing. As with law enforcement, the court may decide to divert some juveniles from the formal justice system. Those cases that progress through the system may result in adjudication and court-ordered probation or out-of-home placement or may be transferred to a crim-

Excerpted from Snyder, Howard N. and Sickmund, Melissa. (1995) *Juvenile Offenders and Victims: A National Report*, pp. 123–137. Washington, DC: Office of Juvenile Justice and Delinquency Prevention.

inal (adult) court. Also, while their cases are being processed juveniles may be held in a secure detention facility.

This chapter quantifies the flow of cases through the juvenile court system, documenting the nature of, and trends in, cases received and the court's response. Sections also explore the nature of juvenile court careers and how the flow of cases differs for courts in urban and rural areas. In addition information is presented on the use of detention, the detention center population, and the conditions of confinement in such facilities.

The case processing information presented in this chapter is drawn from the National Juvenile Court Data Archive's primary publication *Juvenile Court Statistics.* . . .

NATIONAL ESTIMATES MUST BE INTERPRETED CAUTIOUSLY

The data received are not uniform, but reflect the natural variation that exists across court information systems. To develop the national estimates, compatible data are restructured into a common reporting format. However, not all contributed data can support the national reporting requirements. In 1992 national estimates were based on data from more than 1,500 jurisdictions representing approximately 60% of the Nation's juvenile population.

The national estimates of juvenile court activity are not based on a nationally representative sample. Participating courts were not selected through a statistically designed sample. Similar to the approach used in the FBI's Uniform Crime Reporting Program, the court statistics rely on data contributed by all courts able to report. The estimation procedures used are designed to compensate for the potential bias in this type of sample, however, from a purely statistical standpoint, there is no way of determining the validity of the estimates. . . .

MOST, BUT NOT ALL, DELINQUENCY CASES SEEN IN THE JUVENILE COURT ARE REFERRED BY LAW ENFORCEMENT

Delinquency cases are referred to juvenile courts from a number of different sources, including law enforcement, social service agencies, schools, parents, probation officers, and victims. In 1992 the large majority (85%) of delinquency cases were referred to court intake by law enforcement agencies. This percentage has changed little over the past decade.

Nonpolice sources referred a relatively large proportion of disorderly conduct and simple assault cases. Youth charged with escape, contempt of court, and probation violation are generally under the jurisdiction of the court when the offense occurs, so these matters are often brought to the court's attention by court personnel. . . .

U.S. JUVENILE COURTS HANDLE 4,000
DELINQUENCY CASES EACH DAY

In 1992 U.S. courts with juvenile jurisdiction handled an estimated 1.5 million cases in which the juvenile was charged with a delinquency offense—an offense for which an adult could be prosecuted in criminal court.

An individual juvenile may be involved in more than one case during the year. The annual ratio of cases to juveniles is about 3 to 2. Therefore, juvenile courts handled about 1 million individual juveniles charged with delinquency offenses in 1992.

JUVENILE COURTS ARE FACED WITH AN
INCREASING AND CHANGING WORKLOAD

Changes in the nature of the offenders brought to juvenile court in recent years have placed demands on the court's resources and programs. The 26% increase between 1988 and 1992 in the volume of cases that passed through juvenile courts placed a strain on the system. In addition, the courts were asked to respond to not only more cases, but to a different type of caseload.

Over the 5-year period from 1988 through 1992, the juvenile courts saw a disproportionate increase in violent offense cases and weapon law violations, while alcohol and other drug offense cases declined. These changes have required the courts to expand their programs in some areas while decreasing their capacities in others.

MALES ARE INVOLVED IN 8 IN 10 DELINQUENCY
CASES HANDLED EACH YEAR

While only half of the juvenile population, males were involved in about 80% of person, property, and public order offense cases handled by the courts in 1992 and in 88% of drug law violation cases. These proportions did not change substantially between 1988 and 1992.

MALE AND FEMALE CASELOADS INCREASED SIMILARLY

In 1992 for every 1,000 males between the ages of 10 and 17 (who were under juvenile court jurisdiction), the court handled 87 cases involving males. The case rate for females (21 cases per 1,000 females) was one-fourth the rate for males. Between 1988 and 1992 case rates for males and females each increased approximately 20%. Caseload changes were similar for males and females across offense categories.

Youth Were Charged with a Property Offense in the Majority (57%) of the Delinquency Cases Handled by Juvenile Courts in 1992

Most serious offense	Number of cases	Percent of total cases	Percent change 1988–1992
Total delinquency	1,471,200	100%	26%
Person offenses	301,000	20	56
Criminal homicide	2,500	<1	55
Forcible rape	5,400	<1	27
Robbery	32,900	2	52
Aggravated assault	77,900	5	80
Simple assault	152,800	10	47
Other violent sex offenses	9,900	1	60
Other person offense	19,800	1	63
Property offenses	842,200	57	23
Burglary	156,400	11	22
Larceny-theft	361,600	25	16
Motor vehicle theft	73,000	5	34
Arson	8,300	1	24
Vandalism	121,700	8	50
Trespassing	58,500	4	17
Stolen property offenses	28,900	2	−7
Other property offenses	33,700	2	57
Drug law violations	72,100	5	−12
Public order offenses	255,900	17	21
Obstruction of justice	87,100	6	10
Disorderly conduct	69,300	5	50
Weapons offenses	41,000	3	86
Liquor law violations	12,500	1	−26
Nonviolent sex offenses	12,900	1	19
Other public order	33,000	2	−8
Violent Crime Index*	118,600	8	68
Property Crime Index**	599,400	41	20

- Person offense cases accounted for 20% of all delinquency cases handled by juvenile courts in 1992. Cases involving a Violent Crime Index offense accounted for 8% of all delinquency cases.

- Five percent of all cases involved drug law violations.

- Although a substantial portion of the growth in court referrals is related to arrests, changes in juvenile court caseloads are also dependent on other forces. The increases in juvenile court cases were greater than increases in arrests of persons under age 18. Between 1988 and 1992, Violent Crime Index arrests increased by 47%, while arrests for Property Crime Index offenses increased by 8%.

Violent Crime Index: criminal homicide, forcible rape, robbery, and aggravated assault.
**Property Crime Index: burglary, larceny-theft, motor vehicle theft, and arson.
Note: Detail may not add to totals because of rounding. Percent change calculations are based on unrounded numbers.
Source: Butts, J.,et al. (1995). Juvenile court statistics 1992.

THE OFFENSE PROFILE OF WHITE
AND BLACK CASELOADS DIFFER

Court caseloads of black juveniles contained a greater proportion of person and drug offense cases than did the caseloads of other juveniles. Although property cases dominated the caseloads of all racial groups in 1992, this was less true for black juveniles. Among blacks, fewer than half of the cases handled involved property offenses. Among whites and juveniles of other races, just over 60% of cases were property cases.

Blacks had a greater proportion of person offense cases (26%) than either white or other race juveniles (18%). For all groups, drug cases accounted for a relatively small proportion of the caseload: however, the drug proportion was slightly greater for blacks (7%) than for whites (4%) or juveniles of other races (3%). There was little racial variation in the proportion of public order cases.

DELINQUENCY CASE RATES DIFFER SUBSTANTIALLY BY RACE

In 1992 the delinquency case rate for black juveniles (114.2) was more than double the rate for white juveniles (44.9) and nearly triple the rate for juveniles of other races (40.4).

The delinquency case rate among whites increased less between 1988 and 1992 (17%) than did the rates for blacks (29%) and other race juveniles (23%).

Blacks Were Involved in a Disproportionate Number of Delinquency Cases in 1992

	White	Black	Other races	Total
Delinquency cases	65%	31%	4%	100%
Person	57	40	3	100
Property	70	27	4	100
Drugs	52	46	2	100
Public order	65	32	3	100
Juvenile population	80%	15%	5%	100%

- Although the majority of delinquency cases involve white youth, black youth are over represented in the delinquency caseload, given their proportion of the juvenile population.

- The over representation of black juveniles was most prominent in drug and person offense cases.

Note: Detail may not total 100% because of rounding. Nearly all youth of Hispanic ethnicity are included in the white racial category.
Source: Butts, J., et al. (1995). Juvenile court statistics 1992.

DISPARITIES IN WHITE AND BLACK ARREST AND JUVENILE COURT CASE RATES WERE SIMILAR IN 1992

In 1992 the arrest rate of black juveniles for property crimes was double that for white juveniles. Juvenile court referral rates displayed an equal level of racial disparity. Therefore, the level of disparity did not increase between the stages of arrest and juvenile court intake for property offense cases. The level of disparity also held constant for person offenses. The person offense arrest rate for black juveniles in 1992 was 4 times the white arrest rate, equivalent to the disparity in their juvenile court referral rates. For drug law violations, the arrest rate for black juveniles was about 5 times the rate for whites. Roughly the same degree of disparity was found in the juvenile court case rates for these offenses.

DELINQUENCY CASE RATES ROSE SUBSTANTIALLY BETWEEN 1988 AND 1992 IN MOST AGE GROUPS

The 1992 delinquency case rate was 21% greater than the 1988 case rate. Delinquency case rates increased by roughly the same degree in all age groups, with the exception of relatively small increases in the youngest age groups.

6 IN 10 DELINQUENCY CASES HANDLED IN 1992 INVOLVED YOUTH AGE 15 OR YOUNGER

Juveniles age 15 or younger accounted for 62% of person offense cases and 64% of property offense cases. In comparison, they accounted for 53% of public order offense cases and 39% of cases involving drug law violations.

Age at referral	Delinquency cases per 1,000 juveniles in age group		Percent change
	1988	1992	
All ages	45.7	55.1	21%
10	6.0	6.3	5
11	9.8	11.8	21
12	18.8	23.3	24
13	34.8	45.1	30
14	55.3	71.2	29
15	69.3	89.1	29
16	85.3	109.6	28
17	84.6	106.5	26

Source: Butts, J., et al. (1995). Juvenile court statistics 1992.

MORE 16-YEAR-OLDS THAN 17-YEAR-OLDS COME TO JUVENILE COURT—MANY 17-YEAR-OLDS GO DIRECTLY TO CRIMINAL COURT

Although far more 17-year-olds than 16-year-olds were arrested in 1992, the number of juvenile court cases involving 17-year-olds (230,900) was lower than the number involving 16-year-olds (325,400). This lower number stems, in large part, from the fact that in 11 States these youth are excluded from the original jurisdiction of the juvenile court. In these States, all 17-year-olds are legally adults and are referred to criminal rather than to juvenile court. Thus, far fewer 17-year-olds than 16-year-olds are under juvenile court jurisdiction in the U.S.

Even after controlling for their differential representation in the *juvenile* population, the case rates for 16-year-olds were still slightly greater than the rates for 17-year-olds. One reason may be State legislation that enables older juveniles to be processed directly in criminal courts (either via statutory exclusion or concurrent jurisdiction provisions). In these situations, while a youth of juvenile age is arrested, the matter goes before a criminal court rather than before a juvenile court.

INFORMAL PROCESSING INVOLVES THE VOLUNTARY ACCEPTANCE OF SANCTIONS AND INTERVENTIONS

Soon after referral to juvenile court, a decision is made to either handle the case formally or informally. Informal processing is considered when the decision makers (police or probation officers, intake workers, prosecutors, or other screening officers) believe that accountability and rehabilitation can be achieved without the use of formal court intervention.

Informal sanctions are voluntary; the court cannot force a juvenile to comply with an informal disposition. If the decision is made to handle the matter informally (in lieu of formal prosecution) an offender agrees to comply with one or more sanctions such as community service, victim restitution, or voluntary probation supervision. In many jurisdictions, before juveniles are offered informal sanctions, they must admit they committed the alleged act.

When informally handled, the case is generally held open pending the successful completion of the informal disposition. Upon successful completion of these arrangements. the charges against the offender are dismissed. However, if the offender does not fulfill the court's conditions for informal handling, the case is likely to be reopened and formally prosecuted.

THE JUVENILE JUSTICE SYSTEM MAKES BROAD USE OF INFORMAL PROCESSING

Informal handling is common in the juvenile courts. According to *Juvenile Court Statistics* 1992, half (49%) of the delinquency cases disposed by juvenile courts in 1992 were handled informally.

**Percent of cases
handled informally**

	1988	1992
Delinquency	51%	49%
Person	46	45
Property	54	52
Drugs	41	36
Public order	52	49

Source: Butts, J., et al. (1995). Juvenile court statistics 1992.

FEMALES, WHITES, AND YOUNGER JUVENILES ARE MORE LIKELY TO HAVE THEIR CASES HANDLED INFORMALLY

**Percent of delinquency cases that
were handled informally in 1992**

Sex	
Male	48%
Female	61
Race	
White	54%
Black	41
Other race	50
Age at referral	
Under 16	53%
16 or older	46

Note: These patterns do not control for criminal histories that are related to an increased likelihood of formal processing.
Source: Butts, J., et al. (1995). Juvenile court statistics 1992.

CASES ARE MORE LIKELY TO BE HANDLED INFORMALLY IN RURAL AREAS THAN IN LARGE CITIES

In jurisdictions where the population of 10- to 17-year-olds was fewer than 10,000, courts processed 55% of their delinquency cases informally in 1992, while in jurisdictions where the population of 10- to 17-year-olds was greater than 100,000, only 43% of their delinquency cases were processed informally.

A SUBSTANTIAL PROPORTION OF INFORMAL CASES INVOLVE SOME SORT OF VOLUNTARY SANCTION

In 1992 more than half (53%) of informally handled delinquency cases involved some type of intervention services and/or sanctions beyond warning and counseling the youth. In nearly a third (30%) of informally processed cases the youth agreed to a term of voluntary probation supervision, while 23% agreed to other sanctions such as voluntary restitution, community service, or referral to another agency. In a small number of cases the youth and the youth's family agreed to a period of out-of-home placement as a sanction.

INFORMAL HANDLING CAN BE ADVANTAGEOUS TO BOTH THE COMMUNITY AND THE OFFENDER

Programs such as "pretrial diversion" or "deferred prosecution" have attracted increasing interest in recent years. Courts at all levels have found that diverting certain cases from the formal justice system can be cost-effective in terms of both public accountability and offender rehabilitation. Diversion programs reduce the administrative burdens and the costs of prosecution while allowing the justice system to intervene in relatively minor cases. Offenders benefit by avoiding trial and the stigma of formal conviction. Diverted or deferred cases also move through the court system more quickly since they do not involve protracted courtroom procedures.

PETITIONERS ASK THE COURT TO ORDER SANCTIONS IN FORMALLY PROCESSED CASES

Compared with cases that are handled informally, formally processed delinquency cases tend to involve more serious offenses and juveniles who are older and have longer court histories. While more than half of cases involving juveniles above age 13 were formally processed in 1992, formal processing occurred in less than 40% of the cases of younger juveniles. Secure detention between referral and court disposition was used in 28% of formally processed delinquency cases and 12% of informally processed cases in 1992.

If adjudicated, juveniles in formally processed cases may be involuntarily ordered to residential placement or to comply with various conditions of probation. Often diversion has been tried in previous referrals and the youth has returned to court on a new offense.

THE LIKELIHOOD OF FORMAL PROCESSING CHANGED LITTLE FROM 1988 TO 1992

Although the volume of delinquency cases referred to juvenile court intake increased 26% between 1988 and 1992, for most offenses, the proportion of cases referred to court that were formally handled remained about the same.

IN 1992 JUVENILE COURTS FORMALLY PROCESSED NEARLY 744,000 DELINQUENCY CASES

Most serious offense	Percent of 1992 cases that were petitioned	Number of cases petitioned in 1992	Percent change 1988–1992
Total delinquency	51%	743,700	31%
Person offenses	55	165,200	59
Criminal homicide	91	2,300	62
Forcible rape	80	4,300	32
Robbery	85	28,000	63
Aggravated assault	62	48,100	80
Simple assault	42	64,500	46
Other violent sex offenses	68	6,700	50
Other person offense	57	11,300	67
Property offenses	48	400,600	27
Burglary	69	108,300	25
Larceny-theft	37	132,600	17
Motor vehicle theft	69	50,200	42
Arson	51	4,200	35
Vandalism	39	47,300	55
Trespassing	34	20,200	25
Stolen property offenses	62	17,900	1
Other property offenses	59	20,000	57
Drug law violations	64	46,200	-5
Public order offenses	51	131,600	30
Obstruction of justice	69	60,500	8
Disorderly conduct	35	24,000	72
Weapons offenses	54	22,100	107
Liquor law violations	43	5,400	16
Nonviolent sex offenses	48	6,200	11
Other public order	41	13,400	29
Violent Crime Index*	70	82,700	70
Property Crime Index**	49	295,300	24

• As a general rule, the more serious the offense, the more likely the case was to be brought before a judge for formal (court-ordered) sanctioning. For example, 37% of all larceny-theft cases were formally processed in 1992, compared with 69% of all burglary cases.

• The juvenile was charged with an offense against a person in fewer than one-quarter of the delinquency cases formally processed in 1992.

• The relative increase in cases involving Violent Crime Index offenses was more than double the increase in property offense cases.

*Violent Crime Index: criminal homicide, forcible rape, robbery, and aggravated assault.
**Property Crime Index: burglary, larceny-theft, motor vehicle theft, and arson.
Note: Detail may not add to totals because of rounding. Percent change calculations are based on unrounded numbers.
Source: Butts, J., et al. (1995). Juvenile court statistics 1992.

JUVENILES WERE ADJUDICATED IN 427,000 FORMALLY PROCESSED DELINQUENCY CASES IN 1992

A youth referred to juvenile court for a delinquency offense may be adjudicated (judged to be) a delinquent after admitting to the charges in the case, or after the court finds sufficient evidence to prove, beyond a reasonable doubt, that the youth committed the facts alleged in the petition.

In 1992, 57% of all formally processed delinquency cases resulted in an adjudication. Youth were adjudicated delinquent in 53% of person offense cases. This was less than any of the other major categories of offenses— youth were adjudicated delinquent in 58% of property offense cases, 60% of drug law violation cases, and 59% of public order offense cases.

The lower rate of adjudication in person offense cases may reflect intake's unwillingness to divert person offense cases from the formal juvenile justice system until a judge has had the opportunity to review the case.

THE PROPORTION OF CASES ADJUDICATED VARIED BY OFFENSE AND DEMOGRAPHIC GROUP

In 1992, 58% of all formally processed male cases were adjudicated compared with 52% of cases involving females, a pattern that held even after controlling for referral offense.

There were also race and age variations in the proportion of formal cases that were adjudicated in 1992—

* Blacks, 55%.
* Whites, 58%.
* Youth of other races, 65%.
* Juveniles below age 14, 55%.
* 14–15-year-olds, 61%.
* 16-year-olds, 58%.
* 17-year-olds, 52%.

Proportion of Formally Processed Cases that were Adjudicated:

	Males	Females
Delinquency	58%	52%
Person	54	49
Property	59	52
Drugs	61	52
Public order	60	56

Source: Butts, J., et al. (1995). Juvenile court statistics 1992.

The decreasing rate of adjudication in cases involving older offenders is nearly equivalent to the increased probability of judicial waiver for these older offenders. The proportion of formally processed cases that were either waived or adjudicated was relatively constant for juveniles above age 13.

121,000 ADJUDICATED DELINQUENCY CASES RESULTED IN OUT-OF-HOME PLACEMENT, AND 244,000 RESULTED IN FORMAL PROBATION IN 1992

In 28% of adjudicated delinquency cases, the court ordered the youth to residential placement such as a training school, camp, ranch, privately operated placement facility, or group home. Cases involving youth adjudicated for a property offense were least likely to result in out-of-home placement. The relatively high placement rate for public order offense cases was at least partially due to the fact that escapes from institutions and probation and parole violations are included in this offense category.

Once adjudicated, white juveniles were less likely to be ordered to an out-of-home placement than blacks and youth of other races. Females were less likely to be placed than males.

About half (52%) the adjudicated delinquency cases involved detention at some point during processing of the case. These cases were more than twice as likely as cases that did not involve detention to result in out-of-home placement at disposition.

Generally, if adjudicated delinquents were not placed out of home, they were placed on formal probation. Fifty-seven percent of adjudicated delinquency cases resulted in probation. Overall, 85% of adjudicated delinquency cases resulted in either placement or formal probation.

These patterns do not control for criminal histories that are related to increased severity of sanctions.

JUVENILE COURTS ASSIGN PROBATION SUPERVISION TO A WIDE RANGE OF YOUTHFUL OFFENDERS

Probation is the oldest and most widely used community-based, corrections program. Probation may be used at either the "front end" or the "back end" of the juvenile justice system—for first-time, low-risk offenders or as an alternative to institutional confinement for more serious offenders. During a period of probation, a juvenile offender remains in the community and can continue normal activities such as school and work. In exchange for this freedom, the juvenile must submit to a number of conditions.

This submission may be voluntary, where the youth agrees to comply with a period of informal probation in lieu of formal adjudication. Or, once adjudicated and formally ordered to a term of probation, the juvenile must

Proportion of Adjudicated Delinquency Cases in 1992 That Resulted In:

	Out-of-home placement	Formal probation
All cases	28%	57%
Offense		
Person	32	55
Property	25	60
Drugs	32	54
Public order	34	52
Age		
Less than 14	24	63
14	30	58
15	32	56
16	30	56
17	25	54
Sex		
Male	29	57
Female	23	61
Race		
White	25	58
Black	33	56
Other	31	51

Source: Butts, J., et al. (1995). Juvenile court statistics 1992.

submit to the probation conditions established by the court. More than half (54%) of juvenile probation dispositions in 1992 were informal, or enacted without a formal adjudication or court order.

PROBATION CONDITIONS TYPICALLY INCORPORATE ITEMS MEANT TO CONTROL AS WELL AS REHABILITATE

A juvenile may be required to meet regularly with a probation supervisor, adhere to a strict curfew, and complete a specified period of community service. The conditions of probation may also include provisions for the revocation of probation should the juvenile violate the conditions. If probation is revoked, the court may reconsider its disposition and impose stricter sanctions.

PROBATION CASELOADS INCREASED BETWEEN 1988 AND 1992

The total number of delinquency cases receiving probation (either formal or informal) as the most severe initial disposition climbed 23% between 1988 and 1992, from 434,000 to 533,000 annually. The number of adjudicated delinquency cases placed on formal probation increased 24% over this period, from 197,000 to 244,000 annually.

Between 1988 and 1992 probation was the most severe disposition used by juvenile courts in nearly 2 in 5 delinquency cases, and in nearly 3 in 5 adjudicated cases—with the annual proportions remaining constant over this time period. Therefore, the growth in probation caseloads was directly related to the general growth in referrals to juvenile courts.

FORMAL PROBATION CASES DIFFER FROM THOSE RESULTING IN OUT-OF-HOME PLACEMENT

Compared with adjudicated cases that resulted in placement in 1992, adjudicated delinquency cases that resulted in probation involved a higher percentage of whites (63% vs. 55%), females (14% vs. 11%) and youth charged with a property offense (57% vs. 47%).

REFERRAL RATES VARY BY SIZE OF JURISDICTION

To compare case rates for different size counties, counties were ranked by the size of their juvenile population and placed into four groups. Each group contained about 25% of the U.S. juvenile population:

- 2,528 small rural counties.
- 404 small-medium counties.
- 116 medium-large counties.
- 37 large urban counties.

Juvenile courts in large urban jurisdictions handled more cases than courts in rural areas. These differences were not simply the result of the differing population bases. The delinquency case rates (the number of cases processed for every 1,000 juveniles age 10 or older in the population) also differed.

Juvenile courts in small rural counties, on average, received delinquency cases at a lower rate than did courts in larger counties. Referral rates increased with county size except for the large urban stratum, where the rate dropped substantially.

	Delinquency cases in 1992	
County type	Average number	Per 1,000 juveniles ages 10-upper age
Small rural	118	45
Small-medium	865	53
Medium-large	4,044	71
Large urban	9,564	53

DELINQUENCY CASELOADS DIFFER IN
SMALL AND LARGE JURISDICTIONS

To investigate urban/rural variations in court processing, more than 300,000 delinquency case records from 15 States were analyzed. The 1992 caseloads of courts in counties with total populations under 150,000 (rural) were compared with those in counties with populations greater than 600,000 (urban). The analysis found that compared with courts in large urban jurisdictions, the delinquency cases in small rural courts had—

- A smaller proportion of person offense and drug law violation cases.
- A greater proportion of juveniles under age 14.
- A similar percentage of females.
- A smaller percentage of minorities.

THE NATURE OF THE COURT'S RESPONSE DIFFERS
IN URBAN AND RURAL AREAS

Compared with delinquency cases in urban areas, cases in rural areas were—

- Less likely to involve secure detention between referral and case disposition.
- Less likely to be formally processed.
- More likely to be transferred to criminal court if formally processed.
- More likely to be adjudicated if formally processed.
- Equally likely to result in out-of-home placement if adjudicated.

Justice by Geography: Urban, Suburban, and Rural Variations in Juvenile Justice Administration

BARRY C. FELD

I. INTRODUCTION

Although the same statutes and juvenile court rules of procedure apply, juvenile justice administration varies substantially in Minnesota. Juvenile courts' procedural characteristics and sentencing practices relate consis-

Reprinted by special permission of Northwestern University School of Law, *Journal of Criminal Law and Criminology*, Volume 82, Issue 1, pp. 156–210 (1991).

tently to urban, suburban, and rural differences in social structure. Urban courts operate in milieu that provide fewer mechanisms for informal social control than do rural ones; consequently, they place greater emphasis on formal bureaucratized social control. For example, the presence of counsel provides an indicator of a court's legal formality. Attorneys appear in urban courts more than twice as often as they do in rural courts. Structural influences on formal versus informal social control also affect the selection of delinquents and the administration of justice. Urban courts sweep a broader, more inclusive net and encompass proportionally more and younger youths than do suburban or rural courts. Social structure and procedural formality are also associated with more severe sanctions. The more formal, urban courts place over twice as many youths in pre-trial detention and sentence similarly-charged offenders more severely than do suburban or rural courts. As a result, where youths live affects how their cases are processed and the severity of the sentences they receive.

This Article examines the relationships between social structure, procedural formality, and juvenile justice administration and considers the implications of "justice by geography" for juvenile court reform.

A. Social Structure, Crime, and Justice Administration

Crime and delinquency are disproportionately urban phenomena. Criminology uses social structural features to explain variations in the distribution of crime. Classical sociological theory, for example, attributes the greater prevalence of crime in cities to urban anomie. In traditional rural communities, homogeneity and uniformity of beliefs foster informal social control, whereas in urban settings, population density, anonymity, and heterogeneity weaken social cohesion and increase reliance on formal social control. Social ecology, associated with the Chicago School, relates urban structural features such as income inequality, family structure, or racial composition to variations in crime rates.

Urbanization is associated with greater bureaucratization and formal social control as well as with higher rates of crime. Weber associated the formal rationalization of social life with urbanization and bureaucratization and argued that abstract rules would supplant more traditional methods of dispute resolution as law became increasingly rational and functionally specialized. Presumably, urban courts would be more formal and bureaucratized, emphasize rationality and efficiency, and punish on the basis of legally relevant factors such as present offense and prior record. By contrast, rural courts would be less bureaucratized and sentence on the basis of non-legal considerations.

Surprisingly, very little research has been done on the relationships between urbanization, bureaucratization, and justice administration. The few studies available document significant urban-rural differences in sentencing. Hagan found that differential treatment of racial minorities was more pronounced in rural courts than in bureaucratized urban ones. Tepperman reported that rural juvenile courts treated female offenders more leniently than males, but that gender differences declined with urbanization. Austin found that rural criminal courts considered social background factors while urban courts adhered to a more legalistic model of sentencing. Paternoster found that social context influenced charging decisions; rural prosecutors were more likely to seek the death penalty than urban ones. Myers and Talarico reported that urbanization and social context affect criminal court sentencing decisions. In short, these studies support Weberian expectations that similarly situated offenders may be treated differently based upon their locale and that differential processing is more prevalent in rural settings and declines with urbanization and bureaucratization.

Criminology also attempts to explain variations in the administration of justice. Organizations interact with and are influenced by their external environments; for example, the expectations of police, politicians, appellate courts, news media, and the public all affect how courts perform. Criminal justice agencies operate within differing socio-political environments and depend upon their environment for legitimation, resources, and clients. As a result, external social, economic, and political variables constrain even ostensibly similar organizations. Wilson's analyses of urban police practices attributed differences in police behavior to variations in community social structure. Levin compared criminal sentencing in two metropolitan areas and attributed differences in sentencing practices to differences in the cities' political cultures. Eisenstein and Jacob identified the pivotal roles of courtroom work groups on judicial sentencing decisions in different jurisdictions.

B. Social Structural Variations in Juvenile Justice Administration— Formal Versus Informal Social Control

The traditional juvenile court's emphasis on rehabilitating offenders fostered judicial discretion, procedural informality, and organizational diversity. The broad legal framework associated with individualized justice allows judges to apply the same law very differently; descriptions of contemporary juvenile courts continue to emphasize judicial diversity.

With the imposition of formal procedures in *In re Gault* and the emergence of punitive sentencing goals, juvenile courts no longer can be assumed either to conform to the traditional therapeutic model or to be similar to one another. Ethnographic studies of a single juvenile court cannot be generalized to other courts in other settings. Indeed. most juvenile court ethnographies do not provide enough information about a court's social or political context to help explain its behavior.

The few studies that compare juvenile courts in different locales indicate that they are variable organizations that differ on several structural and procedural dimensions. Contrasting traditional therapeutic courts with those holding a more legalistic, due process orientation captures many of the variables in juvenile justice administration. The former intervene in a child's "best interests" on an informal, discretionary basis, while the latter emphasize more formal, rule-oriented decision-making. "Traditional" and "due process" courts may be arrayed across a continuum from informal to formal with corresponding procedural and substantive differences.

Recognizing that juvenile justice is not a uniform system vastly complicates analyses of courts' behavior. Even research that recognizes courts' diversity does not explore either the structural sources or administrative consequences of formal-informal or due process-traditional organizational variation. One recent study examined the impact of counsel on juvenile justice administration. Variations in rates of representation provided an indicator of a formal, due process orientation and were associated with differences in pretrial detention, sentencing, and case processing practices. While the presence of defense attorneys was associated with differences in juvenile justice administration, that study could not account for variations in rates of representation. Although those juvenile courts operated under statutes and rules of statewide applicability, external political, social structural, or legal variables and individual judge's policies apparently influenced courts' procedural and substantive orientations.

The present study provides compelling evidence of "justice by geography." A court's social context strongly influences the ways in which cases are selected, heard, and disposed. Social structure is associated consistently with differences in rates of juvenile criminality, the degree of procedural formality, and juvenile justice administration. These differences are reflected in pre-petition screening of cases, the presence of counsel, pretrial detention, and sentencing practices. In urban counties, which are more heterogeneous, diverse, and less stable than rural counties, juvenile court intervention is more formal and due process–oriented. Urban formality, in turn, is associated with greater severity in pre-trial detention and sentencing practices. By contrast, in the more homogeneous and stable rural counties, juvenile justice administration is procedurally less formal and sentences more lenient. However, rural judges' exercises of discretion also result in gender differences in the processing of female offenders. What are the costs and benefits of formal versus informal dispute resolution? How do these difference in juvenile justice administration affect the lives of young people? Formulating juvenile justice policy requires an appreciation of the structural sources of local variation.

II. THE PRESENT STUDY—DATA AND METHODOLOGY

This study uses data from two sources. Minnesota county census data from 1980 provide indicators of social structure. Data collected in each county by the Minnesota Supreme Court's Judicial Information System (SJIS) for delinquency and status offense cases processed in 1986 provide information on juvenile justice administration. To facilitate analyses between the census and SJIS data sets, the county is the unit of analysis, and counties are then aggregated as urban, suburban, or rural.

... Only formally petitioned delinquency and status cases are analyzed; the SJIS does not include cases referred to juvenile courts which were subsequently disposed of informally without the filing of a petition.

This study uses a youth-based data file that analyzes all 17,195 individual juveniles whose cases were formally petitioned in Minnesota's juvenile courts in 1986.... The data reported here reflect a youth's most current juvenile court referral as well as all petitions, adjudications, and dispositions for at least the preceding two years or more.

In this study, the offenses reported by the SJIS were re-grouped into six analytical categories. The "felony/minor" offense distinction provides an indicator of offense seriousness. Offenses are also classified as being against person or property, other delinquency, and status. Combining person and property with the felony/misdemeanor distinction produces a six-item offense severity scale. When a petition alleges more than one offense, the youth is classified on the basis of the most serious charge. The study uses two indicators of severity of dispositions: out-of-home placement and secure confinement. Out-of-home placement includes any disposition in which the child is taken from his or her home and placed in a group home, foster care, in-patient psychiatric or chemical dependency treatment facility, or correctional institution. Secure confinement is a substantial subset of all out-of-home placements but includes only commitments to county institutions or state training schools.

The classification of counties as urban, suburban and small urban, and rural uses the census concept of Standardized Metropolitan Statistical Area (SMSA) and youth-population density. In this study, counties were classified as *urban* if they were located within an SMSA, had one or more cities of 100,000 inhabitants, and had a juvenile population aged ten to seventeen of at least 50,000 youths. Counties were classified as either *suburban* or *small urban* if they were located within a metropolitan SMSA (suburban) or, if within their own SMSA (small urban), they had one or more cities of 25,000 to 100,000, and had a juvenile population aged ten to seventeen of more than 7,500 but less than 50,000 youths. Counties were classified as *rural* if they were located outside of an SMSA, had no principal city of 25,000 or greater, and had less than 7,500 juveniles aged ten to seventeen.

III. DATA AND ANALYSES

A. Urban, Suburban, and Rural Social Structural Characteristics

This study explores how social structural context influences juvenile courts' responses to delinquency in their county.... Based on the census criteria, Minnesota has two urban counties, eight suburban or small urban counties, and seventy-seven rural counties. More than one-third (34.4%) of the population lives in the urban counties, about one-quarter (25.2%) in suburban or small urban settings, and the remainder (40.4%) in rural counties. . . .

Urban, suburban, and rural counties differ consistently on social structural dimensions which affect both rates of offending and the effectiveness of informal social controls. As contrasted with the urban counties' diversity, rural counties' greater stability and homogeneity suggest they would rely less heavily on formal means of social control. Racial diversity is almost exclusively an urban phenomenon, and a larger proportion of urban households are headed by a single, female parent. While more people in rural counties are poor, they are also more homogeneous and residentially stable. The suburban counties are about as stable and homogeneous as the rural ones, and more affluent than either urban or rural counties. . . .

Crime, especially serious crime, is primarily an urban phenomenon. . . . More than half of the Federal Bureau of Investigation (FBI) Part I offenses in 1980 in Minnesota were committed in the two urban counties. Even after crime rates are standardized for population base, the greater prevalence of crime in the urban counties remains. There were 703.1 serious offenses per 10,000 people in the urban settings as contrasted with only 308.5 per 10,000 in the rural counties.

A similar pattern is evident with respect to juvenile crime. . . . Almost one-half of all the juveniles arrested for serious and less serious offenses (45.6% and 44.5%) reside in the two urban counties. The pattern remains even after controlling for population differences. In the whole state, 297.2 juveniles per 10,000 aged ten to seventeen were arrested for serious felony offenses. However, when this rate is disaggregated geographically, 441.7 urban juveniles per 10,000 were arrested for serious crimes, as compared to 299.4 suburban and only 187.9 rural juvenile serious crime arrests. Similarly, urban juveniles were arrested for less serious offenses 146% more often than suburban youths and 217% more often than rural youths. Thus, it is readily apparent that urban youngsters are both quantitatively and qualitatively more criminally active than their suburban or rural counterparts. . . .

C. Urban, Suburban, and Rural Variations in Juvenile Justice Administration

Because of geographic differences in social structure and case volume, juvenile courts are organized differently throughout the state. In the two urban counties, a full-time district court judge is assisted by other judges, referees, and a large probation staff. Urban judges serve exclusively in juvenile court for several years and provide stability and predictability to courtroom workgroups. Due to lower volume, judges in non-urban counties hear juvenile cases as part of their general caseload and many preside over delinquency matters on a rotating basis. Thus, the urban courts are the most formally organized, bureaucratized, and functionally specialized.

1. Screening Cases—Petitions and Offenses Table 1 reports the numbers of petitions and types of offenses with which juveniles were charged in the state and in the various geographic locales. The largest number and proportion of petitions were filed against juveniles in the rural counties, which reflects both the large number of rural counties and the population age distribution in the state. Slightly more than one-third (36.5%) of the state's "official" delinquents are in urban settings, slightly more than one-fifth (21.4%) are in suburban locales, and the remainder (42.1,%) are in the rural counties. Suburban juvenile courts "underpetition" youths relative to their proportional make-up of the youth population (21.4% vs. 28.2%) while the urban courts "over-petition" juveniles (36.5% vs. 30.6%).

Throughout the state, 18.4% of juveniles were charged with offenses that would be felonies if committed by adults, 54.4% were charged with minor offenses such as misdemeanors and gross misdemeanors, and 27.2% were charged with status offenses. Within the felony category, offenses against property, primarily burglary, predominated. Similarly, within the minor offense category, property offenses such as shoplifting and theft predominated. Less than 10% of delinquency cases involved felony or minor offenses against the person, and more than one-quarter involved non-criminal status offenses.

Different patterns of petitioned offenses emerge when they are examined separately in urban, suburban, and rural counties. Despite the prevalence of reported serious crime and juvenile felony arrests in the urban counties, of those juveniles actually charged, the largest proportion of felony petitions are filed in the suburban, rather than urban, counties. The suburban county courts charge the largest proportion of juveniles with felonies against the person as well as against property. The smallest proportion of felony petitions are filed in the rural settings. Proportionally more rural juveniles charged with felonies are accused of property crimes than are their urban or suburban counterparts. Rural counties charge the largest proportion of status offenders (30.0%) in the state while suburban counties process the fewest (21.2%).

Table 1 also reports the prior record of court referrals. For the entire state, 71.9% of juveniles made their first appearance in juvenile courts; only 1.2% were chronic recidivists with five or more prior appearances. When geographic locale is examined, a different pattern emerges. In urban settings, 64.7% of youths made their first appearance as contrasted with 71.8% and 78.1% of juveniles in suburban and rural counties, respectively. Thus, substantially more delinquency petitions had been previously filed against urban juveniles than had been filed against their non-urban counterparts. . . .

Although urban courts file more petitions overall, suburban and rural courts screen cases more rigorously. While formal petitions were filed in all of the cases analyzed herein, the informal threshold for charging youths may differ by geography. This introduces some important potential sample selection biases into the data. Compared to suburban courts, a smaller proportion of serious offenses and larger proportions of other delinquency and

TABLE 1
Petitioned Offenses and Prior Records

	Statewide	Urban	Suburban	Rural
Juvenile Population Aged 10–17				
% =	100.0	30.6	28.2	41.1
N =	571648	175152	161345	235151
Delinquent & Status Offenders				
% =	100.0	36.5	21.4	42.1
N =	17195[1]	6273	3681	7241
FELONY				
% =	18.4	17.5	23.0	16.9
N =	3153	1095	842	1216
Felony Offense Against Person				
% =	4.0	4.5	5.0	2.9
N =	680	282	185	213
Felony Offense Against Property				
% =	14.4	13.0	17.8	13.9
N =	2473	813	657	1003
MISDEMEANOR				
% =	54.4	55.3	55.8	52.9
N =	9298	3457	2040	3801
Minor Offense Against Person				
% =	5.2	6.0	6.2	3.9
N =	889	376	230	283
Minor Offense Against Property				
% =	32.3	27.3	34.9	35.3
N =	5554	1714	1284	2556
Other Delinquency				
% =	16.6	21.8	14.3	13.3
N =	2855	1367	526	962
STATUS				
% =	27.2	27.2	21.2	30.0
N =	4649	1704	776	2169
Prior Referrals Overall				
0				
% =	71.9	64.7	71.8	78.1
N =	12359	4060	2642	5657
1–2				
% =	23.0	27.1	23.9	19.1
N =	3962	1700	881	1381
3–4				
% =	3.9	6.1	3.5	2.1
N =	669	385	129	155
5+				
% =	1.2	2.0	0.8	0.7
N =	205	128	29	48

[1] *Of the 17,195 total juveniles, 95 are missing data on their present offenses. Those missing offense data include: 17 urban 23 suburban, and 55 rural youths.*

status offenses are charged in urban counties. Differences in urban petitioning rates may be attributable to the filing by police or school administrators of more petty petitions alleging minor and status offenses without
any additional screening.

In addition, the type of behavior required to qualify for official attention in urban settings may be qualitatively more serious than in rural or suburban areas. With substantially higher felony arrest rates, police or other
referral sources in cities may view shoplifting, under-aged drinking, or vandalism as less important, relative to more serious violent and property
crimes, than similar behaviors may appear in suburban and rural areas. With
greater urban anonymity and more bureaucratized social control, minor juvenile deviance may represent less of a tear in the social fabric than it constitutes in more socially cohesive areas. Heavier caseloads and more serious
crimes may lead urban officials to overlook some delinquency that other areas do not ignore. In short, even though all of the youths in this study were
formally charged, geographic differences in rates of apprehension and pre-
petition selection of cases for prosecution suggest that not all "delinquents"
are necessarily equal. . . .

D. Urban, Suburban, and Rural Variations in Rates of Representation—Procedural Formality in Juvenile Court

The Supreme Court in *Gault* held that juvenile offenders were constitutionally entitled to the assistance of counsel, because "a proceeding where
the issue is whether the child will be found to be 'delinquent' and subjected
to the loss of his liberty for years is comparable in seriousness to a felony
prosecution." In the decades since *Gault,* the promise of counsel often remains unrealized. Although there is a scarcity of data, in many states, including Minnesota, less than half of juveniles adjudicated delinquent receive
the assistance of counsel to which they are constitutionally entitled. The
most comprehensive study available reports that in three of the six states
surveyed, only 37.5%, 47.7%, and 52.7% of the juveniles were represented.
The routine presence of defense counsel is the primary indicator of a procedurally formal, adversarial juvenile court with significant consequences
for juvenile justice administration.

1. Rates of Representation   . . . Only 45.3% of juveniles in Minnesota received the assistance of counsel. For the state as a whole, about two-thirds
(66.1%) of juveniles charged with felonies, less than one-half (46.4%) of those
charged with misdemeanors, and about one-quarter (28.9%) of those charged
with status offenses were represented.

Rates of representation differ by geography and offense. In the urban
courts, 62.6% of all juveniles were represented, as were 55.2% of suburban
youths. By contrast, only 25.1% of rural youths had counsel. Of those charged
with felonies, 82.9% had counsel in the urban settings as compared to 67.9%

in the suburban counties and 49.6% in the rural counties. An even sharper drop-off in rates of representation occurred in rural counties for juveniles charged with misdemeanors (23.5%) and status offenses (14.3%). More urban and suburban youths charged with misdemeanors had counsel (64.%, 57.9%) than did rural juveniles charged with felonies (49.6%). More urban and suburban youths charged with status offenses had counsel (45.6%, 33.9%) than did rural youths charged with misdemeanors (23.5%).

Using counsel as an indicator of procedural formality and a due process orientation, the urban courts are the most formal and legalistic while the rural courts adhere most closely to the traditional informal model. Moreover, the actions of various justice agencies are loosely connected; the structural features that determine a court's orientations are likely to be reflected in decisions by other law enforcement agencies as well. This is consistent with the hypothesis that urban courts rely more heavily on formal social control than do courts in other locations.

. . . Comparing the rates of representation at adjudication (arraignment, plea, or trial) with those at disposition reveals that 6.4% fewer juveniles have counsel at sentencing than at earlier proceedings. Virtually all of the decrease in representation at dispositions occurs in the urban counties (62.6% vs. 43.9%). If prosecutors in more bureaucratized courts pre-screen cases using formal legal criteria, then there may be a correspondingly greater legal role for defense counsel at adjudication. Using the "courtroom work group" model, defense counsel are as effective as the juvenile justice system allows them to be. Functioning in a procedurally formal adjudicative context is a more familiar and comfortable role for defense lawyers than is participating in a "messy" social services–dominated dispositional proceeding. Perhaps, urban defense attorneys appreciate that participating at disposition may be futile or even adversely affect the eventual sentence. In any event, once proceedings shift from formal legality to substantive rationality (*i.e.*, social services disposition), urban defense lawyers apparently exit in droves.

E. Urban, Suburban, and Rural Juvenile Court Sentencing Practices

The preceding analyses described some of the characteristics of the courts and juveniles referred to them in different counties. The next analyses explore the consequences for juveniles of being tried in courts in different locations. . . .

For the entire state. 18.5% of all petitioned juveniles are removed from their homes and 11.1% of all juveniles are incarcerated in state or local institutions. However, the urban, suburban, and rural counties differ markedly in their sentencing practices. In urban counties, about one of four (24.0%) juveniles is removed from home. In suburban counties, about one of six (17.5%) is removed. In rural counties, about one of seven (14.2%) is removed. Similarly, urban youths (15.1%) receive secure confinement dispositions more often than do suburban (9.1%) or rural (8.7%) juveniles.

The seriousness of the offense substantially alters a youth's risk of removal or confinement. Despite the court's theoretical commitment to individualized dispositions, actual sentencing practices evidence an element of proportionality. Juveniles charged with felony offenses—person and property—and offenses against the person have the highest rates of out-of-home placements and secure confinement. For the state as a whole, more than one-third (34.3%) of all juveniles charged with a felony offense are removed from their homes, and about one-quarter (24.4%) are incarcerated. Conversely, about half as many juveniles charged with misdemeanors—minor property offenses such as theft and shoplifting, or other delinquency—are removed from home (17.6%) or confined (11.3%). As a result of legal restrictions on the placement of status offenders, they have the lowest proportion of removal from the home or secure confinement. Even though legislation prohibits confining status offenders, 3.5% of them are in county or state institutions.

While there is a direct relationship between the seriousness of the offense and the severity of disposition, there are also marked differences between the sentences imposed in the urban, suburban, and rural counties. For nearly every offense category, urban judges sentence more severely than do suburban or rural judges. For example, of delinquents adjudicated for felonies, urban judges incarcerate one-third (33.3%) as contrasted with only about one-seventh (13.6%) in the suburban counties and one-fifth (20.4%) in the rural counties. Urban judges are nearly as likely to remove juveniles charged with misdemeanors from their homes (21.5%) as suburban judges are likely to remove juveniles charged with felony offenses (23.7%). Urban judges institutionalize more youths charged with misdemeanors (14.1%) than suburban judges do youths charged with felonies (13.6%). Even though suburban courts may prescreen cases to produce a court docket that contains more serious offenses and fewer trivial ones, urban courts still sentence similarly-situated offenders more severely. Only juveniles charged with "other delinquency" receive more severe sentences in suburban courts than they do in urban or rural settings. Rural judges sentence youths charged with felony offenses somewhat more severely than do the suburban judges, but more leniently than do the urban judges. When juveniles are charged with misdemeanor or status offenses, however, rural judges' sentencing practices are comparable to or even more lenient than the suburban judges. Since the largest proportion of rural juveniles are minor and status offenders, overall rural youths receive lenient sentences.

Perhaps there are qualitative differences in offenses which account for the geographical differences in sentencing practices. For example, within comparable offense categories, urban juveniles' crimes may be more serious than rural youths' crimes in ways that statistical controls cannot capture (e.g., amount of injury to victim or value of property stolen) but which may affect sentencing severity. Because there is a greater volume of delinquency, there may be a higher threshold of seriousness before a case is referred to urban juvenile court. However, the scant research on geographic variations in the "quality" of crime concludes that "rural and urban victimizations are similar with respect to their consequences to victims (*e.g.*, injury) and characteristics *(e.g.*, the nature and extent of weapon use). . . ." Alternatively, urban judges see more crime, including serious crime, and may just sentence more severely.

2. Prior Referrals and Dispositions   In addition to the seriousness of the present offense, a history of prior referrals and previous sentences affects a juvenile's disposition. . . . As noted earlier, the rate of prior referrals varied by geographic locale. Compared to the urban juveniles, 7.1% more of the suburban juveniles and 13.4% of rural youths made their first appearance with correspondingly fewer recidivists.

Both overall and controlling for offenses, the length of the prior record affects a youth's likelihood of receiving a more severe disposition; the largest increase occurs between those juveniles with one or two prior referrals and those with three or four. By the time juveniles appear for the third or fourth time, more than half" (52.9%) will be removed from home and more than one-third (39.9%) will be confined. For each offense, there is a linear relationship between additional prior referrals and more severe dispositions. . . .

Even though the relationship between prior referrals and sentencing severity is similar in all types of counties, urban judges remove and confine larger proportions of juveniles than do their suburban and rural counterparts. . . . This further supports the view that urban judges sentence similarly-situated offenders more severely than do their suburban or rural counterparts. The rural judges' dispositional leniency may reflect budgetary constraints, since the costs of placements are borne by county welfare funds. In rural counties, with smaller population and tax bases and greater poverty, extensive, and therefore expensive, intervention may be fiscally prohibitive for all but the most serious or troubled delinquents.

F. Urban, Suburban, and Rural Pre-trial Detention Practices

Several studies examined the relationship between pre-trial detention and subsequent disposition and reported that while several variables affect both decisions, after controlling for their affect, detention *per se* exhibits an independent effect on dispositions. The next analyses examine the relationships between detention, offenses, and dispositions.

1. Detention by Offense   . . . Detention, as used here, refers to a juvenile's custody status following arrest or referral but prior to formal court action— adjudication or disposition. Detention, as distinguished from shelter care, connotes a physically restrictive facility (*i.e.*, a detention center, state institution, or adult jail). Minnesota law and rules allow pre-trial preventive detention if a child constitutes a danger to self or others, or will not keep court appearances. A juvenile's alleged offense is not an explicit criterion for detention except insofar as a juvenile court judge views it as evidence of "endangering" self or others. . . .

The use of pre-trial detention follows a similar pattern in the state as a whole as well as in different geographic locales. While only a small proportion (7.6%) of all juveniles in the state receive a detention hearing, the seriousness of the present offense and the length of the prior record both appear to alter substantially a youth's likelihood of being detained. For the entire state, about twice as many juveniles charged with a felony offense are detained as compared to the overall detention rate (14.9% vs. 7.6%).

A direct relationship exists between prior referrals and rates of detention. However, even when youths are charged with the most serious offenses or have extensive prior records, the vast majorities are not detained. Moreover, larger numbers of minor offenders are detained than are felons. Indeed, for the entire state, slightly more than one-third of detainees are charged with felonies (36.2%), and most are charged with misdemeanors (46.7%) or even status offenses (17.0%). An earlier study found little legal rationale for detention practices and could explain only 9.0% of variance.

When urban, suburban, and rural county detention practices are examined, similar patterns emerge. Youths charged with felony offenses or offenses against the person, and youths with long prior records are detained more frequently than their less delinquent counterparts. However, the largest numbers and proportion of detained juveniles are charged with minor offenses.

While the offense pattern of detention is similar, its geographical use differs substantially. Detention is used most heavily in the urban counties, which detain proportionally two to three times as many youths as do suburban or rural counties. For youths charged with felony offenses, urban courts detain about one of four (25.9%) as contrasted with about one in ten in the rural counties (10.2%) and one of thirteen in the suburban counties (7.4%). Urban counties use detention disproportionately for juveniles charged with misdemeanors (11.5% vs. 3.9% and 3.4%) and status offenses (7.6% vs. 3.9% and 2.9%), as well as for those with prior records.

The heavier reliance on detention in urban settings probably stems from the greater availability of detention facilities. A primary determinant of state or county detention rates is the availability of bedspace. Since there are more detention facilities located in the urban counties, their availability provides an inducement for their greater use. The greater availability and use of detention in urban settings reflects the presence of a critical mass of eligible juveniles, greater reliance on formal mechanisms of control, and a more formal and punitive orientation. Urban courts operate in milieu which provide fewer mechanisms for informal controls, such as stable families to whom youths can return pending court appearances. . . .

IV. DISCUSSION AND CONCLUSIONS— VARIETIES OF JUVENILE JUSTICE

Although the same statutes and court rules of procedure apply, urban, suburban, and rural social structural features relate consistently to substantive and procedural differences in juvenile justice administration. Urban courts operate in communities with more disrupted families, more racially heterogeneous populations and less residential stability, all of which provide fewer mechanisms for informal social control. The urban counties represent less well-integrated, cohesive communities with less "mechanical solidarity" than do the suburban or rural counties. Accordingly, urban counties place greater emphasis on formal, rather than informal, mechanisms of social control. This is reflected in the deployment of police, as well as in juvenile justice administration.

The structural-geographic variation influences juvenile justice administration. In relation to their youth population, the urban courts receive a larger proportion of juveniles in all offense categories. Compared with suburban or rural courts, urban courts received a larger proportion of referrals from non-police sources, particularly probation officers and schools. The diversity of urban referral sources reflects a greater reliance on a more inclusive network of formal social control, which encompasses more troublesome youths in the community. By contrast, the suburban courts, with the lowest overall rate of juvenile court referrals, screened cases more selectively and focussed more on serious offenders and less on status offenders. Perhaps parental affluence and stability, relative to the urban or rural counties, enabled parents and court intake personnel to develop informal, alternative dispositions in lieu of formal court intervention for less serious suburban offenders. Finally, the rural courts dealt with the smallest proportions of juveniles charged with serious crimes and the largest proportion charged with status offenses.

As a result of geographic differences in delinquency, referral sources, and pre-petition screening, the juveniles appearing in the respective courts differ. Urban courts intervened more extensively in the lives of younger juveniles, especially status offenders (43.0%), as contrasted with the suburban (19.9%) or rural (15.7%) courts. Conversely, suburban and rural courts processed more serious young offenders and more older status offenders. The differences in age and offenses suggest that serious crime by younger juveniles in non-urban settings requires an immediate response, whereas for less serious offenses, rural juveniles exhaust informal community alternatives before courts invoke formal processes.

Representation by counsel provides an indicator of a court's formality or due process orientation. While the majority of youths in Minnesota appeared in juvenile courts without counsel (45.3%), geographic diversity in representation existed. The highest rates of representation occurred in the urban courts (62.6%), followed closely by the suburban courts (55.2%), while the rural courts provided only about one-quarter (25.1%) of delinquents with lawyers. The differential presence of counsel suggests basic differences in court orientation—an urban, due process or "formal rationality" model of justice versus a rural, traditional "substantively rational" juvenile court.

Earlier research reported a relationship between procedural formality and sentencing severity. This study provides even stronger support for the formality-severity relationship. The urban courts sentenced youths charged with similar offenses more severely than did the suburban or rural courts. The pattern of urban severity remained even after controlling for the present offense and prior record. Urban courts' greater use of pre-trial detention reflects their reliance on formal controls and more severe intervention. Finally, the regression equations indicate that urban, suburban, and rural courts used similar "frames of relevance." Despite the substantive focus on similar legal variables, however, urban courts sentenced similarly situated offenders more severely. Other research also reports that urbanization exerts a contextual influence on sentences.

Finding "justice by geography" vastly complicates the tasks of criminologists. As this research demonstrates, there is both a theoretical and empirical relationship between variations in social structure and in juvenile justice administration. Studies which analyze and interpret aggregated data without accounting for contextual and structural characteristics may systematically mislead and obscure, rather than clarify. Both theoretically and operationally, it is necessary to refine the relationships between social structure and justice administration. What structural features influence a juvenile court's procedural and substantive orientation? How does the local culture foster a traditional or due process orientation? How do the roles of counsel operating in these diverse socio-legal settings differ?

Finding "varieties of juvenile courts" has important implications for juvenile justice policy. Recent trends in juvenile justice emphasize punishment over rehabilitation with a corresponding increase in procedural formality. What is the relationship between procedural formality and sentencing severity? Does greater urban crime engender more punitive responses, which then require more formal procedural safeguards as a prerequisite? Or, does urban bureaucratization lead to more formal procedural safeguards, which then enable judges to exact a greater toll than they otherwise might? Increases in urban crime may foster a "war-on-crime" mentality that places immense pressures on the justice system to "get tough." Urban racial diversity may foster a more repressive response to crimes by "those people" than in more homogeneous rural settings. While Minnesota traditionally favored a progressive, rehabilitative approach to many social ills, urban formality and punitiveness may reflect a more recent trend in which the ethic of care and treatment is subordinated to restoring social order.

What are the comparative costs and benefits of formal versus informal dispute resolution in juvenile courts? While the formal urban courts imposed the most severe sentences, the suburban courts were nearly as formal and yet sentenced about as leniently as the rural courts did. While the relationship between formality and severity is troubling, an uncritical embrace of the traditional, informal juvenile court does not necessarily follow. In the rural juvenile courts, female juveniles are processed differently and more severely than are either rural males or female offenders in other settings. Does rural "substantive justice" necessarily connote gender-bias and the application of a paternalistic double-standard for which informal juvenile courts are justly criticized?

The policy choices between more or less formal juvenile justice are neither simple nor straightforward. Moreover, if a court's practices are rooted in its social structure, then simply amending laws may not produce the desired change. While diversity rather than uniformity historically characterized juvenile courts, whether such extensive local variation should continue or be encouraged is questionable. Should a system of laws and court rules of procedure be applied generally and uniformly throughout the state? Should local norms and values influence the imposition of sanctions such that youths convicted of similar offenses receive widely disparate consequences? If formal legal guidelines are adopted to structure discretionary detention and sentencing decisions, will they reduce the severity of urban courts' intervention or increase the severity of rural courts? If juvenile sentencing guidelines actually limit judicial discretion, would they produce the worst of both worlds—restricting the efforts of individual judges or communities to rehabilitate their children, while perpetuating more rigid and severe sentences?

Structural Variations in Juvenile Court Processing: Inequality, the Underclass, and Social Control

ROBERT J. SAMPSON
JOHN H. LAUB

Although there is a rich body of theory on crime causation, development of general sociological theory on criminal justice has been sparse. A major reason is that the criminal justice literature is dominated by a focus on individual-level case processing, in particular how "extralegal" factors such as race, social class, and gender influence court decisionmaking. The theoretical significance of these studies for criminal justice theory especially at the

Excerpted from *Law & Society Review*, Vol. 27, No. 2 (1993). Reprinted by permission of the Law and Society Association.

macrolevel—has not been well developed. Hagan contends that the lack of theory is also related to the fact that criminal justice in the United States is organized as a "loosely coupled system," resulting in a seeming randomness in criminal justice decisionmaking.

When one turns attention to the juvenile justice system, the theoretical landscape appears even more barren. Indeed, there is a surprising lack of research on the structural context of the juvenile court—the predominant mode of inquiry concerns individual-level variations *within* courts rather than macrolevel variations *between* courts. Moreover, because of its long-standing commitment to individualized decisionmaking, the juvenile court can be characterized as more "loosely coupled" than the adult system. Studies of juvenile justice decisionmaking thus tend to leave more variation unexplained than comparable studies in the adult arena.

In addition to a theoretical bias in favor of individual-level explanations of juvenile case processing, there is a distinct lack of quantitative data on juvenile courts that are comparable across a large number of jurisdictions. Until recently, juvenile courts have been notoriously unsystematic about recordkeeping in a fashion that would facilitate crossjurisdictional comparisons of case processing. For example, there is only a handful of quantitative studies focusing on structural-level variations with the community or juvenile court as unit of analysis. Moreover, even these existing studies have been severely restricted in the number and representativeness of communities sampled and in the measurement of key dimensions of juvenile processing.

In fact, there is little research on the structural context of crime control in general. As Liska has argued, most macrolevel research in this area has focused on deterrence (i.e., the effect of crime control on crime rates). Only recently have sociologists used collectivities as the unit of analysis and examined how crime control patterns are influenced by social structures. There are excellent ethnographies and historical case studies on macrosocial aspects of crime control, but these "illustrate rather than test sociological perspectives on crime control."

This article addresses the lack of a macrolevel focus on juvenile justice by providing a theoretical framework and empirical assessment of the structural context of juvenile court processing in the United States. Specifically, we derive a macrolevel theory on inequality and official social control that poses the question: How does structural context—especially racial inequality and the concentration of "underclass" poverty—influence formal *petitioning*, predisposition *detention*, and *placement* (confinement) of juveniles? These three dimensions of juvenile court processing, classified by crime type and race, are analyzed in conjunction with structural data for U.S. counties in 1985. Our goal is to lay the groundwork for a better understanding of the relationship between larger societal forces of increasing poverty and inequality and formal systems of juvenile social control.

THEORETICAL FRAMEWORK

We argue that the juvenile court may be fruitfully analyzed by taking an explicitly macrostructural approach to official social control. As Empey has argued, juvenile justice is not a monolithic concept which operates uniformly throughout the United States. Instead, a fundamental fact is that the juvenile court is organized at the local (i.e., county) level, giving rise to potentially important *community-level variations* in juvenile justice. Many other official decisions regarding budgets, criminal justice personnel, and construction of detention centers are also organized at the county level. Consequently, Feld has argued that analyses and interpretations that ignore structural variations across court jurisdictions in justice administration may be systematically misleading. For example, while research has recognized diversity between courts with regard to a "due process" vs. "therapeutic" orientation, we know little about "the structural sources or administrative consequences of . . . [such] organizational variation."

Although "randomness" may be typical in individual case processing, recognition of structural variations at the macrolevel opens a new window on the juvenile court. Generally speaking, a macrosociological perspective suggests that systematic differences in case processing will arise from the social attributes of the communities in which juvenile courts are located. This structural orientation has an analogy in research showing that styles of policing vary according to the demographic, organizational, and political structure of cities. To organize our specific theoretical expectations with respect to juvenile court variations across structural contexts, we integrate three bodies of research.

CONFLICT THEORY: THREATENING POPULATIONS AND THE SOCIAL CONTROL RESPONSE

Most criminal justice research has drawn on consensus and conflict theories of society. In the consensus view there is an assumption of shared values, where the state is organized to protect the common interests of society at large. Criminal law is seen as an instrument to protect the interests of all and punishment is based largely on legal variables (e.g., seriousness of the offense, prior record, etc.). In contrast, conflict theory views society as consisting of groups with conflicting and differing values, and posits that the state is organized to represent the interests of the powerful, ruling class. Criminal law is thus viewed as an instrument to protect the interests of the powerful and the elite, with punishment based largely on extralegal variables (e.g., race, social class, etc.).

One proposition drawn from conflict theory is that groups which threaten the hegemony of middle- and upper-class rule are more likely to be subjected to intensified social control—more criminalization, more formal processing by the criminal justice system, and increased incarceration compared with groups that are perceived as less threatening to the status quo. Furthermore, conflict theorists have argued that minorities (especially blacks), the unemployed, and the poor represent such threatening groups. Irwin defines population groups that are deemed as threatening and offensive to the dominant majority as the "rabble class"—"detached and disreputable persons." Irwin argues that the primary purpose of jails is to manage society's rabble class and hence that this group will be subject to higher rates of confinement.

Although conflict theory has been applied to the realm of juvenile justice, it has been applied less often than to adult criminal justice. Extending the ideas of Platt, Carter and Clelland argue that since its creation the juvenile court has sought to control lower class and minority youth in accordance with dominant class values:

> The juvenile courts' emphasis on the control of morality functions to secure the social, economic and political order by giving sanction to the system of class domination. Therefore, the class bias of the juvenile system of justice is revealed in the functions and consequences of the institutions and policies of that system in relation to the material conditions of capitalist society and subsequent system of class domination, rather than in the conscious class control motives of those who support or directly participate in the juvenile system.

However, like research on the criminal justice system, virtually all the research on juvenile justice processing has involved microlevel studies of individual case processing or studies of contextual effects on individual cases.

In one of the more comprehensive studies relating macro-variables to micro-outcomes, Tittle and Curran examined juvenile justice dispositions in 31 Florida counties. They found differential sanctioning depending on the relative size of the nonwhite and young population, arguing that "nonwhites and youth symbolize to white adults resentment-provoking or fear-provoking qualities like aggressiveness, sexuality and absence of personal discipline." In a study of contextual characteristics of social environments and individual case decisionmaking, Dannefer and Schutt also found racial bias in police processing of juvenile cases in urban counties containing a large proportion of black residents.

In our view, what is important in these studies is the symbolic aspect of social threat. For instance, Tittle and Curran emphasize the perceptions of the threat that "provoke jealousy, envy, or personal fear among elites" rather than the actual threat these groups represent to the political positions of the elite. Similarly, Irwin notes the importance of the subjective perception of "offensiveness, which is determined by social status and context." Revising conflict theory, we argue that "the poor," "the underclass," and "the rabble" are perceived as threatening not only to political elites but to "mainstream America"—middle-class and working-class citizens who represent the dominant majority in American society. As such, we suggest that an assessment of the macrolevel response of the juvenile justice system to the evolving stereotype of threatening young black males dealing drugs in poor neighborhoods across the United States (see below) is especially timely and necessary.

DRUGS AND MINORITIES: A SYMBOLIC THREAT

Peterson and Hagan's analysis of drug enforcement activity during the 1960s and 1970s documents the shifting concerns with drugs and crime in society and illustrates the need to consider historical context in understanding criminal justice operations related to race. More recently, Myers found increased punitiveness for nonwhite drug dealers, underscoring the need to examine race in conjunction with drug use and drug trafficking in a particular historical context.

Two trends emerged during the 1980s that reinforce these claims. The first was the increasing number of black males under correctional supervision and the second saw increasing punitiveness toward drug offenders, especially blacks and users of cocaine. In the 1990s, then, race, class, and drugs have become intertwined; it is difficult if not impossible to disentangle the various elements of the problem. Moreover, the "war" on drugs in the 1980s embodied a different persona than earlier wars, leading to racially discriminatory practices by the criminal justice system. Particularly relevant to our thesis, Tittle and Curran found the largest discriminatory effects in juvenile justice dispositions for "drug/sexual offenses which represent overt behavioral manifestations of the very qualities [that] frighten white adults or generate resentment and envy."

Data from the 1980s support these concerns about the changing dynamics of race and drugs. For instance, while the number of arrests for drug abuse violations for white juveniles declined 28% in 1985 compared with 1980, the number of arrests for drug abuse violations for black juveniles increased 25% over the same time period. Furthermore, data on arrest rate trends by race show that in 1980 the rates of drug law violations were nearly equal for whites and blacks; however, during the decade of the 1980s, white rates declined while black rates increased markedly. Juvenile court data show that the number of white youth referred to court for drug law violations declined by 6% between 1985 and 1986; the number of referrals for black youth increased 42%. The disproportionate increase in the number of black youth detained also seemed linked to the increased number of black drug law violators referred to court. More generally, Blumstein has shown that the dramatic growth in state prison populations during the 1980s was driven in large part by increasing admissions of blacks on drug convictions.

These trends suggest a recent and increasing punitiveness toward drug offenders especially those perceived to be "gang" members from a growing "underclass" population. The existing studies are less clear, however, as to the nature of the juvenile justice system response to drug offenders, especially at the macrolevel. We fill this gap with an examination of the structural context of juvenile justice processing of drug cases.

URBAN POVERTY AND INEQUALITY: THE CHANGING URBAN LANDSCAPE, 1970–1990

Wilson has documented "the rise of social dislocations in inner-city ghettos" over the last 25 years. As Wilson writes, "poverty in the United States has become more urban, more concentrated, and more firmly implanted in large metropolises, particularly in the older industrial cities with immense and highly segregated black and Hispanic residents." Reviewing a host of census data as well as focused studies on poverty, Wilson shows that "the 1970s witnessed a sharp growth in ghetto poverty areas, an increased concentration of the poor in these areas, a substantial rise in the severity of economic hardship among the ghetto poor, and sharply divergent patterns of poverty concentration between racial minorities and whites." Sampson and Wilson also link an increase in poverty and joblessness to social dislocations in family life, community disorganization, and even lower feelings of self-efficacy.

In short, research on urban poverty suggests that the social transformation of inner cities has resulted in a disproportionate concentration of the "truly disadvantaged" segments of the U.S. population—especially poor, female-headed black families with children. Urban minorities have also been vulnerable to structural economic changes related to the deindustrialization of central cities (e.g., shift from goods-producing to service-producing industries; increasing polarization of the labor market into low wage and high wage sectors; and relocation of manufacturing out of the inner city). And with the rise in segregation and income inequality by race, the social milieu of urban life has changed a great deal in the past few decades.

An extension of Wilson's concept of social isolation in inner-city areas of concentrated poverty to the larger macrolevel context of metropolitan areas and counties is supported by Land et al.'s recent findings on the relationships among structural covariates of homicide in the United States. Using principal components analysis, two clusters of variables were found to consistently covary over time and space (i.e., 1960, 1970, and 1980 for cities, SMSAs, and states). The first factor was termed a *population structure component* and consisted of population size and population density. The second factor was labeled *resource deprivation/affluence*, and included three income variables—median income, percentage families below the poverty line, and the Gini index of income inequality—in addition to percentage black and percentage of children not living with both parents. Although these variables seem to tap different concepts, Land et al. found they could not be separated empirically.

Land et al.'s results go beyond Wilson by suggesting that the clustering of economic and social indicators appears not only in 1980 and in neighborhoods of large cities but also for the two previous decennial periods and at the level of macrosocial units as a whole. Moreover, Land and his colleagues present evidence in support of Wilson's argument that concentration effects grew more severe from 1970 to 1980—"the numerical values of the component loadings of percentage poverty, percentage black, and percentage of children under 18 not living with both parents are larger in 1980 than 1970." Recent data also point to the existence of a large underclass population in rural areas, especially the South. Therefore, indicators of disadvantaged "underclass" populations appear to be increasing in their ecological concentration and are present in macrosocial units such as counties and SMSAs—in highly urbanized as well as in rural areas.

The ideas of Wilson and the empirical research of Land and associates have not been integrated with the literature on criminal justice and juvenile justice processing. We believe this is a mistake, for the profound social changes taking place in the wider urban society have distinct ramifications for the major mechanisms of formal social control, namely, criminal and juvenile justice systems. The interesting question that emerges is: What effect do increasing concentrations of poverty and accompanying social dislocations have for juvenile justice processing? Although we plan to examine the effects of increasing "underclass" populations on changes in juvenile justice processing in a larger project, for now we assess the relationship between the concentration of "underclass" populations and juvenile justice processing, especially out-of-home placement. In light of the trends regarding drug offenders discussed above, an examination of the macrolevel confluence of race, underclass concentration, and actions by the juvenile justice system seems especially interesting.

HYPOTHESES AND STRATEGY

Our theoretical integration of these heretofore separate research areas yields a core idea related to the macrostructural context of juvenile justice. That is, the rising concentration of the underclass corresponds precisely with that population perceived as threatening and the population at which the war on drugs has been aimed. Hence our major thesis is that, all else being equal, counties characterized by racial inequality and a large concentration of the "underclass" (i.e., minorities, poverty, female-headed families, welfare) are more likely than other counties to be perceived as containing offensive and threatening populations and, as a result, are subject to increased social control by the juvenile justice system. We further hypothesize that the concentration of racial poverty and inequality will exert macrolevel effects on punitive forms of social control that are larger for blacks than whites and for drug offenses than other delinquencies. As argued above, the dual image of minority offenders and the "drug war" appears to have formed a symbolic yet potent threat to the middle class population.

To test these ideas we examine three post-intake decisions in the juvenile justice process that involve the increased penetration of official social control. Although the first step in the juvenile justice system is referral to the juvenile court, the vast majority of these cases (>75%) stem from police referrals. Drug offenses are most likely to be referred by the police (91%). The remainder are referred by other social control agencies (e.g., probation officers, schools) or by informal parties (e.g., parents). Hence variations in rates of juvenile court referrals are shaped largely by differences in delinquent offending and police decisionmaking, the latter a topic of considerable prior research. By contrast, our purpose here is to study the more "hidden" and unexplored arena of macrostructural variations in postreferral decisionmaking by the court, especially decisions that involve coercive control and deprivation of liberty. To accomplish this goal our strategy is to focus on formal *petitioning*, secure predisposition *detention*, and adjudicated *placement* (confinement) of juveniles. We now turn to a description of the data and more explicit definitions and rationale for these three dimensions of social control.

DATA SOURCES

Our data stem from a larger project in collaboration with the National Juvenile Court Data Archive (NJCDA), located at the National Center for Juvenile Justice in Pittsburgh. A comparative, multijurisdictional approach to the study of the juvenile court was made possible by transforming raw juvenile case records into a common format at the individual level. . . .

By aggregating these individual-level records within each juvenile court of jurisdiction, a data base was created with counties as the unit of analysis. Counties with a minimum population size of 6,000 youth aged 10–17 formed the sample. . . . All regions of the country are represented, and there is a wide range in population size across the 21 states.

Approximately 538,000 individual juvenile case records were aggregated to form theoretically specified variables characterizing these 322 counties in 1985. The general format resulted in the construction of variables relating to the key dimensions of *reason for referral, detention,* and *disposition.* Then, to the extent the data allowed, variables were classified by crime type and demographic characteristics of the juvenile (e.g., age, race, sex). We rely here on the fourfold classification of crimes developed and validated in Snyder et al.—*crimes against property* (burglary, larceny, motor vehicle theft, arson, vandalism, and stolen property offenses), *crimes against persons* (criminal homicide, forcible rape, robbery, and assault), *drug offenses* (unlawful sale, distribution, manufacture, transport, possession, or use of a controlled substance), and *public order offenses* (drunkenness, disorderly conduct, contempt, weapons offenses, prostitution, statutory rape, probation and parole violations). Because of wide fluctuations across counties in reporting procedures for status offenses, the latter were excluded in the creation of court-processing variables and hence all rates refer to delinquency cases. The county-level juvenile court data consisting of both petitioned and nonpetitioned cases were merged with relevant sociodemographic and population data from two other data sets. The first was the Bureau of Census file on County Population Estimates by Age, Race and Sex (1980, 1982, 1984). This data source provided detailed population estimates of age-race-sex breakdowns needed to create referral rates for counties. The second data file is the 1983 *County and City Data Book (CCDB)*, which contains social and economic variables describing each county in the United States.

VARIABLE CONSTRUCTION

Petitioning of Cases

Cases may be placed on the official court calendar in response to the filing of a formal petition, a process that usually involves a hearing before a juvenile court judge. Alternatively, a case may be treated informally through a procedure whereby cases are screened out for adjustment prior to the filing of a formal petition. Depending on the court, this screening is conducted by judges, referees, probation officers, or other designated court personnel.

Although less serious cases carry a higher likelihood of nonpetitioning, there is still considerable variation across counties in the decision to petition a case formally even within the same crime type. When we control for crime type and "input" (i.e, referral rate), we argue that counties which channel a high proportion of cases to the juvenile court via a petition may be conceptualized as having a more formalized, bureaucratized system than counties which treat the same cases informally through a nonpetitioned procedure. In other words, the rate of formal petitioning or what Hasenfeld and Cheung call "judicial handling," may be seen as a quantitative indicator of the extent to which a county has formalized procedures for processing juveniles. To capture these variations we created crime-specific variables representing the proportion of petitioned cases.

Secure Predisposition Detention

Before a case is disposed, a juvenile may be held in secure detention. Although this issue has been explored at the national level, it is central to the operation of juvenile courts at the local level. To address these county-level variations, we constructed proportions of secure detention by dividing the number of cases detained in a county by the total number of referrals in that county. As shown in Snyder et al., detained youth are twice as likely to be petitioned as youth not detained. In fact, many jurisdictions require a formal petition before a youth can be detained. As Snyder et al. thus argue, the decision to detain is closely intertwined with the decision to formally petition the case. As such, logits of secure detention were calculated separately for petitioned and nonpetitioned cases. This eliminates the confounding of the petition-detention decision and allows analysis of the factors that discriminate counties with high rates of detention from counties with low rates of detention among both petitioned and nonpetitioned cases. Because of our focus on the underclass and juvenile confinement, we also created race-specific logits of secure detention.

Placement

Analogous to adult imprisonment, the most serious form of social control exercised by the juvenile court is placement outside of the home. Virtually all such placements (99%) result from formal petitions. Therefore, to explore county-level variations in placement we constructed proportions that divided the number of petitioned cases placed out of the home by the sum of nonreleased, petitioned dispositions (i.e., placement, probation, referral, fine/restitution, and transfer to adult court). Placement rates were classified by type of crime and population subgroup in the same fashion as detention and then transformed into logits.

STRUCTURAL INEQUALITY AND CONTROL VARIABLES

Theoretical considerations coupled with principal components analysis of census data led us to construct three macrolevel variables relevant to assessing our explanatory framework on inequality and symbolic threat. The first is the concentration of resource deprivation, or what many have conceptualized as "underclass" poverty. To represent this dimension with respect to extant theory, we created a standardized scale from six interrelated indicators that, taken together, represent underclass concentration. . . . As was true of Land et al.'s findings, these variables were very highly correlated, clustered together on a single factor, and could not be separated empirically with statistical efficiency.

The second was a racial inequality dimension measured by two variables—the ratio of black to white poverty and the proportion of black families below the poverty level. We created a composite scale where a high value indicates black economic disadvantage relative to whites. Our third inequality-related measure taps the high end of the economic distribution—specifically, the wealth and economic resources of a county.

The juxtaposition of wealth, racial inequality, and underclass poverty provides a unique opportunity to disaggregate the symbolic threat hypothesis. That is, to the extent that poor minorities and racial polarization represent a visible symbol of threat to the middle class, then inequality and underclass poverty should emerge as the major sources of variation in juvenile court processing. On the other hand, if the official social control of juveniles is more responsive to upper-income elites, then a county's wealth should prove the dominant predictor.

To account for competing theoretical perspectives we control for seven key variables. First, Feld has uncovered important urban-rural differences in juvenile justice administration. As Feld writes: "In urban counties, which are more heterogeneous and diverse, juvenile justice intervention is more formal, bureaucratized, and due process–oriented. By contrast, in more homogeneous and stable rural counties, juvenile courts are procedurally less formal and sentence youths more leniently." Given the importance of urbanism in the history of the juvenile justice system and in recent studies of "justice by geography," we examine *urbanism* as a control variable.

Because of our focus on juvenile justice, it is possible that the proportion of youth in a county exerts a contextual influence on court processing. To control for this potential variation we thus created a second composite variable that measures the relative *density of youth* in a county.

Regional variation has always been an important aspect in the historical development of the juvenile justice system, and there is contemporary evidence of the influence of region in both criminal and juvenile justice processing. Hence region (*West* and *South*) is controlled.

Extant theory further suggests that the referral rate will affect the response of the juvenile justice system. According to Hasenfeld and Cheung, the higher the rate of referral, the more demand there is on court services. This creates the need for a "flexible processing technology" and results in more nonjudicial handling of cases. From an organizational perspective this is "the most effective and efficient way of handling large service demands without overburdening organizational resources or undermining court legitimation". On the other hand, Hasenfeld and Cheung argue that the more serious the caseload, the less informality in processing, resulting in the filing of more formal petitions. Whatever the exact relationship, it is crucial to account for *input* in assessing juvenile justice processing. When analyzing formal petitioning, detention, and placement, we thus control for the most relevant input to the system—crime and demographic-specific referrals. This strategy provides a test of the independent effects of social structure on juvenile processing.

In a similar vein, we take into account the *capacity and resources* of the crime control system in assessing the processing of cases. As Hasenfeld and Cheung found, factors relating to the external economy of the court—especially the level of resources—are significant in shaping case processing across decision points in juvenile courts. Although data are unavailable for resources allocated specifically to the juvenile court, we constructed a composite variable that taps per capita county revenues and resources allocated the police and corrections. In all likelihood criminal justice system (CJS) resources are highly correlated with juvenile justice resources. In support of this notion, the wealth of a county is significantly correlated with our CJS resource variable ($r = .33$).

Finally, research from social disorganization theory has identified mobility as an important correlate of crime. Preliminary analysis by Sampson on the structural sources of variation in juvenile justice processing has also shown that mobility is an important factor in juvenile justice decisionmaking at the macrolevel. We thus include *residential mobility* of the county as the seventh control variable. . . .

DISCUSSION

Our major finding is that structural contexts of "underclass" poverty and racial inequality are significantly related to increased juvenile justice processing. This pattern is especially pronounced for secure predisposition detention and adjudicated out-of-home placement. Moreover, our results reveal that the effect of macrolevel structure is generally larger for blacks than whites and appears for drug offenses as well as other delinquencies. Given this higher explained variance, it appears that juvenile justice outcomes are more tightly coupled when targeted against blacks.

Particularly striking are the strong relationships exhibited for rates of black out-of-home placement, the most intrusive intervention possible by the juvenile justice system, for personal, property, and drug offenses. This pattern is consistent with the idea that underclass black males are viewed as a threatening group to middle-class populations and thus will be subjected to increased formal social control by the juvenile justice system. On the other hand, a county's wealth and criminal justice resources offer little to the explanation of juvenile justice processing. This implies that racial polarization and "underclass" poverty are more important than resources as elements of the symbolic threat hypothesis. Nonetheless, it may be premature to dismiss wealth completely given its positive effect on detention and placement rates for blacks processed for drug offenses.

Although intriguing, these findings should be treated as preliminary. We recognize that our models need to be more fully specified and that in general the variance explained in each model was relatively low. One missing dimension concerns information on the administrative structure of the juvenile court. There is a growing body of research suggesting that organizational structure of the court and resource allocations are important in understanding court variations in detention and commitment. To illustrate, Hasenfeld and Cheung have argued that because of community pressures and the possibility of being voted out of office, elected judges respond differently to "dangerous youth." Courts with elected judges may thus have higher commitment rates compared with courts with appointed judges, indicating the necessity of examining court organizational structure in some detail.

Along similar lines, Krisberg and colleagues examined variations in juvenile incarceration rates by state and found that the best predictor of pretrial detention was bed space. This demonstrates the need to control for capacity of the system (i.e., number of beds per referral) as well as reported crime rates. In this regard, Krisberg and his colleagues found that violent and property crime rates had little influence on rates of detention and postadjudication incarceration. Such findings suggest the need to examine the extent to which detention and placement are driven by both organizational structure and resource allocations independent of "input" to the system. These issues must be addressed in order to fully delineate the macrosocial context of juvenile justice processing.

Equally important for future research is the study of change in juvenile justice processing during the last decade. The 1980s saw remarkable changes in many aspects of American life; however, researchers have not yet come to grips with the effects of these changes on formal systems of social control like the juvenile justice system. Our future research will expand the present analyses by examining how macrolevel structural changes have reshaped community contexts and local juvenile justice processing from 1980 to 1990.

CONCLUSION

Despite these limitations, we believe that our results have implications for both theory and policy regarding juvenile justice system processing in the United States. As for theories of social control, our work on the structural context of juvenile justice decisionmaking provides a new dimension in understanding the official social control of juveniles. Until now the juvenile justice system has been largely overlooked in theoretical accounts of formal social control systems at the macrolevel. As for policy, our preliminary results of cross-sectional data suggest that the structural characteristics of counties, especially indicators of underclass poverty and racial inequality, are important in explaining variations in juvenile justice processing. Our article thus demonstrates that macrolevel structural context is an important element in understanding local patterns of juvenile justice processing across the United States.

CHAPTER **3**

Procedural Justice in Juvenile Court

THE CONSTITUTIONAL DOMESTICATION OF THE JUVENILE COURT

Despite occasional challenges and criticism of some conceptual or administrative aspects of juvenile justice, no sustained and systematic examination of the juvenile court occurred until the 1960s. In 1967, however, *In re Gault*, 387 U.S. 1 (1967), began a "due process revolution" that substantially transformed the juvenile court from a social welfare agency into a legal institution. This "constitutional domestication" marked the first step in the convergence of the procedures of the juvenile justice system with those of the adult criminal process.

In re Gault involved the delinquency adjudication and institutional commitment of a youth who allegedly made a lewd telephone call of the "irritatingly offensive, adolescent, sex variety" to a neighbor. The county sheriff took fifteen-year-old Gerald Gault into custody, the juvenile court detained him overnight without notifying his parents, and he appeared at a hearing the following day. The court's probation officer filed a *pro forma* petition that alleged simply that he was a delinquent minor in need of the care and custody of the court. The complaining witness did not appear, the juvenile court did not take any sworn testimony or make a transcript or formal memorandum of the proceedings. The juvenile court judge interrogated Gault, who apparently made some incriminating responses. At no time did the judge advise Gault of a right to counsel, nor did he receive the assistance of an attorney. Following his hearing, the judge returned Gault to a detention cell for several days. At his dispositional hearing the following week, the judge committed Gault as a juvenile delinquent to the State Industrial School "for the period of his minority [that is, until 21], unless sooner discharged by due process of law." If Gault had been tried as an adult, a criminal court judge could have sentenced him to no more than a $50 fine or two months' imprisonment.

In *In re Gault*, the United States Supreme Court examined the realities of juvenile incarceration rather than uncritically accepting the rehabilitative rhetoric of Progressive juvenile jurisprudence. The Court reviewed the history of the juvenile court, noted that the traditional reasons for denying procedural safeguards to juveniles included the belief that the proceedings were neither adversarial nor criminal and that, because the State acted as *parens patriae*, the child was entitled to custody rather than liberty. The Court rejected these assertions, however, and emphasized that a denial of procedures frequently resulted in arbitrariness rather than "careful, compassionate, individualized treatment." Although the Court hoped to retain the potential benefits of the juvenile process, it insisted that the claims of the juvenile court process had to be candidly appraised in light of the realities of recidivism, the failures of rehabilitation, the stigma of a "delinquency" label, the breaches of confidentiality, and the arbitrariness of the process. The Court noted that a juvenile justice process free of constitutional safeguards had not abated recidivism or lowered the high crime rates among juvenile offenders. It also emphasized that the realities of juvenile institutional confinement mandated elementary procedural safeguards. These safeguards included advance notice of charges, a fair and impartial hearing, assistance of counsel, an opportunity to confront and cross-examine witnesses, and a privilege against self-incrimination.

Although the Court discussed the realities of the juvenile system and mandated procedural safeguards, it limited its holding to the adjudicatory hearing—trial—at which a juvenile court judge could find a child to be delinquent. It asserted that its decision would not impair the juvenile court's unique procedures for processing and treating juveniles. But the Court concluded that juvenile proceedings required adversarial procedural safeguards both to determine the truth and to preserve individual freedom by limiting the power of the State.

In contrast to the narrow holding, the basis for the Court's constitutional analysis of what rights must be afforded juveniles in adjudicatory hearings was broad. The Court used the "fundamental fairness" requirements of the Due Process clause of the Fourteenth Amendment to grant juveniles the rights to notice, counsel, and confrontation and did not even refer specifically to the explicit requirements of the sixth amendment. The Court did, however, explicitly invoke the Fifth Amendment to provide juveniles with the protection of the privilege against self-incrimination in delinquency proceedings.

> It would be entirely unrealistic to carve out of the Fifth Amendment all statements by juveniles on the ground that these cannot lead to "criminal" involvement. In the first place, juvenile proceedings to determine "delinquency," which may lead to commitment to a state institution, must be regarded as "criminal" for purposes of the privilege against self-incrimination ... [C]ommitment is a deprivation of liberty. It is incarceration against one's will, whether it is called "criminal" or "civil."

The Court's extension of the privilege against self-incrimination to delinquents provides the clearest example of the dual functions that procedural safeguards serve in juvenile delinquency adjudications: to assure accurate fact finding and to protect against government oppression. In this respect, *Gault* represents a premier example of the Warren Court's belief that expanding constitutional rights and adversary procedures could limit the coercive powers of the State, assure the regularity of law enforcement, and reduce the need for continual judicial scrutiny.

In subsequent juvenile court decisions, the Supreme Court further elaborated upon the criminal nature of delinquency proceedings. In *In re Winship*, 398 U.S. 358 (1970), the Court decided that proof of delinquency must be established "beyond a reasonable doubt," rather than by lower civil standards of proof. Because the Bill of Rights contains no explicit provision regarding the standard of proof in criminal cases, the *Winship* Court first held that the Constitution required proof beyond a reasonable doubt in adult criminal proceedings. The Court then extended the same standard of proof to juvenile delinquency proceedings because the highest standard of proof played an equally vital role there. The Court concluded that the need to prevent unwarranted convictions and to guard against government power outweighed some dissenting justices' concerns that it might hamper the juvenile court's unique therapeutic functions or erode "differences between juvenile courts and traditional criminal courts."

Five years later, the Court in *Breed v. Jones*, 421 US 519 (1975), held that the protections of the Double Jeopardy clause of the Fifth Amendment prohibit the adult criminal prosecution of a youth after a conviction in juvenile court for the same offense. Although the Court framed the issue in terms of the applicability of an explicit provision of the Bill of Rights to state proceedings, it resolved the question by recognizing the functional equivalence and the identical interests of the defendants in a delinquency proceeding and an adult criminal trial.

Only in *McKeiver v. Pennsylvania*, 403 U.S. 528 (1971), did the Court decline to extend the procedural safeguards of adult criminal prosecutions to juvenile court proceedings. The Court in *McKeiver* held that the Constitution did not require a right to a jury trial in a juvenile delinquency proceeding. The Court asserted that "Due Process" required only "fundamental fairness" to assure "accurate fact finding," and concluded that a judge could satisfy this requirement as well as a jury. But, in suggesting that due process in the juvenile context required nothing more than accurate fact-finding, however, the Court departed significantly from its own prior analyses, which relied upon the *dual* rationales of accurate fact-finding and protection against governmental oppression. In insisting that the accuracy of the fact-finding process is the only concern of fundamental fairness, the Court ignored its own analysis in *Gault*, where it held that the Fifth Amendment's privilege against self-incrimination was necessary in order to protect against governmental oppression even though accurate fact-finding might be impeded. Justice Brennan's concurring-dissenting opinion in *McKeiver* notes that protection from governmental oppression might also be afforded by an alternative method, such as a public trial that would render the adjudicative process visible and accountable to the community. The *McKeiver* Court, however, denied that juveniles required protection against government oppression at all, invoked the mythology of the sympathetic, paternalistic juvenile court judge, and rejected the argument that the inbred, closed nature of the juvenile court could prejudice the accuracy of fact-finding.

In denying juveniles the constitutional right to jury trials, the Court in *McKeiver* departed from its earlier mode of analysis and emphasized the adverse impact that this right would have on the informality, flexibility, and confidentiality of juvenile court proceedings. Rather than asking whether the constitutional right in question would have an adverse impact on any unique benefits of the juvenile court, the Court asked whether the right to a jury trial would positively aid or strengthen the functioning of the juvenile justice system. Although the *McKeiver* Court found faults with the juvenile process, it asserted that imposing jury trials would in no way correct those deficiencies and would make the juvenile process unduly formal and adversarial. The Court did not consider, however, whether there might be any offsetting advantages to increased formality in juvenile proceedings or to what extent its earlier decision in *Gault* had effectively foreclosed its renewed concern with flexibility and informality at the adjudicatory stage. The Court also gave no indication why a more formal hearing was incompatible with the therapeutic dispositions that a young delinquent might receive. Although the Court decried the possibility of a public trial, it presented no evidence or arguments to support its conclusion that publicity would be undesirable and that confidentiality of juvenile court proceedings was an indispensable element of the juvenile justice process.

Together, *Gault, Winship,* and *McKeiver* precipitated a procedural revolution in the juvenile court system that has unintentionally but inevitably transformed its original Progressive conception. Progressive reformers envisioned the commission of an offense as essentially secondary to a determination of the "real needs" of a child—the child's social circumstances and environment. Progressives premised intervention on the child's need for rehabilitation and social uplift rather than the commission of an offense. Although *McKeiver* refused to extend the right to a jury trial to juveniles, *Gault* and *Winship* imported the adversarial model, the privilege against self-incrimination, attorneys, the criminal standard of proof, and the primacy of factual and legal guilt as a constitutional prerequisite to intervention. By emphasizing criminal procedural regularity in the determination of delinquency, the Supreme Court shifted the focus of the juvenile court from the Progressive emphasis on the "real needs" of the child to proof of the commission of criminal acts. This shift from "needs" to "deeds" effectively transformed juvenile proceedings into criminal prosecutions and provided the impetus for further substantive as well as procedural convergence between the two systems. Finally, providing a modicum of procedural safeguards in juvenile courts also legitimated the imposition of greater sanctions in juvenile justice.

The articles in this section examine various procedural aspects of juvenile justice administration: pretrial detention; the right to counsel; and the right to a jury trial. Each of these sections contrasts the "law on the books" versus the "law in action." As the Supreme Court noted in *Kent vs. United States*, 383 U.S. 541, 556 (1966), "the child receives the worst of both worlds: [the child] gets neither the protections accorded to adults nor the solicitous care and regenerative treatment postulated for children." These sections reflect the continuing gaps between rhetoric and reality in juvenile justice.

A. PRETRIAL DETENTION

Preventive detention on a predictive basis raises several controversial issues. First, controversy arises from the technical difficulty of accurately predicting which offenders should be detained in order to prevent them from committing further offenses before trial. Second, because detainees experience preventive detention as *punitive* confinement, regardless of the stated regulatory purposes of the practice, pretrial detention raises issues about the propriety of incarceration prior to a determination of guilt, the compatibility of pretrial detention with the presumption of innocence, and the procedural safeguards that the state must provide to legitimate such a practice. Finally, research indicates that a juvenile's pretrial detention status adversely may affect subsequent sentencing decisions by the juvenile court, thus making this one of the most critical decisions a judge makes.

In *Schall v. Martin, 467 U.S. 253 (1984)*, the United States Supreme Court upheld the constitutional validity of a New York statute that authorized a juvenile court to preventively detain a juvenile if the judge found that there was a "serious risk" that the child "may . . . commit an act which if committed by an adult would constitute a crime." In reversing the lower courts that had invalidated the law and upholding the statute, Justice Rehnquist's majority opinion in *Schall* held that "preventive detention under the Family Court Act serves a legitimate state objective, and that the procedural protections afforded pre-trial detainees" satisfies the requirements of due process.

The Court identified a number of "legitimate state objectives" advanced by the preventive detention provisions. It noted that crime prevention is "a weighty social objective," that juveniles commit a substantial amount of crime, and that the "harm suffered by the victim of a crime is not dependent upon the age of the perpetrator." The Court also asserted that, although the statute aimed primarily at crime prevention, it also "protect[ed] the juvenile from his own folly" by preventing the injury that a juvenile offender might suffer from victim resistance or police arrest and by halting a youth's downward spiral into criminal activity. The presence of comparable provisions for juvenile pretrial incarceration in every state bolstered the Court's finding that states evinced a substantial interest in preventive detention of juveniles. The Court in *Schall* clearly recognized that a contrary constitutional holding would invalidate the universal practice of detaining juveniles under much more informal and flexible procedures than those used to hold adult criminal defendants.

Earlier, the court of appeals in *Schall* had concluded that because the juvenile courts dismissed the cases of large numbers of youths detained prior to trial and returned many others to the community following their adjudication that juvenile courts used preventive detention primarily to impose punishment prior to a determination of guilt. The Supreme Court, however, characterized preventive detention as an incident of legitimate governmental regulation rather than as a pretrial imposition of punishment. The Supreme Court suggested that many considerations unrelated to the merits of a delinquency petition could lead to high dismissal rates following pretrial detention. The Court also insisted that no constitutional inconsistency arose between an initial decision to detain and a later decision to release on probation after the court received more information about a youth. Thus, the Court concluded that detention was "consistent with the regulatory and *parens patriae* objectives relied upon by the State and was not used or intended as punishment."

The *Schall* Court also considered whether the procedures used for the detention decision provided adequate "protection against erroneous and unnecessary deprivations of liberty." The majority in *Schall* concluded that the New York procedures for juvenile preventive detention satisfied constitutional "due process" requirements because the juvenile received notice of the charges at an informal initial appearance, the court made a stenographic record of the appearance, a parent or guardian accompanied the juvenile, and the court advised the juvenile of the right to remain silent and the right to counsel. The Court implied that the juvenile court made a probable cause determination at a juvenile's initial appearance, noted that a petition stating probable cause had to be filed at that time, and found that the court conducted a formal probable cause hearing within three days of the initial appearance.

The *Schall* majority also found nothing improper with the preventive detention criteria that allowed the court to detain a youth based solely on a finding that there was a "serious risk" that the juvenile would commit another crime prior to his or her next court appearance. It rejected the district court's view that it is "virtually impossible to predict future criminal conduct with any degree of accuracy" and insisted that "from a legal point of view" courts encountered no difficulties when they predicted future criminal conduct. The Court nevertheless declined to itemize or codify the predictor variables upon which a court should rely in making this prediction, emphasizing that such a list was not necessary.

The *Schall* dissent questioned both the substantive goals advanced by preventive detention and the adequacy of the procedures used. The dissenters agreed with the lower courts' findings that predicting which persons would commit further crimes posed insuperable technical difficulties and that these difficulties made it unlikely that juvenile courts could administer the statute to achieve the public objective of crime prevention. The dissent emphasized that the majority's position that such predictions occur often ignores the important issue of whether those predictions can be made with acceptable accuracy, particularly where the subjects of the prediction have not yet been found guilty of any criminal offense.

The dissent also criticized the majority's characterization of juveniles' liberty interests as inconsequential and its trivialization of the unfavorable conditions in which states detained juveniles. The vast majority of juveniles' institutional contacts occur in pretrial detention centers rather than in post adjudication commitments to training schools or other correctional facilities. Moreover, juvenile courts in nonurban jurisdictions may not have separate juvenile detention facilities and may preventively detain juveniles in adult jails, albeit segregated from adult's offenders. The dissent in *Schall* also expressed concern that the injurious consequences of pretrial imprisonment— deprivation of liberty, stigmatization, negative self-labeling, and prisonization—could impair juveniles' ability to prepare legal defenses. Pretrial detention may increase both a juvenile's probability of conviction and the likelihood of institutional confinement following adjudication.

The *Schall* dissenters also believed that the preventive detention statute provided inadequate procedural safeguards because it did not restrict detention only to juveniles whose present offenses or past conduct indicated a substantial likelihood of immediate future criminality and because juvenile courts routinely detained trivial offenders and those with no prior juvenile court contacts. They also objected that the statute specified neither the nature of the future crimes being predicted nor the burden of proof needed to sustain the prediction, other than requiring that there be a "serious risk" that the juvenile would commit an offense. The lack of statutory standards or criteria about ultimately speculative future behavior remits the detention decision to the individual discretion of each judge. The dissent noted that unstructured discretion creates the danger that judges may detain many juveniles "erroneously" and fosters arbitrariness, inequality, and discrimination in a process that impinges on fundamental liberty interests.

The articles in this section provide a "case study" of the "law on the books" versus the "law in action" and enable the reader to assess the validity of the reasoning used by the majority and dissenting justices in *Schall*. Howard Snyder and Melissa Sickmund provide data on the prevalence and use of detention and the characteristics of youths detained. They also examine recent changes in the types of offenses for which juvenile courts hold youths in detention and the racial disproportionalities that emerge. Jeffrey Fagan and Martin Guggenheim, "Preventive Detention and the Judicial Prediction of Dangerousness for Juveniles," discuss a natural experiment to test the ability of judges to predict youths' future dangerousness. Until later reversed by the United States Supreme Court in *Schall*, the District Court invalidated the New York preventive detention statute. However, the District Court order did not prohibit the judges from making predictive preventive detention decisions, but only enjoined the Commissioner of Juvenile Justice from detaining juveniles ordered into custody based on those predictions. Thus, for three years, juvenile court judges continued to make predictions that certain youths posed a "serious risk" of future criminality and then the detaining authorities released them. Fagan and Guggenheim compare the *Schall* youths with a control sample to assess both the validity of judicial predictions of dangerousness and the amount of crime that might have been prevented under a pretrial detention regime such as that used in *Schall* and most other jurisdictions. *Schall* endorsed standardless judicial discretion to make predictive detention decisions and declined to specify any criteria to guide the decision. One crucial issue is the effect of discretionary decision making on minority youths. Snyder and Sickmund's data indicate that juvenile courts detain a larger proportion of minority youths. In Chapter 5, the article by Donna Bishop and Charles Frazier examines the social and administrative processes that result in disproportionate minority overrepresentation in the detention population, and the impact of pretrial detention decisions on postadjudication dispositional decisions. Recall, too, from the excerpt by Feld, "Justice by Geography," in Chapter 2 that after controlling for other legal variables, a youth's pretrial detention status appears to be an aggravating factor at subsequent sentencing. Moreover, urban communities where disproportionately more minority delinquents live also have greater access to pretrial detention facilities. And, as Sampson and Laub's analyses of "Structural Variations in Juvenile Court Processing" indicated, even within urban contexts, minority youths are disproportionately at risk for greater rates of pretrial detention.

What legal policies would you recommend that a legislature or court adopt to address these issues of prediction, discretion, and racial disproportionality? Would objective "risk assessment" criteria alleviate the disparate impact of juvenile justice decision makers? What factors would you propose?

Detention

HOWARD SNYDER AND MELISSA SICKMUND

WHEN IS SECURE DETENTION USED?

A youth may be placed in a secure juvenile detention facility at various points during the processing of a case through the juvenile justice system. Although detention practices vary from jurisdiction to jurisdiction, a general model of detention practices is useful.

When a case is referred to juvenile court, intake staff may decide to hold the youth in a detention facility while the case is being processed. In general, the youth will be detained if there is reason to believe the youth—

- Is a threat to the community.
- Will be at risk if returned to the community.
- May fail to appear at an upcoming hearing.

The youth may also be detained for diagnostic evaluation purposes. In all States, legislation requires that a detention hearing be held within a few days (generally within 24 hours). At that time, a judge reviews the decision to detain the youth and either orders the youth released or continues the detention.

National juvenile court statistics count the number of cases that involve the use of detention during a calendar year. A youth may be detained and released more than once between case referral and disposition as the case is processed. A youth may also have more than one case involving detention during the year. Juvenile court data do not count "detentions" nor do they count the number of youth detained. In addition, although in a few States juveniles may be committed to a detention facility as part of a disposition order, the court data do not include such placements in the count of cases involving detention.

MOST DETAINED DELINQUENCY CASES INVOLVE CHARGES OF PROPERTY CRIMES

Property cases accounted for the largest volume of cases involving detention. Compared with 1988, the detention caseload in 1992 was made up of a greater proportion of person offense cases.

Excerpted from Snyder, Howard N. and Sickmund, Melissa. (1995) *Juvenile Offenders and Victims: A National Report*, pp. 141–153. Washington, DC: Office of Juvenile Justice and Delinquency Prevention.

Nearly 59,000 More Delinquency Cases Involved Detention in 1992 Than in 1988—Person and Property Offense Cases Each Accounted for About 45% of the Overall Increase

	Number of cases that involved detention				
	1988	**1989**	**1990**	**1991**	**1992**
Delinquency	237,200	256,400	297,700	281,500	296,100
Person	46,000	52,700	65,700	66,600	72,500
Property	112,100	118,400	141,400	136,300	139,200
Drugs	27,100	28,100	26,600	22,900	25,300
Public order	52,000	57,100	63,900	55,700	59,100

Source: Butts, J., et al. (1995). Juvenile Court Statistics 1992.

In 1992, as in 1988, Juveniles Were Detained in 20% of All Delinquency Cases Processed During the Year

	Percent of cases that involved detention				
	1988	**1989**	**1990**	**1991**	**1992**
Delinquency	20%	21%	22%	20%	20%
Person	24	25	27	25	24
Property	16	17	19	17	17
Drugs	33	36	37	36	35
Public order	25	26	27	24	23

- Over the past several years, the likelihood of detention has consistently been greater for drug cases than for cases involving other offenses.

- Property offense cases have the lowest likelihood of detention.

Source: Butts, J., et al. (1995). Juvenile Court Statistics 1992.

MALES WERE MORE LIKELY TO BE DETAINED THAN FEMALES

For both males and females, drug cases had the greatest likelihood of detention in 1992. Among females, however, public order offense cases rather than person offense cases were second to drug cases in the probability of detention. Public order cases involving females were as likely to be detained as those involving males.

As a result of their greater probability of detention in 1992, males were over represented in the detention caseload, compared with their proportion in the overall delinquency caseload.

CASES INVOLVING WHITE YOUTH WERE LEAST LIKELY TO BE DETAINED

Cases involving black youth charged with drug offenses had the greatest likelihood of detention.

While Black Youth Made Up 31% of Delinquency Cases Processed in 1992, They Were Involved in 39% of Detained Delinquency Cases

| | Percent of detained cases | | | |
	White	Black	Other Races	Total
Delinquency	57%	39%	4%	100%
Person	50	46	3	100
Property	62	33	5	100
Drugs	38	61	1	100
Public order	64	33	3	100

Note: Detail may not total 100% because of rounding.
Source: Butts, J., et al. (1995). Juvenile Court Statistics 1992.

| | Percent of cases that involved detention in 1992 | | |
	White	Black	Other races
Delinquency	18%	25%	22%
Person	21	27	29
Property	15	21	21
Drugs	26	47	19
Public order	23	24	22

MOST JUVENILES ENTERING DETENTION CENTERS ARE AWAITING ADJUDICATION

Juveniles may be *detained* prior to adjudication or after adjudication while awaiting disposition or placement, they may be *committed* to the detention facility as part of a court-ordered disposition, and a small proportion of juveniles are *voluntarily admitted*. The majority of admissions to detention centers during the year are detentions as opposed to commitments or voluntary admissions.

One-day count data for February 15, 1991, show that two-thirds of the juveniles detained in public detention centers for delinquency or status offenses were detained while *awaiting adjudication*, and one-third were adjudicated and *awaiting disposition or placement* elsewhere.

THE AVERAGE LENGTH OF STAY IN DETENTION WAS ABOUT 2 WEEKS

The average length of stay for juveniles released from public detention centers in 1990 varied substantially by admission status.

The average length of stay for juveniles released from private detention centers in 1990 was slightly longer—22 days.

MOST JUVENILES IN DETENTION CENTERS ARE CHARGED WITH DELINQUENCY OFFENSES

Fully 95% of the nearly 19,000 juveniles in public detention centers on February 15, 1991, were held for delinquency offenses; 3% were held for status offenses; 2% were not offenders. Among delinquents with a known offense, property offenses made up the largest proportion, followed by person offenses. For status offenders, valid court order violations (such as violating probation conditions) were the largest proportion, followed by runaways.

The offense distribution was not very different in 1991 than in 1983. In 1983 there was a greater proportion of property offenders and a smaller proportion of drug offenders.

Percent of juveniles in public detention centers on February 15, 1991

Offense	Total	Detained	Committed
Delinquency	100%	100%	100%
Person	30	31	22
Violent	20	21	12
Other	10	10	10
Property	36	36	39
Serious	26	25	27
Other	10	10	12
Alcohol	1	1	2
Drugs	10	10	11
Trafficking	6	6	8
Other	4	4	3
Public order	6	6	5
Tech. violation	14	14	20
Other delinq.	2	2	1
Status offense	100%	100%	100%
Running away	33	32	41
Truancy	11	11	13
Incorrigibility	11	12	6
Curfew	2	2	1
Liquor	1	1	3
Valid court order violation	41	42	35
Other status offense	1	1	1

Source: OJJDP. (1993). Children in Custody Census 1990/91 *[machine-readable data file].*

THE DETENTION CENTER POPULATION
GREW 46% FROM 1983 TO 1991

The overall increase in the number of juveniles in detention on a given day stemmed from an increase in residents charged with delinquency offenses. There was a substantially smaller increase in the number of juveniles held for property offenses compared with other delinquency offense categories....

Minorities Made Up Nearly Two-Thirds of the Juveniles Held in Public Detention Centers on February 15, 1991

	Percent of total juvenile residents held	
Race/ethnicity	February 1, 1983	February 15, 1991
Total juvenile residents	100%	100%
White (non-Hispanic)	47	35
Minorities	53	65
White Hispanic	15	19
Black	36	43
Amer. Indian/Alaska Native	1	1
Asian/Pacific Islander	1	2

• In 1983 minorities made up 53% of the public detention population—by 1991 they were 65%.

• The minority proportion was smaller in private detention centers in 1991 than in public facilities, but still accounted for more than half (56%) of the population.

Source: OJJDP. (1985, 1993). Children in Custody Census 1982/83 and 1990/91 *[machine-readable data files].*

There Were Substantially More Minorities Held in Public Detention Centers in 1991 Than in 1983

	Number of juveniles held		Percent change 1983–1991
Race/ethnicity	Feb. 1, 1983	Feb. 15, 1991	
Total juvenile residents	13,048	18,986	46%
White (non-Hispanic)	6,157	6,629	8
Minorities	6,891	12,357	79
White Hispanic	1,943	3,574	84
Black	4,656	8,203	76
Amer. Indian/Alaska Native	154	227	47
Asian/Pacific Islander	138	353	156

• The number of minorities held in public detention centers increased 79% from 1983 to 1991; blacks accounted for the majority of the overall increase in the minority population (65%).

• The groups with the greatest relative increases were Asian/Pacific Islanders and white Hispanics.

Source: OJJDP. (1985, 1993). Children in Custody Census 1982/83 and 1990/91 *[machine-readable data files].*

NEARLY HALF OF ALL YOUTH IN PUBLIC DETENTION CENTERS ON FEBRUARY 15, 1991, WERE IN 4 STATES— CALIFORNIA, FLORIDA, MICHIGAN, AND OHIO

State Variations in the Upper Age of Juvenile Court Jurisdiction Influence Detention Center Custody Rates

Although State custody rate statistics control for upper age of juvenile court jurisdiction, comparisons made among States with different upper ages are problematic. While 16- and 17-year olds constitute approximately 25% of the population ages 10–17, they account for more than 40% of youth arrests, delinquency court cases, and juveniles in custody. If all other things were equal, one would expect higher juvenile custody rates in States where these older youth are under juvenile court jurisdiction.

Demographic variations should also be considered when making State comparisons. The urbanicity and economics of an area are related to crime and custody rates. For example, the District of Columbia's relatively high detention rate must be interpreted with the knowledge that the District is largely urban, with a disproportionate segment of its youth population living in poverty (25% of those under age 18 compared with 18% nationwide).

State variations in the availability of detention beds also may have an impact on State detention rates. For example, just as a change in detention policy would have an effect on the detention rate in a jurisdiction, so a change in the bed space available to a jurisdiction could result in a fluctuation in the detention rate. . . .

THE JUSTICE AND DELINQUENCY PREVENTION ACT LIMITS THE PLACEMENT OF JUVENILES IN ADULT INSTITUTIONS

The Act states that, ". . . juveniles alleged to be or found to be delinquent and [status offenders and nonoffenders] shall not be detained or confined in any institution in which they have contact with adult persons incarcerated because they have been convicted of a crime or are awaiting trial on criminal charges or with the part-time or full-time security staff (including management) or direct-care staff of a jail or lockup for adults. . . ."

Subsequent rulings have interpreted the Act to permit juveniles to be held in secure adult facilities if the juvenile is being tried as an adult for a felony or has been convicted of a felony. In institutions other than adult jails or lockups confinement is permitted, if the juvenile and adult inmates cannot see each other and no conversation between them is possible. This latter requirement is commonly referred to as "sight and sound separation." There is a 6-hour grace period that allows the temporary holding of delinquents in adult jails or lockups until other arrangements can be made, provided there is sight and sound separation. In rural areas, delinquents may

Nationwide, There Were 73 Juveniles Held in Public Detention Centers for Every 100,000 Juveniles in the Population on February 15, 1991

	Number of juveniles on Feb. 15, 1991	Detention rate
U.S. Total	18,986	73
Upper age 17		
Alabama	237	49
Alaska	24	34
Arizona	410	98
Arkansas	38	13
California	5,754	178
Colorado	355	96
Delaware	35	50
District of Columbia	220	478
Florida	1,289	103
Hawaii	22	19
Idaho	29	20
Indiana	351	54
Iowa	56	17
Kansas	130	45
Kentucky	81	18
Maine	0	0
Maryland	233	48
Minnesota	177	35
Mississippi	78	23
Missouri	305	59
Montana	0	0
Upper age 17 (continued)		
Nebraska	45	24
Nevada	169	130
New Hampshire	22	19
New Jersey	569	73
New Mexico	82	42
North Dakota	5	7
Ohio	1,108	90
Oklahoma	76	20
Oregon	196	60
Pennsylvania	520	43
Rhode Island	0	0
South Dakota	35	40
Tennessee	147	27
Utah	162	56
Vermont	17	28
Virginia	616	95
Washington	647	117
West Virginia	56	26
Wisconsin	177	31
Wyoming	0	0
Upper age 16		
Georgia	855	129
Illinois	762	68
Louisiana	271	57
Massachusetts	90	18
Michigan	1,017	108
Missouri	305	59
South Carolina	9	3
Texas	868	47
Upper age 15		
Connecticut	80	34
New York	398	29
North Carolina	163	31

Note: The detention rate is the number of juveniles in public detention centers on February 15, 1991, per 100,000 juveniles ages 10 through the upper age of juvenile court jurisdiction in each State.

Source: OJJDP. (1993) Children in Custody Census 1990/91 [machine-readable data file].

also be held in adult jails or lockups for no more than 24 hours under a certain set of conditions:

- The juvenile is awaiting an initial court appearance.
- There is no alternative placement available.
- There is sight and sound separation.

FEWER JUVENILES WERE HELD IN ADULT JAIL FACILITIES IN 1988 THAN IN 1983

Between 1983 and 1988, the National Jail Census counted those initially subject to juvenile court authority as juveniles *even if they were tried as adults in criminal court*. Nevertheless, National Jail Census data show that fewer juveniles were held in jail facilities in 1988 than in 1983, both in terms of average daily population and admissions.

The number of annual admissions of juveniles reported to the National Jail Census was 38% lower in 1988 than in 1983. It is not known how many of these juveniles were jailed in violation of the jail and lockup removal mandate and how many were held pursuant to its exceptions.

MANY DETENTION CENTER RESIDENTS ARE HELD IN CROWDED FACILITIES

A Substantial Proportion of the Detention Population Is Housed in Rooms That Are Too Small

In 1991 the majority of detention center residents slept in single (70%) or double (20%) rooms. Detention center sleeping rooms ranged in size from less than 30 to 110 or more square feet per juvenile. Overall, 30% of juveniles in detention centers slept in undersized rooms. Of those in undersized rooms, most were in single (57%) or double (34%) rooms as opposed to multiple occupancy rooms. Most undersized double rooms were large enough to meet the 70 square feet standard if they housed only one juvenile instead of two.

THE NUMBER OF JUVENILES IN LIVING UNITS VARIES CONSIDERABLY

In 1991, 47% of juveniles held in detention centers were in facilities where at least some of the living units housed more than 25 residents. Among facilities with living units exceeding the 25-person standard, the size of the largest units varied considerably. Five percent of detention centers had 36 or more residents in their largest units—2 facilities had units with more than 60 residents.

53% of Detention Center Residents Were in Facilities Operating Above Their Design Capacity on February 15, 1991

Public detention centers with a design capacity of:	Facilities		Residents	
	Total	Percent operating above design Capacity	Total	Percent held in facilities operating above capacity
All public detention centers	439	32%	18,986	53%
Fewer than 31 residents	275	21	4,116	31
31–70 residents	102	46	4,552	46
71–220 residents	47	53	5,125	52
More than 220 residents	15	67	5,193	77

- In 1991 32% of detention centers housed more residents than they were constructed to hold—the 1983 figure was 9%.

- The larger a facility's design capacity, the more likely it was to house more residents than it was constructed to hold.

- Facilities designed to house fewer than 31 residents, however, accounted for the largest number of over-capacity facilities.

- In 1991 over-capacity facilities designed for fewer than 31 residents made up 13% of detention centers and held 6% of detention center residents.

- In 1991 over-capacity facilities designed for more than 220 residents were 3% of all detention centers and held 21% of detention center residents.

Note: Data are for February 15, 1991. Design capacity is the number of residents a facility is constructed to hold without double bunking in single rooms and without using areas not designed as sleeping quarters to house residents.
Source: OJJDP. (1985, 1993). Children in Custody Census 1982283 and 1990/91 [machine-readable data files].

SECURITY MEASURES PREVENT ESCAPES AND PROTECT JUVENILES FROM HARMING EACH OTHER OR STAFF

In juvenile facilities, the use of fences, walls, locks, and surveillance equipment is increasingly common, although they do not tend to have the elaborate security hardware often found in adult jails. In 1991, 62% of juveniles in detention were held in facilities with a perimeter wall or fence; in 1987 the figure was 54%. In 1991, 82% of juveniles in detention were in facilities with surveillance equipment; the 1987 figure was 62%.

Locked sleeping rooms and living units provide both internal and perimeter security. Detention centers varied in their use of locks.

COUNTS, CLASSIFICATION, AND SEPARATION ARE COMMON STAFF SECURITY MEASURES— HIGH STAFFING RATIOS ARE LESS COMMON

Accreditation standards for juvenile facilities express a preference for relying on staff, rather than on hardware, to provide security. The guiding principle is to house juveniles in the "least restrictive alternative" placement. Staff security measures include taking periodic counts of the youth in custody, using classification and separation procedures, and maintaining an adequate ratio of security staff to juveniles.

Most juvenile detention facilities use staff to provide security, but relatively few take all the recommended staff security measures (regarding counts, classification and separation, and staffing ratios). Only 1% of juveniles in detention in 1991 were in facilities that met none of the staff security criteria; 32% were in detention centers that met all criteria.

Most detention centers have formal resident counts. Nearly 9 in 10 juveniles in detention in 1991 were in facilities with three or more counts each day. Larger facilities were more likely to have formal counts than were small facilities. Facilities with 20 or fewer juveniles were least likely to have three or more counts a day—facilities with more than 150 juveniles were most likely to meet this criterion.

Most detention centers also use classification and separation as part of their security procedures. Facilities use classification and separation procedures to operate in smaller, more manageable units. By making the living unit the architectural and organizational focal point, the population is broken down into smaller, more manageable groups. Nearly 8 in 10 juveniles in detention in 1991 were in facilities that used classification and separation procedures. Larger facilities were more likely to have established classification procedures than were smaller facilities.

Substandard security staffing ratios were fairly widespread in 1991. Just over half of juveniles in detention were in facilities with at least 1 security staff member for every 10.6 juveniles. If a more relaxed standard of 1 staff member to 12 juveniles is applied, three-quarters of juveniles in detention were in facilities meeting this security staffing ratio.

STAFF PERIMETER CHECKS KEEP RESIDENTS IN
AND KEEP CONTRABAND AND NONRESIDENTS OUT

Most juveniles in detention centers in 1991 were in facilities with perimeter checks by staff (87%). There was little change in the use of perimeter checks since 1987. In that year, 85% of the juveniles in public detention centers were in facilities with perimeter checks.

IN A TYPICAL MONTH, THERE MAY BE
100 DETENTION CENTER ESCAPES

Nationwide, detention centers reported 108 successful escapes and 169 unsuccessful escape attempts during a typical month in 1991. This would translate into an estimated 1,300 escapes and more than 2,000 unsuccessful attempts per year.

The rate of attempted escapes and the rate of successful escapes were virtually the same for detention centers that met the "three or more counts per day" criterion and for those that did not.

Similarly, rates of attempted and completed escapes were the same for facilities with perimeter walls or fences and for facilities without them.

FRISK SEARCHES ARE MORE COMMON THAN
STRIP SEARCHES OR ROOM SEARCHES

There is significant variation in the use of searches across facilities. Nationwide, detention centers reported an average of nearly 40 frisk searches, 30 room searches, and 9 strip searches on any given day for every 100 juveniles. Some facilities, however, reported that no searches were conducted. The highest search rates reported by any detention centers were more than 10 times the average search rates.

MOST DETENTION CENTERS PERMIT THE USE OF
ISOLATION, AT LEAST FOR SHORT PERIODS OF TIME

Three percent of the detention center population was held in facilities that did not permit isolation. Facilities that allowed isolation for up to 24 hours held 50% of juveniles in detention. Facilities holding 15% of juveniles placed no time limits on isolation.

For every 100 juveniles, detention centers reported the equivalent of 3.5 isolation incidents lasting 1 hour or longer each day. The majority of these incidents involved isolations lasting between 1 and 24 hours. These short-term isolations occurred at a daily rate of 3 per 100 juveniles. The rate of isolations lasting more than 24 hours was 1 every other day per 100 juveniles. Facilities holding 10% of juveniles in detention reported at least 6.6 short term isolation incidents per day per 100 juveniles. Facilities that did not use any isolation lasting between 1 hour and 1 day held 2% of juveniles in detention.

MECHANICAL RESTRAINTS—TYPICALLY HANDCUFFS—ARE COMMONLY USED IN JUVENILE DETENTION CENTERS

Nearly three-quarters (72%) of detention centers reported some use of mechanical restraints during 1990. More juveniles were in facilities that used handcuffs than were in facilities using other types of restraint, such as anklets, security belts, or straight jackets.

Facilities that placed no time limits on the use of mechanical restraints held 28% of juveniles in detention. Facilities that permit mechanical restraint use "until the juvenile is calm" held 12% of juveniles. A limit of up to 15 minutes of restraint was imposed by facilities holding 13% of juveniles. The remaining juveniles were held in facilities that placed time limits on the use of mechanical restraints ranging from 16 minutes to more than 1 hour.

Nationwide, detention centers reported using mechanical restraints at an average rate that for a 100-bed facility would translate into 1 incident per week. In comparison, physical restraint (tackling or holds) was used at an average rate that for a 100-bed facility would be the equivalent of nearly 3 incidents per week. The use of physical restraints varied considerably, however. For example, while 36% of detention centers reported no use of physical restraints during the month, 10% had rates above 9 per 100 beds per week. The highest rate reported for physical restraints was 38 per 100 beds per week. . . .

Preventive Detention and the Judicial Prediction of Dangerousness for Juveniles: A Natural Experiment

JEFFREY FAGAN
MARTIN GUGGENHEIM

Since 1970, legislatures have increasingly relied on preventive detention—detention before trial ordered solely to prevent an accused from committing crime during the pretrial period—as an instrument of social control. Prior

Excerpted from Jeffrey Fagan and Martin Guggenheim, *The Journal of Criminal Law & Criminology*, Vol. 80, No. 2, pp. 415–448 (1996), Northwestern University School of Law.

to this period, detention before trial was usually ordered only to assure an accused's presence at trial or to ensure the integrity of the trial process by preventing an accused from tampering with witnesses. Today, the majority of states and the federal system have changed their laws to allow judges to detain arrestees who pose a risk to society if released during the pretrial period. Half of these laws were passed in the 1980s.

The significant increase in the use of detention before trial to prevent crime has not occurred without debate and legal challenge. Two U.S. Supreme Court decisions in the 1980s ensured that preventive detention would continue to be part of legal proceedings in criminal courts throughout the country. *Schall v. Martin* upheld a New York statute authorizing the preventive detention of juvenile delinquents, and *United States v. Salerno* upheld the federal Bail Reform Act of 1984 which authorized the use of preventive detention in federal criminal prosecutions. Although the Supreme Court in both cases rejected the use of detention before trial for *punitive* purposes, it approved its use as a nonpunitive *regulatory* governmental power to prevent future crimes and thereby advance state objectives to protect community safety.

Thus, the degree to which preventive detention furthers its community safety purpose depends entirely upon the *capacity* to predict who will commit a crime over a specified period of time. These short-term predictions of dangerousness are made for defendants awaiting further court appearances. Both *Schall* and *Salerno* challenged the use of preventive detention on the ground that the prediction capacity is too poor to justify its use, but these challenges were squarely rejected. In both cases, the Court concluded that predictions of dangerousness were not so unreliable as to pose due process or equal protection concerns. In *Schall*, the Court emphasized that "there is nothing inherently unattainable about prediction of future criminal conduct"; it also acknowledged that the prediction of future criminal conduct is "an experienced prediction based on a host of variables which cannot be readily codified." However, the validity of judicial predictions of dangerousness is unknown, and the consequences of false predictions of future crimes remain the hidden cost of preventive detention. The predictive validity of judicial determinations of dangerousness inherent in preventive detention is the focus of this research.

A. Bail Reform and the Evolution of Preventive Detention

Preventive detention was part of the second generation of "bail reform" in the 1970s and beyond. Historically, bail statutes were designed to assure the defendant's appearance at court proceedings. This second bail reform effort followed very closely upon the first and differed sharply from it. The first reforms, in the 1960s, were aimed principally at eliminating the unregulated use of pretrial detention, primarily among poor defendants in urban jails....

... The *Schall* and *Salerno* decisions completed the transformation of the purpose of bail from its traditional emphasis on ensuring court appearance to the protection of the public from dangerous persons.

These developments raise two concerns. First, preventive detention statutes reintroduce relatively standardless bases for detention decisions. The bail reforms of the 1960s attempted to eliminate arbitrariness by providing meaningful criteria for judicial consideration in setting bail. Critics of the old cash bail system correctly complained that the absence of such criteria were invitations to disparity and capriciousness.

Unfortunately, the new preventive detention statutes commonly fail to be precise in defining eligibility for detention. Even when statutes are explicit in permitting detention on grounds of "dangerousness," they frequently fail to provide specific standards for determining dangerousness. Terms such as "threat," "danger," and "public safety" are operationally defined in fewer than half the statutes with such references. . . . Most important, the standardless bases for making detention decisions risk false prediction by their broad application to pretrial defendants who may not be reasonably considered "dangerous."

The second concern—and the one which this Article addresses—is the inability to validate the efficacy of judicial predictions of dangerousness made under these statutes. Because defendants are detained prior to committing an act, it has not been possible to validate the prediction of their future wrongdoing. Once a person is detained as dangerous, it is impossible to demonstrate that the detention was unnecessary or wrongful. According to Goldkarnp, the degree to which judges wrongfully detain defendants is unknowable because their decisions "are unfalsifiable.". . . The only way to determine the accuracy of preventive detention predictions is to release defendants who are predicted to commit new crimes during the pretrial period in order to determine the precise degree to which they are risks for future crimes.

1. Definitional Problems   Preventive detention involves a short-term prediction of dangerousness, or the prediction of some future harm. However, many statutes fail to use precise definitions of pretrial danger, the absence of definitional standards makes it difficult to determine what is being prevented, what is the type and magnitude of the harm predicted, and what is the predicted level of risk and the rate of that harm. The product of these variables constitutes "dangerousness."

The development of definitions of danger have focused on two concerns: danger to the public generally posed by the defendant, and danger posed to potential victims or witnesses. . . .

The Supreme Court in *Schall* allowed the preventive detention of juveniles once a judge concluded that there was a "serious risk" that the juvenile would commit *any* crime, no matter how trivial, if released. This breadth is obviously problematic. . . .

Accordingly, preventive detention statutes, even the most specific ones, are inadequate with respect to definitions and decision standards for detention. All agree that preventive detention is justified, if at all, when it succeeds at preventing pretrial violent crimes, including the threat of physical harm. Because the base rate of violence is low, researchers have predicted two effects of the use of preventive detention: over-incarceration (that is, confining people who would not have committed violence if released) and a modest reduction (on the order of one or two percent) in pretrial arrests for "dangerous" or violent crimes.

2. Legal Foundations The theoretical and legal basis for preventive detention rests on the claim that courts can identify those who will commit future crimes during the pretrial period. This goes beyond the assertion that many criminals are recidivists, the basis for predictions of danger that was approved by the Supreme Court prior to *Schall*. In *Jurek v. Texas*, which upheld the use of prediction of future criminality for convicted murderers facing the death penalty, the Court emphasized that sentencing intrinsically involves a prediction of probable future conduct in determining what sentence to impose. This is a long-term prediction of behavior over someone's lifetime. The *Schall* Court relied upon *Jurek* in reaching the very different conclusion that short-term predictions are attainable by using experts who are able to identify particularly dangerous individuals from a larger class. However, predictions of dangerousness of competent persons over the extremely short pretrial detention period raise distinct issues for the state and for the individual from those raised by long-term predictions inherent in sentencing or civil commitment. . . .

3. Predictions of Defendant Risk Morris and Miller distinguish between three types of prediction: "anamnestic," "actuarial," and "clinical." It is not always clear which of these predictions best describes the judicial decisions in preventive detention. Although the predictions in *Schall* resembled clinical predictions made by judges, experts who looked at the New York scheme for assessing pretrial dangerousness criticized the predictions as more closely resembling "hunches" or "guesses."

Jurisdictions typically rely on three factors for determining pretrial dangerousness: prior criminal record, seriousness of the current offense, and judicial discretion. However, there is little empirical evidence that these charge-related bases for detention are good indicators of criminality during the pretrial period. Because judges must focus on the short-term danger posed by the defendant, they must rely on information about unproven prior acts and anticipated future conduct, as well as on subjective information of the personal restraints and social controls that will regulate the defendant's behavior if released. For this reason, juvenile court judges in *Schall* commonly considered such factors as the presence of family members at the detention hearing as an indication of the availability of familial controls during the pretrial period.

As applied, preventive detention reflects some combination of actuarial and clinical predictions. The actuarial component involves a complex framework of judicial experience and normative expectations derived from the accumulation of knowledge from decisions made over lengthy periods of pretrial decision-making. It also reflects a normative consensus among the court's everyday "working group" of decision-makers regarding particular individuals and types of cases. The clinical dimension of the preventive detention decision reflects the judges' professional opinion based on clinical elements that cannot be identified actuarially. These include judgments about the defendants' demeanor, dress, and perceptions of the quality of supervision from parents or caretakers. The *Schall* Court summed up this process as the amalgam of "experienced prediction based on a host of variable factors" that we recognize as a clinical prediction.

A crucial difference, of course, is that traditional clinical assessments by psychological professionals are rendered only after lengthy interviews and reviews of case records. Preventive detention decisions, by contrast, are made by judges often in a matter of minutes and frequently on the basis of unverified information. In *Barefoot v. Estelle*, the Supreme Court noted that "psychiatrists and psychologists are accurate in no more than one in three predictions of violent behavior over a several year period among institutionalized populations that had committed violence in the past." What may we expect when judges are asked to make short-term predictions about a heterogeneous group of defendants where information is sketchy and unverified regarding the elements that comprise risk?

4. The Validity of Judicial Predictions of Dangerousness for Pretrial Defendants The benefit of testing the accuracy of judicial predictions has long been recognized, but the social and personal costs have seemed too high. Simply stated, once an individual has been determined to be dangerous by a judge, the safest recourse is to confine that person. Some studies have tested the accuracy of predictions by mental health personnel. A number of studies have attempted to examine the predictive capacities of bail and pretrial detention by determining the amount of crime committed by persons on release status. This research has been limited to pretrial rearrest rates of persons who have been released by courts on bail or on their own recognizance. These studies have examined what persons released by courts have done during the pretrial period. However, the proposition that courts can identify criminal defendants who are likely to commit crimes before trial if released has never been directly subject to systematic study. As a result, the claim that courts possess the ability to predict pretrial danger of arrestees has become an unfalsifiable assertion as preventive detention becomes more widespread: those deemed dangerous have been denied liberty during the pretrial period and not accorded an opportunity to commit crimes. No study has tested the accuracy of judicial predictions that defendants will recidivate when they are preventively detained.

Efforts to predict both pretrial crime and those defendants who will commit such crimes run headlong into base rate problems. Base rate estimates of pretrial crime are generally low and are especially difficult to compute for juveniles. Indeed, the base rate of pretrial crime among juvenile defendants is unknown and estimates based upon adult pretrial crime rates are problematic as studies of pretrial crime among adults vary depending on the classification of pretrial crime. The rate of pretrial *violent* crime for adults appears to be particularly low, ranging from 3% to 7%. Toborg and colleagues reported a 7% pretrial rearrest rate for *violent* offenses among 3,000 District of Columbia defendants arrested in 1981 for violent offenses. Analyses of more than 4,000 defendants released in Philadelphia between 1977 and 1979 revealed a pretrial rearrest rate for *serious* offenses of 6%. Pretrial rearrest rates for *any* felony vary from 3% to nearly 40%.

Base rates establish probabilities for defined groups, but the epistemology of prediction provides extremely weak grounds for making any prediction about a particular person, especially when the prediction is short-term. When base rates are low—as they appear to be for pretrial juvenile crime—the capacity to make accurate individual predictions of short-term criminality is particularly questionable. Several studies have estimated the accuracy of short-term predictions by using the statutory criteria for detention-eligible arrestees. These studies have concluded that the criteria for detention eligibility is a poor predictor of who will commit a crime during the pretrial period. There is general consensus that the capacity to predict pretrial crime on the basis of statutory standards for determining dangerousness is no better than one in three correct predictions.

The problems are different when base rates are high. In these circumstances, the difficulty involves developing bases to make predictions that improve on randomness. The difficulty of predicting events increases as the base rate falls below 50%. Because violent criminality is a rare event, the establishment of a valid base expectancy rate is critical. When the "true" rate of pretrial violence is one-in-ten, a one-in-three prediction is not a low rate of prediction. In fact, it would be quite high relative to the actual base rate. But a one-in-three prediction is poor relative to a 50% base rate. Even when the base rate is relatively high for a particular group, predicted future dangerousness will vary dramatically within the group. For this reason, the assignment of a threshold for an individual becomes a critical decision in determining which members of the group pose a sufficient risk to justify preventive detention. Given the low base rates of pretrial juvenile crime, the reduction in crime through preventive detention is likely to be quite low unless this threshold is set unreasonably low, close to the low base rate.

In general, predictions of pretrial failure invariably fail to improve on either chance or on the base rate. The Supreme Court acknowledged in *Barefoot v. Estelle* that no study has predicted future criminal behavior for any group over any length of time at greater than one accurate prediction for every two inaccurate predictions. These problems are even more acute for the short-term predictions inherent in preventive detention. Jackson's review of preventive detention notes that "[t]hree noteworthy findings emerge from studies: (1) arrests of pretrial releasees for serious crimes are relatively infrequent; (2) the ability to accurately predict pretrial crime, however measured, is very poor; and (3) the level of pretrial crimes correlates positively with time on release."

Finally, whether rearrest rates alone confirm pretrial crime has been disputed. Rearrest rates may be underinclusive because they do not reflect undetected crimes. However, at the same time, they may be overinclusive because they equate an arrest with guilt. While the number of actual crimes by active offenders may exceed their arrests, there is no basis to conclude that nonarrested juveniles are committing undetected crimes at similar rates, or even any crimes at all. In fact, only about half of those arrested are usually convicted, and often for an offense that is not the primary concern of dangerousness statutes. . . . Nonetheless, rearrest is the only easily obtained and the only legally relevant measure of pretrial criminality. Any other measure or construction, including the use of coefficients to factor in undetected crime and factor out wrongful arrests, involves a level of interpretation that is impossible to resolve satisfactorily and fairly.

5. *The Problems of False Positives and False Negatives*   Finally, the statutory authority for preventive detention in the *Schall* case empowered judges to detain defendants whenever the judge considered their risk of criminality to be high, recognizing that at least in some instances, the juvenile would not commit any crime. The assessment of these predictions is especially important because it provides an estimate of the number of persons detained unnecessarily in order to prevent crime. The threshold at which the number of needlessly detained individuals becomes *too* high is not reducible to a mathematical formula. But it may be useful to view *false positives* as individuals who are deprived of their liberty for utilitarian purposes unrelated to their own danger. Once these individuals are considered to be among a larger group of the "potentially dangerous," they are subject to loss of liberty not because their potential will be realized, but because an indeterminate number of the group will realize theirs.

Accordingly, unconvicted individuals are jailed not to stop them from any wrongdoing but in order to throw a wide enough net to cover others who, if not stopped, would endanger society. It is one thing, *after* conviction, to deprive someone who is no threat to society of his or her liberty for utilitarian purposes. In those circumstances, the convicted person has forfeited liberty based on his or her wrong doing. But *before* conviction, it is difficult to discern how the individual has forfeited anything. The only thing he or she has done, at this point in the criminal justice process, is get arrested.

The recurring errors in predictions must always be balanced by two additional considerations. First, does the cost of trying to prevent pretrial crime outweigh the benefits? Here, the problems of definition and prediction intersect. For these purposes, dangerousness is the product of the crime to be avoided and the predicted rate or odds of its occurrence. When base rates are low, so is the probability that the harm to be avoided would occur. Even within a group where base rates may be higher, the ceiling on predictions within those groups—for example, at one-in-three, as the Supreme Court suggested in *Barefoot v. Estelle*—indicates that the total harm is likely to be insubstantial. When the base rates are actually far lower...the total harm is extremely low, especially when the harm to be avoided is ill-defined and subject to overreach.

In the case of pretrial juvenile defendants, the costs both to the detained adolescent and to his or her community are quite high in terms of foreshadowing their eventual finding of delinquency and serious disposition. Detention causes considerable adverse impact on the detainee, including loss of employment or educational opportunities, separation from family, persistent future disadvantage in the workplace that results in poor job outcomes, and the ordinary inconveniences of being jailed. Pretrial detention of juveniles also has a negative impact on the outcome of the case in court. The conviction rate of detainees is higher, and because detainees are prevented from demonstrating improved behavior in the community, prison sentences are lengthier and more likely. Several studies have concluded that "detention *per se* exhibits an independent effect on dispositions.... In operation, detention almost randomly imposes punishment on some juveniles for no obvious reason and then punishes them again for having been punished before." This bias seems particularly acute for juveniles:

> Detention undermines the fairness of the criminal process in numerous ways. The state's assumption of guilt inherent in detaining before trial becomes a self-fulfilling prophecy. Those detained are more likely to plead guilty, to be convicted if tried, and to receive a prison sentence. Conversely, those released are less likely to plead guilty.

The extent to which false positive and false negative problems exist depends on the accuracy of predictions. Proponents of predictive efficacy minimize the problem of false positives by arguing that defendants are actually involved in more crimes than the police can detect. Proponents also exaggerate the problem of false negatives by assigning a greater weight to these risks than to the costs of other types of error. These arguments persist only because empirical research has not yet tested the precise levels of predictive accuracy. In turn, the assertions that informed the *Schall* and *Salerno* decisions will remain unfalsifiable: "The scientific work necessary to define a group and to assess its base expectancy rate of criminal violence within a given period has not been done." Who then will form a comparison group against which one arrested person's higher base expectancy rate of dangerousness can justify his detention? Will it be other persons arrested for a crime of similar gravity and with similar records? On what standard shall we judge the accuracy of judicial predictions of dangerousness? Morris & Miller suggest that:

> the base expectancy rate of violence for the criminally-predicted as dangerous must be shown by reliable evidence to be substantially higher than

the base expectancy rate of another criminal with a closely similar criminal record and [convicted] of a closely similar crime but not predicted as unusually dangerous.

We agree, and such tests form the basis of the following experiment.

B. This Study

The litigation that led to the *Schall* decision created the circumstances for a natural experiment to test the validity of judicial predictions of dangerousness for juvenile offenders. On June 1, 1981, a federal judge enjoined the preventive detention of juvenile offenders in New York State. The *habeas corpus* writ was issued pursuant to New York Family Court Act § 320.5(3) (b), on behalf of all accused juvenile delinquents who were at that time or who may in the future be detained in the custody of the New York City Commissioner of Juvenile Justice. That section authorized the preventive confinement of accused juveniles whenever a judge concluded that there was a "serious risk" the juvenile would commit a crime during the pretrial period.

The continuing writ of *habeas corpus*, issued at the trial level of *Schall v. Martin*, was in effect for three years. The order declared the New York statute authorizing preventive detention unconstitutional. However, the district court order only enjoined the Commissioner of Juvenile Justice from detaining any juvenile ordered into detention pursuant to the preventive detention statute. Judges remained free to rely on the statute when making detention decisions. Whenever a judge ordered a juvenile to be detained solely for preventive detention purposes, the juvenile was released from custody by the Commissioner of Juvenile Justice without spending any time in the juvenile detention facility. Altogether, seventy-four known juveniles were released in this fashion during the three years, presenting the opportunity to test empirically the assertion in *Schall* that predictions of dangerousness are attainable.

Thus, the restraining order created the conditions for a natural experiment testing the validity of judicial predictions of dangerousness—the release of a cohort of defendants predicted to be dangerous and ordered into incarceration, but not incarcerated. A consistent decision standard and a consistent set of decision-makers were employed in a small number of courts that ordered preventive detention, and the defendants were released prior to their incarceration.

II. METHODS

A. Samples

Samples included (N = 74) juveniles from the Brooklyn and Queens Family Courts in New York City. The juveniles were remanded to custody under the preventive detention statute of the New York Family Court Act during

1981 to 1984, and subsequently released within hours of the detention order pursuant to an injunction obtained in the federal district court for the Southern District of New York.

Schall cases were identified through a procedure that required confirmation by three parties involved in the detention decision. First, judges noted in court minutes that detention was ordered preventively. The judicial order for detention was based on a judicial conclusion that "there [was] a serious risk that [the juvenile] may before the return date commit an act which if committed by an adult would constitute a crime." This judicial finding of serious risk is analogous to a prediction of future behavior. Second, this status was confirmed by attorneys for the prosecuting agency for delinquency petitions in Family Court. Third, when the juvenile was remanded to the custody of the detention authority, counsel for the detention authority validated that this was a *Schall* case. Once validated, the juveniles were released at the courthouse or the detention facility instead of being admitted into the facility.

We assessed the validity of judicial predictions of dangerousness in two ways. First, the arrest histories of the *Schall* cases were examined to determine whether predictions of dangerousness during the pretrial period were accurate. Second, the base rates of rearrest were examined for a matched sample of juvenile offenders drawn from the time period when the *Schall* injunction was in effect. This group was identical to the *Schall* group and provided an estimate of the marginal gain in predictive efficiency from the judicial determination of dangerousness. These offenders were not detained during the pretrial period.

The control group was constructed using a matched-cases procedure. Matching criteria were selected from the results of principal components analyses that determined the legal (offense, prior record) and social characteristics that typified the *Schall* sample. The criteria also were selected to control for social structural factors that are associated with base rates of offenses and arrests. Five variables were identified as matching variables: age, race, gender, committing offense, and prior record (total prior court referrals, prior referrals for violence). The defendant's census tract was added as an additional matching criterion to control for social area characteristics and deployment of police patrol services. . . .

Most offenders were males (over 92%), African-American (about 60%), and 14.5 years of age at the time of the sample arrest. About one-in-three were charged with a violent offense, and over half were charged with nonviolent felony offenses. One-in-ten had no prior record. Defendants with at least one prior apprehension had an average of three prior apprehensions. Over 45% had at least one prior apprehension for a violent offense. Among both *Schall* and control cases, four-in-ten (42.9%) had neither a prior nor a current charge for a violent felony offense, suggesting that the assessment of their "dangerousness" was unrelated to their involvement in violent crimes.

There were no significant differences in any of the social or legal characteristics of the groups. *Schall* and control cases differed only on the judicial determination of risk that the accused would commit a crime if released. The bases for this determination may be reflected in data not available systematically: the defendant's physical appearance and demeanor in the courtroom, the presence of a family member at the detention hearing, presence or use of weapons, or injury to victims.

B. Data and Measures

Social and legal histories were constructed for the *Schall* and control samples from official records in the Kings County (Brooklyn) and Queens County Family Courts in New York City, and the City Probation Department and the Department of Juvenile Justice (the detention authority). Social histories were limited to social structural characteristics since other information (defendants' family composition, school performance, and other social behaviors) was not uniformly available from any of the data sources.

Complete juvenile and criminal histories were compiled for the interval from the subject's first family court appearance through October 31, 1987; those histories were segmented for the periods preceding and following the sample arrest. Family court histories were constructed from the same data sources. Adult criminal histories were constructed from two sources: New York City criminal court arraignments and state criminal justice records. Criminal history information included the dates, charges, and dispositions of all court appearances. Rearrests for PINS offenses or outstanding warrants were excluded since no new crime was alleged.

C. Temporal Criteria for Predictive Efficacy

To validate the prediction inherent in preventive detention, we must be concerned about which crimes might happen in what time interval, should the accused be released. The period of time for which the prediction applies will vary depending on the court system within which the case is located. Definitionally, the maximum time period for pretrial detention is the maximum time period within which the trial must occur. In most adult criminal courts, the speedy trial period is six months. Accordingly, the period of time over which the prediction is being made should be the period of time within which a trial must be held if the individual is *released.*

In New York, the juvenile detention statute expressly authorizes a court to detain preventively if it concludes there is a serious risk that the juvenile may "before the return date" commit a crime. Pretrial detention may be extremely short—as short as three days and as long as seventeen days; whenever a juvenile is detained before trial in New York, trials must take place as soon as three days after the confinement begins for less serious crimes and within seventeen days for the most serious cases. In New York

City, the adjourned date in a delinquency case after an arraignment, *when a juvenile is released*, is commonly between four and six weeks. Even the four to six week period in New York is too short. Cases commonly are adjourned for trial when the juvenile returns to court for the first time after arraignment. When cases are adjourned in this subsequent appearance, ordinarily no new facts about the juvenile's out-of-court conduct will be presented. If the juvenile is on release status for this appearance, he or she virtually always will remain in that status until the trial.

For these reasons, the fairest measure of time within which a judge should be concerned with the juvenile's out-of-court behavior is the maximum time within which the trial must occur—the period from arraignment through the trial. Once the trial has been held, one of two things will occur which will materially change the status of the accused. If the accused is acquitted, the court's power to detain evaporates, even if there still remains reason to believe there is a "serious risk" that he or she will commit a crime. If the accused is convicted, the presumption of innocence has been overcome. If detention is continued, it no longer is pretrial. Detention after conviction, even before final sentencing, may be for punitive purposes. In New York City, the period from initial court appearance through final disposition for delinquency petitions is ninety days. Accordingly, the *Schall* and control groups were compared for all rearrests and specifically for violent offenses within ninety days. To further assess the validity of predictions of dangerousness, we have also looked at rearrests beyond ninety days.

D. Statutory Criteria for Predictive Efficacy

Under the Federal Bail Reform Act, and in many states, confinement to prevent future crimes signifies a judicial determination of "dangerousness.". . .

A problem with the "dangerous" label is its overbreadth as applied in this study. In the *Schall* cases, judges were empowered to order detention whenever they believed there was a risk the juvenile would commit *any* "act which would constitute a crime," including non-violent low-level misdemeanors, as well as behaviors that may expose the juvenile to harm. Many such acts, of course, fall well below the definition of dangerousness. The New York Family Court statute uses an expansive and far-reaching definition of "dangerousness" that includes not only violence but the threat of any violation of penal code statutes. During the period when the *Schall* injunction was in effect, it is unclear the degree to which judges ordered detention to prevent non-violent crimes, or simply to assure the health and welfare of the juvenile. . . . [T]he term "dangerousness" may be overly broad as applied to these cases.

Although the expansiveness of the Family Court statute presages a high prediction rate, particular attention is paid in this study to violent acts because most preventive detention schemes are more narrowly focused than the New York statute authorizing detention for juveniles. Accordingly, we use dangerousness as the criterion variable to assess predictive validity in this study and operationalize it to include violent felony offenses.

III. RESULTS

A. Rearrests Within 90 Days

... *Schall* defendants were more likely to be rearrested within the ninety day period, regardless of the type of rearrest. Over 40% of the *Schall* defendants were rearrested within ninety days, compared to only 15.6% of the controls. For violent offenses, 18.8% of the *Schall* defendants were rearrested, compared to 7.8% of the controls. Evidently, for all rearrests, judges accurately identified a group of defendants that posed a higher risk of subsequent rearrest during the ninety day period when their cases typically reached conclusion.

The marginal gain in predictive efficiency for the *Schall* cases is tempered by the high rate of false prediction evident. . . . Nearly six-out-of-ten (59.4%) of the *Schall* defendants were not rearrested within the ninety day period, compared to about five-out-of-six (84.4%) of the control cases. When violent felony offenses are applied as the standard for evaluating preventive detention decisions, consistent with the Bail Reform Act criteria for dangerousness, the false prediction rate for judicial decisions rises. More than eight-in-ten (81.2%) *Schall* defendants were not rearrested for violent offenses during the ninety day period, compared to more than nine-in-ten (92.2%) control cases. Accordingly, while predictions of subsequent *crime* within ninety days are effective, predictions of *violence* or *danger* are less accurate.

Statutes authorizing preventive detention commonly mention violence as a decision standard for assessing pretrial danger. After controlling for evidence of violence in both the current charge and prior violence, the results suggest even more modest differences. . . .

For defendants charged with other felonies, there were no significant differences in rearrest within ninety days, regardless of prior record or type of rearrest. For defendants charged with misdemeanors, few were rearrested within the ninety day period. In fact, the rearrest rates within ninety days were zero for nearly all groups. The results show that even when defendants meet statutory standards for past dangerousness, predictions of their future dangerousness are unreliable.

B. Time to First Rearrest

Comparisons were made between the time of the first rearrest during the pretrial period to rearrests for either any offense or violent crimes. The analyses controlled for the severity of the current and past charges as well as the total number of prior court referrals. Only defendants with one or more rearrests were included in the analyses. . . .

Schall youths were rearrested more quickly than the controls for both violent offenses and all offenses. The marginal gain in predictive efficiency was significant and consistently high when *Schall* failure rates are compared to controls, regardless of current or prior charges. The mean failure time for any offense for *Schall* defendants charged with violent crimes was 126 days, but was over one year for rearrests for violent offenses. Failure times were predictably higher for *Schall* defendants charged with non-violent felonies, although quite short (seventy-five days) for those with prior violent charges. . . .

Failure times for violent offenses for both *Schall* and control cases were well beyond the ninety day threshold. Since dangerousness is equated with violence in most preventive detention statutes, the results again show that the short-term predictions of subsequent dangerousness during the anticipated pretrial period are inaccurate. While the court was able to accurately predict a group of offenders likely to commit new violent offenses faster than other defendants, the ability to make short-term predictions remains very limited.

However, analysis of failure times estimates differences in group means for those who exhibit at least one failure event and provides an incomplete picture of the differences between groups. Comparisons of failure times do not examine the temporal pattern of recidivism exhibited by the sample, including those who fail and those who do not (those who "survive" until the end of the follow-up period). Unlike failure time analyses, survival or hazard analyses estimate the probability that an individual will fail during a given time period. . . .

In a multivariate model, the efficacy of judicial predictions of dangerousness are tested by introducing legal and extra-legal predictors first, and then determining whether *Schall* cases differ significantly in the estimation of the hazard function. We compared hazard functions for both ninety and 365 day intervals and for rearrests for any offense or a violent offense. . . .

The short-term, ninety day prediction model has direct relevance for assessing the efficacy of preventive decisions that concern the pretrial period. The model for rearrest for *any* crime is significant. Significant predictors in the hazard function include age at first juvenile court contact (younger), and a current charge for a violent felony offense. The coefficient for *Schall* cases is also significant, indicating the greater likelihood of rearrest for *Schall* cases during the ninety day period. However, the model for rearrest for a *violent offense* is not significant, indicating that the model with predictors does not differ significantly from a model with no predictors. In other words, the prediction of pretrial rearrest for a violent crime using these variables is no better than chance.

The long-term prediction models also show that *Schall* cases are more likely to be rearrested for either a violent offense or any offense within 365 lays of their preventive detention. The model for rearrest for any offense within one year is significant. Prior record and current charges for either felony violence or another felony are significant predictors. The coefficient for *Schall* cases is significant, again indicating the greater likelihood of their rearrest. The results are the same for rearrest for a violent offense, although prior record is not significant in that model.

To determine whether the elements of danger were themselves predictors of rearrest during the pretrial period, the analyses . . . were repeated only for the *Schall* cases. The models . . . were not significant, for both short and long-term rearrests. In fact, for short-term rearrests for both *any offense* and *violent offenses*, the results run counter to the operational definitions of dangerousness. In the short-term ninety day model, the coefficients for a current violent felony were negative, while the coefficients for prior violence were not significant. Rearrest for *any offense* was predicted better by a current charge for a non-violent felony. None of the predictors were significant for the models of rearrest for a *violent offense*. The long-term prediction models were significant for rearrest for any offense and also for rearrest for a violent offense. In these models, current violent charges were significant but prior violence was not.

The accuracy of prediction of dangerousness during the pretrial period remains questionable. The prediction models are not significant for violent rearrests once we control prior and current dangerousness. While predictions of a broad range of pretrial crimes are efficient, the prediction of dangerousness is unreliable. Presumably, it is the protection from danger that justifies the false prediction and deprivation of liberty in over half of the *Schall* cases. Yet in using the statutory criteria and definitions for determining dangerousness, we are unable to estimate an efficient model for predicting such danger in the short term. The models were constructed so as to permit assessments of judicial predictions after controlling for the degree of risk or dangerousness in the population. The models fail to demonstrate such efficiency. Even the unmeasured factors inherent in the *Schall* prediction, those that would influence the coefficient after controls for legal and extra-legal factors, do not lead to an efficient prediction of pretrial danger. Whatever additional, unmeasured risks influenced the *Schall* prediction, they were not sufficient to yield an efficient prediction model.

IV. CONCLUSIONS

The capacity to select from among a group of accused delinquents those who pose an elevated risk of criminality in the legally critical interval following arrest is clear from the study. These results are all the more impressive given the limited nature of the information available to the judges at the time of the detention decision. Yet the results are ambiguous with respect to the *marginal* gain in predictive efficiency compared to the base rate of offending for this class of adolescents. The extent of unwarranted detention increases when the statutory basis for preventive detention is narrowed to the dangerousness criteria evident in the Federal Bail Reform Act and in the majority of state preventive detention statutes. The results do not suggest that the judges were wrong in concluding that the class of *Schall* juveniles posed a "serious risk" that they would commit a crime. Rather, this study simply may help us to quantify that term.

A. Absolute and Marginal Gains in Base Rate Predictions

Would an actuarial prediction improve predictive efficiency? When a particular defendant fits the statistical profile for a high base rate group, we could detain that individual based on an actuarial use of prediction with the same predictive validity and efficiency. In this study, that would mean if we detained all of the *Schall* youths without any benefit of a clinical assessment of dangerousness, one-out-of-six detainees would have committed a crime if released. The judges in the *Schall* study clearly improved on this actuarial prediction.

However, this improvement actually means that the judges detained 25% more juveniles who would have committed a crime if released than had the judges detained the entire group based on actuarial predictions. In other words, detaining the entire control group would result in the needless detention of five youths to "catch" the sixth who would have recidivated within the pretrial period. Detaining the *Schall* group would result in the needless detention of six-youths-in-ten to "catch" the four who would have recidivated.

These differences are conservative estimates, since the comparisons were based on criteria that were limited to objective factors and did not include the social and behavioral cues that often guide detention decisions: demeanor, victim injury, parental involvement at the detention hearing, and details about current or past crimes. Had more detailed matching criteria been used, we would expect to narrow the gap in rearrest rates between *Schall* and any type of control group.

B. Constitutional Concerns

When narrowed to violent crimes, the decision standard that guides preventive detention statutes in many state predictions are inefficient and the performance is unacceptable. Over 80% of the *Schall* juveniles were not rearrested for a violent offense within the normative pretrial confinement period. Such performance stands at odds with constitutional concerns over false imprisonment and equal protection: "The high rate of false positives demonstrates that the ability to predict future crimes—and especially violent crimes—is so poor that such predictions will be wrong in the vast majority of cases. Therefore, judges should not use [public safety concerns] as an independent justification for major deprivations of liberty such as detention."

Given the adverse consequences for defendants, we should be quite sure that preventive detention will avoid the commission of a very serious crime. Detaining ten arrestees to prevent six from gambling in public, for example, ought clearly to be unacceptable. Yet, only 36.9% of the *Schall* youths were charged with a violent felony at the time of court appearance. More than six-out-of-ten of the *Schall* youths would have been ineligible for preventive detention under most adult preventive detention statutes. Limiting detention to those accused of violent offenses obviously is fairer to the defendant because this limitation precludes a large class of individuals from eligibility for preventive detention. However, . . . even this limitation on eligibility may be unrelated to the accuracy of the prediction of violence during the pretrial period.

It is difficult to assess this overinclusiveness. The statutes, narrowly interpreted, would suggest that the rate of false positives is unacceptable. It is only when we allow a wide, standardless definition of pretrial danger that the efficacy of the predictions even begins to make sense. In New York, the statute is so vague as to be meaningless with respect to what is being predicted: both petty and minor offenses would comprise the decision standard for dangerousness. This undifferentiated standard runs the risk of predicting everything and nothing at the same time.

It is one thing to disadvantage the accused by detaining him or her to prevent violent felonies. It is quite another to disadvantage a detainee in the outcome of the pending charge. We suggest that this power should be sharply attenuated given the considerable adverse impact detention has on the detainee. Such detention amounts to unregulated punishment.

Ordinarily, the law will not tolerate deprivations of liberty for punitive purposes without a very high degree of certainty of guilt. The *Schall* cases emphasize the importance of this presumption. Although judges had concluded that the *Schall* juveniles posed a sufficient risk to society in order to require detention upon arrest, more than half were never convicted of the crime for which they were arrested (data not shown). It is impossible to determine what these numbers would have been had the *Schall* group been confined (that is, with no federal court intervention). But it is likely that a considerably higher percentage of juveniles would have been convicted. As studies have consistently shown, when one is detained before trial, the case usually results in conviction. We know of no study in which the conviction rate of detainees was below 50%. Preventive detention not only results in unnecessary pretrial incarceration of individuals, it also restricts access to a viable defense, and prejudices case outcomes by detention status. These burdens suggest a careful and conservative use of this power.

There are reasonable and constitutional arguments to incapacitate a presumptively innocent individual when we are certain he or she is dangerous. But whenever a significant number of persons are preventively detained, many individuals will be deprived of their liberty even though they would not have endangered the community. In light of the great cost to defendants in terms of case outcomes and sanctions, and the marginal gains to society in crimes averted, preventive detention appears to be unjustified.

B. THE RIGHT TO COUNSEL

Procedural justice hinges on access to and the assistance of counsel. When the Supreme Court decided *Gault*, attorneys rarely appeared in delinquency proceedings. Despite *Gault's* formal legal changes, however, the actual delivery of legal services continues to lag behind the constitutional mandate. The two articles in this section by Barry Feld, "*In re Gault* Revisited: A Cross-State Comparison of the Right to Counsel in Juvenile Court," and "The Right to Counsel in Juvenile Court: An Empirical Study of When Lawyers Appear and the Difference They Make," provide the most comprehensive studies available of the presence of lawyers in juvenile courts. "*In re Gault* Revisited" provides the only statewide and comparative data on the delivery of legal services. "Right to Counsel" analyzes the legal and court process variables that affect the initial appointment of counsel and the impact of counsel on delinquency dispositions. The latter article also bolsters Feld's earlier observations in "Justice by Geography" that a relationship apparently exists between procedural formality and greater severity in juvenile justice administration.

In 1995, the General Accounting Office replicated Feld's research on the delivery of legal services in juvenile court and corroborated his findings [General Accounting Office, *Juvenile Justice: Representation Rates Varied as Did Counsel's Impact on Court Outcomes* (1995)]. The GAO study analyzed rates of representation in certain counties in three states and found that rates of representation varied among the states, within each state, and across offense and offense histories within each state. The American Bar Association published two recent reports on the legal needs of young people. In *America's Children at Risk* (1993), the ABA reported that "Many children go through the juvenile justice system without the benefit of legal counsel. Among those who do have counsel, some are represented by counsel who are untrained in the complexities of representing juveniles and fail to provide 'competent' representation." A second study sponsored by the American Bar Association, *A Call for Justice* (1995), focused on the quality of representation in juvenile courts and reported that many youths waived counsel and appeared without representation and that the conditions under which lawyers appeared in juvenile courts often significantly compromised youths' interests and left many of them literally defenseless.

In "Right to Counsel," Feld contends that implementing *Gault*'s promise ntails a two-step process. The first is simply to assure that juveniles re-eive the assistance of counsel to which the Constitution entitles them. The econd is to assure that the quality of legal representation satisfies the re-uirements of "effective assistance of counsel." But what is an effective at-orney in juvenile court? How should a lawyer modify her tactics and strate-;ies because her client is a presumptively incompetent child rather than an utonomous and responsible adult? Should an attorney modify her position f a successful suppression motion, for example, results in an acquittal that lenies a youth access to treatment services that only a juvenile court can •rder and pay for?

In re Gault Revisited: A Cross-State Comparison of the Right to Counsel in Juvenile Court

BARRY C. FELD

More than twenty years ago in *In re Gault*, the U.S. Supreme Court held that uvenile offenders were constitutionally entitled to the assistance of counsel n juvenile delinquency proceedings. The *Gault* Court mandated the right to ounsel because "a proceeding where the issue is whether the child will be ound to be 'delinquent' and subjected to the loss of his liberty for years is omparable in seriousness to a felony prosecution." *Gault* also decided that ju-eniles were entitled to the privilege against self-incrimination and the right o confront and cross-examine their accusers at a hearing. Without the assis-ance of counsel, these other rights could be negated. "The juvenile needs the ssistance of counsel to cope with problems of law, to make skilled inquiry into he facts, [and] to insist upon regularity of the proceedings. . . . The child 're-uires the guiding hand of counsel at every step in the proceedings against im.' " In subsequent opinions, the Supreme Court has reiterated the crucial •ole of counsel in the juvenile justice process. In *Fare v. Michael C.*, the Court loted that "the lawyer occupies a critical position in our legal system. . . . Whether it is a minor or an adult who stands accused, the lawyer is the one)erson to whom society as a whole looks as the protector of the legal rights)f that person in his dealings with the police and the courts."

In the two decades since *Gault*, the promise of counsel remains unreal-zed. Although there is a scarcity of data, in many states less than 50% of

Excerpted from Barry C. Feld, in *Crime & Delinquency*, Vol. 34, No. 4; pp. 393–424 (October 1988). Copyright © 1988 by Barry C. Feld. Reprinted by permission of Sage Publications, Inc.

juveniles adjudicated delinquent receive the assistance of counsel to which they are constitutionally entitled. Although national statistics are not available, surveys of representation by counsel in several jurisdictions suggest that "there is reason to think that lawyers still appear much less often than might have been expected."

In the immediate aftermath of *Gault*, Lefstein, Stapleton, and Teitelbaum examined institutional compliance with the decision and found that juveniles were neither adequately advised of their right to counsel nor had counsel appointed for them. In a more recent evaluation of legal representation in North Carolina, Clarke and Koch found that the juvenile defender project represented only 22.3% of juveniles in Winston-Salem, NC, and only 45.8% in Charlotte, NC. Aday found rates of representation of 26.2% and 38.7% in the jurisdictions he studied. Bortner's evaluation of a large, Midwestern county's juvenile court showed that "over half (58.2%) [the juveniles] were not represented by an attorney." Evaluations of rates of representation in Minnesota also indicated that a majority of youths are unrepresented. Feld reported enormous county-by-county variations within the state in the rates of representation, ranging from a high of over 90% to a low of less than 10%. A substantial minority of youths removed from their homes or confined in state juvenile correctional institutions lacked representation at the time of their adjudication and disposition.

There are a variety of possible explanations for why so many youths appear to be unrepresented: parental reluctance to retain an attorney; inadequate public-defender legal services in nonurban areas; a judicial encouragement of and readiness to find waivers of the right to counsel in order to ease administrative burdens on the courts; a continuing judicial hostility to an advocacy role in a traditional, treatment-oriented court; or a judicial predetermination of dispositions with nonappointment of counsel where probation is the anticipated outcome. Whatever the reason and despite *Gault's* promise of counsel, many juveniles facing potentially coercive state action never see a lawyer, waive their right to counsel without consulting with an attorney or appreciating the legal consequences of relinquishing counsel, and face the prosecutorial power of the state alone and unaided.

Even when juveniles are represented, attorneys may not be capable of or committed to representing their juvenile clients in an effective adversarial manner. Organizational pressures to cooperate, judicial hostility toward adversarial litigants, role ambiguity created by the dual goals of rehabilitation and punishment, reluctance to help juveniles "beat a case," or an internalization of a court's treatment philosophy may compromise the role of counsel in juvenile court. Institutional pressures to maintain stable, cooperative working relations with other personnel in the system may be inconsistent with effective adversarial advocacy.

Several studies have questioned whether lawyers can actually perform as advocates in a system rooted in *parens patriae* and benevolent rehabilitation. Indeed, there are some indications that lawyers representing juveniles in more traditional "therapeutic" juvenile courts may actually disadvantage their clients in adjudications or dispositions. Duffee and Siegel, Clarke and Koch, Stapleton and Teitelbaum, Hayeslip, and Bortner all reported that juveniles with counsel are more likely to be incarcerated than juveniles without counsel. Bortner , for example, found that "when the possibility of receiving the most severe dispositions (placement outside the home in either group homes or institutions) is examined, those juveniles who were represented by attorneys were more likely to receive these dispositions than were juveniles not represented (35.8% compared to 9.6%). Further statistical analysis reveals that, *regardless of the types of offenses with which they were charged,* juveniles represented by attorneys receive more severe dispositions."

THE PRESENT STUDY

The present study provides the first opportunity to analyze systematically variations in rates of representation and the impact of counsel in more than one juvenile court or even one jurisdiction. It analyzes variations in the implementation of the right to counsel in six states—California, Minnesota, New York, Nebraska, North Dakota, and Pennsylvania, as well as Philadelphia. These statistical analyses provide the first comparative examination of the circumstances under which lawyers are appointed to represent juveniles, the case characteristics associated with rates of representation, and the effects of representation on case processing and dispositions.

This study uses data collected by the National Juvenile Court Data Archive (NJCDA) to analyze the availability of and effects of counsel in delinquency and status offense cases disposed of in 1984. While 30 states now contribute their annual juvenile court data tapes to the NJCDA, the six states included in this study were selected solely because their data files included information on representation by counsel.

Because of the many hazards and pitfalls in using juvenile court data, an overview of the juvenile justice process and a description of the individual state's data precedes the cross-state comparisons. The NJCDA's unit of count is "cases disposed" of by a juvenile court. Typically, juvenile delinquency cases begin with a referral to a county's juvenile court or a juvenile probation or intake department. Many of these referrals are closed at intake with some type of *informal* disposition: dismissal, counseling, warning, referral to another agency, or probation. These referrals, whether disposed of informally or petitioned to the juvenile court, also generate county record-keeping activities that are reported to the state agency responsible for compiling juvenile justice data.

The sample in this study consists exclusively of *petitioned* delinquency and status offense cases. It excludes all juvenile court referrals for abuse, dependency, or neglect, as well as routine traffic violations. Only formally *petitioned* delinquency and status cases are analyzed because the right to counsel announced in *Gault* attaches only after the formal initiation of delinquency proceedings.

The filing of a petition—the formal initiation of the juvenile process—is comparable legally to the filing of a complaint, information, or indictment in the adult criminal process. Since different county intake or probation units within a state, as well as the various states, use different criteria to decide whether or not to file a formal delinquency petition, the cross-state comparisons reported here involve very different samples of delinquent populations. The common denominator of all these cases is that they were formally processed in their respective jurisdictions ... [T]he proportion of referred cases to petitioned cases differs markedly, from a high of 62.8% in Nebraska to a low of 10.7% in North Dakota.

In most jurisdictions, a juvenile offender will be arraigned on the petition. Since the constitutional right to counsel attaches in juvenile court only after the filing of the petition, it is typically at this stage, if at all, that counsel will be appointed to represent a juvenile. At the arraignment, the juvenile admits or denies the allegations in the petition. In many cases, juveniles may admit the allegations of the petition at their arraignment and have their case disposed of without the presence of an attorney.

The types of underlying offenses represented in the formally filed delinquency petitions differ substantially; the large urban jurisdictions confront very different and more serious delinquency than do the more rural, Midwestern states . In this study, the offenses reported by the states are regrouped into six analytical categories. The "felony/minor" offense distinction provides both an indicator of seriousness and is legally relevant for the right to counsel. Offenses are also classified as person, property, other delinquency, and status. Combining person and property with the felony and minor distinctions produces a six-item offense scale for cross-state comparisons. When a petition alleges more than one offense, the youth is classified on the basis of the most serious charge. This study also uses two indicators of the severity of dispositions: out-of-home placement and secure confinement. . . .

DATA AND ANALYSIS

Part of these analyses treat the availability and role of counsel as a dependent variable using case characteristics and court processing factors as independent variables. Other parts treat counsel as an independent variable, assessing its relative impact on juvenile court case processing and dispositions. These analyses attempt to answer the interrelated questions regarding when lawyers are appointed to represent juveniles, why they are appointed, and what difference does it make whether or not a youth is represented?

Petitions and Offenses   Initially, the appearance of counsel must be placed in the larger context of juvenile justice administration in the respective states. Table 1 introduces the six states' juvenile justice systems, reports

TABLE 1
Petitions and Petitioned Offenses

	California	Minnesota	Nebraska	New York	North Dakota	Pennsylvania	Philadelphia
Number of Referrals	147422	—	6091	—	7741	18926	—
Number of Petitions	68227	15304	3830	21383	831	10168	6812
% Referrals/Petitions	46.3%		62.8%		10.7%	53.7%	
Felony Offense Against % / Person N	8.7 (5946)	2.2 (338)	1.0 (39)	8.2 (1764)	.2 (2)	13.0 (1320)	38.1 (25921)
Felony Offense Against Property	27.2 (18571)	14.3 (2196)	11.1 (427)	14.9 (3192)	15.8 (131)	25.9 (2653)	19.7 (1339)
Minor Offense Against Person	6.1 (4166)	5.0 (766)	3.7 (143)	6.6 (1414)	2.8 (23)	12.5 (1275)	3.7 (255)
Minor Offense Against Property	17.1 (11700)	29.9 (4574)	43.9 (1680)	18.8 (4019)	29.8 (248)	24.9 (2532)	24.9 (1694)
Other Delinquency	38.7 (26376)	20.6 (3148)	9.5 (364)	7.6 (1631)	16.7 (139)	23.5 (2386)	13.7 (932)
Status Offense	2.2 (1468)	28.0 (4282)	30.7 (1177)	43.8 (9363)	34.7 (288)	N/A	

the total number of referrals where available, the total number of petitions, the percentage of referrals to petitions, and the types of offenses for which petitions were filed.

The juvenile courts in the various states confront very different delinquent populations. In part, these differences reflect the nature of the prepetition screening. While California, Nebraska, and Pennsylvania courts formally petition approximately half of their juvenile court referrals, North Dakota juvenile courts only charge about 10.7% of their referrals. The numbers of petitions involved also differ substantially. The large, urban states handle far more cases than the rural Midwestern states. Indeed, Philadelphia alone processes more delinquency petitions than Nebraska and North Dakota together.

The nature of the offenses petitioned also differs substantially among the states. Felony offenses against the person—homicide, rape, aggravated assault, and robbery—are much more prevalent in the large, urban states. In Philadelphia, for example, 38.1% of the juvenile court's caseload involves violent offenses against the person, primarily robbery. By contrast, a substantial portion of the Midwestern states' caseloads consists of minor property offenses such as theft and shoplifting.

The states also differ markedly in their treatment of status offenders. Pennsylvania/ Philadelphia juvenile courts do not have jurisdiction over status offenders. Similarly, status offenders in California appear to be referred to juvenile courts only as a last resort. By contrast, in the Midwestern states, status offenses are the second most common type of delinquency cases handled. The maximum age of juvenile court jurisdiction in New York is 16 years of age, rather than 18 as in the other states. The New York juvenile justice system deals with a significantly younger population, which includes a substantially larger proportion of status offenders.

Rates of Representation   Table 2 shows the overall rates of representation by counsel in the respective states, the percentages of private attorneys and public attorneys—court appointed or public defender—and the rates of representation by type of offense. Although *Gault* held that *every* juvenile was constitutionally entitled to "the guiding hand of counsel at every step of the process," *Gault*'s promise remains unrealized in half of these jurisdictions.

The large, urban states are far more successful in assuring that juveniles receive the assistance of counsel than are the Midwestern states. Overall, between 85–95% of the juveniles in the large, urban states receive the assistance of counsel as contrasted with between 37.5% and 52.7% of the juveniles in the midwestern states. . . .

The first rows of Table 2 report the percentages of private attorneys and public attorneys (court appointed or public defenders) reflected in the overall rates of representation. In every jurisdiction and regardless of the overall rate of representation, public attorneys handle the vast bulk of delinquency petitions by ratios of between 3:1 and 10:1.

TABLE 2
Representation by Counsel (Private, Public Defender/Court Appointed)

	California	Minnesota	Nebraska	New York	North Dakota	Pennsylvania	Philadelphia
% Counsel	84.9[1]	47.7	52.7	95.9	37.5	86.4	95.2
Private	7.6	5.3	13.3	5.1	10.5	14.5	22.0
CA/PD[a]	77.3	42.3	39.4	90.8	27.1	71.9	73.2
Felony Offense							
Against Person	88.7	66.1	58.8	98.5	100.0	91.4	96.3
Private	11.2	9.9	14.7	4.3	—	22.0	29.9
CA/PD	77.5	56.3	44.1	94.2	100.0	69.4	66.4
Felony Offense							
Against Property	86.8	60.6	59.9	98.1	38.9	87.1	95.0
Private	9.0	6.2	14.4	8.3	12.2	15.1	20.5
CA/PD	77.8	54.4	45.5	89.7	26.7	72.0	74.5
Minor Offense							
Against Person	86.7	73.5	41.3	99.0	47.8	89.3	96.1
Private	8.6	7.3	14.9	9.5	17.4	16.4	22.4
CA/PD	78.1	66.1	26.4	89.5	30.4	72.9	73.7
Minor Offense							
Against Property	83.8	46.8	49.6	96.2	38.3	85.5	94.7
Private	6.1	5.3	14.1	6.5	12.5	11.9	16.1
CA/PD	77.7	41.4	35.5	89.7	25.8	73.6	78.7
Other Delinquency	83.4	55.5	48.9	96.8	33.1	82.1	93.2
Private	6.4	5.9	16.0	8.0	10.8	10.8	12.3
CA/PD	77.0	49.6	32.8	88.7	22.3	71.4	80.9
Status Offense	74.1	30.7	56.1	93.8	37.2	N/A	N/A
Private	3.3	3.9	10.3	2.3	7.3		
CA/PD	70.8	26.9	46.3	91.6	29.9		

a. Court Appointed, Public Defender.
1. The California Bureau of Criminal Statistics and Special Services cautions that this rate may **understate** the actual rate of representation, that is, that an even larger percentage of California's juveniles are represented.

Table 2 clearly shows that it is possible to provide very high levels of defense representation to juveniles adjudicated delinquent. More than 95% of the juveniles in Philadelphia and New York state, and 85% or more in Pennsylvania and California were represented. Since the large urban states process a greater volume of delinquency cases, their success in delivering legal services is all the more impressive. While it may be more difficult to deliver legal services easily in all parts of the rural Midwestern states, county by county analysis in Minnesota shows substantial disparities within the state; even the largest county in the state with a well-developed public defender system provides representation to less than half the juveniles. These variations suggest that rates of representation reflect deliberate policy decisions.

Table 2 also shows the rates of representation by type of offense. One pattern that emerges in all of the states is a direct relationship between the seriousness of the offense and the rates of representation. Juveniles charged with felonies—offenses against person or property—and those with offenses against the person generally have higher rates of representation than the state's overall rate. These differences in representation by offense are typically greater in the states with lower rates of representation than in the those with higher rates because of the latter's smaller overall variation. In Minnesota, for example, while only 47.7% of all juveniles are represented, 66.1% of those charged with felony offenses against the person, 73.5% of those charged with minor offenses against the person, and 60.6% of those charged with felony offenses against property are represented.

A second and similar pattern is the appearance of larger proportions of private attorneys on behalf of juveniles charged with felony offenses—person and property—and offenses against the person than appear in the other offense categories. Perhaps the greater seriousness of those offenses and their potential consequences encourage juveniles or their families to seek the assistance of private counsel. Conversely, private attorneys are least likely to be retained by parents to represent the status offenders with whom the parents are often in conflict. . . .

DISCUSSION AND CONCLUSION

Nearly twenty years after *Gault* held that juveniles are constitutionally entitled to the assistance of counsel, half of the jurisdictions in this study are still not in compliance. In Nebraska, Minnesota, and North Dakota, nearly half or more of delinquent and status offenders do not have lawyers. Moreover, many juveniles who receive out-of-home placement and even secure confinement were adjudicated delinquent and sentenced without the assistance of counsel. One may speculate whether the Midwestern states are more representative of most juvenile courts in other parts of the country than are the large urban states. In light of the findings from other jurisdictions, it is apparent that many juveniles are unrepresented.

Clearly, it is possible to provide counsel for the vast majority of young offenders. California, Pennsylvania and Philadelphia, and New York do so routinely. What is especially impressive in those jurisdictions is the very low numbers of uncounseled juveniles who receive out-of-home placement or secure confinement dispositions. While this study shows substantial differences in rates of representation among the different states, it cannot account for the greater availability of counsel in some of the jurisdictions than in others.

There are direct legislative policy implications of the findings reported here. In those states in which juveniles are routinely unrepresented, legislation mandating the automatic and nonwaivable appointment of counsel at the earliest stage in delinquency proceeding is necessary. As long as it is possible for a juvenile to waive the right to counsel, juvenile court judges will find such waivers. Short of mandatory and nonwaivable counsel, a prohibition on waivers of counsel without prior consultation with and the concurrence of counsel would assure that any eventual waiver was truly "knowing, intelligent, and voluntary." Moreover, a requirement of consultation with counsel prior to waiver would assure the development of legal services delivery systems that would then facilitate the more routine representation of juveniles. At the very least, legislation should prohibit the removal from home or incarceration of any juvenile who was not provided with counsel. Such a limitation on dispositions is already the law for adult criminal defendants, for juveniles in some jurisdictions and apparently the informal practice in New York and Pennsylvania where virtually no unrepresented juveniles were removed or confined.

Apart from simply documenting variations in rates of representation, this research also examined the determinants of representation. It examined the relationship between "legal variables"—seriousness of offense, detention status, prior referrals—and the appointment of counsel. In each analysis, it showed the zero-order relationship among the legal variables and dispositions, the legal variables and the appointment of counsel, and the effect of representation on dispositions.

There is obviously multicollinearity between the factors producing more severe dispositions and the factors influencing the appointment of counsel. Each legal variable that is associated with a more severe disposition is also associated with greater rates of representation. And yet, within the limitations of this research design, it appears that in virtually every jurisdiction, representation by counsel is an aggravating factor in a juvenile's disposition. When controlling for the seriousness of the present offense, unrepresented juveniles seem to fare better than those with lawyers. When controlling for offense and detention status, unrepresented juveniles again fare better than those with representation. When controlling for the seriousness of the present offense and prior referrals, the presence of counsel produces more severe dispositions. In short while the legal variables enhance the probabilities of representation, the fact of representation appears to exert an independent effect on the severity of dispositions.

Although this phenomenon has been alluded to in other studies, this research provides the strongest evidence yet that representation by counsel redounds to the disadvantage of a juvenile. Why? One possible explanation is that attorneys in juvenile court are simply incompetent and prejudice their clients' cases. While systematic evaluations of the actual performance of counsel in juvenile court are lacking, the available evidence suggests that even in jurisdictions where counsel are routinely appointed, there are grounds for concern about their effectiveness. Public defender offices in many jurisdictions assign their least capable lawyers or newest staff attorneys to juvenile courts to get trial experience, and these neophytes may receive less adequate supervision than their prosecutorial counterparts. Similarly, court appointed counsel may be beholden to the judges who select them and more concerned with maintaining an ongoing relationship with the court than vigorously protecting the interests of their clients. Moreover, measuring defense attorney performance by dispositional outcomes raises questions about the meaning of effective assistance of counsel. What does it take to be an effective attorney in juvenile court? Why do fewer defense attorney appear at dispositions than at adjudications? How might attorneys for juveniles become more familiar with dispositional alternatives?

Perhaps, however, the relationship between the presence of counsel and the increased severity of dispositions is spurious. Obviously, this study cannot control simultaneously for all of the variables that influence dispositional decision making. It may be that early in a proceeding, a juvenile court judge's greater familiarity with a case may alert him or her to the eventual disposition that will be imposed and counsel may be appointed in anticipation of more severe consequences. In many jurisdictions, the same judge who presides at a youth's arraignment and detention hearing will later decide the case on the merits and then impose a sentence. Perhaps, the initial decision to appoint counsel is based upon the same evidence developed at those earlier stages that also influences later dispositions.

Another possible explanation is that juvenile court judges may treat more formally and severely juveniles who appear with counsel than those without. Within statutory limits, judges may feel less constrained when sentencing a youth who is represented. Such may be the price of formal procedures. While not necessarily punishing juveniles who are represented, judges may incline toward leniency toward those youths who appear unaided and "throw themselves on the mercy of the court." At the very least, further research, including qualitative studies of the processes of initial appointment of counsel in several jurisdictions, will be required to untangle this complex web.

The Right to Counsel in Juvenile Court: An Empirical Study of When Lawyers Appear and the Difference They Make

BARRY C. FELD

INTRODUCTION

The United States Supreme Court's decision *In re Gault* transformed the juvenile court into a very different institution than that envisioned by its Progressive creators. Judicial and legislative efforts to harmonize the juvenile court with *Gault*'s constitutional mandate have modified the purposes, processes, and operations of the juvenile justice system. The Progressives envisioned a procedurally informal court with individualized, offender-oriented dispositional practices. The Supreme Court's various due process decisions engrafted procedural formality onto the juvenile court's traditional, individualized-treatment sentencing schema. Increasingly, as the contemporary juvenile court departs from its original model, it procedurally and substantively resembles adult criminal courts.

Central to the "criminalized" juvenile court is the presence and role of defense counsel. *Gault* held that juvenile offenders were constitutionally entitled to the assistance of counsel in juvenile delinquency proceedings because "a proceeding where the issue is whether the child will be found to be delinquent and subjected to the loss of his liberty for years is comparable in seriousness to a felony prosecution." The Court in *Gault* also decided that juveniles were entitled to the privilege against self-incrimination and the right to confront and cross-examine their accusers at a hearing. Without the assistance of counsel, these other rights could be lost as well. "The juvenile needs the assistance of counsel to cope with problems of law, to make skilled inquiry into the facts, [and] to insist upon regularity of the proceedings. . . . The child 'requires the guiding hand of counsel at every step in the proceedings against him.' " In subsequent decisions, the Supreme Court has reiterated the crucial role of counsel in the juvenile justice process.

In the two decades since *Gault*, the promise of counsel remains unrealized. Although there is a scarcity of data in many states, including Minnesota, less than fifty percent of juveniles adjudicated delinquent receive the assistance of counsel to which they are constitutionally entitled. Although national statistics are not available, surveys of representation by counsel in several jurisdictions suggest that "there is reason to think that lawyers still

Reprinted by special permission of Northwestern University School of Law, *Journal of Criminal Law and Criminology*, Volume 79, Issue 4, pp. 1185–1346 (1989).

appear much less often than might have been expected." The most comprehensive study to date reports that in half of the six states surveyed, only 37.5%, 47.7%, and 52.7% of the juveniles were represented. This Article analyzes variations in rates of representation and the impact of counsel in juvenile delinquency and status proceedings in Minnesota in 1986. These statistical analyses provide the first statewide examination of the circumstances under which lawyers are appointed to represent juveniles, the case characteristics associated with rates of representation, and the effects of representation on case processing and dispositions. Part of these analyses treat the availability and role of counsel as a dependent variable using case characteristics and court processing factors as independent variables affecting rates of representation. Other parts treat the presence of counsel as an independent variable, assessing lawyers' impact on juvenile court case processing and dispositions. Taken together, they provide the most comprehensive analyses available on the role of counsel in contemporary juvenile justice administration. These analyses attempt to answer the interrelated questions regarding when lawyers are appointed to represent juveniles, why they are appointed, and what differences does it make whether or not a youth is represented. . . .

B. The Constitutional Domestication of the Juvenile Court—Procedural Formality and Individualized, Offender-Oriented Dispositions

The Supreme Court's *Gault* decision, which mandated procedural safeguards in the adjudication of delinquency, focused judicial attention initially on the determination of legal guilt or innocence. Following its "constitutional domestication," no longer was "saving" an offender's "soul" at issue, but rather proof of his commission of a criminal offense as a prelude to sentencing or, in the euphemisms of juvenile justice, disposition. In so doing, *Gault* fundamentally altered the operation of the juvenile court. . . .

Several features of the juvenile justice process were critical to the imposition of procedural safeguards and the right to counsel in *Gault*: the fact that juveniles were being adjudicated delinquent for behavior that would be criminal if committed by adults; the attendant stigma of delinquency/criminal convictions; and the realities of juvenile institutional confinement. These realities motivated the Court in *Gault* to mandate elementary procedural safeguards: the right to advance notice of charges; a fair and impartial hearing; the right to the assistance of counsel, including opportunities to confront and cross-examine witnesses; and the protections of the privilege against self-incrimination. . . .

In granting the right to counsel, *Gault* manifested the Warren Court's belief that the adversary process could protect constitutional rights and limit the coercive powers of the state, which, in turn, would assure the regularity of law enforcement and reduce the need for continual judicial scrutiny.

Thus, *Gault* was a specific instance of the Warren Court's general broadening of the right to counsel to preserve individual liberty and autonomy. . . .

C. Implementation of the *Gault* Right to Counsel in State Delinquency Proceedings

When *Gault* was decided, the presence of an attorney in delinquency proceedings was a rare event. In the immediate aftermath of *Gault*, states that had not previously provided for counsel in juvenile court amended their statutes to do so. Despite the formal legal changes, however, the actual delivery of legal services to juveniles lagged behind. Professors Lefstein, Stapleton, and Teitelbaum examined institutional compliance with the *Gault* decision and found that many juveniles were neither adequately advised of their right to counsel nor had counsel appointed for them. In a more recent evaluation of legal representation in North Carolina, Professors Clarke and Koch found that the Juvenile Defender Project represented only 22.3% of juveniles in Winston-Salem, North Carolina, and only 45.8,% in Charlotte, North Carolina. Aday found rates of representation of 26.2% and 38.7% in the two counties of the jurisdiction he studied. Professor Bortner's evaluation of a large, midwestern county's juvenile court showed that "[over half (58.2 percent) [the juveniles] were not represented by an attorney." Evaluations of rates of representation in Minnesota also indicate that a majority of youths are unrepresented. Professor Feld reported enormous county-by-county variations within Minnesota in rates of representation, ranging from a high of over 90% to a low of less than 10%. A substantial minority of youths removed from their homes or confined in state juvenile correctional institutions lacked representation at the time of their adjudication and disposition. Significant numbers of unrepresented juveniles continue to be incarcerated in other jurisdictions as well.

There are a variety of possible explanations for why so many youths are still unrepresented: parental reluctance to retain an attorney; inadequate or non-existent public-defender legal services in nonurban areas; a judicial encouragement of and readiness to find a waiver of the right to counsel in order to ease administrative burdens on the courts; cursory and misleading judicial advisories of rights that inadequately convey the importance of the right to counsel and suggest that the waiver litany is simply a meaningless technicality; a continuing judicial hostility to an advocacy role in traditional treatment-oriented courts; or a judicial predetermination of dispositions with nonappointment of counsel where probation or nonincarceration is the anticipated outcome. Whatever the reasons and despite *Gault*'s promise of counsel, many juveniles facing potentially coercive state action never see a lawyer, waive their right to counsel without consulting with an attorney or appreciating the legal consequences of relinquishing counsel, and face the prosecutorial power of the state alone and unaided.

The most common explanation for nonrepresentation is waiver of counsel. In most jurisdictions, including Minnesota, the validity of relinquishing a constitutional right is determined by assessing whether there was a "knowing, intelligent, and voluntary waiver" under the "totality of the circumstances." The judicial position that a young minor can "knowingly and intelligently" waive constitutional rights is consistent with the Minnesota legislature's judgment that a youth can make an informed waiver decision without parental concurrence or consultation with an attorney.

The right to waive counsel and appear as a *pro se* defendant follows from the United States Supreme Court's decisions in *Johnson v. Zerbst* and *Faretta v. California.* In *Faretta*, the Court held that an adult defendant in a state criminal trial had a constitutional right to proceed without counsel when he or she voluntarily and intelligently elects to do so. The Supreme Court has never ruled on the validity of a minor's waiver of the right to counsel in delinquency proceedings as such, although it upheld a minor's waiver of the *Miranda* right to counsel at the pretrial investigative stage under the "totality of the circumstances." . . .

The crucial issue for juveniles, as for adults, is whether such a waiver can occur "voluntarily and intelligently," particularly without prior consultation with counsel. The problem is particularly acute when the judges giving the judicial advisories seek a predetermined result—the waiver of counsel—which influences both the information they convey and their interpretation of the juvenile's response. The "totality" approach to waiver of rights by juveniles has been criticized extensively. Empirical research suggests that juveniles simply are not as competent as adults to waive their rights in a "knowing and intelligent" manner. Professor Grisso reports that the problems of understanding and waiving rights were particularly acute for younger juveniles:

> As a class, juveniles younger than fifteen years of age failed to meet both the absolute and relative (adult norm) standards for comprehension. . . . The vast majority of these juveniles misunderstood at least one of the four standard *Miranda* statements, and compared with adults, demonstrated significantly poorer comprehension of the nature and significance of the *Miranda* rights.

Grisso also reported that although "juveniles younger than fifteen manifest significantly poorer comprehension than adults of comparable intelligence," the level of comprehension exhibited by youths sixteen and older, although comparable to that of adults, was inadequate. While several jurisdictions recognize this "developmental fact" and prohibit uncounselled waivers of the right to counsel or incarceration of unrepresented delinquents, the majority of states, including Minnesota, allow juveniles to waive their *Miranda* rights as well as their right to counsel in delinquency proceedings without an attorney's assistance. . . .

Even when juveniles are represented, attorneys may not be capable of or committed to representing their juvenile clients in an effective adversarial manner. Organizational pressures to cooperate, judicial hostility toward adversarial litigants, role ambiguity created by the dual goals of rehabilitation and punishment, reluctance to help juveniles "beat a case," or an internalization of a court's treatment philosophy may compromise the role of counsel in juvenile court. Institutional pressures to maintain stable, cooperative working relations with other personnel in the system may be inconsistent with effective adversarial advocacy.

Several studies have questioned whether lawyers can actually perform as advocates in a system rooted in *parens patriae* and benevolent rehabilitation. Indeed there are some indications that lawyers representing juveniles in more traditional therapeutic juvenile courts may actually disadvantage their clients in adjudications or dispositions. Duffee and Siegel, Clarke and Koch, Stapleton and Teitelbaum, Hayeslip, and Bortner all reported that juveniles with counsel are more likely to be incarcerated than juveniles without counsel. Bortner, for example, found that:

> [w]hen the possibility of receiving the most severe dispositions (placement outside the home in either group homes or institutions) is examined, those juveniles who were represented by attorneys were more likely to receive these dispositions than were juveniles not represented (35.8 percent compared to 9.6 percent). Further statistical analysis reveals that, *regardless of the types of offenses with which they were charged*, juveniles represented by attorneys receive more severe dispositions.

Feld's evaluation of the impact of counsel in six states' delinquency proceedings reported that:

> it appears that in virtually every jurisdiction, representation by counsel is an aggravating factor in a juvenile's disposition. . . . In short, while the legal variables [of seriousness of present offense, prior record, and pretrial detention status] enhance the probabilities of representation, the fact of representation appears to exert an independent effect on the severity of dispositions.

. . .

V. DISCUSSION, POLICY IMPLICATIONS, AND CONCLUSIONS

This research provides a comprehensive empirical description and analysis of juvenile justice administration in Minnesota in 1986. It raises a number of disturbing and troubling questions about the quality of "justice" in juvenile courts in Minnesota and, by implication, in many other states. The empirical findings bear on a number of juvenile justice policy issues. What degree of county and judicial diversity in pretrial detention and sentencing is tolerable or desirable within a nominally statewide juvenile justice system? What can be done to improve the mechanisms for delivering legal services to juveniles, especially in rural counties? What legal standards should be used to assess the validity of waivers of counsel, especially those by young juveniles? What can be done to eliminate the impact of prior, uncounselled convictions on subsequent sentencing of juveniles both as juveniles and as adults? What explicit and objective criteria should be adopted to limit the initial use and subsequent impact of pretrial detention? Should "in/out"—commitment and release—and "durational" sentencing guidelines be used in juvenile courts to reduce idiosyncratic and geographical sentencing disparities? The legislative and judicial reforms necessary to address and resolve these problems have profound implications for the juvenile court as an institution.

A. Varieties of Juvenile Justice

The idealized portrayal of the traditional juvenile court is one of procedural informality in the quest of the goals of treatment and rehabilitation. Historically, the predominant focus on characteristics of the young offender fostered judicial discretion and organizational diversity rather than uniformity.

> Since the court intended to rehabilitate the individual delinquent, and not primarily to exact the just measure of the law, the judge's hands could not be tied with procedural requirements. But translated into practice, this grant of authority meant that juvenile courts would be as different from each other as judges were different from each other. . . . The result was a system that made the personality of the judge, his likes and dislikes, attitudes and prejudices, consistencies and caprices, the decisive element in shaping the character of the courtroom. . . . Without rules of evidence, without fixed guidelines, and, in many cases, without the prospect of appeal, the court quite literally had the delinquent at its mercy. The person of the judge himself assumed an altogether novel significance. . . . [A]ny attempt to analyze the workings of a given court demanded a lengthy evaluation of its judge.

Evaluations of contemporary juvenile courts continue to emphasize the diversity of judges and the broad legal framework that allows for "very individualistic interpretation and clearly different application" of laws.

With *Gault*'s imposition of procedural formality and the emergence of punitive as well as therapeutic goals, a state's juvenile courts can no longer be assumed to be in conformity with the traditional model or even to be similar to one another. Intensive ethnographic studies that focus on a single juvenile court cannot be generalized to other courts in other settings. The few comparative studies of juvenile courts reveal some of the complexities of goals, philosophies, and procedures that characterize the juvenile court as an institution.

Recent comparative research by Stapleton and others indicates that juvenile courts are highly variable organizations with observable structural characteristics on a number of dimensions, such as status offender orientation, centralization of authority, formalization of procedure, intake screening discretion, and the like. "[T]he empirical typology of metropolitan juvenile courts reflects the existence of the two major types of juvenile courts ('traditional' and 'due process') suggested in the literature. More important, however, it reveals variations in court structure and procedure that are not captured adequately by existing simplistic typologies." The recognition that a state's juvenile courts cannot be treated as a single, uniform justice system vastly complicates research which must identify and account for these systemic differences as well.

The present study provides additional support for the existence of "varieties of juvenile justice." Even though the same state laws and rules of procedure apply in all eighty-seven counties of Minnesota, it is readily apparent that at the county level the administration of juvenile justice differs substantially. This comparative research design was shaped by variations in rates of representation. The appearance of counsel, as a dependent variable, provides an indicator of structural variation of types of courts on many other dimensions as well. A juxtaposition between a traditional therapeutic and due process orientation summarizes many of the variations in juvenile justice administration. "At one extreme lies the system best described by the concept of *parens patriae*, with an emphasis on 'helping' the child, intervening in his or her best interest. At the other lies the more formal, legalistic system, with a due process model of restricted information flow and precise rules of adjudication." . . .

These procedurally and philosophically different courts operating under uniform state laws implicate a host of socio-legal issues that go far beyond issues of juvenile justice administration. What external political, social, and legal variables influence the procedural and substantive orientation of a court? What are the legal cultures that foster a traditional or due process orientation? What are the comparative costs and benefits of formal versus informal dispute resolution?

This research documents substantial variations within a single state's juvenile justice system in offense screening, detention, sentencing, and the role of counsel in justice administration. While diversity rather than uniformity historically characterized juvenile justice, whether continued justification remains for such extensive local variation is highly questionable. . . .

B. The Right to Counsel and the Waiver of Counsel in Juvenile Court—Shedding Light on the Dark Secret

Empirical evaluations of the impact of Supreme Court decisions on police and courtroom practices indicate that their influence often is limited and their policy goals frequently overridden by the organizational requirements of the affected agencies. Several contemporaneous observers reported the limited influence of *Gault* on the delivery and effectiveness of legal representation. Nearly twenty years after *Gault* held that juveniles are constitutionally entitled to the assistance of counsel, more than half of all delinquent and status offenders in Minnesota still did not have lawyers. Indeed, in only six of Minnesota's eighty-seven counties are even a majority of juveniles represented, and in sixty-eight counties, less than one-third of juveniles have counsel.

Many juveniles who receive out-of-home placement and even secure confinement dispositions were adjudicated delinquent and sentenced without the assistance of counsel. For the state as a whole, nearly one-third of all juveniles removed from their homes and more than one-quarter of those incarcerated in secure institutions *were not represented*. In the sixty-eight counties in the state with low rates of representation, *more than half* of the juveniles who were removed from their homes and who were incarcerated *were not represented*. These very high rates of home removal and incarceration without representation constitute an indictment of all participants in the Minnesota juvenile justice process—the juvenile court bench, the county attorneys, the organized bar, the legislature and especially the Minnesota Supreme Court, which has supervisory and administrative responsibility for the state's juvenile courts.

The United States Supreme Court held in *Scott v. Illinois* and the Minnesota Supreme Court in *State v. Borst* that it was improper to incarcerate an adult offender, even one charged with a minor offense, without either the appointment of counsel or a valid waiver of counsel. Moreover, both the United States and the Minnesota Supreme Courts have described the type of penetrating inquiry that must precede a "knowing, intelligent, and voluntary" waiver of the right to counsel.

Whether the typical *Miranda* advisory and the following waiver of rights under the "totality of the circumstances" is sufficient to assure a valid waiver of counsel by juveniles is highly questionable. Shortly after the *Gault* decision, commentators warned that simply importing adult waiver doctrines into delinquency proceedings was unrealistic and threatened the entire fabric of rights that the *Gault* decision granted. An earlier article that criticized the ease with which juvenile court judges often found waivers of rights by minors noted that:

> considerable doubt remains as to whether a typical juvenile's waiver is, or even can be, "knowing, intelligent, and voluntary." Empirical studies evaluating juveniles' understanding of their *Miranda* [and *Gault*] rights indicate that most juveniles who receive the *Miranda* warning may not understand it well enough to waive their constitutional rights in a "knowing and intelligent" manner. Such lack of comprehension by minors raises questions about the adequacy of the *Miranda* warning [or *Gault's* advisory of the right to counsel] as a safeguard. The *Miranda* warning was designed to inform and educate a defendant to assure that subsequent waivers would indeed be "knowing and intelligent." If most juveniles lack the capacity to understand the warning, however, its ritual recitation hardly accomplishes that purpose.

No doubt, many juvenile court judges in Minnesota concluded that the majority of unrepresented juveniles "waived" their right to counsel in delinquency proceedings. Are the majority of the young juveniles in Minnesota who waived their rights to counsel really that much more competent and legally sophisticated than the eighteen-year-old adult defendant in *Burt v. State* whose waiver was disallowed? Continued judicial and legislative reliance on the "totality of the circumstances" test clearly is unwarranted and inappropriate in light of the multitude of factors implicated by the "totality" approach, the lack of guidelines as to how the various factors should be weighed, and the myriad combinations of factual situations that make every case unique. These factors result in virtually unlimited and unreviewable judicial discretion to deprive juveniles of their most fundamental procedural safeguard—the right to counsel.

There are direct legislative and judicial policy implications of the findings reported here. Legislation or judicial rules of procedure mandating the automatic and non-waivable appointment of counsel at the earliest stage in a delinquency proceeding is necessary. As long as it is possible for a juvenile to waive the right to counsel, juvenile court judges will continue to find such waivers on a discretionary basis under the "totality of the circumstances." The very fact that it is legally possible for a juvenile to waive counsel itself may discourage some youths from exercising their right if asserting it may be construed as an affront to the presiding judge. The A.B.A.–I.J.A. Juvenile Justice Standards recommend that "[t]he right to counsel should attach as soon as the juvenile is taken into custody, . . . when a petition is filed . . . or when the juvenile appears personally at an intake conference, whichever occurs first." In addition, "[the juvenile] should have the 'effective assistance of counsel at all stages of the proceeding,' " and this right to counsel is mandatory and non-waivable.

Some may question the utility of mandatory, non-waivable counsel if, as this research indicates, many of the consequences of representation are negative. Obviously, full representation of all juveniles would eliminate any variations in sentencing or processing associated with the presence of attorneys. Full representation would "wash out" the apparently negative effects of representation. Clearly, a full representation model is quite compatible with contemporary juvenile justice administration. Five counties—urban, suburban, and rural—which process 21% of all of the delinquents in Minnesota already employ a full representation system. The comparisons between the counties with high rates of representation and those with medium and low rates of representation do not indicate that juvenile justice grinds to a halt if juveniles are routinely represented. The systematic introduction of defense counsel would provide the mechanism for creating trial records which could be used on appeal and which could provide an additional safeguard to assure that juvenile court judges adhere more closely to the formal procedures that are now required. Moreover, eliminating waivers of counsel would lead to greater numbers of public defenders in juvenile justice cases. An increased cadre of juvenile defenders would get education, support, and encouragement from statewide association with one another similar to the post-

Gideon revolution in criminal justice that resulted from the creation of statewide defender systems.

More fundamentally, however, since the *Gault* decision, the juvenile court is first and foremost a legal entity engaged in social control and not simply a social welfare agency. As a legal institution exercising substantial coercive powers over young people and their families, safeguards against state intervention and mechanisms to implement those safeguards are necessary. The *Gault* Court was unwilling to rely solely upon the benevolence of juvenile court judges or social workers to safeguard the interests of young people. Instead, it imposed the familiar adversarial model of proof which recognizes the likely conflict of interests between the juvenile and the state. Further, in an adversarial process, only lawyers can effectively invoke the procedural safeguards that are the right of every citizen, including children, as a condition precedent to unsolicited state intervention.

A rule mandating non-waivable assistance of counsel for juveniles appearing in juvenile court might impose substantial burdens on the delivery of legal services in rural areas, such as the sixty-eight counties with low rates of representation. Presumably, however, those counties already are providing adult defendants with representation and standby counsel in criminal proceedings so the organizational mechanisms already exist. Moreover, despite any possible fiscal or administrative concerns, every juvenile is already entitled by *Gault* to the assistance of counsel at every critical stage in the process and only an attorney can redress the imbalance between a vulnerable youth and the state. As the Supreme Court said in *Gault*, "the condition of being a boy does not justify a kangaroo court," especially if the justification proffered for such a proceeding is simply the state's fiscal convenience. The issue is not one of entitlement, because all are entitled to representation, but rather the ease or difficulty with which waivers of counsel are found, which in turn has enormous implications for the entire administration of juvenile justice.

Short of mandatory and non-waivable counsel, a prohibition on waivers of counsel without prior consultation and the concurrence of counsel would provide greater assurance than the current practice that any eventual waiver was truly "knowing, intelligent, and voluntary." Because waivers of rights, including the right to counsel, involve legal and strategic considerations as well as knowledge and understanding of rights and an appreciation of consequences, it is difficult to see how any less stringent alternative could be as effective. A *per se* requirement of consultation with counsel prior to a waiver takes into account the immaturity of youths and their lack of experience in law enforcement situations. In addition, it recognizes that only attorneys possess the skills and training necessary to assist the child in the adversarial process. Moreover, a requirement of consultation with counsel prior to waiver would assure the development of legal services delivery systems that would then facilitate the more routine representation of juveniles.

At the very least, court rules or legislation should prohibit the removal from home or incarceration of any juvenile who was neither represented by counsel nor provided with standby counsel. Such a limitation on disposition is already the law for adult criminal defendants, for juveniles in some jurisdictions, and the operational practice in jurisdictions such as New York and Pennsylvania, where virtually no unrepresented juveniles are removed or confined.

Apart from simply documenting variations in rates of representation, this research also examined the determinants of representation. It examined the relationship between legal variables—seriousness of offense, detention status, prior referrals—and the appointment of counsel. In each analysis, it showed the relationship between the legal variables and dispositions, the legal variables and the appointment of counsel, and the effects of representation on dispositions, while controlling for those legal variables. The regression equations summarized the interrelationship between those variables and their effects on the appointment of counsel and the influence of counsel on dispositions.

There are complex relationships between the factors producing more severe dispositions and the factors influencing the appointment of counsel. Each legal variable that is associated with a more severe disposition is also associated with greater rates of representation. Yet, within the limitations of this research, it appears that representation by counsel is an additional aggravating factor in a juvenile's disposition. When controlling for the seriousness of the present offense, unrepresented juveniles seem to fare better than do those with lawyers. When controlling for the seriousness of the present offense and prior referrals, the presence of counsel produces more severe dispositions. When controlling for offense and detention status, unrepresented juveniles again fare better than do those with representation. When controlling for the effects of all of the independent variables simultaneously through the use of regression techniques, the relationship between the presence of an attorney and receiving a more severe disposition persists. In short, while the legal variables enhance the probabilities of representation, the fact of representation appears to exert an independent effect on the severity of dispositions.

Although other studies have alluded to this phenomenon, this research provides strong and consistent evidence that representation by counsel redounds to the disadvantage of a juvenile. One possible explanation is that the lawyers who appear in juvenile courts are incompetent and prejudice their clients' cases. While systematic qualitative evaluations of the actual performance of counsel in juvenile courts are lacking, the available evidence suggests that even in jurisdictions where counsel are routinely appointed, there are grounds for concern about their effectiveness. Public defender offices in many jurisdictions often assign their least capable lawyers or newest staff attorneys to juvenile courts to get trial experience and these neophytes may receive less adequate supervision than their prosecutorial counterparts. Similarly, court appointed counsel may be beholden to the judges who select them and more concerned with maintaining an ongoing relationship with the court than vigorously protecting the interests of their frequently changing clients.

Measuring defense attorney performance by dispositional outcomes raises questions about the meaning of effective assistance of counsel in a court system in which many of the participants—juvenile court judges, probation officers, and prosecuting attorneys—do not regard an acquittal as a "victory." What does it take to be an effective attorney in juvenile court? Why do fewer defense attorneys appear at the time of juveniles' sentencing than appear at adjudications? Since virtually all juveniles are convicted of some offense, thereby giving the court jurisdictional authority to intervene, how might attorneys for juveniles become more familiar with dispositional alternatives and more effective advocates for the substantive interests of their clients?

Perhaps, however, the relationship between the presence of counsel and the increased severity of disposition is spurious. Obviously, this study cannot control for all of the variables that influence dispositional decision-making. It may be that early in a proceeding, a juvenile court judge's familiarity with a case alerts him or her to the eventual disposition that will be imposed if the child is convicted and counsel may be appointed in anticipation of more severe consequences. In many states and counties, the same judge who presides at a youth's arraignment and detention hearing will later decide the case on the merits and then impose a sentence. Perhaps the initial decision to appoint counsel is based upon the evidence developed at those earlier stages which also influences later dispositions. In short, perhaps judges attempt to conform to the dictates of *Argersinger* and *Scott*, try to predict, albeit imperfectly, when more severe dispositions will be imposed and then appoint counsel in such cases. Even if this somewhat explains the greater severity of sentences of represented juveniles than unrepresented ones, it remains the case that the requirements of *Argersinger, Scott,* and *Borst* are not being fulfilled because many unrepresented juveniles are removed from their homes and incarcerated as well. A fundamental dilemma posed by *Argersinger* and *Scott* is how to obtain the information necessary to determine before the trial whether, upon conviction, the eventual sentence will result in incarceration and thus will require the appointment of counsel without simultaneously prejudging the case and prejudicing the interests of the defendant.

Another possible explanation for the aggravating effect of lawyers on sentences is that juvenile court judges may treat more formally and severely juveniles who appear with counsel than those who do not. Within statutory limits, judges may feel less constrained when sentencing a youth who is represented. Adherence to formal due process may insulate sentences from appellate reversal. Such may be the price of formal procedures. While not necessarily punishing juveniles who are represented because they appear with counsel, judges may be more lenient toward those youths who appear unaided and "throw themselves on the mercy of the court." While such an interpretation is consistent with this data, it raises in a different guise the question of judicial hostility toward adversarial litigants. Why should the fact that a youth avails himself of an elementary, constitutional procedural safeguards result in an aggravated sentence compared to that of an unrepresented juvenile? At the very least, further research, including qualitative studies of the processes of initial appointment and performance of counsel in several jurisdictions will be required to untangle this complex web.

Qualitative studies are also necessary to determine what attorneys actually do in juvenile court proceedings. In light of this research, the right to counsel and the role of counsel in juvenile court entails a two step process. The first is simply assuring the presence of counsel at all. In many jurisdictions, simply getting an attorney into juvenile court remains problematic. Once an attorney is present, however, the role he or she adopts is also fraught with difficulties. While it is beyond the scope of this Article to prescribe the appropriate role for counsel, a number of commentators have questioned whether attorneys can function as adversaries in juvenile courts and, yet, have questioned the utility of their presence in any other role. The reluctance of many to simply apply the role of counsel established in adult criminal courts to juvenile proceedings stems from the perceived differences in sentencing policies and the more "therapeutic" orientation of juvenile courts. Thus, many commentators prescribe different roles for counsel during the factfinding adjudicative stage than for the dispositional process. Whether there are sufficient differences between punishment in criminal courts and treatment in juvenile courts to sustain differences in the role of counsel is certainly open to question. At the very least, however, many more observations and studies of attorneys' actual performance must precede efforts to prescribe appropriate roles. . . .

C. THE RIGHT TO A JURY TRIAL

The right to a jury trial is a critical criminal procedural safeguard for any person charged with a crime and facing the possibility of confinement. However, fewer than a dozen states' case law or statutes grant juveniles the right to a jury trial and the vast majority of states uncritically follow the Supreme Court's lead in *McKeiver v. Pennsylvania* and deny youths access to juries. The *McKeiver* Court emphasized the potential adverse impact of jury trials on the informality, flexibility, and confidentiality of juvenile court proceedings. According to the Supreme Court, requiring a jury trial would render juvenile courts virtually indistinguishable from criminal courts and raise the more basic question of whether any need remains for a separate juvenile court. Although *McKeiver* found faults with the juvenile process, it asserted that jury trials would not correct those deficiencies but would instead make the juvenile process unduly formal and adversarial. The Court simply noted that the ideal juvenile court system is "an intimate, informal protective proceedings," even though courts seldom, if ever realize that "ideal."

Without citing any empirical evidence, the *McKeiver* Court posted virtual parity between the factual accuracy of juvenile and adult adjudications to rationalize denying juveniles a jury trial. But juries provide special protections to assure factual accuracy, use a higher evidentiary threshold when they apply *Winship*'s "proof beyond a reasonable doubt" standard, and acquit defendants more readily than do judges. [*See e.g.*, Harry Kalven and Hans Zeisel, *The American Jury* (1966).] After analyzing the sources of judge and jury differences in decision-making, Kalven and Zeisel concluded that "If a society wishes to be serious about convicting only when the state has been put to proof beyond a reasonable doubt, it would be well advised to have a jury system." A study that compared the arrest disposition rates for similar types of cases in juvenile and adult courts in California concluded that "it is easier to win a conviction in juvenile court than in the criminal court, with comparable types of cases." [Peter Greenwood, et al., *Youth Crime and Juvenile Justice in California* (1983).] Janet Ainsworth, "Re-imagining Childhood," analyzes the right to a jury trial in juvenile courts and offers a variety of reasons why juvenile court judges convict youths more readily than juries convict.

Coupling the differences between "judge reasonable doubt" and "jury reasonable doubt" with the greater flexibility and informality of nonjury, closed proceedings in juvenile court compounds the relative disadvantage for juveniles at adjudication. As we saw in Chapter 3 A, juvenile court judges are exposed to far more prejudicial information about a youth in detention proceedings than a criminal court judge would be, and this may influence both the youth's likelihood of conviction and subsequent institutional confinement. Moreover, the absence of a jury also permits judges to conduct suppression hearings during the trial which allows the introduction of additional information which may be prejudicial for a youth. And, as noted in the previous section, the absence of counsel in many juvenile courts further prejudices the accuracy of the fact-finding process. In response to these concerns, the Supreme Court in *McKeiver* invoked the imagery of the sympathetic, paternalistic juvenile court judge and rejected the argument that the inbred, closed nature of the juvenile court could prejudice the accuracy of fact-finding. "Concern about the inapplicability of exclusionary and other rules of evidence, about the juvenile court judge's possible awareness of the juvenile's prior record and of the contents of the social file; about repeated appearances of the same familiar witnesses in the persons of juvenile probation officers and social workers—all to the effect that this will create the likelihood of pre-judgment—chooses to ignore, it seems to us, every aspect of fairness, of concern, of sympathy, and of paternal attention that the juvenile court system contemplates." *McKeiver*, 403 U.S. at 550.

Quite apart from the factual accuracy or comparability of outcomes of judge and jury decision-making, the *McKeiver* Court ignored that constitutional criminal procedures such as the right to a jury also serve as a check on governmental power. In *Duncan v. Louisiana*, 391 U.S. 145 (1968), the Court held that adult criminal proceedings required a jury to assure both factual accuracy *and* to protect against governmental oppression. *Duncan* emphasized that juries protect against a weak or biased judge or an over-zealous prosecutor, inject the community's values into law, and increase the visibility and accountability of justice administration. These protective functions may be even more crucial in juvenile courts, where judges labor behind closed doors immune from public scrutiny. Appellate courts acknowledge that juvenile cases exhibit far more procedural errors than do adult criminal cases and suggest that secrecy may foster a judicial casualness toward the law that visibility might constrain. The article by Joseph Sanborn, "Remnants of *Parens Patriae* in the Adjudicatory Hearing," examines whether a fair trial is possible in juvenile courts without a right to a jury trial and analyzes some of the structural impediments to procedural justice.

Juries have symbolic significance for the juvenile court out of all proportion to their practical impact, since even in states where juries are available, juveniles seldom use them. A recent review and survey of the exercise of the right in those few jurisdictions that give juveniles access to a jury reported that the rates of usage ranged between less than 1% and 3% of delinquency cases. [Barry C. Feld, "Violent Youth and Public Policy: A Case Study of Juvenile Justice Law Reform," 79 *Minnesota Law Review* 965, 1099–1108 (1995).] As a symbol, providing a jury trial acknowledges that despite our best intention, juvenile justice may be punitive and that even benevolently motivated governmental intervention requires procedural limitations. Finally, after you read the articles in Chapter 5 on juvenile court judges' sentencing practices, juvenile correctional institutions, and evaluations of the effectiveness of "rehabilitative" programs, it will be useful to reconsider to what extent you agree with the *McKeiver* Court's decision to deny juveniles a right to a jury trial because they receive "treatment" rather than "punishment."

Re-imagining Childhood and Reconstructing the Legal Order: The Case for Abolishing the Juvenile Court

JANET E. AINSWORTH

V. LEGAL IMPLICATIONS OF THE RE-IMAGINATION OF CHILDHOOD

As the socially constituted perception of adolescence and childhood has evolved during the late twentieth century, the premises of the *parens patriae* juvenile court no longer correspond to our cultural image of the young.

Excerpted from *North Carolina Law Review*, Vol. 69, pp. 1083–1133. © 1991 North Carolina Law Review Association.

Just as the invention of adolescence at the turn of the century made the Progressives' child welfare law reforms both possible and necessary, so, too, the contemporary change in the images of adolescence and childhood has legal implications that both reflect the change and at the same time reinforce it.

A. The 'Just Desserts' Juvenile Court

1. Rejection of Parens Patriae *Ideology*   The history of correctional philosophy in the second half of the twentieth century is a tale of steadily increasing loss of faith in positivistic penology. The original architects of the juvenile court were confident that juvenile delinquents could be rehabilitated, as long as judges possessed the expertise, information, and resources necessary for proper diagnosis and treatment. Despite several decades of experience with rehabilitative penology in the adult and juvenile justice systems, however, criminal recidivism stubbornly refused to wither away. Dozens of studies were undertaken to find out what program, what methodology, what theory might work. The depressing conclusion, by and large, was that nothing worked.

As a consequence of the general disillusionment with rehabilitative penology, the focus of the criminal justice system turned from assessing the social needs of the offender to assessing the social harm that the offender caused—in short, from rehabilitation to retribution. This trend occurred in juvenile justice systems as well, underscoring the magnitude of change in the social perception of the culpability of young offenders. From a world in which the child by definition was morally incapable of committing a crime, we have now passed to a world in which juveniles are to be held strictly accountable for their crimes. As a result of this shift in juvenile justice philosophy, state juvenile court hearings have come to resemble adult criminal trials.

Consonant with this new philosophy, sentences in the new punitive juvenile court are designed to hold the youth accountable for the offense committed; any rehabilitative services or programs provided during incarceration are incidental to the punishment meted out. The "just desserts" sentencing model bases the length of incarceration on how much punishment the offense merits, not on how long it might take to reform the offender. In rejecting rehabilitation as the justification for incarcerating the offender, determinate sentencing strikes at the very heart of the *parens patriae* dispositional framework. The proliferation of "just desserts" juvenile sentencing laws in the 1980s represents telling evidence of the demise of the older juvenile court model.

2. A Model of the New Juvenile Court   In 1977, Washington state enacted a complete overhaul of its juvenile court system. Washington's Juvenile Justice Act has been called "the most substantial reform of a state juvenile code that has occurred anywhere in the United States." Often cited as the paradigmatic embodiment of the new juvenile court philosophy, the Washington system is widely acknowledged as the model for reforms in juvenile court systems throughout the country.

Washington's Juvenile Justice Act exemplifies a rejection of both the philosophy and practice of the traditional *parens patriae* juvenile court. According to Representative Mary Kay Becker, the principal sponsor of the bill in the state legislature, the new "just desserts" system enacted by the Juvenile Justice Act represents a move "away from the *parens patriae* doctrine of benevolent coercion, and closer to a more classical emphasis on justice.... The presumptive sentencing scheme ... makes *clear that youngsters who are being sentenced*—i.e., deprived of liberty—are being punished rather than 'treated.' " The core provisions of Washington's new system are its determinate sentencing scheme, which sets the length of sentence on the basis of two objective characteristics: the offense, legislatively ranked by level of seriousness, and the prior criminal record of the offender. Judges may deviate from the standard sentences only if mitigating or aggravating factors pertain to the offense; moreover, judges may not base sentencing deviations on their perception of the offender. The law expressly forbids sentencing judges from taking into account information showing that the offender has been abused or neglected. Nor may prosecutors exercise discretion on the basis of such factors. Instead, they must prosecute serious cases regardless of any perceived treatment needs of the child. Even the prosecutorial decision to divert minor offenses from the formal adjudication process cannot be made with reference to social needs of the child in question. In short, the new juvenile justice system has divorced consideration of the social needs of the offender from the issue of imposition or duration of confinement.

The punitive focus of the Juvenile Justice Act was sharpened by Washington's establishment in 1984 of the Juvenile Disposition Standards Commission to implement the 'clear policy' on sentencing called for by the Act. Charged with the responsibility of developing a policy and standards on juvenile sentencing, the Commission produced the *Washington State Juvenile Disposition Standards Philosophy and Guide* in order to "provide direction for the various professionals in the juvenile justice community and help the public understand the reasons and methods behind the juvenile disposition standards." The Commission Guide adopted a youth justice model with three major components: justice and accountability; community safety; and youth development. The Commission Guide emphasized that proportional punishment of offenders both furthers justice and promotes community safety. While acknowledging that providing treatment services during incarceration might be desirable, the Commission Guide cautioned that social services must be only incidental to sanctions, and never the actual rationale for the sentence.

Disposition is not the only aspect of juvenile court to undergo a transformation. Washington replaced the intimate, informal proceeding in which the judge might put his arm around his shoulder and draw the lad to him with procedures that, with one exception, precisely mirror those of the adult criminal trial. The juvenile, like an adult, is charged by prosecutorial information, and must enter a plea of guilty or not guilty. The arraignment hearing is explicitly governed by the same court rules pertaining to adult defendants. Like an adult accused, the juvenile has the right to be represented by counsel and to the services of investigators and expert witnesses necessary to a defense. The juvenile is entitled to the same notice of charges, discovery of prosecution evidence, opportunity to be heard, and confrontation of adverse witnesses as an adult enjoys. Severance and joinder likewise are governed by the same rules that apply in adult criminal cases. Admissibility of evidence is governed by the same constitutional standards, and the normal rules of evidence apply with full rigor. In essence, except for the lack of trial by jury, the juvenile court fact finding in Washington is, by statute and court rule, procedurally identical to that in an adult criminal trial. . . .

C. The Supreme Court and the Juvenile Offender

Examining United States Supreme Court decisions that deal with the juvenile justice system serves two valuable functions. First, because Supreme Court justices are themselves culturally and historically situated actors, tracing the Court's developing juvenile jurisprudence provides tangible evidence of the general social refiguration of childhood. But the Court's opinions are not merely products of larger social processes; these decisions also actively produce social reality. Supreme Court pronouncements have direct, real-world consequences, reshaping institutions or permitting institutions to resist change, according to the Court's decree. Second, and more broadly, the Supreme Court's impact on society transcends the direct consequences of its decisions. The language used in Supreme Court opinions constitutes a powerful rhetorical resource, reconstructing the framework within which public debate is conducted. That being the case, Supreme Court opinions can be seen as both cultural context and content, as artifact and architect of legal reality.

1. The Procedural Challenge to the Parens Patriae *Juvenile Court*   Beginning in the mid-1960s, the Supreme Court undertook a systematic reexamination of the procedural manifestations of the *parens patriae* juvenile court. The opening salvo of the juvenile court's "constitutional domestication" was fired in the 1967 decision *In re Gault.* . . .

The consequences of regulating juvenile court procedure through the due process clause rather than through the sixth amendment became obvious four years after *Gault* in *McKeiver v. Pennsylvania.* In *McKeiver,* the Court held that juveniles are not constitutionally entitled to trial by jury in delinquency hearings. The plurality opinion reaffirmed that the juvenile delinquency adjudication had "not yet been held to be a 'criminal prosecution,' within the meaning and reach of the Sixth Amendment." Thus the Court framed the issue as whether "fundamental fairness" required jury trials under the due process clause. In answering this question, the Court interpreted "fundamental fairness" as mandating only those procedural safeguards that enhanced accurate fact-finding.

As the *McKeiver* plurality recognized, jury trial is the procedural right most inimical to the traditional juvenile court model. With a trial by jury, the juvenile delinquency adjudication would so closely resemble a criminal trial as to make a separate juvenile justice system superfluous. If a state chose to maintain a separate (if concededly unequal) justice system for the young, the Court was unwilling to make that choice constitutionally invalid. . . .

VI. ABOLISHING THE SEPARATE AND UNEQUAL JUVENILE COURT

Having an autonomous juvenile justice system with its own distinctive procedures made sense in a world that viewed the categories of "child" and "adult" as inherently antithetical in their essential attributes. Once the imagined nature of childhood changed and the child-adult dichotomy blurred, however, the ideological justification for a separate juvenile jurisprudence evaporated. With its philosophical underpinnings no longer consonant with the current social construction of childhood, the juvenile court now lacks a rationale for its continued existence other than sheer institutional inertia. All things being equal, inertia might not be an insupportable basis for maintaining the juvenile court. After all, dismantling the system would entail at least some political and economic costs. Indeed, overcoming the vested interests of such an entrenched institution could take a heroic political effort of will. Yet all things are not equal. Perpetuating an anachronistic juvenile court exacts its own costs, both ideological and practical. These costs compel me to conclude that the juvenile court ought to be abolished.

A. Ideological Costs of an Autonomous Juvenile Court

To the extent that today's juvenile court presents its legacy of greater procedural informality than the adult criminal court, the procedural contrast between the two systems is the most salient feature of the juvenile justice system. This contrast may be more of a liability to the juvenile court than traditionally has been assumed, however. When juvenile court practice diverges from that observed in other courts, juvenile court seems less like a court at all. As Martha Minow observed, "[d]ue process notions are familiar to every child in this culture." Raised on a steady television diet of fictional courtroom drama and local news coverage of notorious criminal trials, American young people have an image of what a court proceeding should look like.

The perfunctory bench trial typical of the juvenile court is not what they imagine a trial to be.

The gulf between the archetypical trial and its actualized caricature has significance for juveniles beyond the obvious conceptual dissonance it engenders. Like any other litigants, juvenile defendants invest the legal system with legitimacy only insofar as they see it to be a just system. That perception of justice is affected not merely by the litigants' degree of satisfaction with the outcome of the case, or its distributive justice, but also by their belief in its prescriptive fairness, or its procedural justice.

Extensive sociological research has explored the somewhat counter-intuitive notion that how one is treated in court may be at least as important as the ultimate verdict in shaping one's opinion about whether a system is just. According to these studies, the key factors contributing to a sense of procedural justice are consistency in the process, control of the process by the litigant, respectful treatment of the litigant, and ethicality of the fact-finder. Consistency in the process means both that the system always follows prescribed rules and that everyone is treated equally within the system. Process control is the litigant's ability to determine which issues will be contested and upon what basis the contest will proceed. Respectful treatment of the litigant connotes more than just courteous interchange; it also includes investing the litigant with the full complement of rights possessed by other actors in the system. Ethicality of the fact-finder entails a sense that the judge is honest, non-biased, forthright and non-arbitrary in adjudication.

Even in its current "constitutionally domesticated" version, juvenile court procedural practice cuts against these core notions of procedural justice. Treating juveniles differently from adults—by denying them jury trials, for example—violates the consistency norm of equal treatment for all and reminds the young that they do not have all of the rights assigned to full-fledged members of the society. Similarly, the paternalistic tendencies that juvenile court engenders in its functionaries undermines the norm of litigant process control. From judges to probation officers to defense counsel, juvenile court professionals all too frequently assume that juvenile accuseds are incapable of exercising sound judgment in making the decisions that affect their cases. Confidence in the ethicality of the fact-finder is undercut by the dual roles of the juvenile court judge as finder of fact and sentencing authority. Particularly for the repeat offender, the judge's knowledge of the accused's background and previous criminal record creates the unseemly appearance that guilt has been pre-judged. In the sentencing role, expressions by the judge of paternalistic concern for the juvenile accused coupled with stern judicial sanctioning likewise is inconsistent with the normative model of adjudicatorial behavior. All of these divergences from procedural justice norms strongly suggest that, in the eyes of juvenile respondents, the legitimacy of juvenile court is suspect.

As a consequence of this loss of legitimacy of the juvenile court, the process of legal socialization for a large segment of our youth has broken down. Legal socialization, or the inculcation of a society's approved norms and values regarding the law, has been described as a primary mechanism of social control. The legal system, along with the schools, has been considered the most important institution involved in legal socialization. In a legal culture as deeply permeated by due process concepts as ours, strict observance of procedural rights in and of itself contributes to an inculcation of the values of the social and political order. If juveniles perceive their exposure to the legal system as unjust, however, the legal socialization process fails. Ironically, conserving the current legal order may be possible only at the expense of abolishing the present dual system of adult and juvenile criminal jurisdiction.

B. Practical Consequences of Abolishing the Juvenile Court

1. Jury Trial Availability The most striking difference between juvenile court adjudications and those in criminal court is the lack of jury trial for juveniles. In the majority of states and in the federal system, juveniles are denied jury trial unless they are bound over upon a prosecution request to be tried as adults. Three states give the juvenile judge discretion to allow trial by jury, and thirteen states guarantee juvenile jury trials by case law or statute. Even in those states where juveniles may opt for a trial by jury, such trials are apparently extremely uncommon. The juvenile court ethos exerts powerful institutional and ideological constraints on the accused's exercise of the right to jury trial. The result, whether by legal code or local custom, is that juveniles seldom see jury resolution of the charges against them.

Being deprived of a jury trial hurts juveniles in a number of ways. Juries traditionally have been treasured as a protection against biased judges and overzealous prosecutors, because the jury has no access to background information about the accused which might cause them to prejudge the case. Moreover, because the jury embodies community values, it functions as the symbolic conscience of the community.

Further, it is one of the less well-kept secrets of our criminal justice system that juries acquit more frequently than do judges. In their germinal comparison of judge and jury fact-finding, Professors Kalven and Zeisel empirically demonstrated what every trial lawyer knows: a defendant ordinarily stands a far better chance with a jury trial than with a bench trial. A recent California study comparing juvenile to adult court convictions confirms Kalven and Zeisel's findings; on comparable offenses it is easier to get a conviction in juvenile court than in the adult criminal justice system.

Why do judges convict more often than juries? One explanation is that the nature of judicial decision making is intrinsically different from the process of fact-finding for juries. Judges try hundreds, even thousands of cases every year, while jurors hear only a few during their service. Over and over again, the juvenile court judge hears testimony from the same police and probation officers, inevitably forming a settled opinion on their credibility. Worse yet, the judge may well have heard earlier charges against the accused, and thus may come to hold a fixed view on the juvenile's credibility and character. In any event, the judge hears pre-trial motions to suppress evidence; even if the motions are granted, the judge will have heard the damning information.

Another explanation for the discrepancy in conviction rates between judges and juries is that sitting in high caseload courts such as the typical juvenile court, judges invariably begin to slip into a routine that may make them less meticulous in considering the evidence. Judges grow "weary of fact-finding whereas jurors find it novel and nothing escapes their attention." Not only may judges consider the facts more casually than would jurors, but they also may apply less stringent concepts of reasonable doubt and presumption of innocence.

Moreover, as a general proposition, fact-finding by a single person necessarily differs from that by a group because the sole fact-finder does not have to discuss the law and the evidence with others before reaching a verdict. The back-and-forth, give-and-take of a discussion can cause the fact-finders to reconsider their opinions in light of the arguments and observations of others. Being forced to articulate the basis for an opinion forces the fact-finder to spell out the logical connections between the evidence and conclusions, "giv[ing] contours to items previously apprehended in a fleeting and unclear manner."

Not only is the judicial decision making process different from that of juries, but the personal characteristics of judges differ from those of most jurors. In terms of economic status, social class, race, and gender, it is an understatement to say that judges as a group do not reflect the composition of the community at large. That jury pools include men and women, blacks and whites, adds valued dimension to jury fact-finding that judges cannot share.

Additionally, the litigants in a jury trial may probe the jurors for hidden biases through searching voir dire examination, inquiring about juror attitudes, beliefs, and experiences that may affect the way in which they would hear the case. In a bench trial, no analogous opportunity exists to explore the judge's background. Without voir dire scrutiny to detect the possibility of judicial bias, one must assume that judges are persons of superhuman powers of self-reflection, able to attend to their conscious and unconscious mental processes and set aside any biases they might reveal.

The value of the availability of jury trials for juveniles goes beyond curing the problems of biased judges or disadvantageous fact-finding, however. A jury trial requires the trial judge to articulate in detail the law to be applied in the case through the mechanism of jury instructions. Any error of law in the instructions is reviewable by an appellate court. If no jury instructions exist to make explicit the trial judge's understanding of the law, the reviewing court has no way of knowing whether the juvenile court judge misunderstood or misapplied the law to the juvenile's detriment. As a result, juveniles denied a jury trial lose out twice. They are more likely to be convicted in the first place, and are unlikely to be able to prove an error of law which would allow them to prevail on appeal.

Denying juveniles jury trials has symbolic costs as well, undermining the perceived legitimacy of the judicial process in the eyes of the juvenile. Given the centrality of the jury trial in the popular cultural vision of the legal system, it is not surprising young people share the general public's high regard for the jury trial, ranking it highly among their constitutional rights. Thus, the right to jury trial is important both symbolically and substantively. If abolishing the juvenile court is the only practical means of securing jury trials for juveniles charged with criminal offenses, then abolition would be well worth it for that benefit alone.

Remnants of *Parens Patriae* in the Adjudicatory Hearing: Is a Fair Trial Possible in Juvenile Court?

JOSEPH B. SANBORN, JR.

THE PROBLEM IN PERSPECTIVE

Because of the *parens patriae* doctrine, juvenile defendants historically were denied a right to trial and were usually given perfunctory hearings whose outcomes had already been determined. However, the *In re Gault* decision in 1967 guaranteed that juvenile courts would have to provide meaningful hearings to youths who wanted them. At the same time, however, the *Gault* ruling did not demand that courts adopt all the rules and requirements of criminal court procedure. Nevertheless, 3 years later, the Supreme Court, in *In re Winship*, declared that juvenile court adjudications had to be based on proof beyond a reasonable doubt. Within another year, however, the Court announced, in *McKeiver v. Pennsylvania*, that defendants were not constitutionally entitled to jury trial in juvenile court and that nonadversariness was a positive feature of juvenile courts.

The Supreme Court's vacillation has caused confusion among experts as to precisely what is necessary to achieve due process in the juvenile court's adjudicatory hearing.

From Joseph P. Sanborn, Jr., in *Crime & Delinquency*, Vol. 40, No. 4, pp. 599–615 (October 1994), Copyright © 1994 by Joseph P. Sanborn, Jr. Reprinted by permission of Sage Publications, Inc.

Research into the fairness of the adjudicatory hearing in the post-*Gault* era has yet to be conducted on a comprehensive basis. Most of the empirical work on the adjudicatory hearing has concentrated on the defense attorney's presence in juvenile court. Although some researchers have found that juveniles appearing with defense counsel secured more lenient dispositions than unrepresented youths, others have indicated either that defense lawyers have had little or negative impact on juvenile court outcomes or that judges have refused to appoint counsel in juvenile court. Still other studies have concluded that one type of defense lawyer has performed better than another, or that defense attorneys in general have not done effective work in juvenile court. Similarly, the competency of masters or referees has also been questioned.

Numerous aspects of the adjudicatory hearing itself have been identified as compromising justice: Caseloads have been too large; hearings have been too brief and too confusion ridden or too treatment oriented; defendants have not been advised of their rights; judges have either reviewed youths' school records or probation officers' social reports prior to or during trial or have not observed rules of evidence or the proof beyond a reasonable doubt standard for adjudication; and, delay has been too frequent and too extreme.

Due, perhaps, to the sporadic and isolated inquiries of previous research, contemporary juvenile justice textbooks largely ignore the nature of trial in juvenile court. These books imply there is no cause for concern as to whether defendants are receiving fair trials in juvenile court.

DIMENSIONS OF THE STUDY

Research and Design and Methodology

This study examined the fairness of the adjudicatory hearing, according to the perspectives of various juvenile court workers. Interviewing was chosen as the method of data collection; an open-ended interview was employed. I asked a uniform set of questions to standardize the results and to ensure accurate recording. The interview was administered to 100 workers from three juvenile courts during the summer of 1989; it was designed to last approximately 45 minutes.

Research Sites

Three juvenile courts were selected for this study to determine whether demographic composition or size of the court and its caseload had any bearing on the various perceptions of the juvenile court personnel. The first court was located in a large urban center (Court A), the second was in a suburban setting (Court B), and the third was in rural surroundings (Court C). All three were situated in a northeastern state.

The county in which Court A sat consisted of one major city. In 1989, approximately 9,200 delinquency cases were referred to juvenile court. There were 6 judges, 22 assistant district attorneys (including supervisors), and 17 assistant public defenders (including supervisors) assigned to full-time duty in the urban court; all participated in this study. Court-appointed and privately retained attorneys represented about 25% of the juvenile defendants. A sample of 10 of these lawyers was randomly selected from court lists that depicted the attorneys who appeared most frequently in Court A. Of the 125 probation officers in the urban juvenile court, 10 were randomly selected to be interviewed.

Court B was in a county that served as a major suburban outlet for the community in which the urban court was located. There was one former industrial city within the county limits, but the predominant character of the county was suburban. There were 1,430 petitions filed in 1989. Two masters, four judges, two assistant district attorneys, and two assistant public defenders who handled approximately 70% of the caseload worked part-time in the juvenile court; all participated in this study. Five of the 30 probation officers who worked in Court B and five private attorneys were randomly selected for the interview.

Court C was situated in what was mostly a rural county with two major towns. There were 575 petitions filed in 1989. Two masters, one judge, one assistant district attorney, and one public defender, who handled approximately 85% of the caseload, were assigned to part-time duty in the rural court; all participated in this study. Five of the 25 probation officers who worked in Court C and five private attorneys were randomly selected for the interview.

RESEARCH FINDINGS

The workers were first asked if the judge learned of the defendant's record before trial, and if so, did this discovery prejudice or adversely affect a juvenile's ability to receive a fair trial. Nearly one half of the respondents, particularly defense attorneys, believed the judges learned of the defendants' records through one of three sources: reading the court record, multiple listing of cases (if one case was ready for disposition, the youth must have had at least one prior adjudication), and the presence of probation officers or institutional representatives at trial (which signaled that the child was already subject to a court disposition). Nevertheless, less than two fifths of the court workers believed that these sources of contamination adversely affected a youth's ability to receive a fair trial in juvenile court. Most of the latter individuals were from the defense ranks; however, seven prosecutors, six probation officers, and one judge also perceived an adverse effect on the fairness of trial due to judges having learned about defendants' records before the adjudicatory hearing.

152 PROCEDURAL JUSTICE IN JUVENILE COURT

The workers were then asked if judges remembered juveniles from the latter's previous crimes. Virtually everyone answered positively, whereas almost two thirds of the workers concluded that this recollection adversely affected the child's ability to receive a fair adjudicatory hearing. Although more than one half of the latter group were defense attorneys, they were joined by five judges, 12 prosecutors, and 15 probation officers.

All of the individuals in the suburban and rural courts maintained that judges remembered youths from previous hearings for the current offense, and a majority in each court cited a bias at trial due to this exposure. Included in this group were three judges, eight probation officers, one prosecutor, and nine defense attorneys. The urban court workers were less likely to perceive a possible problem here. This court had recently implemented a policy where judges who conducted detention/preliminary hearings were prevented from presiding at trial for the same defendants. Nevertheless, one judge in Court A was described as regularly trying cases he had heard at the detention level. This is why more than one fourth of the urban court individuals felt that, despite the policy, bias existed at the adjudicatory hearing. One judge, four prosecutors, and two probation officers joined 10 defense attorneys in this group.

Contrary to the findings of other research, everyone in this study insisted that judges did not encourage juveniles to waive their right to counsel. In fact, Court A experienced 100% representation, and members of all three courts argued that judges wanted defense attorneys to appear because, if nothing else, defense representation allowed cases to flow more expeditiously than if the juvenile proceeded without an attorney. The respondents also unanimously agreed that judges did not appoint any particular type of lawyer to represent children who either did not retain their own counsel or who were ineligible for the assistance of the public defender. Rather, appointed counsel were selected by a rotation system over which the judges had no direct influence.

Some aspects of the judges' behavior, however, were noted as negatively affecting the youth's ability to receive a fair trial in juvenile court. Nearly one fourth of the court workers (but only three nondefense people) contended that judges would not dismiss petitions despite a lack of evidence. Instead, the judges either tried to encourage the youth to accept some type of informal probation or passed the case along to trial. Almost the same number of respondents (but, again, only three nondefense people) accused judges of not giving proper attention to defense motions (e.g., a motion to suppress evidence) because to do so would most likely result in an acquittal of the defendant. More than one third of the interviewees (especially urban court prosecutors and defense attorneys) alleged that judges permitted the admission of evidence that was not always competent, relevant, and material and that this undermined the juvenile's ability to receive a fair trial. Even more significantly, almost one half of the court workers, particularly defense attorneys and probation officers, maintained that judges adjudicated juveniles delinquent even when there was not proof beyond a reasonable doubt of their guilt. Most of the individuals who believed judges reduced the conviction standard in juvenile court explained that this occurred due to the judges' desires to help children.

According to a majority of its respondents, the urban court was experiencing a problem with the competency of its judges; all but three prosecutors cited a negative impact on the fairness of trial as did 16 defense attorneys and three probation officers. These workers observed that judges in their court were frequently too inexperienced to know what they were doing and that this was a sword that cut both ways (i.e., helped or hurt defendants). These workers declared that this inexperience has led to judges acting unfairly: ruling poorly on evidence matters and motions, reducing the burden of proof for adjudication, acting carelessly due to a belief that juvenile court adjudications/dispositions did not hurt youths, and believing most adults who testified while disbelieving many or most children who testified simply because of their age. Similarly, nearly three fourths of Court A respondents (and even one half of the judges) acknowledged that judges had done things specifically that had adversely affected a defendant's ability to receive a fair trial. Although some of the complaints simply reiterated previous examples of unfairness (e.g., bad evidentiary rulings), more than one half (50.8%) of the urban court people criticized judges for forcing the prosecution and defense either to trial or a plea bargain, even when both parties were not ready to proceed; abbreviating the adjudicatory hearing by preventing full examination of witnesses; and directly questioning witnesses.

Defense attorneys appeared for every defendant in Court A; no one from that court felt that juveniles were penalized for being represented by counsel. Three fourths of the individuals from Court B estimated that no more than 5% of their cases were processed without the presence of a defense lawyer and that these involved only consent decrees and guilty pleas to misdemeanors. Although no one believed that youths did worse having an attorney, two probation officers thought juveniles did not receive as good a negotiated settlement of the case when they had no assistance of counsel. Nearly all Court C workers (86.7%) offered an estimate of 10% as the proportion of children who appeared without a lawyer. Although all of these people insisted that youths received the same treatment with or without counsel, many acknowledged that guilty pleas to felonies transpired without the benefit of legal assistance in the rural court. Despite the differences among the three courts, the respondents were unanimous in stating that no one was discouraged from hiring an attorney (and that all indigents were assigned either the public defender or appointed counsel), and that defense representation had not meant worse results for defendants in juvenile court.

A vast majority (88%) of the workers conceded that guardian-like defense attorneys sometimes operated in juvenile court; less than one third of the respondents, however, held that the presence of these lawyers adversely affected the ability of defendants to receive fair trials. One interesting con-

trast among the courts was that although members of the urban court referred to private counsel as the only candidate likely to perform like a
guardian, the suburban and rural courts' workers portrayed both public defenders and private lawyers as potential guardians.

Fewer than one fourth (21%) of the workers felt that all types of lawyers
who appeared in juvenile court afforded adequate representation. Interestingly, whereas Court A people were more inclined to grant this recognition
only to public defenders, respondents from Courts B and C were more fa-
vorably disposed toward private counsel. One common perception among the
respondents was that public defenders were the most knowledgeable about
the system but frequently had too many cases to be completely effective. In
the urban court, this caseload problem for defense attorneys had led primarily to rushed representation, perfunctory trials, and, in the eyes of many,
a lack of effective representation and justice. Workers in the suburban and
rural courts concurred that their public defenders were so overworked they
were forced to compromise and to negotiate a plea bargain with the prosecutor. regardless of whether an informal settlement was the appropriate
method by which to resolve the case. Nearly one half of the respondents declared that, overall, defense attorneys did not have an adequate amount of
time in order to be effective in juvenile court. Exacerbating matters here
was the fact that children held in detention pending court action had to be
given an adjudicatory hearing within 10 days (with one possible 10-day continuance) or be released from custody. Private counsel had sufficient time
but often lacked the experience, underestimated the serious consequences
of juvenile court adjudications, and/or simply followed the dictates of their
employers (i.e., the parents).

Nearly one fourth of the workers argued that defense attorneys did not
file motions in appropriate situations or did so less frequently than in criminal court, and that defense lawyers did not vigorously represent juvenile
defendants. Private counsel were usually the target of these accusations.
More than one third of those in the study complained that defense lawyers
actively did something specifically that detrimentally affected a defendant's
ability to receive fair trial in juvenile court. Whereas public defenders were
credited with taking too many cases to be adequately prepared, private counsel were accused of being too inexperienced, listening too much to parents,
not taking juvenile court seriously enough, not fighting for clients, and not
being prepared to represent a client. Not surprisingly, then, more than two
fifths (41%) of the respondents argued that the appearance of a particular
defense lawyer affected a defendant's ability to receive a fair trial. Although
all three courts identified the incompetent (and perhaps the obnoxious) defense attorney as hurting the juvenile's case, urban court workers mentioned
also the public defender's specialized defense unit, which typically represented serious/habitual offenders. One half of the prosecutors and public defenders believed that the presence of this special unit at an adjudicatory
hearing prejudiced the youth's case because it signaled to the judge that the

defendant had either compiled a significant delinquency record or had committed a serious offense.

Similarly, the appearance of a particular prosecutor was noted as a problem in Court A. The urban court had an habitual offender unit within its prosecutor's office. The presence of prosecutors from this unit at the adjudicatory hearing, then, necessarily communicated to the judge that the defendant must have had a significant delinquency record. More than three fourths (78.5%) of the Court A people cited this prosecutor's appearance as adversely affecting a defendant's ability to receive a fair trial.

Prosecutors were accused by almost two thirds (64.6%) of those from the urban court and by more than one third (35%) of those from the suburban court (but by only one person from the rural court) of having done things that undermined the defendant's chances of receiving a fair trial. Respondents complained that prosecutors introduced prejudicial information at the adjudicatory hearing (e.g., the juvenile's having a case ready for disposition as well as for trial) and withheld discovery or evidence. Court A workers, however, attributed maliciousness to their prosecutors that was absent in the perceptions of those from the suburban and rural courts. Specifically, urban court prosecutors were criticized for being overzealous and not caring at all about juveniles or justice, misrepresenting the readiness of a case and/or the existence of evidence, not diverting cases and thus backing up the operation of the court, and using the habitual offender unit and certification (i.e., transfer to adult court) as leverage to intimidate either the judge or the defendant.

Interestingly, although more than three fourths (77%) of the respondents believed that juveniles were unaware of their constitutional rights, less than one third maintained that the youths' ignorance adversely affected their ability to receive a fair trial. Unfairness was not perceived by many primarily because the presence of defense counsel was believed to be sufficient to compensate for the youths' ignorance. The substantial number (30%) who felt that lack of awareness of rights had a negative impact on fairness observed that youths frequently just did what they were told (e.g., pled guilty) without knowing what they were doing or why they were doing it.

More than one half of the interviewees announced that juveniles were pressured to surrender their rights (particularly the right to trial). Whereas participants from all three courts identified defense attorneys (especially private counsel) and parents who prompted defendants to waive their right to trial to receive either help or an outcome believed to be better than that which trial would have produced. Court A workers additionally noted that judges coerced guilty pleas from youths in exchange for denying the prosecutor's certification request.

Fewer than one fourth of the workers felt that the fairness of the adjudicatory hearing was adversely affected by the absence of bail. Primarily it was defense counsel who perceived adverse effects due to a number of biases directed against detained youth: inability to locate witnesses and to have the defendant aid the defense, considerable pressure to resolve deten-tion-related cases much more quickly than matters where the child was re-leased, and prejudice resulting from the juvenile's appearing in detention clothing and handcuffs and entering the courtroom from a cell room. Simi-larly, few individuals discerned unfairness in the adjudicatory hearing due to the absence of the public.

Although more than one half of the respondents argued that there was no meaningful right to appeal a juvenile court adjudication, only one third maintained that this affected the ability to receive a fair trial. The latter were mostly defense attorneys who believed that the lack of appeal en-couraged a cavalier attitude and sloppiness on the part of judges (and even by prosecutors and defense attorneys). By far, trial by jury was perceived as the most significant right that has not been granted juvenile defendants. More than two fifths of the participants insisted that the absence of this right had a negative impact on the fairness of the adjudicatory hearing, but three fourths of these individuals were defense attorneys.

Traditionally, probation officers in the juvenile system have submitted their dispositional treatment plans to court prior to adjudication. One third of the individuals in this study (including 22 defense attorneys and eight pro-bation officers) commented that the availability of these reports adversely affected the fairness of the adjudicatory hearing in two ways. Judges often saw the plans and presumptively concluded that defendants were guilty, whereas defense attorneys frequently opted not to fight cases after they learned of the probation officers' recommendations.

Some juvenile courts allow the same judge to preside over both trans-fer and adjudicatory hearings, even though prejudicial evidence not admis-sible at trial had been revealed during the certification attempt. The urban court had attacked this problem by requiring that denied transfer requests be forwarded to a different judge for trial. Nevertheless, more than one fourth of Court A workers, particularly prosecutors and public defenders, perceived unfairness in this context for three reasons: One judge refused to relinquish control of his certification cases and, in fact, virtually demanded a guilty plea in exchange for his denying transfer; defense attorneys often relaxed after certification was denied and lost interest in fighting against adjudication; and prosecutors regularly advised judges at trial that transfer had previously been denied. Transfer had been rarely denied in the subur-ban and rural courts. A few people from Courts B and C held, nevertheless, that denial of transfer had caused unfairness in the ensuing adjudicatory hearing.

Scheduling of cases had also undermined the fairness of trial according to a majority of the workers; five urban court judges were among this group. Although workers in all three courts mentioned the 10-day trial rule for de-tention cases as an impediment to fairness, Court A individuals also referred to the day-long scheduling of hearings in their court, which necessitated wit-nesses waiting for long periods of time before testifying. Exacerbating matters was the pressure to move cases that was perceived as a problem in all three courts, but particularly so in Court A. More than two thirds of those in Court A maintained that the pressure of moving cases led to many instances of unfairness: judges prematurely forcing both sides to trial, cutting off the examination of witnesses, and making mistakes by hurrying through hearings; and all parties tiring from excessive numbers of cases, not paying attention to the cases, and not doing their job. Finally, when asked whether any particular aspect of juvenile court structure contributed to unfairness in the adjudicatory hearing, more than three fifths of the workers responded affirmatively. Virtually all of the respondents reiterated complaints registered in answers to previous questions.

Except in the urban court, the nature of the adjudicatory hearing itself was not perceived as undermining the juvenile's ability to receive a fair trial. However, nearly one half of Court A individuals thought both that distractions and confusion caused judges to miss testimony and that trials were conducted too quickly. Approximately two fifths of the urban court workers thought that the atmosphere of their adjudicatory hearings was not serious enough, whereas slightly more than one third of these respondents believed that the treatment-oriented atmosphere of the adjudicatory hearings adversely affected a defendant's ability to receive a fair trial. Similar numbers in Courts B and C shared the latter view.

Finally, each worker was asked whether, overall, defendants received a fair trial in juvenile court. One fourth of the respondents answered negatively; urban court people (30.8%) (especially defense counsel) were more than twice as likely as those in the suburban (15%) and rural (13.3%) courts to contend that youths were not afforded fair trials in juvenile court.

DISCUSSION

Unlike other research findings, three items were not perceived in this study as fairness problems in the adjudicatory hearing. Judges neither encouraged defendants to waive their right to counsel nor appointed any particular type of defense lawyer to represent children. Similarly, those youths who appeared in court with an attorney were not seen as being penalized or having fared worse than those defendants who were not represented by counsel.

Moreover, a number of obstacles to fairness that were mentioned by the respondents are not unique to juvenile court. Representation was not complete in the suburban and rural courts, nor was it always effective, competent, and vigorous in all three courts. Not every adult defendant has counsel and some defense attorneys are also not vigorous, effective, and competent in criminal court. The same can be said about juvenile court judges and prosecutors. Finally. much like the situation in adult court, juvenile court was portrayed as being pressured to move a heavy volume of cases, whereas fairness suffered from the scheduling of cases.

Nevertheless, numerous examples of unfairness identified by the study participants are unique to the juvenile court. Workers maintained that judges regularly discovered defendants' records from a variety of sources or remembered defendants from previous crimes or hearings (and were prejudiced by this information) and committed serious mistakes when ruling on motions, evidence, and the burden of proof necessary for adjudication (specifically because of a desire to help the defendant). Defense attorneys contributed to the unfairness by assuming the role of a guardian rather than an advocate and by private counsels' representing the parents rather than the youths. Both judges and defense counsel were credited with attitudes not sufficiently serious in light of what happens in juvenile court.

Unique structural characteristics also influenced the fairness of the adjudicatory hearing, according to the respondents. The absence of jury trial and meaningful appeals was perceived by one third or more of the workers as resulting in unfairness. The respondents argued that judges and defense lawyers frequently have been sloppy and cavalier in the adjudicatory hearing and that judges have been granted tremendous power in the juvenile forum; some unfair trials have resulted from this combination. Another structural feature perceived as contaminating the adjudicatory hearing was the availability of the probation officer's treatment plan prior to adjudication. Overall, the workers, especially from Court A, perceived that there frequently was not enough time to do justice to a case, especially when the defendant was held in custody. Time pressures and the volume of cases, in turn, encouraged judges to both force cases prematurely to trial and to conduct trials too quickly. Finally, the atmosphere of the adjudicatory hearing was said to be too treatment-oriented for fairness to be realized.

Despite these numerous and varied sources of unfairness, three fourths of the workers declared that defendants could receive fair trials in juvenile court. Not surprisingly, complaints emanated mostly from defense attorneys. Nevertheless, virtually everyone cited at least one or two facets of the court's operation that had brought about unfair results in the adjudicatory hearing.

CONCLUSIONS AND IMPLICATIONS

Because this study examined only three juvenile courts, generalizability could be limited and conclusions need to be tempered accordingly. Nevertheless. the results disclosed here largely confirm other piecemeal research efforts on juvenile court practices conducted years ago and raise legitimate concerns regarding fairness in the contemporary juvenile court. One conclusion from this study is that some juvenile courts have retained some characteristics of *parens patriae*, which was the dominant philosophy in the pre-*Gault* era. It would appear that the degree to which *parens patriae* is alive and well depends on how much a particular juvenile court has accepted and furthered the due process renovation that the Supreme Court initiated via *In re Gault.*

A second conclusion is that changes are needed in juvenile courts if fairness is to be realized in the adjudicatory hearing. Two kinds of change seem necessary. The first involves training and attitude adjustment. Judges and defense lawyers who work in juvenile court should know criminal procedure and evidence. They also need to be made aware that adjudications in the juvenile system are very serious for youths. The attitude adjustment would need to include also a reminder to defense attorneys that appellate review is both a necessary and valuable weapon; a warning to private counsel that, regardless of who is paying them, juvenile defendants are their clients; and advice to judges that credibility is not necessarily correlated with the age of the witness. The second change is in the structure of juvenile court; some changes have already been accomplished in some courts. Simple restructuring could guarantee that neither delinquency records nor probation officers' treatment plans are available either to judges or defense attorneys prior to trial. The former would simply not appear in court and the latter would not be devised until after adjudication. Other revisions include not allowing multiple listing of cases if one of them involves an adjudicatory hearing; not sending defendants held in detention to trial in institutional clothing, handcuffs, or through a certain door; and not permitting probation officers or institutional representatives to attend the trial.

A more difficult change would require not allowing the same judge either to conduct both preliminary hearings and trials or to preside over an adjudicatory hearing when he or she has had previous contacts with the defendant. The judge's offer of recusal is not sufficient because the defendant must wait for the judge to recognize and to admit the potential of bias or the defense attorney must risk the enmity of the judge by either requesting recusal or accepting the judge's offer. One solution would be providing for jury trial; another would be to borrow criminal court judges for the adjudicatory stage. In addition. juvenile court officials should discuss the possibility of slowing down the process somewhat so that fairness may be better served.

The most controversial and most difficult change involves the elimination of many of the obstacles to fairness in the adjudicatory hearing: granting the right to jury trial to juvenile defendants. Arguably, jury trial would mean the demise of juvenile court, the fear of which influenced the Supreme Court's ruling in *McKeiver v. Pa.* At the same time, trial by jury would address the two most significant fairness problems: judicial contamination by learning the defendant's record from countless sources and sloppy performances by judges and defense attorneys perpetrated within a private, laissez-faire atmosphere.

These training/attitude and structural changes surely run counter to traditional *parens patriae* notions and would be perhaps prohibitively expensive, both financially and conceptually. Nevertheless, to the extent that *parens patriae* is an obstacle to fairness in the adjudicatory hearing, something has to give way: convenience or fairness. That so many changes may actually be needed in many juvenile courts is perhaps to say no more than that the philosophy of *parens patriae* remains a very viable force in juvenile court, despite *In re Gault* and its progeny. To hold that it is an unlikely prospect that so many alterations will ever occur is perhaps to say no more than that fairness will never be a top priority in the adjudicatory hearings of some juvenile courts.

CHAPTER 4

Transfer of Serious Young Offenders to Criminal Court

The public and politicians perceive a significant and frightening increase in youth crime and violence. Public opinion polls consistently rank "crime" among the top issues that confront the nation and politicians vow to "get tough" on young criminals. Widespread anxiety about juvenile courts' ability either to rehabilitate chronic and violent young offenders or simultaneously to protect public safety accompany the fear of youth crime. These apprehensions drive the current political and policy debate about strategies to "crack down" on youth crime.

The public may view juvenile courts' traditional commitment to rehabilitation as a bias toward leniency often to the detriment of protecting the public or satisfying the victim. Conservatives long have denounced juvenile courts for "coddling" young criminals. Public frustration with the intractability of crime in general, fear of the rise in youth violence, guns, and homicide in particular, and the racial characteristics of violent young perpetrators fuel the desire to "get tough" and provide the political impetus to simplify the process to transfer larger numbers of young offenders to criminal courts for prosecution as adults. The articles in this section examine the boundary of "adulthood" and criminal responsibility and the processes by which states determine whether to prosecute youths in juvenile or criminal courts. Distilled to its essence, how do we decide whether to prosecute a particular young offender as a criminal or as a kid, and what difference does it make for the youths, for public safety, or for the juvenile court?

Virtually every jurisdiction has one or more statutory provisions that allow the state to prosecute some chronological juveniles as adults. These statutory strategies include judicial waiver, legislative offense exclusion, and prosecutors' choice among concurrent jurisdictions. Each type of transfer provision represents an alternative strategy to decide whether to try and sentence a youth as a delinquent or a criminal. Each mechanism reflects different ways of asking and answering similar questions: who are the serious, hard-core youthful offenders; by what criteria should they be identified; which branch of government is best suited to make these sentencing decisions; and how should the juvenile or adult systems respond to them? Each jurisdictional waiver mechanism emphasizes different information about offenders and offenses to decide whether certain youths should be tried as juveniles or as adults. Each of these statutory strategies allocates to a different branch of government—judicial, legislative, and executive—the sentencing policy decision whether a youth is a criminal or a delinquent.

All waiver strategies represent an attempt to reconcile the rhetorical and cultural conception of children as naive innocents with the frightening reality that some youths commit heinous, vicious, "adult"-type crimes. Serious and chronic youth crime highlights the cultural contradiction between a conception of children as dependent and vulnerable, on the one hand, and as autonomous and responsible on the other. Thus, waiver mechanisms choose between these competing constructions of young people, define the boundaries of criminal adulthood, and retrospectively ascribe criminal responsibility to some youths.

The "simple" question whether a particular young offender should be tried and sentenced as a juvenile or an adult poses difficult theoretical and practical dilemmas, and raises almost every juvenile justice policy issue. For example, judicial waiver legislation that requires a judge to decide whether a youth is "amenable to treatment" or poses a threat to public safety, presupposes that judges can predict "dangerousness," that juvenile courts can rehabilitate at least some youths, and that judges possess valid and reliable diagnostic tools that enable them to classify for treatment and determine which youths will or will not respond to intervention. At another level, changes in juvenile court waiver legislation provide a dramatic indicator of the fundamental shift in juvenile court jurisprudence from rehabilitation to retribution, as prosecutorial choice and legislative exclusion statutes emphasize increasingly considerations of the offense rather than the offender. Moreover, jurisdictional waiver that defines the boundary of adulthood implicates not only juvenile court sentencing practices but also the relationship between juvenile and criminal court sentencing practices. Waiver practices require states to develop a coherent sentencing policy to rationalize and integrate the social control of career offenders on both sides of the juvenile-adult divide. Finally, transfer of some youths to criminal court implicates our cultural assumptions about juveniles' criminal responsibility, because waiver of jurisdiction allows juries and judges to impose the death penalty on at least some youths convicted as criminals.

Transfer of juvenile offenders for adult prosecution provides the conceptual and administrative gateway between the more deterministic and rehabilitative predicates of the juvenile justice process and the free will and punishment assumption of the adult criminal justice system. Although the juvenile court theoretically attempts to rehabilitate all of the young offenders who appear before it, a small but significant proportion of miscreant youths resist its benevolent efforts. These are typically older delinquents, nearing the maximum age of juvenile court jurisdiction. Frequently recidivists, these youths have not responded to prior intervention, and successful treatment during the time remaining to the juvenile court may not be feasible. Despite their chronological minority, politicians and the public perceive these youth as mature and sophisticated criminal offenders. Moreover, these "career offenders" may account for a disproportionate amount of all juvenile crime.

Youths whose behavior, experience, and sophistication evince "criminal maturity" and culpability pose even greater challenges to successful rehabilitative intervention. The continued presence of these troublesome youths in the juvenile system conflicts with the presumed immaturity and lesser culpability of juvenile offenders. Retaining serious offenders in the juvenile system with less criminally sophisticated youths may negatively influence the latter, or misallocate scarce treatment resources vis-à-vis more tractable youths.

Finally, highly visible, serious offenses evoke community outrage or fear which politicians believe only punitive adult sanctions can mollify. The availability of a mechanism to prosecute some "hard-core" youthful offenders as adults provides an important "safety valve," permits the expiatory sacrifice of some youths to quiet political and public clamor, and arguably preserves a more benign juvenile system for those who remain. In the absence of some transfer procedures, legislators would experience irresistible pressures to lower the maximum age of juvenile court jurisdiction. Lowering the maximum age sufficiently to reach most of these older, sophisticated juvenile offenders would also sweep many other less serious or persistent youths into the criminal process as well.

While the reasons to create transfer mechanisms seem obvious, the "appropriate" method is less clear. In response to the increases in youth homicide rates in the late-1980s and early-1990s, politicians, members of the public, juvenile justice personnel, and social scientists debated extensively the relative merits of different strategies to transfer some serious young offenders to criminal courts for prosecution as adults. Jurisdictional waiver or divestiture represent a type of *sentencing* decision. Juvenile courts traditionally assigned primary importance to rehabilitation and attempted to individualize treatment. Criminal courts accorded greater significance to the seriousness of the offense committed and attempted to proportion punishment accordingly. All of the theoretical differences between juvenile and criminal courts' sentencing philosophies become visible in transfer proceedings and in legislative policy debates.

Transfer laws simultaneously attempt to resolve both fundamental crime control issues and the ambivalence embedded in our cultural construction of youth. The jurisprudential conflicts reflect much of the current sentencing policy debates: the tensions between rehabilitation or incapacitation and retribution, between focusing on the offender and the offense, between discretion and rules, and between indeterminacy and determinacy. The cultural construction of youth requires us to reconcile the contradiction posed when the child is a criminal and the criminal is a child. How do we select from among our competing images of youths as responsible and culpable, and as immature and salvageable?

Although the details of states' transfer legislation vary considerably, judicial waiver, legislative offense exclusion, and prosecutorial choice of forum represent the three general types of waiver statutes employed. Each statutory strategy emphasizes a different balance of sentencing policy values, relies upon different organizational actors, uses a different administrative process, and elicits different information to determine whether a particular young offender should be tried and sentenced as an adult or as a child.

Judicial waiver represents the most prevalent transfer policy in virtually all jurisdictions. A juvenile court judge may waive juvenile court jurisdiction on a discretionary basis after conducting a hearing to determine whether a youth is "amenable to treatment" or poses a threat to public safety. Judicial case-by-case clinical assessment of a youth's potential for rehabilitation and dangerousness reflects the individualized sentencing discretion characteristic of juvenile courts.

Legislative waiver or offense exclusion constitutes another common transfer mechanism, and frequently supplements judicial waiver provisions. This approach emphasizes the seriousness of the offense committed and reflects the retributive values of the criminal law. Because legislatures create juvenile courts, they possess considerable latitude to define their jurisdiction and to exclude youths from juvenile court based on their age and the seriousness of their offenses. A number of states, for example, exclude youths sixteen or older and charged with murder from juvenile court jurisdiction. Indeed, legislative line-drawing that sets the maximum age of juvenile court jurisdiction at fifteen or sixteen years of age, below the general eighteen year old age of majority, results in the adult criminal prosecution of the largest numbers of chronological juveniles. This type of legislative age line-drawing resulted in the criminal prosecution of about 176,000 youths below the age of eighteen in 1991.

Prosecutorial waiver or concurrent jurisdiction represents a third method some states use to remove some young offenders from the juvenile justice system. With prosecutorial waiver, both juvenile and criminal courts share concurrent jurisdiction over certain ages and offenses, typically older youths and serious crimes. Courts characterize prosecutorial transfer as an ordinary "executive" charging decision. The judiciary does not review routinely discretionary executive decisions because of the constitutional doctrine of separation of powers. Thus, a prosecutor's decision to charge a youth as a juvenile or adult selects the judicial forum. In some jurisdictions, statutes limit prosecutors' charging discretion by age and offense criteria, for example, prosecutors may select the juvenile or adult status for youths sixteen or older and charged with murder on a discretionary basis. To the extent that a prosecutor's discretion to charge the case in criminal courts divests the juvenile court of jurisdiction, prosecutorial waiver constitutes a form of offense-based decision making like legislative offense exclusion.

Each method to decide whether to prosecute a youth as a criminal or delinquent has supporters and critics. Proponents of judicial waiver emphasize its consistency with juvenile courts' rehabilitative sentencing philosophy and contend that individualized judgments provide an appropriate balance of flexibility and severity. Critics object that juvenile court judges lack valid or reliable clinical tools with which to assess amenability to treatment or to predict dangerousness and argue that the standardless discretion judges exercise results in abuses and inequalities, or simply ratify prosecutors' charging decisions.

Proponents of legislative waiver endorse "just deserts" retributive sentencing policies, advocate sanctions based on relatively objective characteristics such as seriousness of the offense, culpability, and criminal history, and assert that offense exclusion fosters greater consistency, uniformity, and equality among similarly situated offenders. Critics question whether legislators can exclude offenses and remove discretion without making the process excessively rigid, and whether politicians can resist their own demagogic impulses to "get tough," adopt expansive lists of excluded "crimes de jour," and thereby substantially increase the numbers of youths whom they transfer inappropriately to criminal court.

Proponents of concurrent-jurisdiction prosecutorial waiver claim that prosecutors can function as more neutral, balanced and objective gatekeepers than either "soft" juvenile court judges or "get tough" legislators. Critics of prosecutorial waiver strategies contend that prosecutors, as locally elected officials, succumb to the same popular and political pressures that afflict legislators to appear "tough" and posture on crime. Moreover, prosecutors often lack the breadth of experience or maturity that judges possess, exercise their discretion just as subjectively and idiosyncratically as do judges, and introduce even greater geographic variability into the process of justice administration. Finally, unlike discretionary judicial waiver decisions, prosecutors' charging decisions lack the redeeming virtues of either a formal record or appellate review.

As the policy debate rages, legislatures increasingly lower the age of eligibility for criminal prosecution, exclude certain combinations of present offense and/or prior records from juvenile court jurisdiction, adopt offense guidelines as presumptive dispositional criteria in judicial waiver proceedings, or delegate to prosecutors the power to decide which youths to prosecute as adults. Judicial waiver focuses on the offender and reflects juvenile courts' rehabilitative ideology. Legislative exclusion and prosecutor's choice emphasize the offense and reflect the criminal law's retributive values. Thus, the choice of waiver strategies implicates many fundamental issues of sentencing policy.

Defining the boundary between juvenile and criminal court depends, in part, on whether policy makers adopt a juvenile or criminal court's jurisprudential "point of view" and focus primarily on characteristics of the offender or of the offense. If policy makers emphasize the criminal law's retributive and punitive values, then the seriousness of the present offense or the offender's prior record control the transfer decision. In that eventuality, transfer decisions lend themselves to relatively mechanical decisional rules like excluded offenses or presumptive sentencing guidelines. In the alternative, if legislators emphasize juvenile courts' commitment to offenders' rehabilitation, then judges must use more indeterminate and discretionary processes to make individualized assessments of youths' "amenability to treatment" or "dangerousness."

Each transfer strategy represents a different approach to the fundamental dilemma posed by the offending youth: is the young person a juvenile or a criminal, and how should the legal systems respond as a result of that classification? Can the juvenile system rehabilitate the young offender or not? Even if clinical efforts theoretically and practically could "salvage" a youth, should condemning the seriousness of the offense take precedence over the possibility of treating the offender? In short, whether certain young offenders should be handled as juveniles or as adults raises tensions between treatment and punishment, and the offender and the offense.

The various articles in this section highlight the policy issues in this ongoing debate. The excerpt "Juveniles and Violence" from the Federal Bureau of Investigation's Uniform Crime Reports, *Crime in the United States 1991* (1992), provides some data on recent trends in youth crime and violence. Although juveniles commit a disproportionate amount of serious crime, beginning in the mid-1980s, the rate of violent youth crime, especially homicides and weapons offenses escalated dramatically. Because the FBI arrest data indicate that black juveniles commit a disproportionate amount of violent crime, legislative policies that emphasize the seriousness of juveniles' offenses inevitably will have a disparate impact on minority youths. The excerpt by Howard Snyder and Melissa Sickmund from *Juvenile Offenders and Victims: A National Report* (1995) gives an overview of the various legislative transfer policies currently employed around the nation and some of the data on changes in rates of waiver. Marcy Podkopacz and Barry C. Feld, "The End of the Line: An Empirical Study of Judicial Waiver," provide a comprehensive analysis of judicial waiver administration. They identify the factors that judges consider when they make transfer decisions, the effects of the waiver process itself on case outcomes, and the sentences young offenders receive when they are subsequently convicted as juveniles or as adults. They note that inconsistencies between judicial waiver policies and criminal court sentencing practices produce a "punishment gap" and allow certain youths to "fall between the cracks" and receive less severe sentences as adults than they might have received as juveniles. Simon Singer, "The Automatic Waiver of Juveniles," examines the administration of a legislative exclusion statute. Singer notes that although the New York offense exclusion legislation reflects a policy to impose more severe sanctions on serious young offenders, the exercise of prosecutorial charging discretion and judicial discretion to "transfer back" some youths often erodes the certainty and predictability of the law. Finally, Donna M. Bishop, Charles E. Frazier, and John C. Henretta, "Prosecutorial Waiver," examine the exercise of prosecutorial discretion in deciding which youths to try and sentence as adults. They conclude that prosecutorial discretion results in highly idiosyncratic and variable decisions which often result in "inappropriate" youths in adult criminal court. In short, each of these studies reveals fundamental flaws in the alternative legal mechanisms to determine which youths are "adults." Is there a solution? Based on this research, what would you propose a legislature do in response to serious or persistent youth crime?

Juveniles and Violence

FEDERAL BUREAU OF INVESTIGATION

Nationwide, there is a growing concern over an escalation in juvenile delinquency, a perception supported by the unprecedented level of juvenile violence confronting the Nation. Historically, the youth of America has had proclivity toward property-related crimes such as motor vehicle theft, larceny, and arson. During the 1980s, however, crimes related to violence became a more significant component of juvenile crime, not only involving disadvantaged minority youth in urban areas but evident in all races, social classes, and lifestyles. In an effort to address this social phenomenon, this study examines the movement in juvenile violence from the mid-1960s to 1990.

Causal factors pertaining to juvenile violence are multifarious. Many social scientists believe that much of the violence reflects a breakdown of families, schools, and other societal institutions. Some studies suggest that 70 percent of juvenile offenders come from single-parent homes. Since 1950, the percentage of single-parent families in the United States has tripled. Moreover, this unprecedented rise in juvenile violence has coincided with a significant increase in the juvenile heroin/cocaine arrest rate, as well as a proliferation in illegal weapon usage. This report measures juvenile violence in terms of arrest rate trends for violent crimes (murder, forcible rape, robbery, and aggravated assault), drug abuse violations, and weapon law violations. Since a specific segment of the U.S. population (i.e., juveniles) is addressed, Uniform Crime Reporting (UCR) arrest statistics are used as an

Excerpted from *Crime in the United States 1991*, pp. 279–289 (1992)

indicator of crime trends. The arrest statistics are based on data reported to the FBI's UCR Program by local law enforcement agencies.

For the purposes of this study, a juvenile is defined as a person between the ages 10–17. Arrest rates expressed per 100,000 in this study are, therefore, based on the population aged 10–17. This age group is viewed to be appropriate in that it accounts for over 98 percent of juvenile violent crime arrests. Consequently, a more definitive trend of juvenile violent crime can be established by omitting children (aged below 10).

VIOLENT CRIME

In 1990, the Nation experienced its highest juvenile violent crime arrest rate, 430 per 100,000 juveniles. . . . The 1990 rate was 27 percent higher than the 1980 rate. . . . [B]oth white and black arrest rates experienced substantial increases from 1965 to 1990. Of particular note is the upward trend that started in 1988 for both white and black youths, as well as the downward trend for those in the other-race category. Overall, for the period 1980–1990, the white juvenile violent crime arrest rate increased 44 percent, as compared to a 19-percent increase for blacks and a 53-percent decline for others. With the exception of robbery, all violent crime categories showed significant increases in juvenile arrest rates during the past decade. In 1990, the juvenile violent crime arrest rate reached 1,429 per 100,000 black juveniles, five times that for white youths. The other-race category registered its lowest violent crime arrest rate in 1990 after peaking in 1978. A crime-by-crime analysis of each violent crime arrest rate follows. In conjunction with this analysis, there is also an examination of the arrest rate trends for juvenile drug abuse violations and weapon law violations.

Murder

The Nation experienced an upsurge in the juvenile murder arrest rate for blacks during the 1980s. . . . This upward trend had a profound impact on the overall juvenile murder arrest rate. . . . Specifically, between 1980 and 1990, the arrest rate for this group increased 145 percent, while the rate for whites rose 48 percent and for other races, declined 45 percent. When considering the difference in the arrest rate for black and white juveniles, the black rate was 7.5 times that of whites in 1990. From a historical perspective, 1965 to 1990, the overall murder arrest rate for juveniles increased 332 percent, from 2.8 to 12.1. Another item of concern is that during the past decade, there has been a 79-percent increase in the number of juveniles who commit murders with guns. In 1990, nearly 3 of 4 juvenile murder offenders used guns to perpetrate their crimes. The juvenile arrest rate trends for weapon law violations and heroin/cocaine violations paralleled the trend for murder since 1980. Murder and illegal weapon usage have become a component of the illicit heroin/cocaine drug trade.

Forcible Rape

The Nation's juvenile forcible rape arrest rate has more than doubled since 1965, from 10.9 to 21.9 in 1990. In more recent years, 1980–1990, the white arrest rate has increased dramatically faster than the black arrest rate, 86 percent versus 9 percent, although the black rate is significantly higher than the white rate. . . . The other racial group category experienced a 66-percent decline since 1980. In fact, this group's rate in 1965 was 27.9 as compared to 3.7 in 1990. The percent distribution for juvenile forcible rape arrestees in 1990 was 53 percent for whites, 46 percent for blacks, and 2 percent for others.

Robbery

Robbery is the second most violent offense, exceeded only by aggravated assault. Consequently, it has the second highest arrest rate among violent crimes. After peaking in 1978 and declining during the middle 1980s, the juvenile robbery arrest rate in the Nation escalated. . . . The upward trend was led by a 54-percent increase in the white arrest rate from 1988 to 1990, when it reached 75 per 100,000, the highest rate for this group during the 26-year period under consideration, 1965–1990. The black arrest rate was 34 percent higher than in 1988 but was 16 percent below the 1980 rate. This was the only decrease experienced by black juveniles for any violent crime category during the decade. Moreover, black juveniles in 1990 constituted 63 percent of juvenile robbery arrests, the highest black percentage for any violent crime category. From a historical perspective, the other racial group category had a relatively high juvenile arrest rate for robbery; but in 1990, its rate decreased to the lowest rate among racial groups . . .

Aggravated Assault

Aggravated assault, the most voluminous violent crime, registered the highest juvenile arrest rate among violent offenses. . . . [T]he rate of juvenile arrests for aggravated assault has increased substantially for both white and black youths, particularly during the past decade. The arrest rate for these two groups increased 59 percent and 89 percent, respectively, from 1980 to 1990. Dissimilar to other violent crimes, the juvenile arrest rate trend for aggravated assault has undulated minimally since 1965. This would suggest that today's youth are more inclined to settle a dispute by engaging in a physical altercation. An exception to this trend was the arrest rate for the other-race category. For this group, the arrest rate declined 39 percent between 1980 and 1990. It now has the lowest aggravated assault arrest rate after peaking in 1978. It should be noted, however, that in terms of total impact, the other-race category represented only 2 percent of the arrests for this crime in 1990.

DRUG ABUSE VIOLATIONS

The pattern of drug abuse in the Nation changed dramatically during the 1980s. . . . Heroin/cocaine violations now represent the predominant drug arrest type for juveniles. A major repercussion of this development has been an extraordinary burden on the juvenile criminal justice system. There is a relationship between juvenile violence and the proliferating drug trade, particularly with regard to cocaine.

Prior to 1980, marijuana was the most abused illegal drug by juveniles for all racial groups. Juvenile marijuana arrest rates rose significantly from 1965 to the mid-1970s, as did those for synthetic drugs and nonnarcotic drugs. Rates for heroin/cocaine arrests were relatively low and rather stable prior to 1980. During the 1980s, however, there was a shift of historical proportion in juvenile arrest rates for marijuana and heroin/cocaine. The marijuana juvenile arrest rate dropped dramatically, while there was an exponential increase in the heroin/cocaine rate. Specifically, between 1980 and 1990, the overall rate for juvenile heroin/cocaine arrests rose 713 percent. When considering this increase by race, the black arrest rate jumped 2,373 percent, followed by a 251-percent upswing for whites, and a 127-percent rise for other races. Conversely, the overall rate for marijuana arrests fell 66 percent. The decline was experienced by all racial groups. It can be suggested that the diverging trends established by these two drug types may not be short-lived. Juveniles will continue to play an instrumental role in the sale and possession of heroin/cocaine, particularly if the opportunity for monetary gain remains.

WEAPON LAW VIOLATIONS

In 1990, nationally there were 151 arrests per 100,000 juveniles for weapon law violations. This was the highest rate ever recorded. It is indicative of a surge in weapon violations by juveniles that commenced during the early 1980s. Both white and black juveniles are responsible for this increase. . . . The arrest rate for whites rose 58 percent between 1980 and 1990, and the black rate jumped 103 percent. The other-race category experienced a 48-percent decline. This group had the lowest arrest rate of any group in 1990, 30 per 100,000 juveniles. This is an interesting development when considering the fact that the other-race rate nearly equalled the black rate in the 1970s. An examination of the percent distribution by race for juvenile weapon law violations arrests in 1990 revealed that whites accounted for 62 percent, blacks for 36 percent, and other races the remainder. As mentioned earlier, the more recent arrest trend for juvenile weapon law violations paralleled the trends for murder and heroin/cocaine violations.

SUMMARY

The Nation is experiencing an unrivaled period of juvenile violent crime that began during the 1980s. Most juvenile arrest rates for crimes related to violence rose substantially between 1980 and 1990 as shown in Table 1. This was particularly true for both white and black youths. The following offenses exceeded or approached their highest juvenile arrest rate in 1990: murder, 12.1; forcible rape, 21.9; robbery, 156.2; aggravated assault, 240.4; heroin/cocaine, 168.1; weapon violations, 151.0. While there was a substantial decline in the arrest rates for the other-race category, arrests of persons in this group accounted for less than 2 percent of violent crime arrests. The decline in this racial category's arrest rates was primarily attributable to a large increase in the number of Asian juveniles. Historically, this group has been the least crime-prone group among juveniles.

While the focus of this study has been at the national level, juvenile arrest data at the state level revealed that three of four states in the Nation experienced significant increases in their overall juvenile violent crime arrest rates between 1980 and 1990. These states covered all geographic regions, which would indicate that the surge in juvenile violent crime arrests has a broad base, not limited to a particular geographic area. Moreover, the juvenile violent crime arrest trend was consistent with the adult upward trend.

The recent increase in the juvenile arrest rate for crimes related to violence may be indicative of future trends when considering concomitant social/demographic trends. Final arrest statistics for 1991, which became available after this study was completed, show that the upward trend in juvenile violent crime continues. The Population group 10–17 is projected to increase

TABLE 1
Percent Changes in Juvenile Arrest Rates* For Crimes Related to Violence, United States, 1990 over 1980

Offense	All races	White	Black	Other
Violent Crime Total	27.3	43.8	19.2	−53.4
Murder	87.3	47.5	145.0	−45.4
Forcible Rape	36.7	85.9	8.5	−66.0
Robbery	−7.5	12.3	−15.6	−67.4
Aggravated Assault	63.7	59.2	88.9	−38.8
Weapon Law Violations	62.6	57.6	102.9	−48.1
Drug Abuse Total	−20.1	−47.6	158.6	−77.0
Heroin/Cocaine	713.4	251.1	2,372.9	126.8
Marijuana	−66.0	−66.7	−47.5	−80.1
Synthetic	−26.5	−34.1	144.7	−77.4
Nonnarcotic	−5.5	−34.6	223.3	−87.5

Arrest rate per 100,000 for the age group 10–17.

significantly between 1990 and 2000. This development may lead to further escalation in juvenile crimes/arrests. Similarly, it is widely believed that prevailing social conditions with regard to family stability, education, and other societal institutions have an effect on the behavior of juveniles.

Transfer

HOWARD SNYDER AND MELISSA SICKMUND

ALL STATES ALLOW JUVENILES TO BE TRIED AS ADULTS IN CRIMINAL COURT UNDER CERTAIN CONDITIONS

There Is More Than One Path to Criminal Court

A juvenile's delinquency case can be transferred to criminal court for trial as an adult in one of three ways:

* Judicial waiver.
* Prosecutorial discretion.
* Statutory exclusion.

In a given State, one, two, or all three transfer mechanisms may be in place.

TRANSFERS TO CRIMINAL COURT HAVE BEEN ALLOWED IN SOME STATES FOR MORE THAN 70 YEARS

Some States have permitted juvenile offenders to be transferred to criminal court since before the 1920s—Arkansas, California, Colorado, Florida, Georgia, Kentucky, North Carolina, Ohio, Oregon, and Tennessee. Other States have permitted transfers since at least the 1940s—Delaware, Indiana, Maryland, Michigan, Nevada, New Hampshire, New Mexico, Rhode Island, South Carolina, and Utah.

Traditionally, the decision to transfer a youth to criminal court was made by a juvenile court judge and was based upon the individual circumstances in each case. Beginning in the 1970s and continuing through the 1990s, however, State legislatures increasingly moved young offenders into criminal court based on age and offense seriousness without the case specific as-

Excerpted from Snyder, Howard N. and Sickmund, Melissa. (1995) *Juvenile Offenders and Victims: A National Report*, pp. 154–156. Washington, DC: Office of Juvenile Justice and Delinquency Prevention.

sessment offered by the juvenile court process. In half the States, laws have been enacted that exclude some offenses from juvenile court and a number of States have also expanded the range of excluded offenses. One-quarter of the States have given prosecutors the discretion to charge certain offenses either in juvenile or criminal court.

JUDICIAL WAIVER IS THE MOST COMMON TRANSFER PROVISION

In all States except Nebraska and New York, juvenile court judges may waive jurisdiction over a case and transfer it to criminal court. Such action is usually in response to a request by the prosecutor; however, in several States, juveniles or their parents may request judicial waiver. In most States, statutes limit waiver by age and offense.

STATUTES ESTABLISH WAIVER CRITERIA OTHER THAN AGE AND OFFENSE

Most State statutes also limit judicial waiver to juveniles who are "no longer amenable to treatment." The specific factors that determine lack of amenability vary, but typically include the juvenile's offense history and previous dispositional outcomes. Many statutes instruct juvenile courts to consider the availability of dispositional alternatives for treating the juvenile and the time available for sanctions, as well as public safety and the best interests of the child when making waiver decisions. The waiver process must adhere to certain constitutional principles of fairness. . . .

CRIMINAL COURTS OFTEN MAY RETURN TRANSFERRED CASES TO JUVENILE COURT OR ORDER JUVENILE SANCTIONS

Several States have provisions for transferring "excluded" or "direct filed" cases from criminal court to juvenile court under certain circumstances. This procedure is sometimes referred to as "reverse" waiver or transfer. In many States juveniles tried as adults in criminal court may receive dispositions involving either criminal or juvenile court sanctions.

FEW STATES ALLOW PROSECUTORIAL DISCRETION, BUT MANY JUVENILES ARE TRIED AS ADULTS IN THIS WAY

In some States, prosecutors are given the authority to file certain juvenile cases in either juvenile or criminal court under concurrent jurisdiction statutes. Thus, original jurisdiction is shared by both criminal and juvenile

Most States Have Broad Age and Offense Provisions for Judicial Waiver

Key:
- ● Provision is specifically mentioned in State's Juvenile Code.
- ☐ Provision applies only if the other condition similarly shaded is also met.

See Example below for information on how to read the graphic.

| State | Minimum age | Any criminal offense | Certain offenses | | | | | | | Prior delinquency adjudication or criminal conviction |
			Capital crimes	Murder	Person offenses	Property offenses	Drug offenses	Weapon offenses	Felony offenses	
AL	14	14								
AK										
AZ										
AR	14	16							16	
CA	14		14	14	14			14		
CO	14			14	14			14		
CT	14						14			☐
DE	14	16							14	☐
DC		16[a]							14	
FL		14							15	
GA	13	15	13			15				
HI	16	14							16	
ID	14	13								
IL	13	14								
IN		14		10					16	☐
IA	14	16								
KS	14						14			
KY	14				15	15			14	
LA	15		14	15					14	
ME		15								
MD						14				
MA	15				14				14[b]	

State	Minimum age (by offense/crime restriction)
MI	15
MN	14 13
MS	13
MO	14
MT	12 12 14
NV	16 16
NH	16
NJ	14 14 14 14 14
NM	15 15c 15c 15c 15c
NC	13 14 14
ND	14 16 14
OH	15 16
OK	
OR	15 15
PA	14 14
RI	
SC	16 14 16
SD	16
TN	14 14 14
TX	15 14 15
UT	14 14
VT	10 10 10 10
VA	14 14 14
WA	
WV	14 16 14 14 16
WI	14 14 14
WY	

Example: Alabama permits judicial waiver for any delinquency case involving a juvenile 14 or older. Connecticut permits waiver of juveniles age 14 or older charged with certain felonies if they have been previously adjudicated delinquent.

aWaiver conditional on the juvenile being under commitment for delinquency.

bWaiver conditional on a previous commitment to the Department of Youth Services.

cProvisions differ from traditional judicial waiver in that juveniles are adjudicated in juvenile court and at disposition are "subject to adult or juvenile sanctions."

Note: Analysis conducted 10/94; some provisions effective 1/1/95. Ages in the minimum age column may not apply to all the restrictions indicated, but represent the youngest possible age at which a juvenile may be waived to criminal court. For States with a blank minimum age cell, at least one of the offense restrictions indicated is not limited by age. When a provision is conditional in prior adjudications, those adjudications are often required to have been for the same offense type (e.g., class A felony) or a more serious offense.

Source: Szymanski, L. (1994). Waiver/transfer/certification of juveniles to criminal court: Age restrictions–crime restrictions (1994 update).

courts. State appellate courts have taken the view that prosecutor discretion is equivalent to the routine charging decisions made in criminal cases. Thus, prosecutorial transfer is considered an "executive function," which is not subject to judicial review and is not required to meet the due process standards established in *Kent*.

Prosecutorial discretion is typically limited by age and offense criteria. Often concurrent jurisdiction is limited to those charged with serious, violent, or repeat crimes. Juvenile and criminal courts often share jurisdiction over minor offenses such as traffic, watercraft, or local ordinance violations as well.

There are no national data at the present time on the number of juvenile cases tried in criminal court under concurrent jurisdiction provisions. There is, however, some indication that in States allowing such transfers, they are likely to outnumber judicial waivers. Florida, which has both judicial waiver and concurrent jurisdiction provisions, filed two cases directly in criminal court for each one judicially waived in 1981. By 1992 there were more than six direct filings for each case judicially waived.

STATUTORY EXCLUSION ACCOUNTS FOR THE LARGEST NUMBER OF JUVENILES TRIED AS ADULTS IN CRIMINAL COURT

Legislatures "transfer" large numbers of young offenders to criminal court by statutorily excluding them from juvenile court jurisdiction. Although not typically thought of as transfers, large numbers of youth under age 18 are tried as adults in the 11 States where the upper age of juvenile court jurisdiction is 15 or 16. An estimated 176,000 cases involving youth under the age of 18 were tried in criminal court in 1991 because they are defined as adults under State laws.

Many States exclude certain serious offenses from juvenile court jurisdiction. State laws typically also set age limits for excluded offenses. The serious offenses most often excluded are capital and other murders, as well as other serious offenses against persons. Several States exclude juveniles charged with felonies if they have prior felony adjudications or convictions. Minor offenses, such as traffic, watercraft, fish, or game violations, are often excluded from juvenile court jurisdiction in States where they are not covered by concurrent jurisdiction provisions.

Currently there are no national data on the number of juvenile cases tried in criminal court as a result of these types of statutory exclusions. In States where they are enacted, however, the number of youth affected may exceed those transferred via judicial waiver. For example, Illinois lawmakers amended the jurisdiction of the juvenile courts in 1982 to exclude youth aged 15 or older charged with murder, armed robbery, or rape. In the 7 years prior to 1982, the Cook County juvenile court judicially waived an average of 47 cases annually to criminal court. In the first 2 years following

Several States Allow Prosecutors to Try Juveniles Charged with Serious Offenses in Either Criminal or Juvenile Court

Key: ░ Provision is specifically mentioned in State's Juvenile Code.
☐ Provision applies only if the other condition similarly shaded is also met.
See Example below for information on how to read the graphic.

State	Minimum age	Any criminal offense	Certain offenses							
			Capital crimes	Murder	Person offenses	Property offenses	Drug offenses	Weapon offenses	Felony offenses	Prior felony adjudication
AR	14		14	14	14				16	
CO	14				14			14	14	
DC	16			16[a]	16[a]	16[a]				
FL		16[b]	c	14	14	14		14	16	
GA	15									
LA					15	16				
MI		16[b]								
NE		16[b]								
NH										
SD										
UT	16	16	16	16					16	
VT	16	16	16	16						
WY	13	13								

Example: In Florida prosecutors have discretion to file in criminal court those cases involving juveniles 16 or older charged with felony offenses (or misdemeanors if they have prior felony adjudications) as well as those 14 or older charged with murder, certain other person offenses, or certain property crimes. Juveniles of any age charged with capital crimes are tried in criminal court following grand jury indictment. In New Hampshire prosecutors may file in criminal court any juvenile case involving a felony charge.

[a]*Statutory exclusion language interpreted as concurrent jurisdiction provision.*
[b]*Provision applies to misdemeanors only.*
[c]*Provision is conditional on grand jury indictment.*

Note: Analysis conducted 10/94; some provisions effective 1/1/95. Ages in the minimum age column may not apply to all the restrictions indicated, but represent the youngest possible age at which a juvenile's case may be filed directly in criminal court. For States with a blank minimum age cell, at least one of the offense restrictions indicated is not limited by age. When a provision is conditional on previous adjudications, those adjudications are often required to have been for the same offense type (e.g., class A felony) or a more serious offense.
Source: Szymanski, L. (1994). Concurrent jurisdiction (1994 update).

Many States Exclude Certain Serious Offenses from Juvenile Court Jurisdiction

Key:

□ Exclusion is specifically mentioned in State's Juvenile Code.

⌐ Exclusion applies only if the other conditions similarly shaded is also met.

See Example below for information on how to read the graphic.

State	Minimum age	Murder	Certain offenses						Previous	
			Person offenses	Property offenses	Drug offenses	Weapon offenses	Felony offenses	Capital crimes	Felony adjudication(s)	Criminal conviction
AL	16				16		16	16	□	
AK	16		16	16					□	
CT	14	14					14 □			
DE										
GA	13	13	13	15 □						
HI	16	16							□	
ID	14	14	14		14					
IL	15	15	15		15	15	15 □		□	
IN	16	16	16			16	16 □		□	
KS	16		16*	16*			14			
KY	14									
LA	15	15	15							
MD	14		16			16				
MN	14	16					14 □	14		
MS	14									□

State					
NV	16				16
NM	7	13	13		7
NY	13	13	13		13
NC	16	16	16	16	16
OH	16				16
OK	16	16	16	16	
PA	16				
RI	16	16			
UT	14	14	14		
VT	16	14			
WA	16				

Example: In North Carolina, juveniles age 13 or older charged with certain felonies are excluded from juvenile court jurisdiction. In Hawaii, juveniles age 16 or older charged with murder are excluded if they have prior felony adjudications, as are those 16 or older charged with certain felonies who have prior felony adjudications.

*Exclusion applies only to juveniles charged with commiting offenses while in custody in juvenile institutions.

Note: Analysis conducted 10/94; some provisions effective 1/1/95. Ages in the minimum age column may not apply to all the exclusions indicated, but represent the youngest possible age at which a juvenile may be excluded from juvenile court. For States with a blank minimum age cell, at least one of the exclusions indicated isn ot restricted by age. When an exclusion is conditional on previous adjudications, those adjudications are often required to have been for the same offense type (e.g., class A felony) or a more serious offense.

Source: Szymanski, L. (1994). Statutory exclusion of crimes from juvenile court jurisdiction (1994 update).

the enactment of the exclusion legislation, criminal prosecutions of juveniles more than tripled, climbing to 170 per year, 151 of which resulted from the exclusion provision.

THE NUMBER OF JUVENILES TRANSFERRED TO CRIMINAL COURT HAS GROWN SUBSTANTIALLY IN RECENT YEARS

Juveniles charged with serious offenses, with lengthy records of prior offenses, or who are unreceptive to treatment in the juvenile justice system are sometimes transferred to criminal court. The methods used to move juveniles into the adult system vary. In recent years, many States modified their laws to transfer more young offenders into the criminal courts. Increasingly, young offenders are moved into the adult system by legislative or prosecutorial actions rather than by judicial waiver.

THERE HAS BEEN A SUBSTANTIAL INCREASE IN WAIVED CASES

Between 1988 and 1992, the number of cases judicially waived to criminal court increased 68%.

FEWER THAN HALF OF THE CASES JUDICIALLY WAIVED TO CRIMINAL COURT INVOLVE PERSON OFFENSES

Although several factors may result in young offenders being transferred to criminal court, the offenses involved in such cases often do not match the expectations of elected officials or the public. In 1982, for example, a national survey of criminal court transfers found that 32% of judicial waivers involved violent offenses against persons, while 62% involved either property charges or public order offenses. A similar pattern existed in 1992 when, according to *Juvenile Court Statistics*, person offense cases accounted for just over

Most serious offense	Number of waived cases		Percent change
	1988	**1992**	
Delinquency	7,000	11,700	68%
Person	2,000	4,000	101
Property	3,700	5,200	42
Drugs	700	1,400	91
Public order	500	1,000	90

Note: Detail may not add to totals because of rounding. Percent change was calculated using unrounded numbers.
Source: Butts, J., et al. (1995). Juvenile court statistics 1992.

one-third of judicially waived cases. Two-thirds of the delinquency cases judicially waived in 1992 involved either property offenses, drug law violations, or public order offenses as the most serious charge.

INFORMATION ON THE CRIMINAL COURT'S RESPONSE TO TRANSFERRED JUVENILES IS NEARLY 10 YEARS OLD

Research capturing court practice in the mid 1980's found that, while transfer to criminal court was reserved for the most serious offenders, these youth were handled more leniently, probably because they were appearing in criminal court for the first time and at a relatively young age. In addition, juveniles tried as adults gain the right to bail, increasing their chances of release from pretrial custody when handled in the criminal system.

Fewer Than 2% of All Formally Processed Delinquency Cases Are Judicially Waived to Criminal Court

Offense	Percent of petitioned delinquency cases that were waived				
	1988	1989	1990	1991	1992
Delinquency	1.2%	1.4%	1.3%	1.6%	1.6%
Person	1.9	2.0	2.1	2.4	2.4
Property	1.2	1.2	1.1	1.2	1.3
Drugs	1.5	2.8	2.7	4.4	3.1
Public order	0.5	0.5	0.6	0.7	0.8

Source: Butts, J., et al. (1995). Juvenile court statistics 1992.

Judicially Waived Cases Generally Involve Older Males

	Percent of waived cases				
	1988	1989	1990	1991	1992
Age at Referral					
15 or younger	7%	11%	10%	9%	12%
16 or older	93	89	90	91	88
Sex					
Male	96%	95%	96%	96%	96%
Female	4	5	4	4	4
Race					
White	54%	49%	45%	46%	47%
Black	43	49	52	52	50
Other	2	2	3	2	3

Note: Detail may not total 100% because of rounding.
Source: Butts, J., et al. (1995). Juvenile court statistics 1992.

A 1978 national survey by Hamparian and others found that the majority of transferred cases sentenced in criminal court received probation, fines, or other alternatives to incarceration. This study found that 46% of cases waived by juvenile court judges and 39% of those filed directly by prosecutors resulted in a criminal court sentence that involved incarceration.

A study by Bortner examined the cases of 214 juveniles who were waived to adult court in 1980 and 1981 and found that the majority (63%) of these cases received probation as the primary disposition. Jail or prison terms were ordered in 32% of cases, fines in 1%, and dismissal in 4%.

Some studies have found adult courts more likely to incarcerate. A study by Fagan compared juvenile and criminal court handling of 15- and 16-year-old felony offenders during 1981–82 in four neighboring counties in two States—New York where such felons are excluded from juvenile court jurisdiction and New Jersey where they are not. The study found that sanctions imposed by juvenile courts in New Jersey were half as likely to include incarceration as were sentences imposed on similar age youth by criminal courts in New York. For example, New Jersey juvenile courts incarcerated 18% of robbery cases, while criminal courts in New York incarcerated 46%. In a more recent sample of cases handled in the same counties during 1986–87, however, the Fagan study found that robbery cases were more likely to receive incarceration in juvenile court (57% vs. 27%).

IF INCARCERATED, TRANSFERRED JUVENILES
DO NOT ALWAYS RECEIVE LONGER SENTENCES

A 1986 study by Rudman and others analyzed case outcomes for a sample of 177 violent youth considered for transfer in four urban jurisdictions. In 71 cases, the transfer was denied and the youth was handled in juvenile court. The study found that criminal court sentences were longer than those imposed by juvenile courts. While 43% of the youth handled in juvenile courts received terms of incarceration exceeding 2 years, this was true for 88% of the transferred youth. However, as with other studies that have employed this research design, part of the difference in sentencing could have resulted from the juvenile courts being more likely to transfer more serious cases.

Other studies have compared the length of juvenile and criminal court sentences and found them to be more similar. Fagan examined the sentences imposed by juvenile and adult courts in cases of felony burglary or robbery and found no significant differences in the minimum and maximum terms ordered. In robbery cases, juvenile courts ordered terms of confinement with an average minimum of 11 months and an average maximum of 34 months. Criminal court sentences had average minimum and maximum terms of 11 and 32 months, respectively.

PROCEDURAL DIFFERENCES BETWEEN JUVENILE AND CRIMINAL COURTS MAKE COMPARISONS DIFFICULT

Comparing case outcomes in juvenile and adult courts is problematic. A 1983 study by Greenwood and others examined court dispositions of juveniles and young adults (ages 16–21) charged with armed robbery or residential burglary in three large California jurisdictions. The study found that adult court sentences were more severe on average, but the difference was partly due to the juvenile court's differentiated handling of youth charged with the same offense. When offenders had a prior record, the juvenile court's response was far more severe, while criminal court dispositions varied much less with the offender's prior record.

In Los Angeles, for example, robbery cases that involved two or more aggravating factors were nearly 3 times as likely to result in incarceration in juvenile court as those having no aggravating factors. Aggravating factors had less effect on the severity of criminal court dispositions.

TRANSFERRING YOUNG OFFENDERS TO THE CRIMINAL COURTS MAY NOT IMPROVE THE DETERRENT EFFECT OF COURT SANCTIONS

The Fagan study, for example, compared postrelease outcomes for 15- and 16-year-olds charged with felony robbery or burglary in criminal courts and juvenile courts. The probability of rearrest and reincarceration was no different for youth charged with burglary, regardless of which court handled their case. Offenders charged with robbery, on the other hand, were significantly less likely to be rearrested and reincarcerated if they were handled as juveniles. Among the offenders who recidivated during the study's followup period, the length of time before rearrest was significantly longer for youth who received juvenile court sanctions.

STUDIES ON THE IMPACT OF CRIMINAL COURT TRANSFER HAVE NOT YIELDED DEFINITIVE CONCLUSIONS

The debate over the efficacy of criminal court transfer has been underway for at least 50 years. Yet, there are still no definitive answers to basic questions about the effects of the practice. In many ways, policymakers are operating in the dark on this issue.

Although there have been few reliable studies on the impact of transfer and the studies describe behavior that predates recent large increases in violent juvenile crime, the most common findings of these studies indicate that transferring serious juvenile offenders to the criminal justice system does not appreciably increase the certainty or severity of sanctions. While transfer may increase the length of confinement for some of the most serious offenders, the majority of transferred juveniles receive sentences that are comparable to sanctions already available in the juvenile justice system. More importantly, there is no evidence that young offenders handled in criminal court are less likely to recidivate than those remaining in juvenile court.

A. JUDICIAL WAIVER

The End of the Line: An Empirical Study of Judicial Waiver

Marcy Rasmussen Podkopacz
Barry C. Feld

I. INTRODUCTION

When young offenders commit serious or violent offenses, should the justice system respond on the basis of "just deserts" or on the "real needs" of the offender? Waiver decisions ... require a sentencing policy choice between punishment in adult criminal court or rehabilitation in juvenile court. If one adopts a criminal court's point of view, the emphasis on punishment prevails, and the seriousness of the present offense or one's prior record controls the decision to transfer adolescents from juvenile to adult court. When offense considerations dominate, transfer decisions lend themselves to relatively mechanical decisional rules or presumptive sentencing guidelines. Alternatively, if one adopts a juvenile court's point of view, the emphasis on rehabilitation predominates, and individualized assessments of an offender's "amenability to treatment," "dangerousness," and future welfare control the sentencing decision. When offender characteristics are paramount, courts require more open-ended, indeterminate, and discretionary processes.

The recent increase in youth violence has provoked legislative reactions to "get tough" or to find the "right" solution. Every state has adopted one

Reprinted by special permission of Northwestern University School of Law, *Journal of Criminal Law and Criminology*, Volume 86, Issue 2, pp. 449–492 (1996).

or more statutory strategy to transfer some chronological juveniles to criminal courts. The alternatives include: (1) judicial waiver of juvenile court jurisdiction; (2) legislative exclusion of specific offenses from jurisdiction in juvenile court; and (3) prosecutorial choice of forum between concurrent jurisdictions in deciding whether a youth is a criminal or a delinquent.

Judicial waiver is the most common waiver mechanism across the nation. A juvenile court judge may waive juvenile court jurisdiction on a discretionary basis after a hearing to determine whether a youth is "amenable to treatment" or poses a threat to public safety. A judge's case-by-case clinical assessment of a youth's rehabilitative potential and dangerousness reflects the individualized sentencing discretion characteristic of juvenile courts.

Proponents of judicial waiver emphasize its consistency with juvenile court sentencing philosophy and contend that individualized judgments provide an appropriate balance of flexibility and severity. By contrast, critics argue that juvenile courts lack valid or reliable clinical tools with which to assess amenability to treatment or to predict dangerousness, and that the standardless discretion courts exercise results in abuses and inequalities.

As the public debate about serious and violent delinquents intensifies, legislatures increasingly exclude certain combinations of present offense and prior record from juvenile court jurisdiction or emphasize offense criteria to structure judicial discretion in waiver hearings. Despite these legislative modifications of the most consequential sentencing decisions juvenile courts make, there is remarkably little research on the determinants of waiver, the sentences that young offenders received in juvenile or criminal courts, or their subsequent criminal careers.

This Article addresses this paucity with an analysis of judicial waiver policy and processes in Hennepin County (Minneapolis), the largest metropolitan county in Minnesota. First, we discuss the legal framework for judicial waiver decisions and describe prior research on waiver practices. Second, we explore significant determinants of the waiver decision, analyzing 330 transfer motions filed between 1986 and 1992 to identify the offender and offense variables that affect judicial waiver decisions. In our analysis we include indicators of the judicial waiver process, including: the timing of the process, the role of clinical assessments, and the ways in which individual judges affect transfer decisions. Finally, we examine the subsequent juvenile or criminal court processing, sentencing, and recidivism of youths against whom prosecutors filed waiver motions.

II. JUDICIAL WAIVER

Two United States Supreme Court cases provide the constitutional framework for making the individualized sentencing decisions involved in judicial waiver hearings. In *Kent v. United States*, the Court held that states must provide juveniles with some procedural due process protections in judicial waiver hearings, thereby "formalizing" this special sentencing decision. In *Breed v. Jones*, the Court applied the double jeopardy provisions of the Constitution to the adjudication of juvenile offenses and required states to decide whether to try a youth in juvenile or criminal court before proceeding on the merits of the charge.

Although *Kent* and *Breed* provide the procedural framework for judicial waiver decisions, the substantive bases for these decisions pose much greater difficulties. Most jurisdictions allow juvenile court judges to waive jurisdiction based on assessments of a youth's dangerousness or amenability to treatment. These discretionary decisions focus on the offender's age, the amount of time left for treatment within juvenile jurisdiction, treatment prognosis as reflected in clinical evaluations, and threat to others as reflected in the seriousness of the present offense and prior record.

Asking the court to decide whether a youth is dangerous or amenable to treatment implicates some of the most difficult issues of sentencing policy and juvenile jurisprudence. The underlying legislative assumptions that effective treatment programs exist for serious or persistent juvenile offenders, that classification systems can differentiate the treatment potential or dangerousness of various youth, and that validated and reliable diagnostic tools enable a clinician or juvenile court to determine the proper disposition for a particular youth—are all highly problematic and controversial. Alternatively, waiving juvenile court jurisdiction because a youth poses a threat to public safety assumes that courts reliably and accurately can predict future dangerousness.

Juvenile courts exercise broad, standardless discretion when making waiver decisions on the basis of statutory criteria such as amenability to treatment or dangerousness. Adding long lists of amorphous and contradictory substantive factors, such as the standards appended in *Kent*, reinforces rather than constrains judicial discretion because courts can justify any decision by selectively emphasizing one set of attributes over another.

The subjective nature of waiver decisions allows unequal application of the law to similarly situated youths without any effective check. Juvenile courts cannot administer these discretionary statutes on a consistent, even-handed basis. Hamparian's nationwide analysis of waiver in 1978 provides compelling evidence that judicial waiver practices are inherently arbitrary, capricious, and discriminatory. In addition, a juvenile's race may also influence the waiver decision. Furthermore, Jeffrey Fagan reports that the length of time from age at offense to the jurisdictional age limit, rather than the offender's prior record, strongly influences judicial transfer decisions; courts transfer juveniles where the seriousness of the offense requires a longer sentence than is available in the juvenile court.

A second problem posed by discretionary waiver is the inconsistency between the criteria used to make transfer decisions and the criteria used by criminal courts to impose prison sentences. Despite public concerns in many jurisdictions about youth violence, most youths judicially waived to criminal court are chronic property offenders rather than violent offenders. When criminal courts sentence recidivist property offenders who appear as adult first-offenders, these youths often receive shorter sentences as adults than they could have received in juvenile court. This lack of integration between juvenile court waiver and criminal court sentencing practices gives rise to a "punishment gap" when chronic young offenders make the transition from one system to the other.

A. Judicial Waiver in Minnesota

Minnesota's judicial waiver statutes, criteria, and procedures typify the way most states decide to prosecute some chronological juveniles in criminal courts. Subject to the constitutional constraints of *Kent* and *Breed*, Minnesota's statute and Juvenile Court Rule 32 govern the process of waiving juvenile court jurisdiction and prosecuting a young offender as an adult. The county attorney initiates a reference proceeding by filing a motion for adult prosecution. Following a finding of probable cause, the juvenile court may order a social study of the child and within thirty days of filing the motion must conduct a hearing to determine whether the youth meets the waiver criteria. The juvenile court may grant adult reference if it concludes that the child is "not suitable for treatment" or that "public safety is not served" by retaining the youth in juvenile court.

Prior to 1980, Minnesota's waiver law provided minimal guidance for juvenile courts trying to decide whether to certify a youth for criminal prosecution. In *In re Dahl*, the Minnesota Supreme Court confronted some of the procedural and substantive problems in the juvenile waiver process. The court clearly indicated to the legislature that the waiver criteria needed modification and greater specificity, concluding that "re-evaluation of the existing certification process may be in order."

In 1980, the Minnesota legislature amended the certification process. The revised juvenile code retained, unchanged, the basic waiver criteria of nonamenability to treatment or dangerousness, and placed the burden of proof on the prosecution to establish by "clear and convincing evidence" that juvenile court jurisdiction should be waived. However, the legislature added a third subdivision to the certification statute to enable prosecutors to establish a *prima facie* case, or rebuttable presumption, of nonamenability and dangerousness by proving that a youth possessed various combinations of present offense and prior record. Despite the legislative attempt to use offense criteria to rationalize waiver decisions, the rebuttable presumption strategy did not reduce judicial discretion.

Evaluations of Minnesota's waiver process before and after the 1980 legislative amendments characterized judicial waiver decisions as idiosyncratic, geographically variable, and in conflict with criminal court sentencing practices. These studies consistently found that the largest group of juveniles waived to adult court throughout Minnesota were property offenders, not violent offenders, and that the criteria for transfer differed between urban and rural jurisdictions. Moreover, because waived juveniles committed less serious offenses and had less extensive criminal history scores, they often received shorter sentences in adult courts than they could have received in juvenile court. . . .

The next section of this Article analyzes judicial waiver practices between 1986 and 1992, when the prima facie case or rebuttable presumption law prevailed. It provides a comprehensive assessment of judicial discretion in operation in an urban context.

III. EMPIRICAL ANALYSES OF JUDICIAL WAIVER PRACTICES

Minnesota's judicial transfer law and process is typical of the waiver strategy used by a majority of other states. Accordingly, the information we collected and analyzed may generalize to the many other jurisdictions that make similar judicial transfer decisions. Various methodological short-comings limit the usefulness of past studies, such as small samples, limited access to critical variables, a reduced view of the offense both in terms of the present offense (including only violent felonies for instance) and in the prior record of offenses. This analysis focuses on the single most populous county in Minnesota, Hennepin County, which is composed of Minneapolis and its surrounding suburbs, and mirrors many other major metropolitan urban areas. Hennepin County accounts for over a quarter of the state's population and over a third of the FBI Part I crime. Over 42% of Part I Violent Crime for the state occurs in Hennepin County, and juveniles accounted for nearly a quarter of all clearances for these violent crimes.

For this study, we pre-tested an extensive data collection protocol and then gathered data from Juvenile Court files. Court psychologists conducted a psychological examination and wrote a full report for about half of the juveniles against whom the prosecutors filed a reference motion. The Juvenile Probation department completed an in-depth reference study on almost all of those juveniles evaluated by Psychological Services. The Juvenile Court files contained the psychological report and the reference study, as well as information on delinquency charges, adjudications, dispositions, and social history reports. In addition, we reviewed all disposition reports, probation progress reviews, program progress reviews, and program exit summaries for any other information to supplement the primary sources; these various reports provided rich sources of information for this study. We also interviewed the various participants in the waiver process and observed court proceedings and pre-hearing conferences.

Although prima facie case statutory definitions attempt to guide prosecutors' selection of which juveniles to file motions against for adult reference, prosecutors are neither expected to charge all youths whose delinquency background fits the criteria, nor precluded from charging other youths who do not meet the criteria. Thus, the prosecutors' initial discretion necessarily defines the population of youth included in this study and determines their characteristics. Our sample includes all juveniles against whom the prosecutors filed a reference motion for the first time between 1986 and 1992.

... [D]uring the period of our study, white juveniles comprised 81% of the ten to seventeen year old youth population in Hennepin County. African-American adolescents comprised 9% and other minority adolescents an additional 10% of the county's youth. However, police apprehension of juveniles in Hennepin County for FBI Part I Index offenses reveals a different pattern. Police arrested white youths for 55% of all serious crimes, African-American youths for 32%, and other minority youths for the remaining 12%. This disproportionality between population percentages and arrest percentages is striking and becomes even greater when viewing the percentages of youths motioned for adult reference. Of those youths against whom prosecutors filed transfer motions, 28% were white, 55% were African-American, and 17% were of some other minority group.

Additionally, there are differences in the type of offense common to the various racial groups. Police cleared most of the property crimes with arrests of white juveniles (57%), and cleared most of the violent crimes with arrests of African-American juveniles (54%), indicating that race-crime specificity is evident at very early stages of the juvenile justice process. When we analyze the racial characteristics of youths against whom the prosecutors filed reference motions, the race-offense nexus emerges even more graphically. Although about one-third (34%) of the arrests for violent crimes involved white juveniles, less than one-fifth (19%) of the violent offenders against whom prosecutors filed reference motions were white. While African-American youth account for a majority (54%) of all juvenile arrests for violent crimes, they made up nearly two-thirds (65%) of the population against whom prosecutors filed reference motions for felonies against the person. The percentage of arrests and motions for serious property crimes are similar.

These differences reflect both the prosecutors' decision to file reference motions predominantly for violent crimes, as well as a different and larger proportion of violent offenses in African-American juveniles' prior records. ... Although the three racial groups appear very similar in terms of the proportion that had any type of past felony adjudication and the average number of past felony adjudications or out-of-home delinquency placements, they do differ in their likelihood of having a prior person felony. Twice as many minority youths as white youths (34%, 31% vs. 15%) had an adjudication for a felony against a person, whereas whites were twice as likely as African-Americans (50% vs. 27%) to have a delinquency history of property felonies. Juveniles other than whites or African-Americans had a less crime-specific delinquency background than either of the latter groups; they were as likely as African-

Americans to have a history of person felonies and nearly as likely as whites to have a background of property felonies.

The Minnesota Sentencing Guidelines used to sentence adult offenders presume that defendants convicted of certain violent crimes, for example, murder, criminal sexual conduct, or felonies using a firearm, should be committed to prison. We ascertained whether the juveniles against whom prosecutors filed reference motions were charged with presumptive commitment to prison offenses or had these types of offenses in their prior delinquency records. Using this criteria, prosecutors filed reference motions for presumptive offenses against 66% of the African-American juveniles, 18% of other minority juveniles, and 16% of white juveniles. While only 15% of all the juveniles had a prior adjudication for a presumptive commitment offense, African-American youths constituted three-quarters of that group. Twenty percent of all African-American juveniles had presumptive commitment offenses in their delinquency history compared with 11% of other minority juveniles and 7% of white juveniles. This is a significant difference in past adjudications for presumptive offenses by racial groups.

[The study] also reports information on the average number of prior delinquency out-of-home placements for each racial group. Children classified as other minorities had the highest average of prior delinquency placements and differed significantly only from the average for African-Americans. White youths were placed out of their home for delinquency related matters nearly as often as other minority youths. The average number of out-of-home placements is larger than the average number of felony adjudications, indicating that youths may be placed out of the home for misdemeanor level adjudications as well.

Although the racial groups differ qualitatively in terms of the type of present offenses charged and prior delinquency records (person offenses for African-Americans and property offenses for whites), they appear very similar in terms of the quantity of their prior delinquency involvement (average number of prior felonies, percent of each group that had any prior felonies, and the average number of prior juvenile court placements). Finally, ... 71% of white juveniles against whom prosecutors filed a motion for referral to adult court were certified, compared with 63% of African-American and 64% of other minority juveniles. The racial difference in referral rates was not statistically significant. Possibly, this indicates a ceiling of total felony level offenses acceptable within juvenile court, regardless of the specific type of felonies.

Prosecutors typically filed a reference motion against a youth for a single delinquent incident, although they may allege more than one offense. In the typical case, the juvenile appears in court on the reference motion on the present offenses with no other unresolved outstanding offenses; 85% of the cases fit this pattern. For the remaining 15% of the youths, prosecutors simultaneously filed multiple reference motions for crimes arising out of several different behavioral incidents, or they filed a single motion with other outstanding charges pending.

A. Rate of Transfer

... The juvenile court handled an average of forty-seven reference motions per year, and waived about two-thirds (65%) of these youths for adult prosecution. Except for 1988, when prosecutors filed a larger number of reference motions, the certification rate from 1986 through 1990 was relatively stable and above 70%. The transfer rate was somewhat lower in 1991 and 1992.

Two factors account for the change in certification rates in the later years. First, the judge who presided from 1986 until 1990 left the juvenile court bench. In the remaining two years, three other judges heard most of the reference motions. Second, the County Attorney's Office changed its reference motion filing policy in 1991 to concentrate primarily on youths who met the prima facie offense criteria.

B. Offense Characteristics

1. Present Offense In 1991 and 1992, the County Attorney's Office filed more reference motions against youths who met the prima facie case criteria, emphasizing the seriousness of the present offense rather than the cumulative record of persistence. As a result, the percentage of cases that met the serious offense criteria increased from less than 3% in 1986–1988 to about half of the cases in 1991–1992.

Reflecting this policy change, prosecutors charged significantly more youths with presumptive commitment offenses. Between 1986 and 1990, prosecutors filed reference motions against about half of the juveniles for presumptive commitment offenses; while by 1991 and 1992, they charged nearly three quarters of all juveniles (73% and 74%, respectively) with presumptive commitment offenses.

Prosecutors filed reference motions most often for felonies against the person (63%). The proportion of reference motions filed for violent crimes increased from about 60% in the earlier years to about 80% by the end of our study. Prosecutors filed reference motions against 25% to 30% of the youths for property felonies in the earlier years, but these charges declined significantly by 1991 and 1992 to only about 10% of the reference motions filed. Although about one-third (31.2%) of the reference motions alleged only a single felony, prosecutors filed multiple counts against most of the youths in this sample and charged over one quarter (26.4%) of the juveniles with four or more felonies.

2. Weapons Prosecutors filed most reference motions for violent crimes; the juveniles used some type of weapon in about half (48.2%) of these offenses. This percentage remained relatively constant across the study years until the final year of 1992 when the percent of juveniles who used weapons increased to nearly 70%. Our multivariate analyses indicate that a juvenile's use of a weapon significantly influenced the court's decision to refer to adult court.

C. Offender Characteristics

1. Prior Delinquency Adjudications   We used three different indicators of juveniles' past delinquency records. First, to measure seriousness, we determined whether the prior record included a presumptive commitment offense. Second, to measure persistence, we simply counted the number of prior misdemeanor or felony adjudications and weighted all felonies equally. Third, we distinguished prior offenses by the type of crime, such as felony offenses against the person, property, or drugs. We classified juveniles' prior record on the basis of the most serious crime and used these alternative constructions of prior records to test whether the court considered the "quality" of the delinquency history or simply the "quantity" in making reference decisions.

There is a straightforward trade-off between charging policies emphasizing seriousness and persistence; the seriousness of the present offenses and the length of the prior record are inversely related. As prosecutors' reference motion policy emphasized the seriousness of the present offense rather than cumulative persistence, the number of prior felony adjudications in the juveniles' delinquency records decreased significantly over time, from 2.11 prior felonies in 1986 to 1.57 in 1992.

Most juveniles did not have prior adjudications for violent crimes, and this did not change over the course of the study. Only about 15% of all the motioned juveniles had prior adjudications for presumptive offenses. However, the proportion of juveniles with prior property felony adjudications significantly decreased, and the number of juveniles with prior drug felony convictions increased between 1986 and 1992.

Interviews with the prosecutors, judges, and court service personnel indicated that prosecutors filed reference motions against two "types" of juveniles. One group consisted of "persistent" offenders: juveniles with an extensive prior delinquency history, mainly property offenses, who were motioned on another property offense that simply constituted the "last straw." These chronic offenders had exhausted the juvenile treatment programs and resources. The other group consisted of "serious" offenders: juveniles with a limited prior delinquency history who were motioned on a presumptive commitment violent crime. . . . These two categories combined comprise over two-thirds of the motioned juveniles. In the earlier years of the study, prosecutors filed reference motions mainly against non-presumptive offenders with two or more prior delinquency adjudications, but by the end of the study, this flipped and prosecutors charged over half of the juveniles, who had a limited (one prior felony or less) delinquency history, with presumptive offenses.

This trend is reflected in the average number of prior out-of home placements across the study years as well. The persistent offender of the earlier years averaged nearly three and one-half delinquency placements prior to the filing of the reference motion. In 1991, the average had dropped to only about one and one-half prior placements before the prosecutor filed the reference motion, and the overall decrease in the number of past program placements was significant. Conversely, the percent of motioned juveniles with no prior placements increased from only 15% in 1986 to 48% and 40% in 1991 and 1992, respectively.

2. Racial Background   The County Attorney's policy change to emphasize the seriousness of the present offense affected the proportion of minority juveniles over the period of our study because of the greater propensity of minority youths to be arrested for and charged with the most serious, violent crimes. Even in 1986, minority juveniles comprised nearly two-thirds (64%) of the youths against whom prosecutors filed reference motions; by the end of our study period, minority juveniles comprised nearly nine out of ten (88%) of the youths whom prosecutors sought to waive.

3. Age of Motioned Juveniles   The juvenile's age at the time of the present offense is an important variable in the waiver process, because it indicates the length of time remaining to treat the youth in the juvenile system. The minimum age to file a reference motion is fourteen years old; at the time we conducted this research, the juvenile court's maximum dispositional jurisdiction extended until age nineteen. Prosecutors in Hennepin County filed very few reference motions against juveniles younger than sixteen years of age. Indeed, in the seven year span of our study, prosecutors filed reference motions against only thirty-four juveniles (10%) for crimes they committed when less than sixteen years of age; twenty-four of those youths were fifteen years old and only ten were fourteen years old. The vast majority of juveniles (296 youths or 90%) against whom prosecutors filed a reference motion were sixteen or seventeen years old at the time of the present offense; fully 60% of juveniles were seventeen years old.

D. Court Process Variables

Despite the number of studies that analyze waiver outcomes, surprisingly few examine the process by which courts reach those decisions. We examined the impact of the presiding juvenile court judge and the effects of clinical and psychological evaluations on the most important sentencing decision of juvenile courts.

1. Court Service Evaluations and Studies   At the request of juvenile court, either the Juvenile Probation or the Psychological Services divisions of the Department of Community Corrections evaluates the personal or psychological characteristics of the offender, family background, education, and delinquency background of youths against whom the prosecutor files a reference motion.

The Juvenile Probation department may provide a detailed social report, called a reference study. The juvenile court requested reference studies in only 43% of the cases, although the number of reference study requests increased to about 50% in the final two years of our study, when more youths faced charges for violent crime. A request for a reference study did not significantly affect the outcome of waiver decisions. The court retained jurisdiction over 34% of those juveniles for whom it requested reference studies and over 37% of those juveniles for whom it did not request a study. Probation officers collected and summarized the available social, behavioral, and clinical information about the youths and recommended retention or transfer to the juvenile court. Probation officers' recommendations statistically influence juvenile court decisions. These consistent relationships may reflect either heavy judicial reliance on probation staff's recommendations, or the probation staff's familiarity with and anticipation of judicial waiver and practices.

The juvenile court ordered psychological evaluations for nearly all of the youths for whom it requested reference studies, and for a few additional youths as well. Overall, the courts requested psychological evaluations of 46% of the juveniles with some increases in the latter years of our study (63% in 1991 and 57% in 1992). . . .

2. Juvenile Court Judge   One judge presided over the juvenile court for about half of the period covered by our study and several other judges served for shorter tenures. The four judges . . . heard 85% of all the first reference motions filed. Judge #1 handled over half of all the reference cases in our study (55%) and referred about three quarters (75%) of the youths against whom prosecutors filed a reference motions. By contrast, Judge #4 referred only about half (54%) of the cases he decided. Thus, the presiding judge's judicial and administrative philosophy may be an important variable affecting the reference process.

The variability of waiver rates requires further explanation. There is no standard waiver rate, and research in other jurisdictions indicates substantial variation. The seriousness of youth crime, County Attorney charging policies, defense attorney plea negotiation strategies, and juvenile placement options all affect transfer rates. In our study, for example, prosecutors filed reference motions alleging presumptive commitment to prison offenses against only 46% of the juveniles whose cases Judge #1 decided, compared with 74% of those Judge #2 decided, 69% that Judge #3 heard, and 77% of those before Judge #4. Juveniles charged with presumptive commitment offenses are often younger offenders who have less extensive prior records and fewer treatment placements; consequently, the decision whether to waive them to criminal court may be more difficult.

The philosophy and policies of the presiding judge also affect referral rates. For example, after controlling for the seriousness of the reference motion offense, Judge #1 referred 76% of those youths charged with presumptive commitment to prison offenses, while Judge #2 referred 64% of the youths charged with presumptive offenses, Judge #3 referred 79%, and

Judge #4 waived 55%. The juveniles in the latter years also had less extensive prior delinquency records. Moreover, the waiver decision is only part of the overall sentencing process. In many instances, after the juvenile court judge refers a youth for adult criminal prosecution, he or she will preside as a criminal court judge over the adult component of the case. Because the waiver decision often is part of a plea-bargained "package deal," reference decisions cannot be viewed in isolation from \the subsequent sentences of a youth as a juvenile or as an adult.

Table 1 shows each of the six independent variables found to be significant in our multivariate analysis. We defined these six indicators as part of the court process, attributes of the offender, or characteristics of the offense. This Table examines each of the three categories of variables individually. These bivariate analyses report the percentage of juveniles that were referred to criminal court within the various combination of characteristics.

The first part of the Table shows the court process variables; the rows indicate which judge presided over the reference decision. Because Judge #1 presided over 55% of the reference decisions and referred juveniles at a higher rate than the other judges, we created a dummy code for Judge #1. The columns describe the type of recommendation made by the probation department and psychological services.

These professionals evaluated about half of the juveniles against whom prosecutors filed reference motions and recommended whether the court should refer or retain them. A request for a clinical evaluation was not a *de facto* waiver decision; youths who received additional clinical services are neither more nor less likely to be certified because they are evaluated.

To detect agreement or disagreement between court services personnel, we combined their appraisals. We constructed the categories as follows: 1) both the probation officer and the psychologist agreed that the juvenile should be referred to adult court; 2) both court employees agreed the youth should remain in juvenile court; 3) the probation officer and the psychologist disagreed on the reference recommendation; and finally, 4) neither conducted an assessment. . . .

The first part of Table 1 indicates that Judge #1 referred juveniles at a much higher rate (75%) than the other judges as a group (50% referral rate). This difference was even more striking when there were no recommendations solicited from the probation department or psychological services (Judge #1 referred 80% while other judges referred 40%). In addition, when the court service personnel recommended transfer, there was near certainty that a juvenile would be referred to criminal court regardless of which judge presided. Likewise, when these court officers recommended retaining a juvenile, very few judges opposed that decision. Clearly, including variables that assess court processes in the analysis of the factors determining certification are important.

The second section of Table 1 displays the age and prior placement history of the offenders in this study. The court referred to adult court only

TABLE 1
The Certification Rate of Motioned Juveniles (Percent of Juveniles in Each Cell Transferred to Adult Court)

1. The effect of COURT PROCESS variables

What are the probation/psychologist recommendations?

Who is the judge?	Both juvenile N = 54	No recommendation* N = 189	Both adult N = 87	Total N = 330
Judge #1 N = 179	8%	80%	100%	75%
Other judges N = 151	14%	40%	93%	50%
TOTAL	11%	63%	97%	65%

2. The effect of OFFENDER CHARACTERISTICS

Number of prior out-of-home delinquency placements

Age of offender	None N = 111	One to three N = 113	Four or more N = 106	Total N = 330
14 or 15 Years Old N = 34	31%	17%	17%	24%
16 Years Old N = 98	48%	47%	82%	61%
17 Years Old N = 198	62%	76%	85%	74%
TOTAL	54%	62%	80%	65%

3. The effect of present OFFENSE CHARACTERISTICS

Type of present offense and whether a weapon was used

Number of charges	Non-person N = 121	Person-no weapon N = 54	Person-weapon N = 155	Total N = 330
Two Felonies or Less N = 192	51%	55%	70%	59%
Three Charges or More N = 138	83%	68%	73%	74%
TOTAL	59%	61%	72%	65%

The no recommendation category includes the eleven juveniles who were evaluated and the probation officer and psychologist disagreed on the court recommendation. In the multivariate model these eleven youth are kept as a unique category.

about one quarter of the younger motioned offenders, 61% of the sixteen year old youths, and 74% of those who were seventeen when they committed their present offense. There are several possible explanations for the relationship between age and waiver decisions. First, a youth's age may act as a proxy for prior delinquency: older juveniles have a longer opportunity to acquire a more extensive prior record. Second, a youth's age determines the length of time remaining for treatment within juvenile jurisdiction. Finally, judges may view younger offenders as less culpable for their crimes and decline to certify them as readily.

We analyzed a number of alternative measures of prior delinquency history. Because a youth's "amenability to treatment" is a crucial issue in the waiver decision, the extent of previous dispositions may indicate a juvenile's exhaustion of treatment resources and provide a rationale to transfer a youth to criminal court. We found that prior program placement was the most robust indicator of prior juvenile court involvement. It was highly correlated with prior delinquency record (r = .7), and when we included both variables in the model, we gained no additional information from prior delinquency history. We included only prior program placements in our model as the single indicator of past juvenile justice involvement, because it provided a stronger predictor of the reference decision than prior delinquency.

Juvenile court referred about half (54%) of those youths with no prior delinquency placement history. This referral rate jumped to 80% for those youths with four or more prior delinquency placements. The cells inside the Table indicate that sixteen year old juveniles were transferred as frequently as seventeen year olds when they both had four or more placements (82% and 85%, respectively). Therefore, as important as age is in determining who is certified, at a certain point, prior history with the juvenile court becomes as important.

The final part of Table 1 reports information about the offense most common to other certification studies. We analyzed both the number of charges alleged in the reference motion and the type of crime charged. The court referred three quarters (74%) of the youths against whom prosecutors filed three or more charges, compared with 59% of those juveniles charged with two or fewer felony offenses. We first categorized the present offense into non-person and person offenses and secondly considered whether or not a weapon was used. The transfer rate for juveniles charged with a non-person offense (59%) was very similar to the transfer rate for those youths with a person offense who did not use a weapon (61%). The rate increased to 72% for those youths charged with a person felony who used a weapon.

The highest referral rate in the third section of Table 1 occurred for youths who were charged with a non-person offense and who had three or more charges against them on the present offense (83%). These particular juveniles had significantly more prior delinquency placements than either of the other two offense categories (3.2 prior placements for those whose present offense was non-person, 2.3 for person offense with no weapon, and 1.3 for person offense with a weapon), which may explain the high certification rate. . . .

F. Significant Variables

1. Court Services Recommendations   One of the most powerful variables in our model was the recommendation given by court services personnel. When the probation officer and psychologist agreed on a recommendation either to retain juvenile court jurisdiction or to refer the youth to adult court, there was a statistically significant probability that the court would follow that advice. In particular, if both the probation officer and the court psychologist recommended that a juvenile should be tried as an adult, the highly significant logistic coefficient (4.7) indicates that transfer was a near certainty. When both court personnel recommended that the juvenile court retain jurisdiction over the youth, the odds of transfer to criminal court decreased significantly. . . .

2. Juvenile Court Judge   Which juvenile court judge presided over the reference process constituted another significant process variable. We saw from Table 1 that Judge #1 referred juveniles at a higher rate than other judges who presided in subsequent years. But that view could have resulted because Judge #1 made decisions under different conditions than the other judges. Multivariate analysis allows us to test this proposition. When we control for all the other factors in our model, . . . youths who appeared before Judge #1 had significantly higher odds of being referred when compared to the other judges as a group (1.4). This finding is consistent with our contention that judicial waiver is a highly individualized, discretionary sentencing decision in which the outcomes depend significantly upon who is the judge.

3. Age at Present Offense   A youth's age at the time the prosecutor filed the reference motion constituted a significantly powerful variable influencing reference decisions. The older the youth, the greater the likelihood that the judge would refer the case to criminal court. This was not an entirely linear relationship, however. Fourteen and fifteen year old youths were much less likely to be certified than seventeen year old youths. The logit coefficient for sixteen year old youths, though not as strong as the younger ages, also reflected reduced odds of being referred when compared to a seventeen year old youth.

4. Prior Program Placements   We categorized prior out-of-home placements into three groupings: 1) no prior delinquency placements; 2) one to three prior placements; and 3) four or more prior placements (the excluded category). We found that both of the first two categories differed significantly from the final category. Youths with no prior placements and with only a few (one to three) prior placements experienced significantly lower odds of being certified to adult court than did those youths in the alternative category of four or more program placements. Effectively, prior placements did not become a significant factor in the certification decision until a youth crossed a threshold of four or more placements.

5. Number of Present Offense Charges We dichotomized the number of present charges alleged in the reference motion into two or fewer felonies (the excluded category) and three or more felonies. The number of felony charges that the prosecutor alleged in the reference motion significantly affected whether or not the court certified a juvenile; the odds of transfer were greater when the prosecutor alleged three or more charges against a youth. Multiple charges may provide an additional indicator of the seriousness of the case pending against a youth.

6. Present Offense Characteristics We analyzed several different indicators of the seriousness of the present offense and ultimately constructed three categories of offenders alleged by prosecutors: 1) those who committed a felony offense against the person *and* used a weapon; 2) those who committed a felony offense against the person but did not use a weapon; or 3) those who committed a felony (e.g., property or drug) other than a crime against the person. Recall that prosecutors charged nearly two-thirds (63%) of the juveniles with some type of violent crime. Whether the prosecutor charged a youth with a crime against the person did not necessarily increase the likelihood of transfer. In an urban setting in which prosecutors file reference motions against most juveniles for violent offenses and courts certify youths on the basis of their cumulative delinquency records, the seriousness of the present offense alone may be a secondary consideration. When we controlled for the other variables, the juvenile court was no more likely to certify youths charged with a felony offense against the person than to waive those charged with property offenses, provided that the juvenile did not use a weapon. However, if the prosecutor alleged that the youth committed a crime against the person *and* used a weapon in the commission of the offense, then the court was significantly more likely to waive the youth to criminal court. Thus, a weapon appears to be a necessary component of the seriousness of the offense. . . .

I. Post-Waiver Juvenile or Criminal Court Sentencing of Young Offenders

Once juvenile court decides whether or not to transfer a juvenile, what happens to the case? We followed the justice system careers of each youth to determine whether a conviction ensued in juvenile or criminal court, what sentence was imposed, and the impact of juvenile or adult sentences on subsequent recidivism.

1. Dispositions and Sentences of Youth in Juvenile and Criminal Court
Juvenile courts transfer some youths to criminal court so that they may receive longer sentences as adults than are available in the juvenile system. However, several studies report a "punishment gap" and question whether criminal courts impose more severe sanctions on waived youths than juvenile courts would if they retain jurisdiction. Chronic property offenders who constitute the bulk of waived juveniles in most states receive shorter sentences as adults than do property offenders retained in juvenile court. By contrast, youths convicted of violent offenses in criminal courts receive substantially longer sentences than do their juvenile counterparts. For juveniles and adults convicted of comparable crimes, both types of disparities—shorter sentences for waived youths than for retained juveniles adjudicated of property offenses, and longer sentences for convicted waived youths than for retained juveniles adjudicated of violent crimes—raise issues of sentencing policy and justice. Are either types of disparities justified? Are there any policy rationales for the disjunction?

We examined the types of sentences juvenile and criminal courts imposed on retained and referred youths, the proportion of offenders they incarcerated in correctional facilities, and, of those confined, the length of sentence they received. By comparing the commitment rates and sentence lengths between the two systems, we can assess the efficacy of social control.

The juvenile court sentenced most (54%) of the delinquents to some type of long-term juvenile correctional facility. The court sentenced an additional one-fifth (20%) of the retained juveniles to some type of short-term local program, in-patient treatment facility, work camp, or ranch. The court placed on probation 12% of youths who did not receive sentences that resulted in out-of-home placement or correctional confinement, and imposed conditions such as a fine, letter of apology, work squad, day treatment program, or stayed sentence to a correctional facility. The remaining 14% of the retained juveniles had charges dismissed.

Of the 215 certified youths, the criminal courts sentenced 82% to a local or state correctional facility. The adult court can sentence certified youths to state prison where the minimum sentence length is one year or longer or to county jails where the maximum sentence length is one year. However, the criminal courts also ordered stayed prison terms for virtually all of the youths confined in local jails. If those young offenders violated the terms of their probation following release from jail, their stayed prison terms could be executed to extend their confinement. . . .

Criminal courts incarcerated certified youths at much higher rates than the juvenile courts. This was true even when the severity of the offense was controlled. Eighty-five percent of the convicted referred youths were incarcerated whereas only 63% of the adjudicated retained youths were placed in a correctional facility. The adult criminal courts incarcerated 93% of the youths convicted of a presumptive offense, while the juvenile court imposed long-term confinement on 65% of the youths retained in juvenile court who were adjudicated for a presumptive offense. The adult criminal courts confined 78% of youths convicted of non-presumptive offenses in jail or prison, whereas the juvenile court committed only 61% of non-presumptive delinquents to a correctional facility. Thus, for both presumptive and non-presumptive offenses, criminal courts incarcerated youths convicted as adults significantly more often than did the juvenile court. Although the waiver process selects youths on the basis of seriousness, the differences in rates of dismissal, conviction, and incarceration between the two systems are striking.

2. Length of Sentence In addition to the differences in probabilities of conviction and certainty of confinement for juveniles and adults, we calculated the actual lengths of sentences imposed on those youths incarcerated in both justice systems. We defined the sentence length as the amount of time a court ordered an offender committed or confined for the offense(s) for which the prosecutor filed the reference motion.

Our analyses of juvenile and criminal court sentences replicate the sentencing disparities reported in other studies.... Those youths convicted as adults of presumptive offenses received sentences substantially longer than those imposed on juveniles convicted of comparable offenses. By contrast, the juvenile court-sentenced youths were found delinquent for non-presumptive, property offenses for terms longer than their adult counterparts.

Because the adult and juvenile systems differ, it is difficult to directly compare sentence lengths in custodial facilities. Criminal courts have two correctional confinement options—prison or jail—while juvenile courts have only one incarceration option—long-term correctional facilities. Criminal courts sentenced most youths convicted of presumptive offenses to prison (51%) and imposed a median sentence length of 1,459 days—about four years. When they made a mitigated downward departure from the presumptive sentences, they confined those referred youths for a median sentence of one year—the maximum allowed for jail confinement.... By contrast, juvenile courts sentenced youths retained and adjudicated for presumptive offenses to median terms of incarceration of 266 days, or about nine months. Thus, youths sentenced as adults either to prison or to jail served substantially longer terms than their juvenile counterparts who were adjudicated of comparable offenses.

For youths convicted as adults of non-presumptive offenses, criminal courts sentenced the vast majority (95%) to local jails for median terms of 120 days, or about four months, and made aggravated, upward departures to send youths convicted of non-presumptive offenses to prison in only four cases (5%). By contrast, the juvenile court incarcerated the thirty-one juveniles adjudicated delinquent for non-presumptive offenses to median terms of 182 days, or about six months. Transferred youths have a higher conviction rate and a higher certainty of incarceration for all types of offenses than youths retained in juvenile jurisdiction. Youths sentenced in adult court also receive substantially longer incarcerative sentences for presumptive offenses than retained juveniles, but this is not the case for nonpresumptive offenses. The juvenile courts imposed longer sentences on less serious property offenses than did the criminal court.

3. Recidivism   Do waiver policies or criminal sentencing strategies reduce subsequent recidivism by offenders? Because we individually tracked the subsequent criminal careers of each youth against whom prosecutors filed a first reference motion between 1986 and 1992, we constructed an accurate record of the subsequent official delinquent and criminal justice responses for this group of serious young offenders. We coded as recidivism all offenses that occurred after the offense for which the prosecutor filed the initial reference motion. Although other studies use rearrests as an indicator of recidivism, we used a more conservative definition of recidivism—actual adjudications or convictions.

We defined "street time" as two full years of non-incarceration time following the sentence or disposition on the motioned offense, allowing a standardized opportunity for new crime. We excluded youths motioned in 1992 since data collection stopped in 1993, and also excluded 10% of youths in our data who because of their prison times did not have two or more years at risk to commit a new crime. This means our recidivism levels are under-estimates of the recidivism level for the referred youths. Assessing the recidivism within a two year "window of opportunity" following sentencing and release standardizes the length of time available for all remaining juveniles. In this analysis, post-reference motion conviction or adjudication for any subsequent offense constituted recidivism. Using this conservative definition of recidivism, over half (52%) of the youths who had an opportunity to commit additional crimes did so. These reconviction recidivism levels fall within the broad range of re-conviction recidivism levels reported in other studies of juvenile recidivists. Within the two year window following the initial reference motion offense, there were no statistically significant differences in recidivism levels between members of different racial groups. Fifty percent of the African-American youths recidivated, as did 52% of the white youths, and 60% of the youths of the other minority group.

Finally, we compared the recidivism levels of those youths waived to adult criminal court with those youths over whom the juvenile court retained jurisdiction. A larger proportion of certified youths committed new offenses within two years than did those who remained in the juvenile justice system. Nearly three-fifths (58%) of the youths referred by juvenile court for criminal prosecution as adults committed an additional crime, compared with 42% of those who remained in juvenile court. There are several possible explanations of the differences in recidivism levels in the two systems. First, because juvenile courts emphasized youths' total record of offending, including the prior treatment attempts to make certification decisions, they used a valid and reliable tool with which to identify high base-rate career criminals who had a greater probability of subsequent recidivism. Thus, the discretionary certification process did a reasonably good job of identifying the most chronic and prolific offenders within the population of serious offenders. Secondly, the adult incarceration experience may better train further criminality than the juvenile correctional experience. Thirdly, some might attribute the lower recidivism levels among the retained juvenile population to the "effectiveness of treatment" within the juvenile correctional system. However, the population selection biases inherent in the waiver process and the absence of a control group make it difficult to attribute the differences in recidivism rates between the juvenile and adult groups to "treatment" effects. On the other hand, if legislatures and courts intend to deter youths from committing additional offenses by subjecting those who persist in delinquency to the more severe punishment of the adult criminal justice system, our data indicate that they are not achieving that goal.

IV. CONCLUSIONS

This study presents a complete and comprehensive analysis of the judicial waiver process and juvenile/criminal court sentencing policies. Our research improves on previous studies in a number of important respects. The quality of our data enable us to use multivariate analytic techniques to disaggregate the factors that lead juvenile courts to refer some youths to criminal court and retain jurisdiction over others. Logistic regression is specifically designed for analyses employing a dichotomous dependent variable—refer or retain. Moreover, we refined the specification of the dependent variable to analyze judicial waiver decisions the first time prosecutors file a reference motion against a juvenile, because courts' reactions to second and subsequent motions differ substantially. We collected considerable delinquency and criminal data for motioned youths from sources outside of Hennepin County when necessary and, therefore, have completed a better delinquency picture of more mobile youths. Additionally, because we also collected information about these youths' prior program exposures and exhaustion of placement options, we demonstrate the salience of prior dispositions as an operational indicator of "amenability to treatment."

Our analyses also examine the influence of court processes on waiver decisions by exploring the ways in which juvenile court judges affect waiver decisions. Within the same urban county and court, the various judges decided the cases of similarly-situated offenders significantly differently. These judicial differences influenced both the characteristics of youths waived or retained, and the subsequent sentences imposed on them as juveniles or adults.

Our analyses also document the crucial role that probation recommendations and psychological evaluations play in the "individualized" waiver process and outcomes; probation officers' and psychologists' recommendations to the court to retain or refer a youth significantly affect the eventual judicial waiver decision. More importantly, the statistical model including recommendations from court service personnel allowed better predictions of both categories of juveniles, referred and retained, but substantially improved the prediction of youths who were retained.

Future waiver studies should include variables that tap various court process indicators. Clearly, the judge who presides over juvenile waiver issues makes a difference, as do the recommendations provided by probation officers and clinical evaluators.

We followed and compared the subsequent sentences that these youths received as juveniles or as adults. Referred youths were incarcerated at a higher rate than retained youths, regardless of whether the conviction was for a presumptive or non-presumptive crime. Youths tried and convicted as adults for violent crimes for which the Sentencing Guidelines presume commitment to prison received sentences dramatically longer than did their juvenile counterparts convicted of similar offenses. However, for youths adjudicated of nonpresumptive offenses, the juvenile courts imposed longer sentences than did the criminal courts for most young adult offenders. Thus, for non-violent offenders, the lack of integration between juvenile waiver criteria and criminal court sentencing practices perpetuate the "punishment gap" and allows chronic property offenders to "fall between the cracks." Both types of disparities for similarly-situated offenders—longer adult sentences for violent offenders and longer juvenile sentences for property offenders occurred because the two systems lack a coherent sentencing policy that spans both.

B. LEGISLATIVE OFFENSE EXCLUSION

The Automatic Waiver of Juveniles and Substantive Justice

SIMON I. SINGER

Contemporary juvenile justice reforms include the transfer or waiver of juveniles into the adult criminal court. The most common waiver procedure is one that places waiver decisions in the hands of the juvenile court judge.

From Simon I. Singer, in *Crime & Delinquency*, Vol. 39: pp. 253–261 (April 1993), copyright © 1993 by Simon I. Singer. Reprinted by permission of Sage Publications, Inc.

This traditional form of waiver is typically called judicial waiver. Although the vast majority of states maintain this form, it has been criticized as inappropriately extending the discretionary decision-making power of juvenile justice officials to waiver decisions.

Barry Feld, for example, in his comprehensive review of waiver legislation, argues that judicial waiver is too closely linked to the individualized, substantive justice approach of juvenile court. As a consequence, judicial waiver decisions are based less on offense seriousness and more on the nonoffense-related substantive concerns of juvenile justice officials. Feld concludes that "judicial waiver statutes reveal all of the defects characteristic of individualized, discretionary sentencing schema."

There is considerable support for Feld's assertion that judicial waiver reflects the individualized, discretionary sentencing practices of juvenile court. Based on national data, Hamparian et al. report that only 32% of judicial waivers in 1978 were for violent offenses. Osbun and Rode report that transferred juveniles in Minnesota included many "juveniles whose records do not appear to be very serious." They conclude that juvenile court judges are unable "to identify many juveniles whose records are characterized by violent, frequent, and persistent delinquent activity." Feld reports that in Minnesota, offense seriousness and prior arrests explain very little (3%) of the variance in judicial waiver decisions. Drawing on a multivariate analysis of data on violent juvenile offenders in cities with judicial waiver statutes, Fagan and Deschenes also conclude that "judicial waiver statutes empower the juvenile court judge to make a transfer decision without applying objective criteria."

Feld further argues that the punishment-oriented objectives of waiver are best met in states that have adopted legislative waiver reforms. In those states, the criminal prosecution of juveniles is based on technical definitions of violent offense categories that automatically exclude juvenile offenders from prosecution under juvenile delinquency statutes. Also, Bishop and Frazier suggest that one way to introduce "greater equity and predictability to the transfer process would be to look to the legislature to bring more offenses (or offense/prior record combinations) within the ambit of the legislative exclusion statute."

In contrast to most states, which have developed judicial waiver procedures, a few states have enacted legislative waiver procedures for specific categories of offenses. In these cases, criminal justice officials, rather than juvenile justice officials, decide the appropriateness of charging juveniles as adults. Legislative waiver places eligible juveniles into the criminal justice process from the point of arrest. Thus legislative waiver bypasses the juvenile court and is believed to eliminate the initial discretionary power of juvenile justice officials.

Critics of legislative waiver argue that its reverse waiver procedure reproduces the same discretionary avenues of justice that exist in juvenile court among juvenile justice officials. In criminal court, prosecutors have the option simply not to charge eligible juveniles as juvenile offenders. As with adult offenders, they may merely dismiss all arrest charges. Prosecutors also can transfer jurisdiction over juveniles to juvenile court by reducing the severity of charges, or by shifting designated felony offenses to nondesignated offenses for which juveniles are not criminally responsible. Finally, they can invoke a formal "reverse" waiver hearing based on their assessment of the amenability of juveniles to treatment in juvenile court.

Thus Zimring argues that sources of discretion in the waiver process are shifted from juvenile justice to criminal justice officials:

> Systems that attempt to cope with this problem by providing judicial or prosecutorial discretion to transfer back to juvenile court (a common "safety valve to the safety valve") are no less discretionary because the reference back occurs after a waiver decision. They simply reallocate discretion, generally from a juvenile court judge to prosecutors or criminal court judges.

Insight into a nonoffense-related substantive source of juvenile justice discretion is provided by David Matza in his classic work on delinquency and juvenile justice. Matza suggests that parental support is the most important nonoffense-related determinant of the juvenile court's decision to place delinquents in state custody:

> Whether a juvenile goes to some manner of prison or is put on some manner of probation ... depends first, on a traditional rule-of-thumb assessment of the total risk of danger and thus scandal evident in the juvenile's current offense and prior record of offenses; this initial reckoning is then importantly qualified by an assessment of the potentialities of "out-patient supervision" and the guarantee against scandal inherent in the willingness and ability of parents or surrogates to sponsor the child.

Specifically, Matza hypothesizes that "those with adequate [parental] sponsorship will be rendered unto probation, and those inadequately sponsored to prison."

Similarly, criminal justice officials are faced with last-resort decisions regarding the status of juveniles in criminal court. Criminal justice officials must decide if the potentially harsher placement of juveniles in criminal court is an appropriate last-resort penalty. Drawing on Zimring's point that discretion in waiver decisions is reallocated to criminal justice officials and Matza's insight into the determinants of juvenile justice decision making, I hypothesize that juvenile offenders from nontraditional families are more often waived into criminal court. I assume that parental support is greater among traditional families where both parents are present than among those in which only a single parent is available. If criminal justice officials respond to juveniles in a manner similar to that of juvenile justice officials, then nonoffense- as well as offense-related characteristics should dominate the waiver process.

LEGISLATIVE WAIVER IN NEW YORK

In 1978, New York state legislators mandated legislative waiver or waiver by exclusion of violent offense categories. New York's juvenile offender (JO) law lowered the age of criminal responsibility to 13 years for murder and 14 years for a wide range of other violent offenses (Crime Package Bill of 1978 [1978 NY Laws, 481]). For juveniles charged with any designated felony, the court of initial jurisdiction is technically criminal court. However, as in other states with legislative waiver, juveniles in New York can be removed from the criminal justice process and petitioned or charged in the juvenile court (technically called Family Court).

If the arrest charges are reduced to nondesignated offenses, then removal to juvenile court is automatic, because juveniles cannot be charged with offenses for which they are not legally responsible. Although the transfer of juveniles to juvenile court for serious crimes, such as murder and rape, requires the consent of the criminal court judge, prosecutors have considerable discretion in the charging process for a wide range of less serious JO offenses.

METHODOLOGY

Data and Variables

I collected data on 103 JO arrests that occurred between September 1, 1978 and December 31, 1985 in Buffalo, New York. The designated felonies with which these juveniles were charged first required a preliminary hearing in the city's court. As with adult offenders, juveniles charged with designated felonies were initially subject to the prosecutor's decision to seek a grand jury indictment.

The dependent variable is the prosecutor's decision to seek a grand jury indictment for juveniles arrested for JO offenses. A grand jury indictment is required in all felony cases brought before the criminal court whether they involve juvenile or adult offenders. The grand jury is led only by the prosecutor, because the defense has no opportunity to present evidence.

Nonoffense-related independent variables are the offender's race and the marital status of the JO's parents. Marital status is based on the number of parents with which JOs reside. As previously stressed, I assume that there is less parental support for JOs residing in single-parent households. Race is coded into White and non-White JOs. Prior research argues that race is linked to the development and implementation of the JO law.

Legally relevant variables include the extent of injuries inflicted on the victim(s) by the offender and prior felony arrests. Injuries are coded on an ordinal scale ranging in value from 1 to 5 (1 = no injuries, 2 = minor injuries, 3 = treated and discharged, 4 = overnight hospitalization, and 5 = death). Prior offenses are measured by the offender's number of prior recorded arrests.

Finally, I consider as an additional indicator of offense seriousness the publicity JOs received at the time of arrest. Arrested JOs are not protected by the juvenile court's traditional requirement of confidentiality. I expect the presence of publicity compounds the perceived severity of offenses, and consequently affects the prosecutor's initial decision to charge juveniles as adults. Media attention is measured by whether the name of arrested JOs appeared in one of the two daily newspapers that existed at the time of the arrest (0 = no; 1 = yes).

JO Characteristics

More than three quarters of arrested JOs were non-White and 85% were from single-parent households; 54% of non-White JOs were referred to the grand jury compared to 38% of Whites; 59% of JOs from single-parent households were referred to the grand jury compared to 27% of JOs from double-parent households.

The bivariate relationships between grand jury referral and indicators of seriousness were in the expected direction. The more serious the injuries to the victim, the more likely it is that JO cases were referred to the grand jury. All four juveniles arrested for murder were referred to the grand jury. Among JOs charged with serious injuries against their victims, 71% were referred to the grand jury, compared to 41% of JOs arrested for minor injuries or no injuries to their victims. Similarly, 56% of JOs with a prior offense were referred to the grand jury compared to 45% without a prior felony arrest. Surprisingly, media attention appears to have had little impact on the decision to bring a JO case forward to the grand jury; 63% of publicized JO arrests were referred compared to 58% of nonpublicized arrests.

Multivariate Analysis of Grand Jury Certification

To determine the predictors of the prosecutor's referral of juveniles to the grand jury, a logistic regression was estimated. . . . [T]here was an inverse relationship between the number of parents a JO resided with and the JO's probability of being referred to the grand jury. Juveniles from single-parent homes were more often referred to the grand jury than juveniles from households living with both parents. In contrast to parental marital status, race had no significant effect on the charging process for arrested JOs.

The only offense-related variable that is significant was the extent of injuries. But the possible effects of prior felony arrest and media coverage were not significant. When the four JO cases involving homicide were excluded from the analysis, the effect of offense seriousness was no longer significant. The only statistically significant predictor of grand jury referral for nonhomicide cases was the number of parents in the JO's household. In homicide cases, the number of parents with which JOs resided had no effect on their referral to the grand jury.

CONCLUSION AND IMPLICATIONS

Based on the initial processing of juveniles arrested for serious offenses, the data analysis for this upstate New York city seems to lend partial support to the argument of legislative waiver critics. Nonoffense-related considerations were not eliminated by legislative or automatic forms of waiver. Rather, legislative waiver seems to have duplicated the discretionary decisions of juvenile justice officials with those of criminal justice officials. In these data, the number of parents with which arrested JOs live, a nonoffense-related, substantive determinant of legal discretion, was significantly related to the prosecutor's referral to the grand jury.

Thus these findings support Matza's insight on the effect of parental support on legal decision making, but with a population of juveniles in the adult criminal justice system. In other recent research by Mark Jacobs, parental marital status was also found to be an important predictor of last-resort dispositions but in a contemporary juvenile court. In a multivariate analysis of juvenile court dispositions, Jacobs concludes that

> children from nontraditional families and children living apart from their parents are at risk of out-of-home placement entirely out of proportion to the risk of recidivism they pose. There may be compelling organizational and institutional reasons for this sort of treatment, but they are not correctional in nature. (p. 216)

The results of this analysis similarly suggest that organizational and institutional interests in substantive justice follow juveniles into the criminal justice system. Despite legislative attempts to accomplish the reverse by getting tough on juvenile crime, substantive justice reemerges in the decision making of criminal justice officials. The effect of parental support on the waiver of juveniles suggests support for Zimring's argument that legislative waiver shifts substantive sources of legal discretion from juvenile justice officials to criminal justice officials.

There are other unmeasured substantive factors influencing legal decision making that were not coded here that might also relate to prosecutorial decision making in waiver decisions. Interviews with prosecutors reveal that they routinely call school officials to ask about the arrested JO's school-related behavior. Similarly, a criminal court judge related that older-looking juveniles are more often waived into criminal court. Also, several variables might have been more precisely measured. The effects of media coverage might have been significant if the amount of newspaper coverage rather than just mention of the arrested JO's name was coded. Similarly, the type of legal representation might have been related to parental support in that JOs from dual-parent households might be better able to afford a private attorney.

Future research on the criminal justice processing of juveniles needs also to consider the context in which case processing decisions are made. In contrast to Buffalo, the effects of substantive justice or parental support may be of less significance in New York City where specialized offense bureaus exist to handle a much larger number of juvenile-designated felony arrests. Decisions in large urban areas may be more routinized, and, therefore, the effects of offense-related variables in the charging process may be of greater significance.

In support of legislative waiver, it should be noted that all juveniles referred to the grand jury were charged with serious violent offenses. With legislative forms of waiver, a criminal court conviction is only possible for those juveniles charged with designated felony offenses. As previously mentioned, the national survey by Hamparian et al. reveals that nearly all reported waivers in states with legislative waiver were for violent offenses. Legislative waiver precludes the possibility that juveniles will be sentenced in criminal court for less than violent offenses.

Still, in New York only a minority of juveniles arrested for violent offenses as JOs are charged as adults. By examining decision making early in the criminal justice process, I uncovered areas of official discretion that would not appear as statistically significant at later stages in the criminal justice process. Use of a more homogeneous group of indicted JOs would mask any difference in nonoffense-related effects in the initial criminal justice decision-making process. Although waiver reforms produced diverging legal avenues in which juveniles can enter the criminal court, the results of this analysis suggest that the roads to criminal court quickly merge whether they begin in systems of juvenile or criminal justice.

C. PROSECUTORIAL WAIVER

Prosecutorial Waiver: Case Study of a Questionable Reform

DONNA M. BISHOP
CHARLES E. FRAZIER
JOHN C. HENRETTA

In the last two decades, the transfer of juvenile offenders to criminal courts has become increasingly controversial. Highly publicized negative appraisals of correctional treatment programs have challenged the rehabilitative ideal

From Donna M. Bishop, Charles E. Frazier, and John C. Henretta, in *Crime & Delinquency*, Vol. 35, pp. 179–198 (1989), copyright © 1989 by Donna M. Bishop, Charles E. Frazier, and John C. Henretta. Reprinted by permission of Sage Publications, Inc.

n which the juvenile justice system is based and provoked strong pleas for punitive response to youthful misbehavior. Confidence in rehabilitation nd, concomitantly, in the juvenile court, has been undermined further by ramatic increases in juvenile crime in the 1970s. One of the signs of mount-1g disillusionment with rehabilitation is the transfer of young offenders to riminal courts for prosecution and punishment. Over the period 1971–1981 ransfers increased nationally from less than 1% to more than 5% of juve-ile arrests.

The transformation from juvenile to adult status has serious conse-uences for affected youths. The status of "juvenile" carries with it a shield rom publicity and protection against extended pretrial detention and post-onviction incarceration with adults. In addition, it provides protection gainst loss of civil rights, against disqualification for public employment, nd against the personal status degradation and restriction of legitimate op-ortunities that often follow a criminal conviction. Feld has summarized suc-inctly what is at stake with his observation that, compared to youths rocessed in the juvenile justice system, youths treated as adults have a reatly reduced probability of surviving adolescence with their life chances ntact.

Historically, the transfer of juveniles to criminal court has been accom-lished most commonly by judicial waiver. The practice of judicial waiver as reviewed by the United States Supreme Court in *Kent v. United States*. n that decision, the Court characterized waiver as "critically important" nd mandated a number of procedural safeguards to protect the interests of he child—the right to a hearing that meets the essentials of due process nd fair treatment, representation by counsel, access to information consid-red in reaching the waiver decision, and a statement of reasons for the vaiver. Although *Kent* was decided on procedural grounds, the Court also numerated several substantive criteria to guide judges in making transfer ecisions. Many states have incorporated these criteria into their juvenile odes either *verbatim* or with minor modifications. These standards reduce he likelihood of arbitrary dispositions and ensure some degree of equi-ability to the transfer process. When a state seeks to transfer a youth to riminal court via judicial waiver, it bears the substantial burden of mar-halling evidence sufficient to convince a presumably treatment-oriented ju-enile court judge that a youth poses a serious danger to the community and s not amenable to treatment within the juvenile justice system.

In keeping with today's growing trend toward punitive responses to lelinquency, many jurisdictions recently have taken steps to facilitate the rosecution of youths in criminal courts. Three streamlined methods of trans-er are now in use that bypass the uncertainties and inconveniences of the vaiver hearing in juvenile court. One method involves the exclusion by tatute of certain categories of offenses—most often, capital offenses and najor felonies—from juvenile court jurisdiction. Another method provides or grand jury indictment of juveniles charged with certain major felonies. Under either of these alternatives, youths charged with any of the enumerated offenses are automatically tried as adults. The third and most controversial transfer mechanism consists of prosecutorial waiver or "direct file" statutes. This method, which has been adopted in at least 13 states, delegates to prosecutors the nonappealable discretion to file charges in either juvenile or criminal court. While some prosecutorial waiver statutes include clear and restrictive criteria for their application, others provide only vague guidelines.

Not surprisingly, prosecutorial waiver statutes have been the object of sharp criticism. First, there is fear that provisions allowing quick and easy transfer will be abused. For example, Mylniec charges that "the speed with which [transfer] decisions are often made in the prosecutor's office, the absence of standards, and the potential for conscious abuse or negligent misapplication of the statute result in decision making that is fraught with the dangers of arbitrariness." Second, there is concern that youths who might respond to therapeutic interventions or simply "mature out" of juvenile misconduct may be prosecuted in criminal courts and confined with adults under circumstances that may have decidedly negative effects on young offenders. Third, prosecutorial waiver statutes greatly expand the power of prosecutors who historically have been more concerned with retribution than with rehabilitation. Consequently, widespread use of prosecutorial waiver signals a fundamental shift in delinquency policy away from the *parens patriae* philosophy that is the cornerstone of the juvenile court and toward a retributive orientation characteristic of criminal courts. In a real sense, then, prosecutorial waiver threatens the very existence of a separate justice system for juveniles.

This article is a case study of prosecutorial waiver in Florida. Florida enacted limited prosecutorial waiver legislation in 1979 and amended it in 1981 to grant prosecutors almost unlimited discretion in deciding which 16- and 17-year-olds should be denied juvenile status. In addition to providing for judicial waiver and grand jury indictment of certain juvenile offenders, the Florida Juvenile Justice Act permits the prosecutor to file a bill of information in criminal court on any child 14 years of age or older who has previously been adjudicated delinquent for one of several violent felonies and who is currently charged with a subsequent such offense, and on any 16- and 17-year-old charged with any violation of Florida law "when in his judgment and discretion, the public interest requires that adult sanctions be considered or imposed" (Florida Statutes Annotated Chapter 39.04(2)(e)(4)). Remand from criminal court to juvenile court is possible upon request of the child only if he or she is charged with a misdemeanor and does not have two prior delinquency adjudications, one of which involved a felony.

In sum, the prosecutor has the power to transfer any 16- or 17-year-old charged with any felony. Any 16- or 17-year-old charged with a misdemeanor or even a local ordinance violation may also be charged as an adult if he or she has had two prior adjudications of delinquency, one of which involved a felony. This extremely broad discretionary power is carried out without a hearing, without any statement of reasons, without counsel, and without any proof that the youth is either dangerous or nonamenable to treatment within the juvenile justice system. "The ease with which jurisdiction over juveniles in this state may be moved from a juvenile to an adult court constitutes a fundamental and direct challenge to the most central precepts that distinguish these very different types of courts."

While there have been several studies of waiver of jurisdiction by the juvenile court, only one prior empirical study has focused on prosecutorial waiver. Thomas and Bilchik conducted an analysis of cases filed in 1981 in Dade County, Florida. The present study relies on broader and more recent individual-level case data as well as interview data to explore further this relatively new and not yet well understood trend in juvenile justice.

Our study is divided into three parts. In the first part, records of juveniles transferred to criminal court statewide for the period 1979–1987 are reviewed. These data provide a basis for exploring the impact of changes in the law on trends in transfer rates and practices. Second, we report the results of interviews conducted with prosecutors in the juvenile divisions of each of the state's twenty judicial circuits. Finally, we examine individual-level case data for a three-year period in two large counties and describe the characteristics of transferred youths and the dispositions of their cases.

TRANSFERS IN FLORIDA, 1979–1987

Table 1 provides data on transfer trends in Florida over a nine-year period that spans the 1981 expansion of Florida's direct file provisions. Prior to this change, only a small proportion (1%–3%) of delinquency filings were transferred to criminal court. The rate of transfer increased dramatically in 1982, when nearly 9% of the court's caseload was channeled to criminal court. Since

TABLE 1
Transfers in Florida, 1979–1987

Year	Total delinquency filings	Number transferred	Percentage transferred	Percentage of transfers direct filed
1979	66,504	860	1.29	48
1980	42,797	1198	2.80	54
1981	48,105	1360	2.83	61
1982	41,088	3637	8.85	68
1983	38,398	3067	7.99	77
1984	41,492	2209	5.32	78
1985	46,599	2615	5.61	85
1986	50,289	3224	6.41	88
1987	57,298	4214	7.35	88

that time, smaller but nonetheless substantial proportions of delinquency filings have been turned over to the criminal courts.

Much of the increase in the transfer rate is no doubt attributable to the changes in Florida law that expanded prosecutorial transfer powers. During the period 1979–1981, when prosecutors' direct file powers were more limited, 54% of transfers were direct files. The remainder of the transfers involved judicial waivers (39%) and indictments (7%). In 1982, however, direct files increased sharply to 68% of all transfers. In each successive year, direct files constituted an increasingly greater proportion of transfer cases. In 1987, nearly 90% of transfers in the state were made through direct file. Proportionate declines in both indictments and judicial waivers occurred over this time period, with the decline in judicial waivers being most striking—down to 11% in 1987.

It is important to note that transfer of cases from juvenile to criminal court does not seem to be related to juvenile court caseload pressures. As can be seen in Table 1, delinquency filings declined between 1979 and 1982, while transfers increased substantially. Between 1983 and 1987, delinquency filings increased steadily, while transfers fluctuated.

INTERVIEWS WITH JUVENILE PROSECUTORS

Studies of the effects of legal change are too often limited to examinations of changes in aggregate rates such as those reported above. While such data are both necessary and critical to any sophisticated impact assessment, they leave several very important questions unaddressed. For example, how do key juvenile justice officials (in this instance, prosecutors) interpret the change in the law? What are their views regarding its utility and appropriateness? How do their interpretations of the change in the law relate to their personal philosophies of and orientations toward juvenile justice? Did the change in the law have any impact on their perceived ability to achieve valid and desirable goals? What effects do they believe the change in the law had on their actual practices? In sum, aggregate data do not tell us enough about either the relationship between changes in law and changes in practice or about the reasons behind changes in practice.

Some insight into these issues may be gained through analyses of telephone interviews with juvenile prosecutors in each of the state's twenty judicial circuits. The individuals interviewed were either the chiefs of juvenile divisions or they were in substantial ways responsible for developing and implementing prosecutorial policy relating to juvenile transfer. In a number of cases, the researchers were already acquainted with the interviewees and their colleagues, and had previously discussed with them informally many issues relating to juvenile transfer.

It is clear that prosecutors generally were pleased with the 1981 change in transfer provisions, primarily because it expanded their discretion. Some felt that the law should have gone even further. For example, while virtually all of the respondents indicated in closed-ended responses that the changed transfer provisions were "adequate," half indicated in open-ended responses that the law should have been more far reaching. Most of this latter group wished that the law had made it easier to transfer juveniles under 16 years of age. A smaller number thought that 16–17-year-old misdemeanants lacking prior felony adjudications should also have been made eligible for direct filing. One prosecutor expressed the opinion that there should be no age or offense restrictions whatsoever on who could be transferred.

Equally interesting were the views of those who did not feel that further expansion of the law was desirable. Approximately half of the respondents expressed concern that provisions of the current law have considerable potential for abuse. They worried that persons less ethical than themselves—or those who were sometimes overzealous in seeking harsh punishments for juvenile offenders—would use the direct file provisions inappropriately. Such concerns seemed to be tied to the perception that most prosecutors decide which cases to transfer without clear standards to guide them. Indeed, our interviews indicated that this fear was not without foundation.

Most prosecutors had not, in fact, established any formal policies. With one clear exception, juvenile division chiefs at best reported having established informal policies that called for them to review all transfers initiated by attorneys under their supervision. They thought this review process sufficient to ensure that staff members initiated prosecutorial waiver only in appropriate cases. However, several of these same division chiefs expressed considerable doubt that their counterparts in other circuits were as careful as they in overseeing staff. Not only was it a common perception among prosecutors that operations in other circuits were not managed as well as their own, but it was also common for prosecutors to suggest that levels of care and standards used by others in the exercise of discretion were too low. There is reason to believe that prosecutors' reservations about practices outside their own jurisdictions were not without foundation: Prosecutors in the state have fairly frequent exchanges and develop a broad familiarity with each others' operations.

Our interviews also provided a basis for examining the relationship between prosecutors' perceptions of the expanded direct file provisions and their personal orientations toward juvenile justice. At the end of each interview, we asked semi-fixed response and open-ended questions designed to determine what goals prosecutors hoped to achieve in transferring juveniles to criminal court and what philosophies of juvenile justice they held. These questions obviously tapped an area of considerable interest to our respondents in that most of them took care to think through their answers, some responding for more than a half hour.

Prosecutors' philosophies of juvenile justice varied widely. Not too surprisingly, however, their orientations tended to resemble models that are currently the source of considerable nationwide debate by policymakers.

Their philosophies may be categorized as falling under a "pure"just deserts model, a "modified" just deserts model (i.e., one that ties together just deserts with some utilitarian goal such as deterrence), and a traditional rehabilitative model of juvenile justice.

Prosecutors holding the pure just deserts viewpoint argued that some measure of punishment is necessary in virtually all juvenile cases and that transfer of jurisdiction, at the very least, assures the achievement of this goal. They believed that traditional juvenile justice responses, as routinely applied, had no beneficial effects. In fact, they tended to believe that juveniles were made worse by the juvenile system's tendency toward leniency. Prosecutors in this group made no mention of utilitarian goals such as the desire to protect the community through incapacitation or deterrence. They did not insist on or express any interest in whether juveniles were incarcerated as a part of an adult disposition, nor did they expect punishment to lead to reform. Their attraction to the expansion of direct file provisions was simply that it provided a convenient mechanism through which they could move juveniles from a system where real punishment was not possible to a system that had punishment as a primary goal.

The second group of just deserts prosecutors held just as strongly as the first to the view that punishment was essential. Unlike the first group, however, they saw punishment as a means to protect the community and deter future crimes. Some deterrence potential was attributed to transferring a juvenile case even if a conviction was not achieved. Filing an information in criminal court virtually assured lengthy pretrial detention in adult jails for the vast majority of transfers At the least, these prosecutors claimed, transfer "sent a message" to youths that they risked very serious adult punishments. Further, if youths were ultimately convicted, transfer opened the possibility of incarceration in jails and prisons. Unlike the pure just deserts advocates described above, this group of prosecutors held out some hope that punishment would have beneficial deterrent and incapacitative effects.

Both the pure and the modified just deserts types espoused viewpoints that are completely antithetical to the basic precepts underlying juvenile justice. In our interviews many of these prosecutors expressed contempt for the juvenile justice system, most especially for the social service personnel who staff the majority of juvenile justice positions (e.g., intake workers, detention staff, probation officers, training school personnel). These punishment-oriented prosecutors, who make up nearly half of our respondents, and who are charged with representing the state's interest in delinquency cases, constitute a continuing challenge to those who defend the traditional juvenile justice system.

The third philosophy, one held by a slight majority of respondents, endorsed completely the traditional principles of juvenile justice. It was this group's view that Florida's direct file provisions should be used only as a last resort. Transfer to adult court jurisdiction was considered appropriate only in the rarest cases, reserved for offenders who had already failed to benefit and could not now benefit from the alternatives available in the juvenile justice system. Once prosecutors in this group defined transfer as necessary, they hoped for rehabilitation, but most worried that simple punishment and incapacitation were all that were certain in the adult system.

Policymakers would like to believe that a prosecutor's opinions about juvenile crime and transfer of jurisdiction would provide some basis for predicting actual practice. However, we found that prosecutors' philosophies and their perceptions of their own practices tend to be almost totally unrelated. Indeed, those prosecutors holding a "pure" or a "modified" just deserts philosophy implied that they would use the direct file option often, in a high proportion of the eligible cases. In fact, however, if we use their own estimates of the proportion of eligible cases in which the direct file option is actually exercised, these prosecutors generally were no more inclined to use direct file than those who adhered to a "last resort" stance. Even though half the prosecutors believed that juveniles should be transferred only as a last resort, many of them reported transferring as high a proportion of cases as those prosecutors holding to a more punitive stance. Virtually every prosecutor, regardless of orientation toward juvenile justice, reported having increased the use of transfer following the 1981 change in the law.

While it may seem paradoxical that the "last resort" prosecutors transferred as many juvenile offenders as more punitive types, this result makes sense when one understands that many rehabilitation-oriented prosecutors believed that they must turn to transfer sooner than they would like. They pointed out that some liberal juvenile justice reforms—for example, deinstitutionalization—have had the unintended consequence of reducing rehabilitative options in the juvenile justice system, thus making transfer more likely. Like many other states, Florida recently has closed several training schools and, because of this, many prosecutors observed that there is a real need for alternative residential treatment programs for juvenile offenders. They feared that increased use of transfer might be mistakenly interpreted as rejection of a rehabilitative philosophy, when in fact transfer would be much less desirable were treatment programs available in secure juvenile facilities. They were keenly aware that Florida's expanded direct file provisions had shifted the spotlight of attention away from those who adhered to traditional precepts of juvenile justice and toward those with more punitive orientations.

In sum, our interviews revealed clearly delineated general philosophies of juvenile justice held by juvenile division prosecutors in Florida. Regardless of philosophy, however, almost all prosecutors approved of the additional discretionary power brought about by the 1981 change in the law. Moreover, while we found evidence of three distinct philosophies among the prosecutors whom we interviewed, no respondents perceived a conflict between their application of Florida's transfer provisions and their orientations toward juvenile justice. Indeed, each group reported using transfer more frequently once the law was changed to make it easier to do so.

When we asked prosecutors to indicate the criteria they used in deciding which cases to file in criminal court, we were surprised to find that they tended to stress the same considerations, regardless of their philosophies of juvenile justice. All reported that they placed heavy emphasis on the seriousness of the offense—particularly whether a felony against persons was involved—and the juvenile's prior adjudications of delinquency. In addition, and consistent with their philosophy, prosecutors who viewed transfer as a last resort indicated that an important consideration for them was whether the youth had previously been committed to a residential facility.

A large number of other factors were also mentioned. For example, many indicated that age was an important factor in the transfer decision, independent of offense seriousness or prior record. Because juvenile court jurisdiction in Florida terminates when youths reach age 19, many prosecutors were inclined to transfer youths who committed offenses shortly before their 18th birthdays. In such cases, they felt that the juvenile system could accomplish little in the time remaining between disposition and loss of jurisdiction.

Somewhat surprisingly, only one respondent indicated that the recommendation of the state's Department of Health and Rehabilitative Services was routinely considered in making the filing determination. Others indicated that when a decision had been made to transfer a juvenile based on offense and prior record considerations, his or her accomplices might also be transferred primarily because of concern for equitable treatment. Still others reported that the presence of an adult codefendant made transfer more likely because it suggested criminal sophistication of the juvenile offender.

Equally interesting were some of the reasons given for not transferring a case, or for terminating processing after a transfer had been initiated. Some prosecutors mentioned that they were unlikely to transfer juveniles who were "boyish" or youthful in appearance, for fear that they would be acquitted by sympathetic criminal court juries. Several indicated that transfers, once initiated, were withdrawn in exchange for guilty pleas in juvenile court. Many defended this practice of using the threat of transfer as a plea negotiation tactic.

TRANSFER PRACTICES IN TWO COUNTIES

In this section, the implementation of expanded prosecutorial waiver provisions is examined with individual-level case data from two Florida counties. Information was drawn from prosecutors' files and clerks of court's records in two Florida counties, as well as data provided by the Florida Department of Health and Rehabilitative Services (DHRS). In each county, we began with prosecutors' records of cases in which a transfer to criminal court was initiated by the juvenile division. Clerks' records were then checked for case processing information. Prosecutors' and clerks' records included information regarding sociodemographic characteristics of juveniles transferred, charges filed in criminal court, criminal court adjudication, and sentence. From DHRS' statewide computerized data base, information was obtained on the previous offenses for which each youth had been referred to the juvenile justice system, as well as the disposition of each prior referral.

The two counties from which the data were collected include a midsized urban area in the mid-Atlantic region and a large urban area in the center of the state. The two sites were selected in part because the juvenile division chiefs in each area had held their positions since the first prosecutorial waiver legislation was passed and had maintained a careful log containing information on all cases in which transfer to criminal court had been initiated. In both counties, we examined all cases in which direct file proceedings were initiated by juvenile division state attorneys during the period beginning January 1,1981, and ending December 31, 1984. Although we anticipated that practices and outcomes in the two counties might be sufficiently different to warrant separate presentation of findings, they were so similar that, for most purposes, we have combined the data to simplify the presentation. The total number of cases is 583 (198 from the smaller county, 385 from the other).

Processing of Transfer Cases by Criminal Division Attorneys

If transfer is based on the desire to protect the public from dangerous youths and to deliver harsh sanctions to intractable offenders, we would expect official actions commensurate with these goals. An initial question, then, is whether cases in which transfer was sought by juvenile division attorneys were actually adjudicated in criminal count. Criminal prosecutors may evaluate cases very differently from juvenile prosecutors. For example, criminal division attorneys may view cases of transferred juveniles as relatively minor, either because they involve "first offenders" or because their offenses are less serious than those of adult offenders whose cases they routinely review. Thus substantial numbers of transfer cases may "fall through the cracks," acted upon in neither juvenile nor criminal court.

In the smaller of the two counties, almost a third (32%) of the cases in which transfer was initiated by the juvenile division were not prosecuted in criminal court. In half of these, the criminal division prosecutor took no action in the case after it had been forwarded by the juvenile division. In the remainder, the criminal division prosecutor initially filed a bill of information but later terminated processing through a nolle prosequi. While some of these cases may have come back to the juvenile division for filing at a later date, our interview data suggest that the vast majority were not prosecuted in either court and consequently received neither treatment nor punishment for their alleged offenses.

In contrast, only 14% of the cases transferred in the larger county were not prosecuted in criminal court. This level of case attrition is quite low, especially when one considers the variety of factors that may come into play in decisions not to prosecute (e.g., insufficiency of the evidence, lack of victim cooperation, inability to locate witnesses, exchange of immunity from prosecution in return for testimony in cases involving codefendants).

The difference in the criminal court handling of juveniles in the two counties is largely attributable to differences in bureaucratic practices, rather than to differences in the seriousness or perceived prosecutorial merit of transfer cases. In the smaller county, juvenile division prosecutors screened cases for transfer and forwarded them to the criminal division with a recommendation for criminal prosecution. Criminal division attorneys then decided whether to accept the juvenile division's recommendation. In many cases, the criminal division did not act in a timely fashion and the case was lost for violation of speedy trial rules. By contrast, in the larger county, the juvenile division chief personally filed bills of information. The transfer took place unless a criminal division attorney directly intervened to stop it. Thus juvenile offenders in the two counties were at different levels of risk for criminal prosecution largely because of the different ways the two prosecutors' offices were organized.

Characteristics of Cases Filed in Criminal Court

We turn now to an examination of the characteristics of cases filed in criminal court. Nearly all (93%) of the transferred youths were male, and a majority (63%) were white, somewhat less than the proportion white in the juvenile population in the two counties. A majority (60%) of the youths transferred were 17 at the time of their offenses, many of them very close to their 18th birthdays. A smaller number (37%) were 16, and only 3% were under 16.

The most common rationale surrounding transfer of juveniles anticipates that youths remanded to criminal court are a particularly intractable group of dangerous offenders who cannot benefit from further juvenile justice intervention. In addition, because the primary purpose of prosecutorial waiver provisions is to protect the public, and because lengthy incarceration appears to be the only criminal justice disposition not available within the juvenile justice system, one would expect the vast majority of transferred youths to be sentenced to lengthy terms of incarceration. The reality of the situation differs considerably from these expectations. We consider these issues here because they are central concerns both of most policymakers endorsing Florida's direct file provisions and of most of the law's critics as well.

Advocates of transfer assume that the selection process identifies youthful offenders who are dangerous. Indeed, in both counties studied, the chief prosecutors assured us that this was the case. However, if the criterion of dangerousness used is the commission of a violent felony, our findings show that only 29% of the juveniles transferred via prosecutorial waiver met this standard. Most (55%), in fact, were charged with property felonies. Half of these property felony cases involved grand theft (commonly, auto theft) and the remainder involved unarmed burglaries of automobiles and unoccupied dwellings. A small proportion (11%) involved felony drug charges and a few transferred juveniles (5%) were charged with misdemeanors.

Moreover, the trend over the years has been to transfer increasingly greater proportions of nonviolent offenders and misdemeanants. For example, in 1981, 7% of youths transferred were charged with felony drug offenses and 2% were charged with misdemeanors. By 1984, these proportions had more than doubled, to 15% and 7%, respectively. The proportion of felony property offenders remained relatively stable, while felony person offenders declined substantially. In 1981, 32% of transferred youths were charged with felonies against persons, compared to 20% in 1984. Based on the offense charged, few of the juveniles transferred to criminal court via prosecutorial waiver would seem to be the kinds of dangerous offenders for whom transfer is most easily justified.

To explore the question of whether transferred youths are intractable and not amenable to treatment in the juvenile justice system, we first ask whether the juvenile justice system has been given an opportunity to exhaust the resources available to it prior to prosecutorial waiver. Second, we examine the offense histories of transferred youths to look for evidence of chronic offending.

Whether the juvenile justice system has exhausted its resources is best measured by whether a youth has been committed to a residential facility (e.g., training school). Once this sort of institutionalization has failed, a reasonable argument may be made that transfer to criminal court is appropriate. Only 35% of transferred youths previously had been committed to a residential facility. Most youths (58%) previously had been placed on probation or had received court-ordered sanctions such as restitution or community work service. In 23% of the cases, youths were transferred for a first offense without the benefit of any juvenile justice treatment programming. In the vast majority of the cases, then, the full range of dispositional alternatives available to the juvenile court had not been exhausted prior to transfer.

However, the data do indicate a trend toward greater selectivity. In 1981, for example, 29% of transferred youths had been previously committed, compared to 49% in 1984.

With regard to chronicity of offending, we have already noted that 23% of the youths transferred were first offenders. Slightly more than a third (34%) had one or two prior referrals. Less than half (41%) had three or more prior referrals.

We noted above that there has been a shift in recent years toward transferring youths charged with less serious offenses. There has also been a trend toward transferring youths with longer records of offending. For example, in 1981, 27% of youths transferred had three or more priors. In 1984, 60% of youths transferred had three or more priors. The offenses of transferred youths have not become more serious—fewer than 20% had records of felony person offenses. However, their prior records suggest that they were a more intractable group than was the case in the early years of direct file.

In sum, our findings from analyses of practices in two counties show that, in the period immediately following the change in Florida's direct file provisions, transferred youths generally were not unequivocally dangerous. While most were charged with felonies, only a small proportion were charged with violent offenses against persons. In addition, there is little evidence that they were intractable: Nearly one-fourth had no prior record and very few had multiple prior offenses. More recently, prosecutors have transferred greater numbers of youths charged with lesser offenses, that is, possessory drug felonies and misdemeanors. At the same time, however, they appear to be selecting youths whose records include signs of intractability.

Criminal Court Disposition of Transfer Cases

A high proportion (96%) of transferred youths were convicted in criminal court. Nevertheless, transfer did not ensure severe sanctions for the vast majority of offenders. While some postconviction incarceration occurred in 61% of the cases, nearly half of these involved jail sentences of short duration. Prison sentences were ordered in only 31% of the cases. Of those receiving prison terms, 54% were sentenced to 1–3 years, 31% received 4–6-year sentences, and 15% received 7 or more years. It should also be noted that Florida law includes very generous gain time provisions. Once these are applied, sentences actually served are substantially shorter than those ordered.

Moreover, as might be expected from transfer trends mentioned earlier, the rate of incarceration has declined in successive years as transfer charges have become less serious. For example, 81% of those convicted in 1981 were sentenced to terms of incarceration, compared to only 51% of those convicted in 1984.

DISCUSSION AND CONCLUSIONS

Direct file provisions in Florida law afford prosecutors extraordinary power to transfer 16- and 17-year-old youths to criminal court. The law provides no guidance for the exercise of discretion other than to direct prosecutors to transfer cases "when the public interest requires it." Given the scope of the authority they are given and the lack of clear standards or guidelines, Florida prosecutors are in a position to alter fundamentally the juvenile justice system. As other states move in the direction of instituting direct file provisions, understanding the trends in and relationships among events in Florida may serve better to inform their decisions. All those concerned with juvenile justice policy and reform efforts should be interested in both our general and specific findings. At the general level, our analyses indicate that the cases in which the direct file provisions have been utilized are seldom the serious and chronic offenders for whom transfer is arguably justified. An important specific point for discussion is why it is that so few of those eligible are transferred, at the same time that so many of those who are transferred seem inappropriate.

Our interviews suggest several reasons for the restraint shown by prosecutors in the application of Florida's direct file provisions. First, a small majority of prosecutors held firmly to the traditional philosophy underlying the juvenile justice system. That is, they were inclined to exhaust the resources of the juvenile justice system completely before considering transfer to criminal court. Even then, they invoked the direct file power as an undesirable last resort, having little confidence that anything "good" would come of the transfer. It is interesting that so many prosecutors in juvenile divisions accepted so completely precepts of juvenile justice favoring rehabilitation, especially when it is recognized that there is little institutional support for such viewpoints among prosecutorial workgroups. For example, several rehabilitation-oriented respondents indicated that they are viewed in pejorative terms by their associates (i.e., as the "soft on crime, social worker types"). A few even indicated that they believed their prospects for promotion and enhancement in the office were impaired by their views.

In the first year following the broadening of direct file provisions, sharp increases in juvenile transfers occurred. Following that first year, however, a number of internal and external factors appeared to persuade prosecutors to exercise greater restraint. One immediate pressure occurred following the initial increases in the use of transfer when prominent and vocal members of the Florida judiciary openly attacked what they considered excessively large numbers of transfers. These officials were successful in bringing statewide attention to the direct file issue, a by-product of which was the appointment by the governor of a special adviser on juvenile justice who was a widely recognized critic of Florida's new direct file provisions. In addition, at least three other agencies of government officially identified direct file as a critical issue and organized lobbying efforts aimed at revising the law to reduce prosecutorial discretion. In the face of this public attention, in 1983 prosecutors began reducing the proportions of cases transferred.

In some regions of the state, intraorganizational pressures also played a part in inducing prosecutors to select transfer eases more carefully. In many jurisdictions, the initial reaction of juvenile division prosecutors to the expanded direct file provisions greatly increased the workload of criminal division prosecutors. There was nothing in the revision of the Juvenile Justice Act that anticipated substantial shifts in caseload pressures, so staff resources in criminal divisions tended to remain stable. Some juvenile division prosecutors reported responding to accusations from their counterparts in criminal divisions that they were "dumping" their caseloads into the adult system.

Still other factors may account for (1) the reductions in transfer rates between 1983 and 1984, (2) the slow but steady increase in transfer rates since that time, and (3) the recent primacy of offenders' prior records in selecting cases for transfer. Perhaps most important is the implementation of sentencing guidelines, which became effective in 1983. The guidelines made it unlikely that offenders without extensive and serious prior records would receive prison sentences. Consequently, transfer became a less desirable option, especially for first- and second-time offenders. The institution of sentencing guidelines was, for some prosecutors, the occasion to consider and develop a calculus designed to optimize the timing of transfer. Acting on their perception that it is easier to obtain convictions in juvenile than in adult court, prosecutors began to delay transfer to accumulate points in juvenile court that could later be applied for criminal sentencing purposes." After a lag time to allow offenders to accrue convictions in juvenile court—in the words of one prosecutor, "giving them enough rope to hang themselves"—transfers to criminal court have recently begun to accelerate toward 1982 levels.

Despite the restraint exercised by prosecutors, another important finding of this study is that many prosecutorial waiver cases are inappropriate when evaluated in terms of the traditional justifications for transfer of jurisdiction. In the two counties studied, fewer than 20% of youths transferred were charged with felonies against persons. Moreover, of those charged with other offenses, the trend was toward transfer of juveniles charged with less serious felonies and misdemeanors. We did find a trend toward transfer of youth with lengthier histories of offending and with prior commitments to juvenile institutions. However, in the most recent year examined, a substantial proportion of transferred youths had fewer than three prior offenses and fewer than half had previously received the most severe disposition available in the juvenile justice system.

We also found that many 17-year-old juveniles who had neither committed serious felonies nor accrued lengthy prior records were transferred. The chief reason appeared to be that they were nearing their 18th birthdays. This reason would not likely be considered a valid basis for concluding that the protections traditionally afforded juveniles should be denied or that the public interest requires transfer. It is clear in these cases that prosecutors were exploiting the lack of guidelines in the direct file provisions and, in effect, rewriting the law that sets the upper age limits of juvenile court jurisdiction.

Our analyses suggest several reasons for the fact that so many arguably inappropriate cases are direct filed. First, Florida's Juvenile Justice Act mandates that juveniles charged with capital and life felonies be transferred to criminal court via grand jury indictment. Consequently, in selecting cases for direct file, prosecutors of necessity choose from a pool of eligibles from which the most dangerous and violent offenders have already been excluded.

Second, when the law changed in 1981, some prosecutors felt that they had been given a mandate to transfer larger proportions of delinquency cases to criminal court. Prior to 1981, prosecutorial discretion over the transfer of 16- and 17-year-olds was carefully circumscribed by offense and prior record restrictions. The removal of these restrictions may have led many prosecutors to conclude that the legislature's intent was that they transfer less serious offenders.

Third, the closure of training schools and other secure juvenile facilities in Florida has contributed to increased rates of transfer. Even prosecutors who favor rehabilitation and who are in principle reluctant to utilize the direct file option find that they must do so because of the lack of treatment resources.

Finally, the ease with which prosecutorial waiver can be accomplished contributes to its use. Interview data attest to this point as indicated by the many respondents who expressed uneasiness about the ways that the direct file provisions were being applied. Both the lack of statutory criteria to aid in selecting cases for direct file and prosecutors' ability to bypass judicial oversight of direct file decisions encourage less care and thoughtfulness than is desirable in the application of the law.

CHAPTER 5

Sentencing Delinquent Offenders

The Progressive reformers envisioned a broader and more encompassing system for youths than a criminal justice system that simply punished them for their offenses. As Judge Julian Mack's excerpt in Chapter 1 indicated, juvenile courts invoked the ideology of *parens patriae* and attempted to combine social welfare with penal social control in one institution. The "rehabilitative ideal" envisioned specialized judges who made therapeutic dispositions in children's "best interests." Because reformers' entertained benevolent aims and individualized their solicitude, they did not circumscribe narrowly the power of the state. To the contrary, they minimized procedural safeguards and maximized discretion to provide flexibility in diagnosis and treatment. They accorded secondary significance to proof of guilt of an offense and focused primary attention on youths' social circumstances.

Despite the juvenile court's historical discourse of "compassionate care" and "individualized treatment," the Supreme Court in *Gault* emphasized the disjunction between rehabilitative rhetoric and punitive reality. Subsequent analysts note that juvenile courts often resemble an assembly-line justice system in which judges quickly dispose of large numbers of delinquent youngsters with only a few, inadequately funded treatment options. The articles in Chapter 5 explore the disjunctions between juvenile courts' rhetoric and reality, between theory and practice. These articles raise the questions whether the sentences imposed and the facilities and programs provided to delinquents convicted of crimes differ significantly from those of adult offenders and whether intervention produces positive effects in youths' future behavior.

In the past two decades, states' sentencing laws and juvenile courts' sentencing practices toward delinquents have become increasingly more punitive. Juvenile courts' "triage" policies that divert or remove status offenders from the juvenile justice system, and waive serious younger offenders to criminal courts also allow juvenile courts to "get tough" with the remaining criminal delinquents. Perhaps ironically, *Gault's* expansion of delinquents' procedural and legal rights legitimated the imposition of more severe sanctions in juvenile courts.

For the Supreme Court in *McKeiver*, the differences between juvenile treatment and criminal punishment provided the primary rationale to deny jury trials in delinquency proceedings and to maintain a juvenile system separate from the adult system. While most people readily understand that "punishment" simply involves an involuntary and coerced loss of personal liberty or autonomy because a person committed a crime, the Supreme Court in *McKeiver* found the issue much more complicated. Justice White's concurring opinion in *McKeiver* highlighted the distinctions between "treatment" in juvenile courts and "punishment" in criminal proceedings.

> [T]he juvenile justice system rests on more deterministic assumptions [than the criminal justice system]. Reprehensible acts by juveniles are not deemed the consequence of mature and malevolent choice but of environmental pressures (or lack of them) or of other forces beyond their control. Hence the state legislative judgment not to stigmatize the juvenile delinquent by branding him a criminal; his conduct is not deemed so blameworthy that punishment is required to deter him or others. Coercive measures, where employed, are considered neither retribution nor punishment. Supervision or confinement is aimed at rehabilitation, not at convincing the juvenile of his error simply by imposing pains and penalties. Nor is the purpose to make the juvenile delinquent an object lesson for others, whatever his own merits or demerits may be. A typical disposition in the juvenile court . . . may authorize confinement until age 21, but it will last no longer and within that period will last only so long as his behavior demonstrates that he remains an unacceptable risk if returned to his family. Nor is the authorization for custody until 21 any measure of the seriousness of the particular act that the juvenile has performed (*McKeiver*, 403 U.S. at 552 (White, J. concurring).

The indeterminate and non-proportional length of juvenile dispositions and the "eschewing [of] blameworthiness and punishment for evil choices" satisfied Justice White that "there remained differences of substance between criminal and juvenile courts" (*McKeiver*, 403 U.S. at 551–52). The Court in *McKeiver* uncritically accepted the rhetoric of *parens patriae*, described juvenile justice theory rather than reality, defined punishment narrowly, and then failed to analyze either the differences between punishment and treatment or whether juvenile courts actually provided the latter. Because *McKeiver* assumed that juvenile courts afforded only positive rehabilitative treatment, it did not provide youths with criminal procedural protections against state coercion.

Part of the Court's failure to distinguish between treatment and punishment stemmed from its own lack of analytical clarity about the conceptual and practical differences between the two. Justice White's opinion, quoted above, explains the theoretical premises of rehabilitation but provides few practical indicators whether juvenile courts realize their aspirations. Perhaps the Court refrained from systematically analyzing the differences between punishment and treatment because it realized that effectively no substantial differences might exist. But, if the Court could not distinguish between these contradictory justifications, then the Constitution would force it to invalidate a staple institution of states' social control of youths. Perhaps more charitably, the Court simply had less access to information about the reality of juvenile justice administration than we do today. Courts adjudicate constitutional rights primarily in the realm of legal abstractions. Lawyers often are ill-equipped to marshal and present complex social science data and experiences in ways that make those abstractions a reality in the judicial process. The President's Crime Commission, *The Challenge of Crime in a Free Society* (1967) had only begun to reveal the practical deficiencies of the juvenile courts' treatment ideology. And, as the previous sections reveal, nearly three decades of judicial, legislative, and administrative changes have dramatically transformed the juvenile courts and correctional institution that *McKeiver* appraised. Whatever the Supreme Court thought the purposes and practices of juvenile justice were at the time of *McKeiver*, they clearly differ now.

Barry C. Feld, The Juvenile Court Meets the Principle of Offense: "Punishment, Treatment, and the Difference It Makes," provides a theoretical framework for examining juvenile court sentencing laws and practices. Feld argues that recent decades have witnessed a fundamental shift in juvenile justice policies from rehabilitation to retribution, from dispositions based on individualized assessments of characteristics of the offender to more proportional sentences based on the seriousness of the offense. The "Just Deserts" movement, which led to determinate sentences for adults, also has spilled over into the juvenile justice process as well as. The article summarizes the implications of "get tough" legislative policies on changes in juvenile sentencing laws and some of the empirical research on juvenile court sentencing practices.

The Juvenile Court Meets the Principle of Offense: Punishment, Treatment, and the Difference It Makes

BARRY C. FELD

... This article analyzes the changing sentencing practices of the juvenile court. Contemporary juvenile courts increasingly focus on the offense committed—the "Principle of Offense," rather than on the youth's "best in-

Excerpted from the *Boston University Law Review*, Volume 68:5, pp. 821–896 (1988). Reprinted with permission. © 1988 by Boston University Law Review, Boston University. Forum of original publication. Boston University bears no responsibility for any errors that may have occurred in reprinting, translation, or editing.

terests"—in their sentencing decisions. Changes in juvenile courts' "purpose clauses" to emphasize characteristics of the offense rather than the offender reflect the ascendance of the Principle of Offense. Moreover, the trend of juvenile courts to employ a "justice model," which prescribes the appropriate sentence on the basis of "just deserts" rather than "real needs," reflects a movement away from a rehabilitation-treatment based model. Recent legislative changes in juvenile sentencing statutes and correctional administrative guidelines emphasize proportional and determinate sentences based on both the present offense and prior record, and dictate the length, location, and intensity of intervention. The shift in emphasis from treatment to punishment is also illustrated in dispositional decisionmaking processes and the harsh reality of juvenile correctional confinement.

These changes serve to both indicate and advance the substantive and procedural criminalization of the juvenile court. Emphasis on punishment, rather than treatment, of delinquents raises fundamental questions about the adequacy of procedural protections in the juvenile court. Affording juveniles procedural parity with adults as a prelude to punishment, however, raises the issue of whether there is any need for a separate juvenile court system. . . .

III. THE PRINCIPLE OF OFFENSE IN JUVENILE COURT: JUST DESERTS IN SENTENCING PRACTICES

. . . The fundamental justification for denying jury trials in delinquency proceedings and, more basically, for maintaining a juvenile justice system separate from the adult one is based on the differences between punishment and treatment. Yet, part of the *McKeiver* Court's failure to distinguish between punishment and treatment in the contemporary juvenile justice system stems from a lack of analytical clarity about the conceptual differences between the two justifications for intervention. Punishment involves the imposition by the State, for purposes of retribution or deterrence, of burdens on an individual who has violated legal prohibitions. Treatment, by contrast, focuses on the mental health, status, and future welfare of the individual rather than on the commission of prohibited acts.

Conceptually, punishment and treatment are mutually exclusive penal goals. Both make markedly different assumptions about the sources of criminal or delinquent behavior. Punishment assumes that responsible, free-will moral actors make blameworthy choices and deserve to suffer the prescribed consequences for their acts. Punishment imposes unpleasant consequences because of an offender's *past offenses*. By contrast, most forms of rehabilitative treatment, including the rehabilitative ideal of the juvenile court, assume some degree of determinism. Whether grounded in psychological or sociological processes, treatment assumes that certain antecedent factors cause the individual's undesirable conditions or behavior. Treatment and therapy, therefore, seek to alleviate undesirable conditions in order to improve the offender's *future welfare*.

In analyzing juvenile court sentencing practices, it is useful to examine whether the sentencing decision is based upon considerations of the past offense or the future welfare of the offender. When a sentence is based on the characteristics of the offense, it is typically determinate and proportional, with the objective of retribution or deterrence. The decision is based upon an assessment of past conduct—the present offense and any prior criminal record. When a sentence is based upon characteristics of the offender, however, it is typically open-ended, non-proportional and indeterminate, with the goal of rehabilitation or incapacitation. The decision is based upon a diagnosis or prediction about the effects of intervention on an offender's future course of conduct.

It is also useful to distinguish the bases of such dispositions. David Matza has described the Principle of Offense as a principle of equality: an effort to treat similar cases in a similar fashion based on a relatively narrowly defined frame of relevance. Matza observes:

> The principle of equality refers to a specific set of substantive criteria that are awarded central relevance and, historically, to a set of considerations that were specifically and momentously precluded. Its meaning, especially in criminal proceedings, has been to give a central and unrivaled position in the framework of relevance to considerations of *offense* and conditions closely related to offense like prior record, and to more or less preclude considerations of status and circumstance.

By contrast, the Principle of Individualized Justice differs from the Principle of Offense in two fundamental ways. First, the Principle of Individualized Justice is much more inclusive;

> [i]t contains many more items in its framework of relevance.... The principle of individualized justice suggests that disposition is to be guided by a *full understanding* of the client's personal and social character and by his "individual needs." [Secondly, t]he consequence of the principle of individualized justice has been mystification.... [I]ts function is to obscure the process of decision and disposition rather than to enlighten it.

By including all personal and social characteristics as relevant, without assigning controlling significance to any one factor, individualized justice relies heavily on the "professional judgment" of juvenile court administrators.

In the adult dispositional framework, determinate sentences based on the offense increasingly supersede indeterminate sentences as "just deserts" displaces rehabilitation as the underlying sentencing rationale. The Progressives' optimistic assumptions about human malleability are challenged daily by the observation that rehabilitation programs fail to consistently rehabilitate and by volumes of empirical evaluations that question both the effectiveness of treatment programs and the "scientific" underpinnings of those who administer the enterprise.

Proponents of "just deserts" reject rehabilitation as a justification for intervention for a number of reasons. First, they argue that an indeterminate sentencing scheme vests too much discretionary power in presumed experts. Second, they point to the inability of such clinical experts to justify their differential treatment of similarly situated offenders based on validated classification schemes with objective indicators. Finally, opponents of rehabilitation emphasize the inequalities, disparities, and injustices that result from therapeutically individualized sentences. "Just deserts" sentencing, with its strong retributive foundation, punishes offenders according to their past behavior rather than on the basis of who they are or who they may become. Similarly situated offenders are defined and sanctioned equally on the basis of relatively objective and legally relevant characteristics such as seriousness of offense, culpability, or criminal history.

The same changes in sentencing philosophy are appearing in the juvenile process as well. However, "just deserts" sentences for juveniles have important implications for *McKeiver*'s therapeutic rationale and procedural implementations. The inability of proponents of juvenile rehabilitation to demonstrate the effectiveness of *parens patriae* intervention has led an increasing number of states to incorporate "just deserts" sentencing principles into their juvenile justice systems. The underlying premises of "just deserts" are that a juvenile's personal characteristics or social circumstances do not provide a principled basis for determining the length or intensity of coercive intervention and that "only a principle of proportionality (or "deserts") provides a logical, fair, and humane hinge between conduct and an official, coercive response."

Whether a juvenile receives punishment based on his past offense or treatment based on his personal characteristics may be answered by examining several aspects of juvenile courts' sentencing practices: the decision whether a youth should be transferred to criminal court for prosecution and punishment as an adult; the explicit legislative purposes of contemporary juvenile codes; the sentencing framework used for making juvenile dispositions; the actual sentencing practices of the juvenile court; and the conditions of confinement in juvenile institutions. Such an examination reveals that despite persisting rehabilitative rhetoric, the dispositional practices of the contemporary juvenile court increasingly are based on the Principle of Offense and reflect the punitive character of the criminal law.

Concluding that juvenile courts punish rather than treat raises fundamental questions about the quality of procedural justice in juvenile courts, since the failure to provide all criminal procedural safeguards is justified by the "alternative purpose" of treatment. Moreover, many juveniles currently may serve longer sentences than do their adult counterparts convicted of similar offenses. Juveniles' equal protection challenges to legislative classifications imposing longer terms for juveniles than for adults for similar offenses consistently have been rejected on the grounds that juveniles receive "treatment" rather than punishment. If juvenile courts punish, then the underlying basis for distinguishing juvenile and adult sanctions is eliminated. Finally, if juvenile courts in fact punish without safeguards of the criminal process in a fashion frequently more severe than could be legally imposed upon a similarly situated adult, is there any remaining justification for a separate system for adjudicating young offenders for committing criminal offenses?

A. The Purpose of the Juvenile Court—Distinguishing Punishment from Treatment

The Progressives envisioned, and the *McKeiver* decision endorsed, a model of the juvenile court as a benevolent treatment agency making dispositions in the "best interests of the child." Because the *McKeiver* Court subscribed to the view that juvenile courts rehabilitate rather than punish, it did not analyze further the differences between "treatment" and "punishment." . . .

Most states' juvenile court statutes contain a "purpose clause" or preamble, a statement of the underlying rationale of the legislation intended to aid the courts in interpreting the statute. Thus, examining a juvenile code's purpose clause provides one insight into the goal of juvenile court intervention. Since the creation of the original juvenile court in Cook County, Illinois, in 1899, the historical purpose of juvenile court law has been

> to secure for each minor subject hereto such care and guidance, preferably in his own home, as will serve the moral, emotional, mental, and physical welfare of the minor and the best interests of the community; to preserve and strengthen the minor's family ties whenever possible, removing him from the custody of his parents only when his welfare or safety or the protection of the public cannot be adequately safeguarded without removal; and, when the minor is removed from his own family, to secure for him custody, care, and discipline as nearly as possible equivalent to that which should be given by his parents. . . .

Many states included this statement of purpose from the original Illinois juvenile court act in the preamble to their juvenile codes. Some states provided the additional purpose of "remov[ing] from a minor committing a delinquency offense the taint of criminality and the penal consequences of criminal behavior, by substituting therefore an individual program of counselling, supervision, treatment, and rehabilitation."

Forty-two of the states' juvenile codes contain a statement of legislative purpose or similar preamble. Within the past decade, however, ten state legislatures—almost one-quarter of states with a legislative purpose statement or preamble in their juvenile law statutes—have redefined the purpose of their juvenile courts. These recent amendments of juvenile code purpose clauses downplay the role of rehabilitation in the child's "best interest" and acknowledge the importance of public safety, punishment, and individual accountability in the juvenile justice system. One of the distinguishing characteristics of the "new" juvenile law is that "in many jurisdictions accountability and punishment have emerged among the express purposes of juvenile justice statutes."

... [S]tates have redefined the purpose of their juvenile courts to include the following objectives: "correct juveniles for their acts of delinquency"; "provide for the protection and safety of the public"; "protect society ... [while] recognizing that the application of sanctions which are consistent with the seriousness of the offense is appropriate in all cases"; "render appropriate punishment to offenders"; "protect the public by enforcing the legal obligations children have to society"; "protect the welfare of the community and to ... control the commission of unlawful acts by children"; "protect the community against those acts of its citizens which are harmful to others and ... reduce the incidence of delinquent behavior"; and "reduce the rate of juvenile delinquency and ... provide a system for the rehabilitation or detention of juvenile delinquents and the protection of the welfare of the general public."

Some courts recognize that these changes in legislative purpose clauses signal basic changes in philosophical direction, "a recognition that child welfare cannot be completely 'child centered.'" Courts, as well as legislatures, increasingly acknowledge that "punishment" may be an acceptable purpose of a juvenile court's "therapeutic" dispositions. In *State v. Lawley*, the Washington Supreme Court reasoned that "sometimes punishment is treatment" and upheld the legislature's conclusion that "accountability for criminal behavior, the prior criminal activity and punishment commensurate with age, crime and criminal history does as much to rehabilitate, correct and direct an errant youth as does the prior philosophy of focusing upon the particular characteristics of the individual juvenile." Similarly, in *In re Seven Minors*, the Nevada Supreme Court endorsed punishment as a legitimate purpose of its juvenile courts:

> By formally recognizing the legitimacy of punitive and deterrent sanctions for criminal offenses juvenile courts will be properly and somewhat belatedly expressing society's firm disapproval of juvenile crime and will be clearly issuing a threat of punishment for criminal acts to the juvenile population.

The court suggested that, in order to effect this purpose, "[j]uvenile courts should be able to fashion reasonable punitive sanctions as part of dispositional programs in delinquency cases." Possible sanctions include restitution, compensation for crime victims, and incarceration in detention facilities and jails. ...

[M]any legislatures and courts fail to consider adequately whether a juvenile justice system can explicitly punish without simultaneously providing criminal procedural safeguards such as a jury trial. Although a legislature certainly may conclude that punishment is an appropriate goal and a legitimate strategy for controlling young offenders, it must provide the procedural safeguards of the criminal law when it opts to shape behavior by punishment. Any ancillary social benefit or individual reformation resulting from punishment is irrelevant to the need for such procedural protections.

Confinement of a juvenile for a determinate sentence based on the nature of the offense committed still entails a loss of liberty imposed explicitly to punish violations of the criminal law, regardless of whether the length of confinement is shorter than for a similarly situated adult and the place of incarceration is not called a "prison."

B. Dispositional Practices and the Juvenile Court's Sentencing Framework

While the legislative purpose clause states whether the intent behind a juvenile's disposition is punishment or treatment, analyzing the juvenile court's statutory sentencing framework and dispositional practices may also indicate whether there is a therapeutic "alternative purpose." When based on the characteristics of the offense, the sentence usually is determinate and proportional, with a goal of retribution or deterrence. When based on the characteristics of the offender, however, the sentence is typically indeterminate, with a goal of rehabilitation or incapacitation. The theory that correctional administrators will release an offender only when he is determined to be "rehabilitated" underlies indeterminate sentencing. When sentences are individualized, the offense is relevant only for diagnosis. Thus, it is useful to contrast offender-oriented dispositions, which are indeterminate and non-proportional, with offense-based dispositions, which are determinate, proportional, and directly related to the past offense.

1. Indeterminate Sentencing in Juvenile Court   Historically, the premise of sentencing in the juvenile court system was the "best interests" of the child-offender implemented through indeterminate and non-proportional dispositions.

> The problem for determination by the judge is not, Has this boy or girl committed a specific wrong, but What is he, how has he become what he is, and what had best be done in his interest and in the interests of the state to save him from a downward career. It is apparent at once that the ordinary legal evidence in a criminal court is not the sort of evidence to be heard in such a proceeding.

Judicial inquiry focuses not on a youth's prior conduct but rather on the development of a program to alleviate the conditions that caused the youth's delinquency. The delinquency disposition entails a variety of assumptions: the causes of the "delinquency," its course if left untreated, the appropriate forms of intervention to alter those conditions, and the ultimate prospects of success; in short, it requires diagnosis, classification, prescription, and prognosis. Because one cannot predict accurately the length of rehabilitative therapy necessary to ensure success, sentences are characteristically indeterminate. . . .

Most juvenile sentences are indeterminate; confinement ranges from one day to a period of years until the offender reaches the age of majority or some other statutory age. In *Gault*, for example, fifteen-year-old Gerald Gault allegedly made "lewd phone calls" for which he was committed to the State Industrial School "for the period of his minority [that is, until age 21], unless sooner discharged by due process of law." An adult convicted of the same offense would face a fine of fifty dollars or imprisonment for a maximum of two months. While the majority of indeterminate juvenile sentencing statutes continue for the duration of minority or some other maximum age, a minority prescribe a statutory maximum sentencing period for juvenile offenders, typically two years with judicial authority to extend for an additional two years or more. Most adolescent offenders, however, reach the age necessary for statutory termination of their sentence before the initial maximum sentencing period, plus any extension can be completed. Within the broad range of sentences authorized by the juvenile law statutes, the judge's authority is virtually unrestricted. . . .

2. Legislative and Administrative Changes in Juvenile Court Sentencing Statutes—De Jure Dispositional Decisionmaking   The punishment–treatment dichotomy is most explicit in the context of the decision whether to imprison juveniles. In the vast majority of indeterminate jurisdictions, the judge's sentencing power ends with a commitment to the state's juvenile correctional agency. Thereafter, the juvenile correctional authority or a parole board determines when a youth should be released from custody. . . .

Indeterminate sentencing schemes typically include an unspecified period of confinement with a wide range between the minimum and maximum length; a release decision made after incarceration and based, in part, on behavior during confinement; and a release decision based on progress toward rehabilitation rather than on formal standards. . . .

In contrast to the indeterminate sentencing schemes, a determinate sentencing framework usually includes a presumptive sentence or narrow dispositional range; an early determination of length of institutional stay set either at the time of adjudication or shortly thereafter; and a sentence based on formal, articulated standards that are proportional to the seriousness of the youth's present offense, any prior record, and age. To the extent that the length of the sentence is determined by a judge at trial or shortly after commitment, it reflects the offender's prior conduct. Alternatively, if the sentence is determined by an administrative agency during the later stages of confinement, it is more likely to reflect the offender's conduct during confinement.

. . . [A]bout one-third of the states currently use offense-based criteria to regulate decisions on juvenile institutional commitment and release. These determinate and mandatory minimum sentencing provisions require judges to consider the present offense, the prior record of the youth, or both.

(A) DETERMINATE SENTENCES IN JUVENILE COURT   For most of this century, theories of positivism and the use of confinement for utilitarian, preventive, or rehabilitative purposes dominated sentencing practices. Indeterminate sentences were the norm as long as the view prevailed that offenders should be treated rather than punished, that the duration of confinement should relate to rehabilitative needs, and that therapists possessed the scientific expertise to determine an offender's progress toward reform. Indeterminacy is based on the assumption that the goal of rehabilitation can be achieved and that the technical means to achieve it are available.

The precipitous decline of support for the rehabilitative ideal in the 1970s stemmed from dissatisfaction over empirical results. The apparent failure of the rehabilitative effort reawakened the quest for penal justice. Courts sentenced similarly situated offenders on the basis of relatively objective factors such as their offenses. In a justice system in which reform of offenders remains elusive, the quest for consistent sentencing acquires greater allure.

1) Washington The most dramatic departure from traditional *parens patriae* juvenile rehabilitation occurred in 1977, when the State of Washington enacted just deserts sentencing principles for its juvenile justice system. The primary goals of the new legislation were to assure individual and systemic accountability through presumptive sentencing guidelines. Legislative guidelines emphasized uniformity, consistency, proportionality, equality, and accountability, rather than rehabilitation. Under these guidelines, presumptive sentences for juveniles are determinate and proportional to the age of the offender, the seriousness of the offense, and the juvenile's prior record.

... [T]he Washington juvenile code creates three categories of offenders—serious, middle, and minor—with presumptive sentences and standard ranges for each. A sentencing guidelines commission developed dispositional and presumptive length-of-stay guidelines in the form of standard ranges (in weeks) that are proportionate to the seriousness of the present offense, age, and prior record. The sentencing judge has the responsibility of classifying a youth as a minor, middle, or serious offender, but he cannot set indeterminate sentences for the offenders. Instead, the judge refers to a dispositional schedule that prescribes the standard range of sentences for a youth with that offense record. The judge may deviate from the presumptive guidelines only by finding with "clear and convincing evidence" that following the dispositional guidelines would produce a "manifest injustice." Any disposition outside of the standard range may be appealed by the State or the juvenile. The guidelines provide that a first or "minor" offender may not be institutionalized, while the most menacing "serious" offender must be institutionalized for 125 weeks to three years. After a youth is incarcerated, institutional staff make security level assignments, facility placements, and program recommendations. A release date must be set by the time a youth has served sixty percent of the minimum sentence imposed.

An evaluator of the revised Washington code concluded that it improved juvenile sentencing practices: "Sentences in the post-reform era were considerably more uniform, more consistent, and more proportionate to the seriousness of the offense and the prior criminal record of the youth than were the sentences in the rehabilitation system which existed before 1978." The evaluation also reports that while referrals to juvenile courts increased, commitments to correctional facilities declined, resulting in "a substantial and marked reduction in the severity of sanctions. . . ." Another study of Washington's sentencing practices noted a clear correlation between the seriousness of the offense and a youth's length of stay. . . .

(B) MANDATORY, MINIMUM TERMS OF CONFINEMENT BASED ON OFFENSE . . . . [I]n addition to experimenting with determinate sentencing, a number of jurisdictions have altered their juvenile sentencing statutes and practices. The changes emphasize characteristics of the offense rather than the offender as the formal determinant of dispositions. This has been accomplished through the adoption of either offense-based determinate sentences for some offenders, offense criteria as sentencing guidelines, or mandatory minimum sentences for certain offenses. All of these limit individualized consideration of a juvenile's "real needs."

Under many of the mandatory minimum sentencing statutes, the judge retains discretion to commit a juvenile to the state's department of corrections. If the judge does decide to incarcerate a youth, she may also prescribe the minimum sentence to be served for that offense. In several jurisdictions, however, the mandatory sentence is non-discretionary, and the judge must commit the juvenile for the statutory period. These nondiscretionary mandatory minimum sentences are typically imposed on juveniles charged with serious or violent present offenses or those who have prior delinquency adjudications. The mandatory minimum sentences may range from twelve to eighteen months, until age twenty-one, or until the adult maximum sentence for the same offense. . . .

(C) ADMINISTRATIVELY ADOPTED DETERMINATE/PRESUMPTIVE OR MANDATORY MINIMUM SENTENCING GUIDELINES. . . . Another trend in juvenile sentencing practices is the adoption of guidelines for determining length of confinement by a state's department of corrections or juvenile parole authority. These administrative guidelines use offense-based criteria to structure institutional release decisions. While the adult corrections process has employed parole release guidelines for several decades, their use in the juvenile process is more recent.

3. Empirical Evaluations of Juvenile Court Sentencing—De Facto Dispositional Decisionmaking Assessing the relative impact of the Principle of Individualized Justice or the Principle of Offense on dispositions requires ascertaining the relationships between legal variables—present offense and prior record—and disposition, and social characteristics or "extra-legal" variables—race and social class—and dispositions. However, "even a superficial review of the relevant literature leaves one with the rather uncomfortable feeling that the only consistent finding of prior research is that there are no consistencies in the determinants of the decisionmaking process." The studies, having been conducted in different jurisdictions at different times and employing different methodologies and theoretical perspectives, yield contradictory results; however, two general findings emerge from this research. The first is that the Principle of Offense accounts for most of the variance in dispositions that can be explained. The second is that after controlling for present offense and prior record, discretionary individualization is often synonymous with racial discrimination.

Juvenile court judges answer the question "what should be done with this child?" in part, by reference to explicit statutory mandates. The discretionary decisionmaking powers of the judge, however, are also tempered by practical and bureaucratic considerations. Administrators of justice in juvenile courts enjoy greater discretion than do their adjudicatory counterparts at the adult criminal level because of the presumed need in juvenile justice proceedings to look beyond the present offense to the "best interests of the child" and because of paternalistic assumptions about the ability to rehabilitate children.

The relevance given to individualized justice in the adjudication of juvenile offenses, however, raises concerns about the impact of discretionary decisionmaking. Lower-class and nonwhite youths are substantially overrepresented in the juvenile justice system. Basing the severity of a juvenile's sentence on social characteristics such as race or socioeconomic status raises issues of fairness, equality, and justice. When practitioners of "individualized justice" base discretionary judgments on social characteristics or race, rather than legal variables, their decisions frequently redound to the disadvantage of the poor and minorities and lead to charges of discrimination. This discrimination is reflected in differential processing and more severe sentencing of minority youths relative to whites.

An alternative explanation for the disproportionate overrepresentation of minorities in the juvenile justice process is that, despite the juvenile system's nominal commitment to individualized justice, dispositional decisions are based on the Principle of Offense rather than on an assessment of individual needs. If that is the case, then overrepresentation of minority and lower-class youths in the juvenile system may be attributed to real differences in rates of delinquent activity by these youths.

An obvious question, then, is to what extent legal factors—present offense and prior record—or social characteristics—race, sex, or social class—influence judges' dispositional decisionmaking. Evaluations of dispositional practices suggest that the Principle of Offense pervades practical decisionmaking throughout the juvenile justice system, whether the decision is made by the police, during intake, or at adjudication. Historically, the juvenile justice system premised its dispositional decisions on the characteristics of the offender. Contemporary research, however, suggests the system has shifted its emphasis from the characteristics of the offender to the offense committed. As a corollary, juvenile courts increasingly seek formal rationality in decisionmaking by using general rules applicable to categories of cases rather than pursuing individualized substantive justice.

A number of studies report that minority or lower-class youths receive more severe dispositions than white youths even after controlling for relevant legal variables. One report notes that initial decisions as to screening, detention, charging, and adjudications are strongly influenced by the Principle of Offense. The report concludes, however, that as cases progress in the adjudicatory process, race and class directly affect dispositions, with minority youths receiving more severe sentences. Another study, conducted with a control for legal and processing variables, found that a juvenile's race had a direct effect on decisions made at several processing junctures. Others have concluded that when legal variables are held constant, the juvenile court's individualized justice "typically applies harsh sanctions to blacks, those who have dropped out of school, those in single parent or broken homes, [and] those from lower socioeconomic backgrounds...." A study of the impact of extralegal factors, particularly race, on decisionmaking at six points in the juvenile process found that "minority youth receive consistently harsher dispositions." The study concluded that

[t]he evidence for racial discrimination ... is compelling. Its sources may lie in the individual attitudes of decisionmakers in the system's independent agencies, but it is unlikely that these seemingly isolated decisionmakers of substantially different backgrounds would produce such consistent, systemic behaviors. Rather than a chance convergence of independent behaviors, they seem to reflect a sociological process, if not a generalized perspective, shared across decisionmakers of disparate backgrounds. Like other societal institutions, the justice system is not blind to ethnic and racial differences.

Other research has found race affects only the dispositions of minor offenders, while for serious or repeat offenders, sentencing disparities between the races decline. Contrary to expectations, a few studies report that white youths receive more severe dispositions than blacks. Some studies report that substantive factors such as "family and school problems," along with legal criteria, explain variations in sentencing. Summarizing this research, the Principle of Offense appears to be the most significant factor influencing juvenile court dispositions, with a substantial amount of sentencing variation related to a juvenile's race.

The elevation of the Principle of Offense to a dispositional standard received tacit endorsement in 1967 from the report of the President's Commission on Law Enforcement and the Administration of Justice, which explicitly recognized the punitive character of juvenile court intervention. Subsequently, several juvenile justice policy groups have recommended the replacement of indeterminate sentences with formal dispositional criteria and sentences proportional to the seriousness of the offense; in short, a shift from substantive justice to formal legal rationality.

The elevation of the Principle of Offense has also received practical administrative impetus from bureaucratic imperatives—the desire of juvenile and criminal justice agencies to avoid scandal and unfavorable political and media attention. Several scholars have noted the constraint that "fear of scandal" imposes on juvenile court dispositions. One such scholar has observed that

> juvenile court decision-making comes to be pervaded by a sense of *vulnerability to* adverse public reaction for failing to control or restrain delinquent offenders.... [Fear of scrutiny and criticism increases pressures] to impose maximum restraints on the offender—in most instances incarceration. Anything less risks immediate criticism. But more than this, it also exposes the court to the possibility of even stronger reaction in the future. For given any recurrence of serious illegal activity, former decisions that can be interpreted as "lenient" become difficult to defend.

The Principle of Offense and scandal avoidance encourage formal and restrictive responses to the more serious forms of juvenile deviance. "[W]hether a juvenile goes to some manner of prison or is put on some manner of probation ... depends first, on a traditional rule-of-thumb assessment of the total risk of danger and thus scandal evident in the juvenile's current offense and prior record of offenses...."

Finally, juvenile courts necessarily develop bureaucratic strategies to reconcile their need for highly individualized assessments with their pursuit of often contradictory formal goals.

> Time after time after time procedures emerge which permit officials in these organizations to classify and categorize those who come to their attention as swiftly and simply as they can. The form of these categorization processes is commonly defined by the types of information which organizations routinely capture as a basis for forming or, equally often, defending the decisions they are obligated to make.

Because the present offense and the prior record of delinquency are among the types of information routinely and necessarily collected in juvenile court processing, it is hardly surprising that they provide a type of decisional rule.

A survey of juvenile sentencing practices in California reported that, despite claims of individualization, juvenile dispositions appear to be based primarily on the youth's present offense and prior record. The study concluded that

> comparisons of juvenile and adult sentencing practices suggest that juvenile and criminal courts in California are much more alike than statutory language would suggest, in the degree to which they focus on aggravating circumstances of the charged offense and the defendant's prior record in determining the degree of confinement that will be imposed.

While legal variables exhibit a stronger statistical relationship to dispositions than do social variables, a substantial amount of variation in the sentencing of juveniles cannot be explained. Present offense and prior record are the best predictors of dispositions, yet they only account for approximately one-quarter of the variance in sentencing. With respect to the large amount of unexplained variation, commentators have observed that "the juvenile justice process is so ungoverned by procedural rules and so haphazard in the attribution of relevance to any particular variables or set of variables that judicial dispositions are very commonly the product of an arbitrary and capricious decision-making process." The absence of any explanatory relationship between legal or social variables and dispositions may be interpreted as true "individualized justice," where every child receives a unique disposition tailored to his or her individual needs. "Given the philosophy of the juvenile court system, this finding might be interpreted as quite positive in the sense that it could imply that judges consider a broad spectrum of both legal and social variables in their attempt to individualize decisions." This discretionary "individualization" has important consequences, however, such as the disproportional effects of race on sentencing.

An equally plausible interpretation, however, is that there is no rationale to dispositional decisionmaking; it consists of little more than intuition, guesswork, and hopes, constrained marginally by the youth's present offense and prior record. In such a case, individualization is simply a euphemism for arbitrariness and discrimination:

> [T]hese findings also suggest the possibility that those who share various social characteristics will be treated in a significantly different fashion from those drawn from other categories in the population; those against whom complaints are filed by one type of complainant will be treated differently than those who have engaged in comparable behavior, but whose offense has been brought to the attention of social control agencies by a different complainant; and those who come before one judge will be disposed of differently than those who appear before another judge, regardless of who they are or what their present and past offense record might be.

A system of justice in which the most powerful explanatory variables—present offense and prior record—have a relatively low correlation to variations in sentencing remains highly discretionary and, perhaps, discriminatory. It means that there is substantial attenuation between a youth's criminal behavior and the severity of the disposition; minor offenders can receive much more severe dispositions than serious offenders. Similarly situated offenders, in terms of their present offense or prior record, can receive markedly dissimilar dispositions. . . .

4. Summary of Changes in Juvenile Court Sentencing Practices   The preceding analysis of de jure and de facto juvenile justice sentencing practices demonstrates a very strong nationwide movement, both in theory and in practice, away from therapeutic, individualized dispositions toward determinate or mandatory sentences based on the Principle of Offense. This very strong trend has emerged only since the *McKeiver* decision. When *McKeiver* was decided in 1970, no states used determinate sentencing statutes, mandatory minimum sentencing statutes for serious juvenile offenders, or administratively promulgated sentencing and release guidelines. Today, nearly one-third of the states employ one or more of these sentencing strategies. . . .

Viewed as a whole, the various legislative and administrative changes and operational practices described thus far have eliminated virtually all of the significant distinctions between sentencing practices in the juvenile and adult criminal processes. The use of determinate sentences based on the present offense and prior record of the juvenile, whether de jure or de facto, calls into question any possible therapeutic "alternative purpose" for juvenile dispositions. The use of mandatory minimum statutes to sentence on the basis of the seriousness of the juvenile's offense avoids any reference to the offender's "real needs" or "best interests." The revision of purpose clauses in juvenile justice statutes, with greater emphasis placed on the integrity of the substantive criminal law or the need to protect public safety, eliminates even rhetorical support for the traditional rehabilitative goals of juvenile justice. These changes were succinctly summarized by a California court in *In re Javier A.*, which concluded that "the purposes of the juvenile process have become more punitive, its procedures formalistic, adversarial and public, and the consequences of conviction much more harsh."

One of the most comprehensive studies of state juvenile sentencing practices reports:

> Numerous states have, by statute, adopted determinate sentencing policies for serious or violent offenders, and several states have now either adopted determinate sentence statutes or have created administrative release guidelines that establish explicit time or ranges of time to be served for any delinquent who has committed an act that would be a crime if committed by an adult.
>
> *These policies contradict some of the basic assumptions of the original juvenile court: that juvenile offenders should be handled quite differently than adult offenders, that the juvenile court and youth corrections are designed to operate and therefore function in the best interest of the child, that the objective of the juvenile justice system is rehabilitation of the youth and not applying fixed time of punishment, and that rehabilitation is an open-ended process requiring treatment of each youth as an individual, thus "time served," as it were, is indeterminate depending on the successful rehabilitation of the youth.*

In short, these changes call into question the underlying rationale of the *McKeiver* decision that juvenile dispositions are for the "alternative purpose" of rehabilitation.

C. "Get Tough" Legislation and Conditions of Confinement in Juvenile Institutions

Formal legislative and administrative sentencing criteria, as well as the operational practices they foster, contradict the traditional individualized, offender-oriented sentencing rationales of the juvenile court. This conflict is further reflected in the conditions of confinement in the institutions to which juvenile offenders are committed for rehabilitation. Studying the institutional reality of juvenile corrections, the supposed locus of "rehabilitation," advances the punishment versus treatment inquiry.

Examining juvenile correctional facilities helps to determine whether institutional confinement constitutes punishment or a therapeutic "alternative purpose." Indeed, it was the reality of institutional conditions that motivated the Court in *Gault* to afford juveniles procedural safeguards. There, the Supreme Court noted:

> The fact of the matter is that, however euphemistic the title, a "receiving home" or an "industrial school" for juveniles is an institution of confinement in which the child is incarcerated for a greater or lesser time. His world becomes a building with whitewashed walls, regimented routine, and institutional hours. . . ." Instead of mother and father and sisters and brothers and friends and classmates, his world is peopled by guards, custodians, state employees, and "delinquents" confined with him for anything from waywardness to rape and homicide.

In *Gault*, the Court belatedly recognized conditions that have long persisted. The *Gault* Court's emphasis on incarceration and institutional confinement is relevant to the issue of punishment and underlies its fifth amendment holding. The Court has never held that involuntary confinement per se constitutes punishment. The *Gault* Court, however, correctly perceived incarceration per se as a severe penalty, a substantial deprivation of autonomy, and a continual reminder of one's delinquent status, all of which are punitive in nature.

The contradictions between the rhetorical affirmation of rehabilitation and the reality of custodial institutional confinement have characterized the juvenile court since its inception. Rothman's study of the early juvenile training schools describes institutions that not only failed to rehabilitate but were scarcely distinguishable from their adult penal counterparts. Schlossman provides a similarly pessimistic account of the reality of juvenile correctional programs under the aegis of Progressivism. Indeed, the juvenile court's lineage of punitive, custodial confinement in the name of rehabilitation can be traced back to its institutional precursors in the Houses of Refuge.

Gault's criticism of the adequacy of juvenile correctional programs is not simply a historical artifact. Evaluations of juvenile correctional facilities in the years since *Gault* reveal a continuing gap between the rhetoric of rehabilitation and its punitive reality. The author's study of juvenile institutions in Massachusetts describes facilities in which staff physically abused inmates and were frequently powerless to prevent the worst aspects of inmate abuse by other inmates.

> [T]he lives of the low-status inmates in the custody-oriented cottages were miserable. . . . The direct physical assaults and abuse were substantial and

real. The attendant psychological trauma was equally apparent. These victims of terrorization were afraid of other inmates. Their fear emboldened others who, by their aggression, reinforced their fear.

A study in Ohio reveals a similarly violent and oppressive institutional environment for the "rehabilitation" of young delinquents.

Extensive scrutiny of the Texas juvenile correctional system during the 1970s revealed patterns of staff and inmate violence and the subjection of inmates to degrading make-work tasks. The California Youth Authority conducted extensive reviews of its institutions and concluded that "a young man convicted of a crime cannot pay his debt to society safely. The hard truth is that the CYA staff cannot protect its inmates from being beaten or intimidated by other prisoners." The research attributed the violence to inappropriately designed facilities, inadequate staffing, and substantial overcrowding, all of which "promote the formation and ascendancy of prison gangs." Despite the rhetoric of rehabilitation, the daily reality of juvenile offenders confined in many "treatment" facilities is one of staff and inmate violence, predatory behavior, and all of the attendant punitive consequences of custodial incarceration.

During the period of these post-*Gault* evaluation studies, a number of lawsuits challenged the conditions of confinement in juvenile correctional facilities, alleging that the conditions violated the committed inmates' "right to treatment" and inflicted "cruel and unusual punishment." The "right to treatment" is a logical extension of the state's invocation of its *parens patriae* power to intervene for the purported benefit of the individual. In settings other than juvenile correctional facilities, such as institutions for the mentally ill and mentally retarded, states confine individuals "for their own good" without affording them the procedural safeguards required for criminal incarceration. In all of these settings, it is the promise of benefit—a therapeutic "alternative purpose"—that justifies the less stringent procedural safeguards. Thus, failing to deliver the promised treatment results in simple custodial confinement—punitive incarceration and a loss of liberty—which is the essence of a due process violation.

The "right to treatment" and "cruel and unusual punishment" cases provide another view of the reality of juvenile corrections. In *Nelson v. Heyne*, the court found that inmates were routinely beaten with a "fraternity paddle," injected with psychotropic drugs for social control purposes, and deprived of minimally adequate care and individualized treatment. In *Inmates of Boys' Training School v. Affleck*, the court found inmates confined in dark, cold, dungeon-like cells in their underwear, routinely locked in solitary confinement, and subjected to a variety of punitive practices. In *Morales v. Turman*, the court found numerous instances of physical brutality and abuse, including hazing by staff and inmates, staff-administered beatings, exposure of inmates to tear gas, homosexual assaults, extensive use of solitary confinement, repetitive and degrading make-work, and minimal clinical services.

In *Morgan v. Sproat*, the court found that youths were confined in padded cells with no windows or furnishings and only flush holes for toilets, and denied access to all services, programs, or materials except a Bible. In *State v. Werner*, the court found that inmates were locked in solitary confinement, beaten and sprayed with mace by staff, required to scrub floors with a toothbrush, and subjected to punitive practices such as standing and sitting for prolonged periods without changing position.

Unfortunately, these cases are not atypical, as the list of judicial opinions documenting institutional abuses demonstrates. Rehabilitative euphemisms, such as "providing a structured environment" and a therapeutic "alternative purpose," cannot disguise the punitive reality that characterizes confinement in a juvenile institution. Although not as uniformly bad as adult prisons, juvenile correctional facilities are certainly not so benign and therapeutic as to justify depriving those who face commitment to them of procedural safeguards. While the prospect of incarcerating juveniles in barbarous adult facilities is not appealing, the well-documented prevalence of violence, aggression, and homosexual rape in juvenile facilities is hardly consoling.

Evaluations of juvenile corrections have consistently found violent inmate subcultures to be a function of institutional security arrangements; the more authoritarian controls are imposed to facilitate security, the higher the level of covert inmate violence within the subculture. Juveniles sentenced to long terms under "get tough" legislation are the most serious and chronic offenders, yet facilities designed to handle them often suffer from limited physical mobility, inadequate program resources, and intense interaction among the most problematic youths in the system. The result is a situation that can easily give rise to a juvenile corrections "warehouse" with all of the worst characteristics of adult penal incarceration.

The changes in juvenile court sentencing legislation have exacerbated all of the deleterious side effects that institutional overcrowding produces. Changing sentencing practices without simultaneously accounting for their impact on the correctional system is a prescription for disaster.

> Not only were more youth being sent to training schools, they were also staying longer. Whereas training school average length of stay declined from 260 days in 1974 to 238 in 1979, length of stay rose back up to 256 days by 1982. . . .
>
> . . . [T]he proportion of minority youth in the nation's training schools has [also] increased. In 1977 whites made up 53% of the public training school population; by 1982 the proportion of whites in training schools had declined to 46%.

Longer terms of confinement in custodial warehouses increasingly populated by minority youths is hardly the therapeutic "alternative purpose" envisioned in *McKeiver*. . . .

A. JUVENILE COURT SENTENCING PRACTICES

The articles in Chapter 5 A provide both qualitative and quantitative analyses of juvenile court sentencing practices. Recall from Chapter 2, judges can only dispose of the cases that reach them and several other individuals make decisions that affect a young offender's progress through the juvenile justice process. Police officers may adjust a case informally on the street or at the station house, divert it, or refer the youth to intake for formal processing. Juvenile court intake, in turn, may dispose of the case through informal supervision or diversion or refer a youth to the juvenile court for formal adjudication. Finally, even after formal adjudication, the juvenile court judge may choose from a wide array of dispositional alternatives ranging from continuing a case without a finding of delinquency, probation, or commitment to a state training school. Dispositional decisions cumulate; decisions made by the initial participants—police or intake—affect the types of decisions made by subsequent participants.

Juvenile court judges decide what to do with a child, in part by reference to statutory mandates. Moreover, practical bureaucratic considerations and paternalistic assumptions about children influence their sentencing decisions as well. Robert Emerson, "Role Determinants in Juvenile Court," provides a qualitative assessment of the processes of juvenile court decision making. Emerson emphasizes the local context within which judicial decision making occurs and the organizational constraints on judges' dispositions. Practical bureaucratic considerations provide an impetus to base youths' sentences on the seriousness of their offenses and prior records. Avoiding scandals and unfavorable political and media attention constrain juvenile court judges to impose more formal and restrictive sentences on more serious delinquents. Emerson's essay also provides an important linkage to the articles in Chapter 2, by Feld, "Justice by Geography," and Sampson and Laub, "Structural Variations in Juvenile Court Processing," that identified the relationships between a court's political and social structural context and the administration of juvenile justice.

The exercise of broad discretion associated with individualized justice raises concerns about its discriminatory impact. It is virtually a truism that minority youths are disproportionately overrepresented at every stage of the juvenile justice process. In 1988, Congress amended the Juvenile Justice and Delinquency Prevention Act to require states receiving federal funds to assure equitable treatment on the basis, inter alia, of race and family income and to assess the sources of overrepresentation of minorities in juvenile detention facilities and institutions (42 U.S.C. § 5633(a)(16)(1993

Supp.)). In response to the OJJDP mandate, a number of states examined and found racial disparities in juvenile justice administration. An analytic assessment of the juvenile court sentencing research literature concluded that "there is substantial support for the statement that there are race effects in operation within the juvenile justice system, both direct and indirect in nature." [Carl Pope and William Feyerherm, *Minorities and the Juvenile Justice System* 41 (1992).] The broad discretion inherent in a *parens patriae* system of individualized justice raises concerns that the cumulative impact of decisions contributes to the substantial overrepresentation of minority youths in the juvenile justice process. Accounting for the prevalence of and reducing racial disparities in juvenile court case processing and sentencing constitute a major juvenile justice policy objective.

Donna Bishop and Charles Frazier, "Race Effects in Juvenile Justice Decision-Making," attempt to ascertain the reasons why juvenile court judges disproportionately sentence minority youths to juvenile correctional institutions relative to white youths. These analyses of juvenile court dispositional practices pose a number of difficult questions. Do discretionary sentences based on social characteristics result in more severe sentencing of minority youths? Or, despite a theoretical commitment to individualized justice, do judges base youths' sentences on their present offenses or prior records, and does racial disproportionality result from real differences in rates of offending by race? Or does the structure of justice decision making—for example, racial differences in rates of intake screening, pretrial detention, or representation by counsel—act to the detriment of minority juveniles? In short, to what extent do legal offense factors, socio-demographic variables, or system-processing variables influence juvenile court judges' sentencing decisions and account for the racial disparities? Two general findings emerge from these studies. First, the present offense and prior record account for most of the variance in juvenile court sentencing that these analysts can explain. Second, after controlling for these offense variables, the individualized justice of juvenile courts often produces racial disparities in the sentencing of minority offenders. While legal variables exhibit a stronger relationship with disposition than do youths' social characteristics, most of the variation in sentencing juveniles remains unexplained. The recent changes in juvenile sentencing statutes summarized by Feld, "The Juvenile Court Meets the Principle of Offense: Punishment, Treatment, and the Difference it Makes," may reflect disquiet with the underlying premises of individualized justice and the idiosyncratic exercises of judicial discretion. In particular, combining "get tough" sentencing trends that emphasize the seriousness of youths' offenses, differences in rates of offending by juveniles of different races, and the cumulative impact of a juvenile's race on screening and processing decisions has significant implications for the disproportionate overrepresentation of minority youths in juvenile correctional institutions.

Role Determinants in Juvenile Court

ROBERT M. EMERSON

Reflecting an optimistic faith in the ideal of individualized justice, humanitarian reformers pushed the creation of juvenile courts throughout the country during the first decades of this century. Following the model of the first juvenile court established in Illinois in 1899, the philosophy of the new courts emphasized treatment and rehabilitation as the appropriate goals of state intervention in the lives of youth, the use of wide-ranging "scientific" diagnostic inquiry to identify the causes of delinquency problems, and informal, flexible procedures for conducting courtroom hearings in pursuit of these goals. The judge was to function as a fatherly clinician, conducting the hearing so as to maximize personal rapport with the child, directing the investigation into the causes of the delinquency, and implementing a detailed treatment plan giving priority to the care, guidance, and protection of the youth. Illegal offense was to be subordinate to social background. . . .

Underlying this philosophy was the assumption that the juvenile court, since it dispensed treatment not punishment, had no interest other than that of the child. Rather than facing charge and punishment, the youth "is alleged to have committed an offense and a petition is filed in his behalf." While under some circumstances counsel might participate, adversary concerns were antithetical to the nature of court proceedings. The protections afforded by the rules of criminal procedure were unnecessary, and strict rules of evidence, cross-examination of witnesses, and the right to remain silent were not guaranteed.

The strong humanitarian concerns of the founders of the juvenile court, however, were inlaid with authoritarian assumptions and practices. An emphasis on "discipline" and control underlay their efforts to "save" youth from the vices, crimes, and sins prevalent on the urban scene. . . . Moreover, underlying the early juvenile-court movement were strong, if often tacit, class and ethnic commitments, apparent in the concern with reforming the way of life of the poor and the foreign. . . .

As the crusading fervor of this "child-saving movement" declined and the juvenile court became an established institution, skepticism toward the realities of juvenile court practice grew. More and more observers noted that punishment and control were frequent, if not dominant, concerns in the court, that despite the growing professionalization of treatment in the court, rehabilitation often existed in name only, and that the interests of the child were routinely subordinated to the organizational requirements of court and probation bureaucracies and to community and law-enforcement pressures

Excerpted from *Handbook of Criminology* (1974), pp. 621–638.

for order and punishment. By the 1960s this skepticism and discontent had coalesced into two complementary forces for change, one primarily procedural and the other substantive in focus.

The procedural critique of the juvenile court . . . emphasized the reality of the punishments and sanctions imposed by the court in arguing for the need to reinstitute the protections of due process . . . [T]he major impetus was provided by the 1967 U.S. Supreme Court decision in the *Gault* case. This ruling held that a minor had to be told the specific charges against him, had a right to an attorney, to confront and cross-examine complainants and witnesses, and could not be forced to make self-incriminatory statements. Since the *Gault* decision the movement toward procedural due process in the juvenile court has made marked if nonuniform, progress: a number of constitutional protections have been extended to youth, proceedings have taken on a more formal and "legalistic" character, and lawyers have come to play a regular, if uneasy, role in hearings.

A second, more substantive discontent with the juvenile court focused on its efforts to prevent delinquency. In intervening to help youths who seem headed toward delinquency, the court could act in self-defeating ways. Too often court actions effectively stigmatized youths as delinquent in ways that tended to establish and perpetuate, rather than cure, their delinquency. In practice, contact with the juvenile court constituted a stigma that "gets translated into effective handicaps by heightened police surveillance, neighborhood isolation, lowered receptivity and tolerance by school officials, and rejections of youths by prospective employers." This observation led to the policy recommendation that the juvenile court explicitly abolish prevention as a goal in favor of a philosophy of "judicious nonintervention." . . . In this way juvenile-court operations would be narrowed and explicitly organized around its control functions. . .

THE LOCAL CONTEXT OF COURT ACTIVITIES

Perhaps one of the strongest themes of recent research on the juvenile court is the need to view the court as it operates within and is affected by its local environment. The juvenile court does not function as an isolated, largely autonomous institution. Rather its activities take place in and are shaped by its local institutional and community context and the pressures and demands emanating therefrom.

Local pressures on the juvenile court take two different forms, reflecting distinct orders of local ties and interests in its activities. On the one hand are fairly diffuse pressures and expectations from the local community, frequently mobilized and expressed by the news media and local political figures. On the other hand are the more focused, concrete demands from local institutions specifically concerned with the control and care of youth.

The Community Setting One striking feature of many juvenile courts is their strong ties with the local political system. Judges are elected in some states and appointed by the state governor in others. . . . Juvenile-court probation positions are often regarded as prime patronage appointments, although increasingly subject to civil service requirement in many areas. . . . Furthermore, juvenile courts require more financial support from local government than local criminal courts, where fines may offset much of their operating costs. In many areas juvenile-court judges, probation officers, and court clerks actively participate in political party affairs.

In general, dependence upon the political system tends to increase court sensitivity to pressures for *controlling and restraining delinquent youths.* Here the demands and interests of politicians, the press, and community seem to complement and reinforce one another: local politicians often use the occurrence of sensational crimes committed by youths or local "crime waves" as occasions to oppose "crime in the streets" and to press for a "get tough" policy on the part of the courts. The local press often provides the initial opportunity for such tactics, giving intensive coverage to some crime, identifying and publicizing "crime waves" and prominently displaying "law and order" statements by politicians. Here both politician and the press tend to organize and shape community concern over these issues, as well as to reflect and express it. As a result of these processes, the juvenile court and "delinquency" typically become live local issues with demands for upholding public order. . . .

One consequence is that juvenile-court decision-making comes to be pervaded by a sense of *vulnerability* to adverse public reaction for failing to control or restrain delinquent offenders. Such public concern often is focused on cases involving violent, perhaps dramatic, and newsworthy offenses. These cases become publicly visible, and the juvenile-court's decisions may be subject to specific scrutiny and criticism. Under these circumstances the court staff feels strong pressure to impose maximum restraints on the offender—in most instances, incarceration. Anything less risks immediate criticism. But more than this, it also exposes the court to the possibility of even stronger reaction in the future. For given any recurrence of serious illegal activity, former decisions that can be interpreted as "lenient" become difficult to defend. . . .

In its routine activities, however, the court's decisions are not directly affected by such pressures. For by and large, the insulating mechanisms of the juvenile-court structure—the exclusion of the public and press from hearings, nondisclosure of names of juveniles—along with the minor nature of most delinquent offenses, give most court decisions extremely low visibility in the community at large. Thus, these locally generated pressures on the court for control and restriction are not constant and pervasive.

However, even where the current offense is not particularly violent or serious, the court becomes vulnerable should the delinquent commit such a highly visible act in the future. Thus, any particular disposition, no matter how obvious, appropriate, and defensible it was at the time, can subsequently become evidence of the court's "coddling," overleniency in failing to "protect the community," or outright gullibility, if and when the youth involved commits a newsworthy and sensational offense.

The kinds of pressures analyzed above often introduce a fundamental restrictiveness into the court's handling of its cases. Particular decisions have to anticipate possible adverse public and political reaction. Decisions that might open the court to criticism constitute risks and may well be avoided. Indeed, "risk" specifically reflects the court's vulnerability to criticism for having failed to control and restrain. The "safe," defensible disposition is the restrictive, protect-the-community one: to make any other disposition thus comes to involve "taking a chance." The chance is the unknown consequence that may "blow the lid right off," opening the court and its personnel to basic attack and criticism. The court's political and communal ties place presumptive value on restraint and control.

Complainant Pressures More pertinent than these general community and political pressures for the juvenile-court's day-to-day activities are the immediate demands and interests of those initiating delinquency complaints. For while the juvenile court is fairly well shielded "from generalized public pressures," by that very fact it becomes particularly "exposed to the demands of those units with which it has most frequent contact." Moreover, pressures from these sources, including police, schools, social agencies, and parents, are specific and case-focused. Dealing with their immediate complainant demands is a pervasive and recurrent concern for the court, and constitutes a fundamental constraint on how it processes cases.

Some complainant interests involve highly situational and short-run concerns. The police, in particular, often seek court support against visible challenges to their authority; e.g., they may push to have a youth who has been "fresh" with them held in detention pending hearing. The court may accede to such pressure perhaps, in part, to allow the complainant to cool off. The strength of complainant pressures, even on such short-run issues, becomes a critical consideration in the court's disposition of cases. In such instances, the basic sense in which the court comes to attend to and deal with cases as *complaints about trouble* becomes apparent. At an extreme, decisions may be made not so much to control or help a delinquent as to placate or satisfy an irate and/or powerful complainant. In less extreme instances as well, the court is fundamentally oriented to this sense in which it is being asked to "do something" about a trouble by taking some account of the interests and pressures of complainants. Thus, it can be suggested that one problem confronting the juvenile court is exactly that of *showing complainants that they are doing something.*

But there are also complainant pressures for more consequential and long-term action by the court, reflecting a different set of control contingencies. The situation of the police is particularly critical here.

Many delinquency cases are initiated by juvenile officers, police officers assigned to handle all complaints about youths or investigations of offenses felt to involve youths. Rarely, if ever, making on-the-spot apprehensions of delinquents, the work of the juvenile officer centers on investigating and solving the wide variety of complaints about youthful misbehavior and trouble-making. A school is broken into, a neighbor complains that kids are breaking his windows, a bike is stolen, storekeepers complain about petty shoplifting or gatherings of youths who intimidate customers. These are the routine kinds of matters that juvenile officers handle.

In dealing with and disposing of such cases, police concern often lies in "keeping peace" rather than in "enforcing the law." The power to arrest and to initiate juvenile-court cases is routinely a tool or threat used to maintain or establish some kind of order in the local community. Particularly where minor infractions are involved, juvenile officers typically try to deal with the case informally, where this may entail mediating between the youth and the complainant in order to settle the differences between them. Thus, the juvenile-officer's job involves not so much solving crimes committed by youths as *dealing with* and trying to *settle complaints* about legally ambiguous troubles attributed to youth. (This proceeds within the dual constraints of stopping further complaints and keeping the youth from making further trouble.) . . .

In dealing informally with community troubles, the power to arrest and to initiate court action becomes a strategic weapon used to cajole and negotiate settlements, often by threatening the youth into better behavior. Official action provides a resource for influencing behavior, and may be invoked only as a "last resort." In these terms court action is often initiated when the police feel that mediation and attempts at informal handling have failed or are inappropriate. In the first instance, attempts to mediate a settlement may fail when a complainant refuses to compromise and insists on official action, or when the accused youth or his parents resist such settlement. . . .

Under a variety of circumstances, however, the police come to feel that informal handling is inappropriate. Thus, court action may be initiated when a policeman has his authority assaulted or challenged in what otherwise might be an inconsequential encounter with a youth. Or, when a youth seems to be regularly getting into trouble and has received a number of "breaks" with unofficial handling of prior incidents, even trivial matters may be seized on in order to get him before the court.

In these situations, where unofficial control and settlement procedures have not worked or are inappropriate, the police go to court to get backing for their control efforts. Court backing may take either a routine or an extreme form. In the former, the police want and expect the court to use its authority to sanction and intimidate those juvenile troublemakers who have continued to generate complaints and hence disturb the local peace. In this sense, the police bring into court youths they have had difficulty in managing informally and pressure the court to supplement their controlling efforts with its own supervision and authority. In these instances, the police expect the court to find the youth delinquent, give him a stiff lecture, put him on probation or give him a suspended sentence, and supervise and control his activities in such a way as to discourage him from making more trouble.

More extreme "backing up" is sought where both internal control measures and the threat of court sanction fail (or are felt to be too costly). Here pressure is exerted to have the court remove from the community those persistent troublemakers who have come to be regarded as "uncontrollable" and hopeless. Thus, the police pressure the court to incarcerate the delinquent who has committed a large number of offenses or who has committed a particularly vicious and serious one.... In such cases the police want the youth "off the streets," i.e., out of the community where his misconduct is producing a constant stream of complaints from citizens.

Similarly, a number of other community institutions regularly bring cases to court in order to support and reinforce their internal efforts to control youthful troublemakers. In the public school system, one of the most important of these institutions, court complaints may be initiated by vice-principals or deans in charge of school discipline, truant officers assigned to enforce compulsory attendance laws, and administrators of special schools for those youths who have been expelled from the regular school system. As with the police, these school agents generally take court action after initial attempts to correct the problem have failed. Thus, delinquency charges are used after a period of unsuccessful pressuring and bargaining to settle the trouble....

Court cases initiated by other school agents often reflect similar contingencies of institutional control. While school complaints frequently cite a specific incident of trouble, even a clear legal violation, such as assaulting a teacher or another student, formal court action often represents a more general appeal for supportive action in dealing with what is felt to be a longstanding control problem. The court is entreated either to use its authority to get the youth to conform, or to get rid of him. In the first instance, the court is expected to provide a realistic, supplementary threat to a tenuous situation of control; in the second, to remove a disruptive troublemaker.

Similar control problems and pressures often appear in incorrigible or runaway complaints initiated by parents against their children. What emerges in these situations is often a request that the court back up parental authority and control, which are felt to be under attack or ineffectual. Thus, parents may complain that their offspring refuse to obey them, stay out late without permission, hang around with the wrong friends, or date undesirable boys. In all cases they are requesting the court to throw its support behind their efforts to control or put a stop to such behaviors.

Finally, child-care institutions, particularly the child-welfare agencies, may initiate complaints of runaway and incorrigible children for substantively similar reasons. Here it must be emphasized initially that the court's relations with the variety of treatment resources dealing with children tend to be funneled through the public agencies. Private child-welfare agencies have close control over client selection, tending both to avoid undesirable and difficult cases and to shift the most troublesome to public agencies. . . .

Dealing with the least desirable and most troublesome children, control becomes the dominant organizational problem for the public child-welfare agencies. Under these circumstances, the court's capacity to apply coercive sanctions provides a necessary and even essential service. On the one hand, cases may be taken to court to reinforce the internal control regime of a public institution. Thus, incorrigibility complaints may be filed against youth who have made little or no effort to adjust to the rules of the institution. On the other hand, where a youth is felt to be unmanageably disruptive, perhaps even with court backing and support, court action may seek his incarceration in reform school. These contingencies are particularly pressing for the older boys who had moved through and been rejected by many of the local residential placements. The juvenile court and reform schools ultimately help public agencies eliminate these "hard-to-place" youths who have exhausted all placement options, including those usually regarded as "last resorts."

In conclusion, agencies in regular contact with the juvenile court typically appeal to it for control purposes. Demands for more effective coercive sanctions, and not directly or immediately for treatment, lie behind many delinquency complaints. More generally, the most sought-after power the court has is exactly its control of access to the state's correctional system. Primary control agents often come to feel that even the court's supplemental control efforts are inadequate and press to have troublemakers regarded as unmanageable, time consuming, or dangerous taken off their hands completely by incarceration. In an important sense, then, the court has the ability to serve these primary control agencies by eliminating from their case loads those youths who have proved persistently difficult or unmanageable. In this way the state youth correctional system comes to serve as an institutionally vital "dumping ground" for youths judged "hopeless" or uncontrollable by routine control methods, including those invoked by the court itself.

TREATMENT AND INTERINSTITUTIONAL DEPENDENCE

Whether and to what extent the court goes along with or resists complainant pressures depends in large part upon the specific relations and obligations it develops with the complaining organization. Briefly, when the court becomes dependent upon another organization for services or resources, pressures and demands emanating from that organization cannot be easily ignored. And somewhat paradoxically, the court incurs such obligations and enters into more dependent relations with these organizations largely in pursuit of goals central to its own distinctive treatment commitments. Specifially, the juvenile court has two general strategies available for providing services to help or treat delinquents: first, to try to develop autonomous court programs and facilities; second, to develop access to existing community facilities and resources. In either case, however, the juvenile court is drawn into relations with local institutions which often involve obligations at odds with its helping and treatment purposes.

The local political system provides one main avenue for securing and expanding treatment facilities. Judges may draw heavily on their knowledge and connections in local politics to press for court programs and services. For example, through political contacts and pressure, a judge may obtain a court clinic to test and evaluate delinquent youth. Such a result reaffirms and strengthens ties to the political system and to the public pressures emanating from it.

In addition, court treatment goals require routine cooperation with community agents concerned with the control and/or care of children. For example, juvenile-court staff have to rely heavily upon both police and schools in trying to work with delinquents on probation in the community. In the first place, probation officers are often almost totally dependent upon community sources, especially the police and the schools, for information about the day-to-day activities of their probationers (e.g., whether a boy is drinking frequently, taking drugs, hanging around with undesirable peers, or having trouble with his family). Second, the juvenile court is dependent on the police and other local institutions for more active support in its decisions about how to handle cases in the community. This becomes critical when probation officers begin to "work with" a youth, and may have to call upon police and other officials for support and cooperation. Successful probation work often entails both continuing negotiations with police over what is being done with a particular youth and persistent pleadings to put up with a certain amount of trouble during this time.

Similar relations arise with the schools. A probation officer may want to keep a youth in school, and yet find that the school regards the youth as a troublemaker and wants to get rid of him. The commitment to treatment then leads court personnel to urge the school to accept or keep a delinquent who would otherwise be expelled. These problems may be accentuated in dealings with special schools for problem pupils within the public-school system. Juvenile courts frequently develop close ties with such schools and thereby are more able to obtain this kind of tolerance. But in so doing the court incurs obligations to the school, generally to go along with its requests for restrictive court action in other cases involving more "serious problems."

Third, the juvenile court actively seeks to establish close working ties with a variety of local institutions for the specific purpose of influencing the selection and recruitment of court cases. Associated with the court's treatment goals is a commitment to preventing delinquency, leading, in turn, to a concern with *predelinquency*. Court staff feel they should deal not only with the obviously delinquent but also with youths moving toward delinquency or having "delinquent tendencies." Yet the court knows that these agencies that regularly initiate delinquency complaints tend to pass over just these cases; their interest centers more on immediate troublemakers than on currently manageable youths. "Predelinquents," then, are just those youths least likely to be brought before the court, and special efforts must be made if this selection process is to be modified. . . .

In summary, the juvenile court's quest for treatment services and resources draws it into a network of mutual obligations and dependencies with local organizations. As well as tending to undermine judicial autonomy in ways stressed by Vinter and others, increased susceptibility to local pressures generally pushes the court in restrictive, even punitive, directions in accord with the recurrent control interests of the organizations involved. But while the court must usually take these demands into account, it does not simply give in to them. While the police may press to have a "troublemaker" taken off the streets, or a welfare agency may want a problem ward sent to reform school, the court employs its own standards for assessing the appropriateness of such actions. In particular, whatever the strength of complainant pressure, the court feels it either premature or inappropriate to incarcerate youths who do not appear to them either "hopelessly" or "seriously" delinquent. In this sense demands for control are filtered through the court's own procedures for judging the seriousness of any particular case and the necessity for any particular response. The following sections will consider these procedures for processing delinquency cases.

TROUBLE, MORAL CHARACTER, AND DELINQUENT CAREERS

Basic to juvenile-court processing of youths charged with delinquency is a distinction between mild and serious cases. This distinction does not rest simply on the delinquent offense. Acts that would constitute felonies if committed by adults comprise a very small percentage of juvenile-court case loads. When such cases do come before the court, the gravity of the offense and the accompanying publicity and controversy set them off as exceptional. Serious offenses are handled as special cases, receiving special care and procedures that differ fundamentally from the ways of handling more routine delinquencies. Verbally court staff underline this distinction by noting, for example, that certain procedures are normal "unless it's an extremely vicious act."

Most petitions brought before the juvenile court involve minor offenses in strict legal terms—"kid's stuff"—including less serious misdemeanors and youth-specific violations, such as runaway, incorrigible, and curfew infractions. In their routine work with these cases, concerns with personal, family, and community "problems," "not the notion of serious crime, seem to orient the probation officer's definition of juvenile delinquency." Specifically, the juvenile court routinely attends less to the legal offense than to the presence of "problems" or "trouble." Thus, a judge noted that in conducting hearings:

> we look for tip-offs that something is really wrong. We get some tip-offs just from the fact-sheet: truancy, school attendance, conduct and effort marks.... If you get something wrong there, you know there's trouble. When you get truancy and bad conduct plus the delinquency, there's definitely something wrong.

In practice, court inquiry typically shifts at an early point from the delinquent act as a legal offense to finding out what the act indicates for the offender, in short, to "what is the problem here?"...

The judge's feeling that there is "real trouble" reflects an assessment that the ... activities and situations not only entail some marginal delinquency, but more importantly, may lead to full-blown delinquency. That is, in these activities and situations the judge detects certain indicators of "the short-run and long-run courses of action the suspect is likely to pursue." These indicators suggest "real trouble"—possible movement toward a further *delinquent career*. In so doing the court relies upon typifications of the causes, circumstances, and processes whereby youths may progressively move from innocuous beginnings into "serious delinquency." ... Through the use of such typified constructs of delinquent careers, the court interprets what present behavior or "problems" portend for the youth's future behavior. In so doing the court begins to identify what should be done in response to that particular case.

Moreover, assessment of "real trouble" as the possibility of movement toward "serious delinquency" depends in large part on judgments of *what kind of youth* is involved. Thus, the court's use of concepts of typical delinquent careers implies a fundamental concern with the youth's *moral character*. Moral character involves the judgment of what a person "really is," what his "essential nature" is, as distinct from the role-specific identity implied by any particular behavior or performance. With the partial exception of "serious offenses," mere violation of a law does not make a youth a "real delinquent" in the eyes of the court staff. As a probation officer noted about one youth: "There are delinquents and there are delinquents.... All children steal things. She's not a delinquent." Thus, a "real delinquent" is seen as not simply a youth who has committed a delinquent act, but as one whose actions indicate he or she is the kind of person who has or will become regularly and seriously engaged in delinquent activity. Character assessments of this kind thus underlie the court's handling of cases, particularly its identification of cases as "serious problems." In this sense, a "real," "hardcore" delinquent is a youth who comes to be seen as fundamentally criminal in character by court staff. While such a youth may already be heavily involved in serious delinquent activity, he need not be, and may show only minor delinquent conduct. Nonetheless, he may be felt to be "the kind of kid who will go bad," the kind of youth who in time will become a real delinquent, regularly engaged in serious, perhaps violent, delinquent activity.

Different assessments of the offender's moral character may lead the court to make very different interpretations of the meaning and implications of the same delinquent act. On the one hand, the delinquency may be viewed "as, a manifestation of criminal (that is, purposely irresponsible) social character." In this case the delinquent offense tends to be seen as more "serious," and confirms the underlying imputation of criminal character upon which it is based. On the other hand, imputation of "normal character" may serve to insulate a youth from the criminal implications of his behavior. Here the offense may be viewed as the product of a basically "good kid," but "due to circumstances that the juvenile presumably cannot easily control." Under these circumstances, even with involvement in recurring, perhaps increasingly serious, delinquency, court staff continue to feel that the possibility of such a youth becoming a "real delinquent" is unlikely and or preventable.

Assessments of career stage and moral character are not static and absolute in nature, but rather assume a changing, tentative, emerging character. For moral character is not simply judged at one point, e.g., on first contact, and that judgment perpetuated thereafter. Rather, initial judgments are made and acted upon with consequences that may drastically modify (as well as confirm) these first assessments. The court itself assumes that initial assessments of trouble and moral character are highly tentative and subject to change, and may respond as to allow explicitly for further evidence and reevaluation, e.g., continuing minor offenses, such as shoplifting, without a finding "in order to see if there is a serious problem." Assessments of moral character, then, constantly change, as the court attempts to deal with the trouble, reassesses its judgments in light of the success or failure of these remedies, and tries new ways of dealing with the youthful troublemaker appropriate to one of that now-recognized character.

It should be emphasized that the juvenile court's concern with trouble, a delinquent career, and moral character is fundamentally *practical* rather than theoretical in nature. For these assessments are made in and as part of the process of deciding what to do about the variety of cases coming before the court. Locating "real trouble," specifying a career stage, or assessing moral character are not ends in themselves, but are used in deciding what should and can be done with specific cases. That is to say, determining what to do with a particular youth does not involve simply assessing what he has done in the past and trying to anticipate what he will or might do in the future. *Rather, such assessments are made in light of and directed toward deciding among the actual courses of action that are available and appropriate in this particular case.*

One way of indicating what is involved here is to suggest that identifying real trouble and making assessments of a delinquent career stage and character are not final decisions but first steps for the juvenile court's practical task of actually doing something about the cases brought before it. Determining just what a delinquent has done and what he will in all likelihood do and become in the future serves not to dispose of a case, but to identify a range of "realistic" and "appropriate" options for working out a disposition to the case. For example, in deciding that a youth is only marginally involved in delinquency, the court effectively judges that one of a range of mild, routine responses—some variant of routine probationary supervision—is appropriate. Conversely, to identify a youth as at a late stage of delinquency is to narrow the range of possible ways of dealing with his case to these involving major action, perhaps incarceration. In these ways the court's determination of the career stage and moral character serves to specify institutionally proper and reasonable ways of dealing with delinquency cases.

INITIAL ASSESSMENTS AND COURT CAREERS

In distinguishing between minor and serious delinquency and in determining initial lines of response to cases, court staff attend to a variety of possible signs of trouble and of delinquent moral character. These include features of the delinquent offense, the youth's general pattern of behavior, the personal impression he makes on court staff, and his wider social circumstances.

Court conceptions of the typical features of delinquent acts provide a resource for attending to and making sense of cases. Court personnel come to hold certain stereotyped conceptions about the typical situations, motives, and character of perpetrators of a given kind of delinquent offense. These "stereotypes" embody the court's locally acquired, common-sense knowledge of delinquency situations. By determining that a particular offense falls in such a known class of acts, the court comes to anticipate a particular set of motives, circumstances, and techniques for the act, and a particular kind of delinquent actor. . . .

In this way, certain typical offenses lead the court to expect delinquent offenders of a particular moral character. Thus, when the court detects (nontypical) elements of preplanning and professional techniques in "use without authority" cases, or their lack in handbag snatches, the usual expectations do not hold and further probing into the offense may seek to establish what kind of youth was committing it.

Beyond inferences from the offense, the court turns to a youth's "record" in assessing trouble and moral character. Almost the first step made by a probation officer in processing a new complaint is to find out whether the youth involved has had prior contact with the juvenile court. This "record" plays a fundamental role in the court's subsequent assessment and handling of the case. A youth without a prior record is usually presumed to be normal in character and his case will typically be handled routinely on some form of perfunctory probation. A lengthy record (even of minor offenses) or conviction for one or two serious offenses is taken to imply commitment to or movement toward serious delinquent activity.

Even when there is no official record, the court may identify general patterns of delinquent activity and hence possible criminal moral character. What is critical is tying a current act to prior incidents of the "same kind." In this way, for example, reference to prior unreported incidents of some delinquent behavior may transform a current act from an isolated incident into evidence of a recurrent pattern. . . .

Court staff read and interpret records of delinquent activity in reference to their conceptions of a delinquent career. Thus, just as it is assumed that minor delinquency may lead to serious delinquency, so it is assumed that the occurrence of serious delinquency will have been preceded (and caused) by minor delinquency. Court staff then expect a youth who is currently charged with a fairly serious offense, such as handbag snatching or armed robbery, to have a prior record of less serious delinquent activity building up toward the present offense. These common-sense notions of how delinquent careers develop also allow identification of anomalous patterns. For example, when a serious delinquent offense is committed without any apparent progression through the normal prior delinquent stages, court staff often feel that the delinquent offender may be disturbed rather than criminal in character. Similarly, unevenness in the appearance of delinquent activity, such as a concentration of offenses in a short period of time, is generally felt to indicate some psychological problem rather than developing criminality. In either instance, psychiatric referral may be forthcoming, with the court clinic expected to fill in the missing background in psychological terms.

Court assessments of trouble and moral character depend not only on how past behavior is interpreted, but also upon immediate impressions of the youth. . . . Probation interviews, in fact, regularly serve as means for interpreting a youth's character. Delinquents who behave politely, show respect for both parents and the probation officer, acknowledge the officer's authority and right to ask questions, and appear convincingly remorseful—in short, who behave in ways reflecting a "good attitude"—will tend to be judged as normal in character and inspire the probation officer as someone who can be worked with, perhaps even in the face of recurring delinquencies. In contrast, the youth who persists in acting "fresh," defiantly, who refuses to become repentant or who does so with visibly less than full conviction, will become identified as "hardened," criminally inclined, and will quickly lose the protection and support of the probation officer if he gets into much further trouble.

Finally, court staff also expect the problems and misconduct of youths headed toward serious delinquency to surface in behavior in school and at home. One probation officer noted, for example, that she identified "severe cases" by "late hours, stubbornness, resentment to the parents, 'D' in conduct." The school reports routinely obtained by probation and court staff provide detailed records of performance, trouble incidents, psychological and other testings, and less formal teacher and staff evaluations, all of which may be organized to document the developing disruptive and delinquent tendencies of the youth involved.

Of further interest here is the pervasive assumption of court personnel that "something wrong in the home" is both a cause and a sign of possible future delinquency. Court personnel attend very closely to the family situations of the youths coming before them. "Broken homes," including divorced or separated parents, are frequently identified as the probable source of delinquent misconduct. But the court also recognizes a somewhat broader category of "bad home situations" promoting delinquency. Parents may be judged "weak," disinterested, uncaring, or simply immoral in ways that lead to delinquency by lack of control, neglect, or example. Or some more psychological "family problem," such as strain with a stepparent or an objectionable personality trait of one or both of the parents, may be identified as the source of difficulties and tensions. In general, the integrity and morality of the delinquents' family life is reviewed, evaluated, and cited in justification of official intervention by court staff. A "bad home situation" becomes an expected background feature in serious, "hardcore" delinquency, and its apparent absence may even suggest to the court that the youth's problem is psychological, not criminal. Concretely, a "bad home" is often treated as an indicator of "real trouble" and serious delinquency by court personnel, leading to a more severe response to the case, while an apparently "good home" and parents' reports of "good behavior" at home tend at first to minimize court perceptions of serious delinquency.

In conclusion, the regular use of a youth's family situation by court and probation staff to identify "real delinquents" has basic implications for sociological research and theories of delinquency. With other things (e.g., the offense) equal, a "broken home" or "bad family situation" increase a youth's risks of being identified and treated as a "real delinquent" at critical points in his contacts with the juvenile court. As opposed to a youth from a "good" family, he is more apt to be brought to court on a formal petition rather than receive informal handling, to be given intensive rather than routine probation, and incarcerated rather than kept in the community. Identification not only of a "broken home," but also of a "bad neighborhood," "trouble in school," and "bad peer associations," may lead to differential court responses to delinquency cases. In this way, "the ideologies and policies of law-enforcement officials selectively assemble juveniles for probation evaluation according to existing theories shared by the community and social scientists." Theories of delinquency are not an exclusively sociological prerogative: juvenile-court and probation personnel develop and hold similar theories of the causes of delinquency. And it is the court staff, acting upon and responding to cases on the basis of their theories, that produce the data that the sociologist works with, data such as correlations between official rates of delinquency and family instability, poor neighborhoods, school problems, and the like.

CHARACTER AND ROUTINE PROBATION

In identifying cases involving "real trouble" and problematic character, the juvenile court begins to allocate its time, effort, and resources differentially between cases. Facing a large number of complaints about delinquency with limited staff and resources, the court comes to deal with most cases in minimal and perfunctory terms, and must distinguish these from the few to which more costly and demanding responses have to or should be undertaken. The great majority of delinquency cases are seen as manageable with only a minimum of staff time and effort devoted to overseeing the activities and situation of the delinquent. . . .

By and large, probationary supervision provides the juvenile court with its initial and routine alternatives for dealing with cases. Such supervision comes to center around the enforcement of a minimal set of standard rules aimed at forestalling further troublemaking on the part of the youth. These rules generally include: report periodically to the probation officer; attend and behave in school; get a job if out of school; and observe curfew. In addition, the youth may be warned to behave at home and to obey his parents, cautioned to stay out of trouble in school, and encouraged to complete his school work. Association with undesirable friends may be prohibited. Finally, participation in some after-school program, usually for recreation, may be arranged.

Given relatively high case loads making even supervision on these terms impossible on any large scale, probation officers come to depend heavily on indirect procedures. In particular, they routinely shift responsibility for direct and regular control of delinquents to other agents. Routine probation, in fact, explicitly involves trying to integrate (or reintegrate) the delinquent into those institutions that normally control and regulate youths' activities. The family and the schools are considered crucial here. . . . In this way the probation officer both relies upon and seeks to reaffirm the authority of these primary control institutions.

Thus, indirect probationary control regularly seeks to subject the delinquent to as continuous adult supervision and control as possible. The court makes an effort to involve delinquents in YMCA recreation programs, settlement-house activities, summer camps, etc., simply as a means of occupying and organizing their free time, keeping them off the streets and out of trouble. Similarly, out-of-school delinquents are required to work, since jobs occupy their time and place them in an adult-supervised setting.

In addition, these primary community institutions are relied on not only for day-to-day control and supervision, but also for maintaining surveillance over the youth's activities. In effect, the probation officer tries to enlist the aid of parents, teachers, school officials, social workers, and police to report to him any problems or troubles involving the youth. This gives probation an essentially reactive character: the probation officer assumes that a delinquent is staying out of trouble until or unless reports of misconduct reach him from these sources.

From this it should be apparent that the control regime employed in routine probation rests on the assumption that the delinquent involved is of *fundamentally normal character*. It is assumed that this routine, cursory probation will work with youths who are not "really delinquent." Strategic considerations in allocating probation resources over an extremely high case load seem critical here. For *as a practical matter*, there is neither sufficient time nor resources to provide intensive help and supervision to all those youths who appear on the surface to be "good kids." In addition, the payoffs that can be anticipated from such a strategy are small, for most of these youths are expected to be deterred from further delinquency by their court experience. And while the court obviously recognizes that some will get into further, perhaps serious, trouble, this will involve only a very small percentage that can still be identified early enough to be worked with effectively on more intensive probation. Moreover, ordinary probation serves as a test for the normalcy of such character. It is organized on the basis of control practices adequate for preventing further trouble by a normal youth. With no more than minimal supervision, such a delinquent is expected to proceed through the course of probation without incident (e.g., "I never see them again"). Thus routine probationary control assumes that a normal youth will be deterred by the probation officer's direct assertions of authority, intimidated by his lectures and warnings, and motivated to do better (or at least not make trouble) in his contacts with primary control institutions.

"More trouble" tends to threaten and perhaps invalidate these assumptions. More trouble indicates that routine measures are not working. As a result tighter supervision and control may be imposed.

INTENSIVE PROBATION AND MOVEMENT TOWARD INCARCERATION

As trouble continues, formal controls may be increased (e.g., a suspended sentence imposed), and closer supervision maintained. The probation officer will make frequent checks with parents and school about current behavior and new problems. The youth may be required to report more regularly to the probation officer on his doings and difficulties, and to participate actively in such court-sponsored programs as tutorial sessions and group therapy.

"Trust," relevant to cursory probation only in that the youth is assumed to be normal and hence expected to stay out of trouble, becomes critical if the probation officer wishes to move beyond a formal relationship of authority to establish a basis for helping the youth and changing his behavior.

Intensive probation, in fact, hinges upon the development and maintenance of a "trust relationship" between delinquent and probation officer. Such a relationship presumes a youth of normal moral character, a youth who "can be worked with" and probably "saved" despite his current delinquency. Probation staff will continue to tolerate and support the youth who through continued cooperation and a "good attitude" conveys normal character. Thus assessments of moral character remain critical during this phase of the delinquent's court career, particularly in the face of continuing delinquency. A youth who can maintain a good attitude and show sincerity toward the probation officer's attempts to help and supervise his activities will usually be kept on probation despite new problems.

"Good reasons" will be found in his personal circumstances to explain his shortcomings, while "more trouble" from a youth whose character has become suspect will confirm his inherent criminality, providing "documentary evidence of the 'hopelessness' of the case."

In contrast, a trust relationship and intensive probation are not developed with delinquents judged to be too far "gone" to be effectively helped and treated. For court and probation staff to get involved in such "hopeless cases"—youths well into criminal pursuits or who appear too "hardened" to be "saved" or "rehabilitated"—is a dubious expenditure of time and effort. Instead, a practical policy of "letting it go" may be preferable. . . .

Even in cases not considered "hopeless," however, more active court intervention and involvement are neither automatic nor inevitable because the court routinely attends to and seeks out *alternatives to its own programs* and controls as ways of dealing with delinquents. Psychiatric care is regarded as a particularly desirable form of help or treatment, for example, and the court will frequently withdraw from a case on the condition that the family agree to have the youth begin therapy. But even where the alternative course of action offers little or no treatment advantage, the court may accept it as a practical, feasible way of disposing of the case. . . . Often these kinds of solutions are seen to offer nothing more than a change of scene, and perhaps a chance to start over without the prejudice of an acquired record. Thus, the court hopes that such action *might* end further delinquency problems. But more importantly, where the youth has moved out of its jurisdiction, the court will not be held accountable even in the face of serious and dramatic offenses. In these ways the court is open to a fairly wide variety of "making do" practices for dealing with its cases.

As a case moves through a court and routine remedies are either rendered inappropriate or exhausted, the court staff may begin to consider more serious dispositional alternatives. If the youth does not seem to be adjusting in the community, incarceration becomes an increasingly live issue, and an active search for alternatives to supplement and/or replace intensive probation may be begun. Distinctively "helping" concerns may hasten, or even themselves lead to, the feeling that "something has to be done." For example, a youth's family situation may appear so untenable or pathological that some other arrangement appears imperative to the court staff. The more desirable and/or therapeutic the placement institution, the greater its attractiveness to court personnel as an alternative to keeping the youth at home in the community.

Arranging placement, however, can involve a difficult, complex, and extremely unpredictable set of negotiations. In the first place, the desires of both youth and family may have to be considered, and their support and cooperation obtained. Probation officers' efforts to arrange what they regard as an extremely desirable placement are easily undermined when the delinquent feels coerced and "messes up" a hard-won admission interview. Second, an institution considered appropriate for the youth and his problems with vacancies must be found. Third, institutions must often be convinced to accept the delinquent. Here many placement institutions have formal or informal policies about the specific kinds of cases they will and will not take. Depending on agency idiosyncracies, delinquents whose records include drug use, overt sexual behavior, violence, or even recurrent runaways may be either turned down directly or looked upon with disfavor. Admission regularly requires a process of negotiation where the court tries to convince the institution of the youth's basically desirable moral character and suitability for their program.

As a result, an underlying tentativeness and reversibility marks the placement process. The court, having decided that a youth has to be taken out of his home or community, begins to search out an appropriate placement. But the preferred placement simply may not be what the youth wants, may not want him, or may have openings only at some uncertain point in the future. What to do about the case, then, must be reevaluated taking these developments into account. Faced with the alternative of placement at the second-best institution, keeping the youth in his home may reemerge as the best available solution. For example, it may be decided that placement in a psychiatric facility is desirable, but for one of the reasons suggested, it cannot be obtained. The court may then reconsider what to do in terms of a choice between leaving the youth in his home and "on the streets" as against trying to work out some less palatable placement, and on balance may decide in favor of the former. Further trouble may lead to another reevaluation plus pressure to follow up on the previously discounted alternative.

With continued problems of adjusting in the community or in more desirable placements, that "something has to be done" may take on an even stronger and more fixed sense. Court personnel come to see absolutely no alternative but to take the youth out of the community, institutional placement of some form becomes unavoidable, and the issue shifts to what is the best available institution given the circumstances of the case. Especially serious offenses regularly confront the court in just these terms: where a violent crime has been committed, the court operates on the presumption that the youth must be taken off the streets. Immediate return to the community is a remote if not quite unimaginable disposition, primarily because of vulnerability to public criticism if something goes wrong.

Complainant and other outside pressures may also play an important role here. Clearly such pressures involve a key dimension in the disposition of serious offenses. Yet community pressures may arise even without the publicity and attendant visibility of a serious offense. As a youth gets into more and more serious troubles, and the usual community and institutional remedies seem ineffective, local pressures that "something be done" may become stronger and more persistent. . . .

As incarceration appears increasingly imminent and unavoidable, the court staff will frequently make frantic efforts to arrange some alternative institutional placement. Other agencies will be pressured to find some "closed" residential facility that would accept the youth: although with agency reluctance and the residence of most such institutions to "hardcore delinquents," there may be very little chance of success. A more viable option frequently involves trying to get the youth admitted to a noncorrectional state institution providing some kind of special care or training. Referrals to the court clinic are made regularly, for example, to determine whether the youth is retarded or psychotic, and hence possibly qualified for admission to state schools for the retarded or mental hospitals. Some residential placement is sought almost without regard to the nature of the delinquent's problems, as any program and focus is assumed to be more desirable than commitment to a state correctional facility.

In addition, as incarceration becomes a live issue, the ability of the families of delinquents to provide the court with alternative courses of action becomes increasingly critical. Here class differences become crucially important, as middle-class parents have more resources to mobilize in the effort to keep their child out of a state institution. Intensive psychiatric care or placement in a residential military school may be arranged by family members with the encouragement and advice of court staff in order to avert threatened or impending commitment to reform school.

In some cases commitment to the state correctional institution is viewed by court personnel as necessary to restrain a delinquent of hopelessly criminal and dangerous character. Here court and probation personnel see "no alternative" to incarceration. In other instances, however, it is not so much the delinquent's moral character as *the lack of any other practical option* that makes such commitment a necessary and unavoidable decision. . . . Youths not felt to be "really" hopeless or criminal-like by court staff, nonetheless, may eventually be incarcerated. . . .

CONCLUSION

Recent substantive criticism of the juvenile court has challenged the premise that court actions will necessarily benefit and help youth in trouble. Damaging stigma is held to be a more frequent result of court intervention than effective treatment. The negative consequences of official identification as delinquent may far outweigh any benefits of court help and treatment, particularly with the marginal offender or the predelinquent. In extreme instances, such intervention may reinforce and stabilize behaviors that in all likelihood would have been abandoned with time and increasing maturity.

With the shift of the prevailing model of the juvenile court from benevolent parent-therapist to overreaching stigmatizer came a reformulation of the court's proper approach to delinquency. Early intervention easily undertaken in the presumed interest of the youth has given way to a more cautious, restrained stance. Only serious, "last resort" cases in which the advantages of help clearly outweigh the negative consequences of court contact are appropriate objects of official action. Less serious problems of misconduct should be diverted out of the legal system into unofficial agencies for help and service. . . .

Race Effects in Juvenile Justice Decision-Making: Findings of a Statewide Analysis

Donna M. Bishop
Charles E. Frazier

I. INTRODUCTION

Overrepresentation of minorities in the juvenile justice system is well-established. On a national level, minority youths are arrested in numbers greatly disproportionate to their numbers in the general population. While black youths comprise approximately 15% of the ten to seventeen year old population at risk for delinquency, recent figures indicate that they constitute approximately 28% of youths arrested. Further, according to the Office of Juvenile Justice and Delinquency Prevention's (OJJDP) "Children in Custody" census, minority overrepresentation increases dramatically as one moves beyond arrest to later stages in processing. For example, minorities constitute approximately 62% of youths held in short-term detention facilities, and approximately 60% of those committed to "deep end" long-term institutional programs.

Quite apart from issues related either to the extent or causes of differential minority involvement in crime, a number of researchers have ex-

Reprinted by special permission of Northwestern University School of Law, *Journal of Criminal Law and Criminology*, Volume 86, Issue 2, pp. 392–413 (1996).

pressed concern about whether the juvenile justice system operates with a selection bias that differentially disadvantages minority youths. The research reported here is intended to add to the growing body of literature addressing that question. However, this research differs in significant respects from past research because it focuses on differences between the processing of delinquency and status offense (dependency) cases, rather than simply the juvenile justice system in general. Additionally, we supplement our statistical analyses with qualitative data to aid in understanding sources of racial disparity.

Our discussion is divided into two parts. In Part I, we report the findings of quantitative analyses conducted using official records of cases processed through the juvenile justice system in Florida. In Part II, we supplement and provide a basis for a more detailed interpretation of the quantitative findings, drawing upon in-depth interviews with system insiders—juvenile judges, state's attorneys, public defenders, and social service personnel. Based on those interviews, we explore the social and organizational processes underlying the findings reported in Part I.

II. PART I

A. Considerations Guiding the Quantitative Analysis

Because the juvenile justice system consists of multiple decision points, it is essential that researchers track cases from arrest to final disposition through as many stages as possible. This is desirable for at least two reasons. First, decisions made at different points reflect the actions of different decision-makers—such as social service workers at intake, prosecuting attorneys at case filing, judges at court disposition—whose professional philosophies, organizational subcultures, and discretionary authority differ in ways that may render either intentional discrimination or institutional discrimination more or less likely to occur. The identification of more and less problematic decision points may facilitate both an understanding of sources of racial disparity as well as the development of strategies to reduce it.

Second, if a researcher examines only a single decision point, such as judicial disposition, the researcher's analyses may underestimate or altogether miss the effect of race. If disparities occur at early decision points that are not examined, analyses of late-stage outcomes are likely to produce findings of no discrimination.

Another consideration guiding the quantitative portions of the research is the importance of estimating multivariate models that include controls for legally-relevant factors that might explain or justify race differentials in processing outcomes. At a minimum, we wanted to include as precise a measure of offense severity as the data would permit, as well as a measure of offense history that would take into account both the frequency and severity of individuals' prior records.

A final consideration guiding the quantitative analyses is the possibility that the effect of race might be conditioned by other variables. Frequently, those who have explored racial disparities in justice system processing have restricted their estimates of additive or main effects models, which can obscure substantial race differences in treatment. Suppose, for example, that nonwhites and whites charged with serious offenses receive similar dispositions, while nonwhites charged with minor offenses receive harsher dispositions than whites. In this instance, an additive model might show little or no racial impact, while an interactive model would reveal a significant race effect contingent upon offense severity.

B. The Data Set

Data for the quantitative portions of this study were obtained from the Client Information System maintained by Florida's Department of Health and Rehabilitative Services (DHRS). The data set includes the total population of youths referred for juvenile intake processing throughout the state between January 1, 1985 and December 31, 1987. Because Florida law requires that all juvenile complaint reports be processed through the intake division, the data set is quite comprehensive and includes records of all police contacts other than those resulting in informal field adjustments, as well as referrals from parents, school officials, and other nonpolice sources. The case records were organized to permit tracking of decisions made at multiple stages in processing, from initial intake through judicial disposition.

Because the Client Information System tracks referrals rather than individuals, we reorganized the data set around individuals so that multiple referrals of a youth to the juvenile justice system over the three year period could be chronicled and examined. We accomplished this by restricting our analyses to the last delinquency referral in 1987 for each individual, a procedure that allowed us to capture at least two full years of offense and processing history information for each youth. The total number of individuals at the point of initial intake is 161,369. This includes 137,028 youths referred for delinquent acts. . . .

In the analyses that follow, the juvenile justice system is viewed as a series of decision points, each of which is simplified to represent a dichotomous contrast. Four stages are involved in delinquency case processing. . . .

1. Delinquency Case Processing

1. INTAKE SCREENING   DHRS officials review all referrals originating from police arrests or from complaints by nonpolice sources. In addition to reviewing the facts presented in each referral, they are expected to interview the juvenile and his/her parents or guardians. They then make nonbinding recommendations to the state's attorney regarding the preferred method of handling each case. Intake officers may recommend that a case

be closed without action, that it be diverted from the juvenile justice system for informal handling, or that it be referred to court for formal processing. . . .

2. DETENTION STATUS   Decisions regarding detention status are made shortly after delinquency referrals are received. Detention decisions are made jointly by intake staff, law enforcement officials (when referrals are police-initiated), and state's attorneys. . . .

3. PROSECUTORIAL REFERRAL   State's attorneys decide whether a delinquency case proceeds to court, . . . cases in which a decision was made to file a formal petition of delinquency or to seek transfer to adult court. . . .

4. JUDICIAL DISPOSITION   The final stage in the processing of delinquency cases modeled in these analyses is judicial disposition of cases. Although the court has a wide range of options, our analyses compare youths who were returned to the community, (e.g., those ordered to do community work service, placed on informal probation, placed on formal probation), with those who were committed to residential facilities (e.g., youth camps, training schools) or transferred to adult criminal court. . . .

3. Independent Variables

SOCIODEMOGRAPHIC CHARACTERISTICS   The *RACE* categories in the Client Information System include "white," "black," "American Indian," "Asian or Pacific Islander," and "unknown." Because the number of persons classified as "American Indian," "Asian or Pacific Islander," and "unknown" was very small (less than 1% of the cases), we restrict the analysis to blacks, whom we hereafter refer to as nonwhites, and whites. Other sociodemographic characteristics included in the analysis are *GENDER* and *AGE*.

For the analysis of delinquency cases, we used the most serious offense cited in the arrest or complaint to characterize the *CURRENT OFFENSE*. We coded this variable using the following scoring scheme: felony offense against person = 6; felony property offense = 5; felony offense against public order = 4; misdemeanor offense against person = 3; misdemeanor property offense = 2; misdemeanor offense against public order = 1. . . .

We operationalized *PRIOR RECORD* by measuring the severity of prior referrals to the juvenile justice system. This measurement allowed us to account for both the frequency and severity of prior offending, and we constructed it by adding the severity scores of all offenses in each prior referral (using the same severity values as described above for CURRENT OFFENSE), then dividing by the number of prior referrals.

Where appropriate, we also included case processing outcomes as independent variables in the analyses. That is, we explored the effects of decisions made at earlier stages in processing on subsequent stage outcomes (e.g., the effect of being held in secure detention on judicial disposition). This procedure allowed us to identify and assess possible indirect effects of race on case outcomes.

C. Analysis and Findings

Because we defined each of the processing outcomes in terms of a dichotomous contrast, we used logistic regression as the method of estimation. In addition to estimating the main effects of each predictor in additive models, we also estimated models for each processing outcome that included all two-way interactions involving race. These interaction models allowed us to determine whether the influence of race at each decision point is conditioned by values of other variables in the model. We report models containing interaction terms in the tables only where the interaction model produced a significant increment in fit over the additive model.

... [I]t is important to note that nonwhites comprise 21% of the population at risk (ages ten to seventeen) and 29% of the group referred to delinquency intake, but only 19% of the group referred to dependency intake.

... [A]mong those referred for delinquent acts, a greater proportion of nonwhites than whites received the more severe disposition at each successive stage in processing. Racial disparities are most pronounced at intake screening and judicial disposition. For example, 53% of nonwhite youths referred to intake are recommended for referral to court, compared to 42% of white youths. At judicial disposition, 31% of nonwhite youths are incarcerated or transferred, compared to 18% of white youths. The cumulative effect of these decisions is that the racial composition of the cohort becomes increasingly nonwhite as it moves through the system: while nonwhites make up 21% of the population at risk (ages ten to seventeen) and 29% of the cohort referred to delinquency intake, they make up 44% of the cohort incarcerated or transferred...

... [R]esults for intake referral outcomes ... indicate that the seriousness of the current offense weighs heavily in intake decision-making, and is the strongest predictor of outcomes at this stage. As might be expected, intake officers also consider youths' prior records of offending and are more likely to recommend formal processing for youths with lengthy and serious prior records. In addition, however, there is evidence that individual characteristics of youths influence intake referral decisions. Nonwhites, older youths, and males are significantly more likely to be recommended for formal processing than are whites, younger adolescents, and females.

Because logistic regression coefficients do not have a clear, intuitive interpretation, it is helpful to discuss the effect of race on the probability that intake will recommend a case for formal processing. To do this, we illustrate with the case of a typical youth referral: we calculate the predicted probability of a recommendation for formal processing for white and nonwhite youths with values of other variables in the model set at their respective means. In these data, the typical youth referred to delinquency intake is a fifteen year old male referred for a misdemeanor against person (e.g., simple battery), with a prior record score consistent with having one prior referral for a misdemeanor against property (e.g., criminal mischief). The probability that a white youth with these characteristics will be recommended for formal processing is 47%. For a similar nonwhite youth, the probability of a recommendation for formal processing is 54%—a substantial difference of seven percentage points.

... [D]etention decisions are influenced to a modest degree by race when other important variables are controlled. For the typical case, the probability of being held in secure detention is 12% for a white youth, compared with 16% for a nonwhite youth. The strongest predictors of detention status are the legal variables of current offense and prior record. Gender and age are also significant predictors, although, as is the case with race, their effects are modest.

... [T]he effect of race on detention status is conditioned by both gender and prior record. Nonwhite males and females are handled much more similarly than are white males and females: among whites, the probability of being detained for females is significantly lower than is the case for males. Nonwhite females, on the other hand, are detained at a rate that approximates that of nonwhite males. The effect of race is also conditioned by severity of a youth's prior record. When youths have no prior record, or their prior record is not serious, nonwhites and whites are rarely detained, and there is little difference in their detention rates. When the prior record is indicative of serious or frequent offending, however, the risk of being detained is much higher for nonwhites than for whites.

Two illustrations may help to clarify the nature of these interaction effects. Consider, for example, a white male with a relatively high prior record score of eight. His probability of detention is 17%. A nonwhite male with the same prior record has a probability of detention of 23%, a difference of six percentage points. A nonwhite female with a similar prior record has a detention probability of 21% (higher than that of the white male), while a similar white female has a probability of detention under these circumstances of 16%. When the prior record score is low, however, these race and gender differences are almost nonexistent.

... [At] the prosecutorial referral stage ... offense seriousness and prior record each have significant effects on prosecutorial decision-making, as do gender and age. The impact of race is very modest: the typical white youth has a 32% chance of being referred to court, compared to a 34% chance for the typical nonwhite youth. After controlling for other variables, being detained has the effect of increasing the likelihood of referral to court. Consequently, some of the influence of race on prosecutorial decision-making is subsumed by the effect of detention status. Nonwhites are more likely than whites to be detained, and those who are detained are more likely to be prosecuted. Thus, racial inequality at the prosecutorial referral stage is more pronounced than the race coefficient in this model would suggest.

... [F]or judicial disposition [t]he ... severity of the current offense and prior record each have significant, though fairly modest, effects on dispositional outcomes. Juveniles who are detained are also more likely to receive dispositions of incarceration. Once again, race, operating through detention status, indirectly affects disposition. Those found in contempt also are significantly more likely to receive harsher judicial dispositions. At this final stage in processing, each of the sociodemographic characteristics has a significant effect on case outcomes, the effect of race being relatively strong. The typical white delinquent has a 9% probability of being committed or transferred, compared to a 16% probability for nonwhites.

The results for judicial disposition become considerably more complex when we examine ... three significant interaction terms in a better fitting model. The effects of race on case outcomes at this stage are conditioned by gender, prior record, and contempt status. To summarize briefly, while nonwhite and white youths with more serious prior records are dealt with similarly, nonwhite offenders with nonserious prior records are more likely to be incarcerated or transferred than white offenders with nonserious prior records. The findings also indicate that the treatment of nonwhite females more closely approximates the treatment accorded nonwhite males than does the treatment of white females approximate the treatment of white males. Finally, being held in contempt increases the likelihood of a more severe outcome selectively among whites, but not among nonwhites. . . .

D. Summary of Findings of the Quantitative Analysis

Our analysis points to clear disadvantages for nonwhites at multiple stages in delinquency case processing. While the magnitude of the race effect varies from stage to stage, there is a consistent pattern of unequal treatment. Nonwhite youths referred for delinquent acts are more likely than comparable white youths to be recommended for petition to court, to be held in preadjudicatory detention, to be formally processed in juvenile court, and to receive the most formal or the most restrictive judicial dispositions. . . .

III. PART II

A. Interview Data

To supplement and provide a basis for interpreting our quantitative findings, we conducted telephone interviews ranging in length from one to four hours with a randomly selected sample of thirty-four juvenile justice officials. The sample includes intake supervisors, assistant state's attorneys assigned to juvenile divisions, public defenders assigned to juvenile divisions, and juvenile court judges from each judicial circuit. A primary reason for conducting the interviews was to examine more deeply and from different perspectives the race differences uncovered in the quantitative portion of our analyses. We wanted to determine what officials working in the system observed and believed with regard to race effects, as well as how they interpreted these effects. Although most of our respondents are seasoned insiders with years of experience in juvenile justice, the explanations they offer must be considered tentative, because the sample is small. We are confident, however, that their observations point to potentially fruitful avenues for further research.

Findings of race differentials in processing, while consistent with the notion of intentional race bias or discrimination, are subject to a number of other interpretations as well. It would be too simplistic to conclude that our findings provide evidence of widespread racial prejudice. As we shall see, the reasons offered by justice officials for the racial disparities that we have observed are multiple and complex.

A majority of the juvenile justice officials whom we interviewed were quick to indicate that our findings of racial disparities in processing were consistent with their experiences and observations. There was, however, variation by functional role. For example, all of the DHRS caseworkers and defense attorneys in the sample perceived race disparities in processing. A smaller proportion of prosecutors and judges perceived race effects. There was also variation in interviewees' perceptions of the kinds of racial bias present in the juvenile justice system. Some respondents, for example, believed the main problem was individuals who held and applied prejudicial attitudes. Many more saw the problem as endemic to the system, the consequence of well-intended policies and practices that impact differentially on whites and nonwhites.

This latter group of respondents suggested that racial disparities in delinquency case processing are in part a result of agency policies and practices that focus on family support and family cooperation as considerations for diversion, for detention, and for final disposition. They noted that, in some instances, these considerations are incorporated into formalized agency decision criteria.

For example, DHRS policy renders youths referred for delinquent acts ineligible for diversion programs if their parents or guardians (a) cannot be contacted, (b) are contacted but are unable to be present for an intake interview, or (c) exhibit attitudes and styles of behavior that are perceived as uncooperative to intake staff. It is important to note that availability of a telephone and access both to transportation to DHRS offices and child care for young children who must remain at home are all taken for granted in this diversion policy.

DHRS intake supervisors reported that minority parents often are single working mothers or single mothers on welfare with other young children at home. If employed, they are often employed in low-paying, low-status occupations; unlike those in managerial and professional positions, these parents often lack the flexibility to take time from work to be interviewed. In addition, many may be embarrassed to make such requests of their employers. Those who are unemployed and on welfare frequently lack access to child care for young children remaining at home. Many must depend on public transportation which may not operate near their homes or DHRS offices. Some do not have telephones and this makes it more difficult for DHRS officials to contact them. Intake officials also indicated that minority parents tend more often than white parents to be distrustful of the juvenile justice system. Intake staff tend to see these families as less cooperative with DHRS. Similar references to family support and cooperation were cited by prosecutors as key considerations in detention decisions. Generally, these considerations have a negative and differential impact on nonwhite delinquents. Typical is the view illustrated in the following comment by a delinquency intake supervisor:

> Our manual told us to interview the child and the parent prior to making a recommendation to the state's attorney. We are less able to reach poor and minority clients. They are less responsive to attempts to reach them. They don't show. They don't have transportation. Then they are more likely to be recommended for formal processing. Without access to a client's family, the less severe options are closed. Once it gets to court, the case is likely to be adjudicated because it got there. It's a self fulfilling prophecy.

Thus far, we have noted that respondents identified criteria for diversion and detention that render nonwhite offenders more likely to be recommended for formal processing and held in secure detention. It is interesting to note the interface between these comments and the findings of our quantitative analyses. Note, for example, that race had no direct effect on prosecutorial filing decisions, and that both prosecutorial filing decisions and judicial dispositional decisions to incarcerate were influenced by detention status. The race effect on both the decision to formally prosecute and on the judicial decision to incarcerate appears to emanate in no small part from decisions made at earlier stages in the system—decisions to recommend formal prosecution and secure detention—that are tied to well-intended but inadvertently discriminatory front-end agency policies.

Many of the interviewees were aware that policies of Florida's juvenile justice system locked them into decisions that ultimately disadvantage nonwhites. Respondents from all levels of the system commented on the unfairness of a structure which renders nonwhite youths more vulnerable to formal processing because their families are unable to comply with agency policies.

Many respondents also reported that juvenile justice decisions in delinquency cases are affected by differentials in access to retained counsel and private treatment resources, differentials that impact negatively on low-income—especially minority—clients. Especially in later stages of delinquency processing, respondents observed that the system emphasizes treatments (e.g., psychological counseling, drug treatment) that are often best obtained through private agencies. Youths from affluent families may take advantage of these treatment options and avoid formal processing. Minority youths who are less affluent can only obtain comparable services by being adjudicated delinquent and then committed to residential facilities. As one of the judges in our sample observed:

> Minorities and low income kids get more [juvenile justice system] resources. If parents can afford [an expensive private treatment facility], the child gets probation. If not, he gets committed. Income is significant in that a lot of early interventions are directed to middle income groups. If a child needs constructive activity, a middle class family can afford it. Maybe there is institutional bias.

As might be expected, some respondents were very critical of practices which resulted in minorities receiving harsher treatment by justice officials. Others argued that these practices were quite defensible. In their view, justice officials were merely trying to provide needed services to the disadvantaged that wealthy families could purchase on their own. To become eligible for these services, however, youths had to be formally processed—e.g., referred to court, adjudicated delinquent, and placed on formal probation or committed to residential programs. Only then could these services be provided at state expense. Moreover, this sort of policy negatively impacts on nonwhites anytime they come back to the system on a subsequent charge. A juvenile's prior record and prior disposition history are primary predictors of (and primary justifications for) formal processing and more severe sanctions. What may begin with good intentions at an earlier stage ultimately becomes a self-fulfilling prophecy. The influence of race is obscured as decisions to formally prosecute and detain in the past are used to justify more severe sanctions for youths returning to the system.

In addition, many respondents indicated that juvenile justice officials make decisions influenced in part by perceptions (or misperceptions) of youths' family backgrounds and circumstances. Respondents frequently reported that delinquent youths from single-parent families and those from families incapable of (or perceived to be incapable of) providing good parental supervision are more likely to be referred to court and placed under state control. In other words, when justice officials perceive that there is family strength and support, they are more likely to select less intrusive treatments and sanctions. For the most part, our respondents believed that these distinctions were fair and appropriate. They also indicated that, at least in delinquency cases, black family systems generally tend to be perceived in a more negative light, that pre-disposition reports give disproportionate attention to assessments of family situations, and that judges rely heavily on pre-disposition reports in reaching dispositional decisions.

Several comments made by state's attorneys and judges are instructive:

> Judge: "Inadequate family correlates with race and ethnicity. It makes sense to put delinquent kids from these circumstances in residential facilities."

> State's Attorney: "Detention decisions are decided on the basis of whether the home can control and supervise a child. So minorities don't go home because, unfortunately, their families are less able to control the kids

... I think the way the system sets up programs shows some institutional bias. If family stability was not a prerequisite to admission to less severe program options, race differences would be less."

State's Attorney: "In black families who the dad is, is unknown, while in white families—even when divorced—dad is married or something else. The choices are limited because the black family is a multi generational non-fathered family. You can't send the kid off to live with dad."

One of the key findings of our quantitative analyses was that nonwhites are disadvantaged in delinquency case processing. . . .

B. Conclusions

Our findings show clear indications of race differentials in justice processing. The quantitative analyses demonstrate appreciable effects of race on delinquency case processing that disadvantage minority offenders. These findings are consistent with perceptions of juvenile justice officials at all levels of professional involvement. That minority offenders are disadvantaged is not surprising. A number of previous studies have reported similar findings. . . .

Had we only the quantitative data, these contrasts would have caused us concern; we would have had no basis for offering an explanation. Interviews with justice officials conducted as a second phase of this research have offered an intriguing glimpse into the dynamics of justice work, into organizational policies, practices, and philosophies, and into the possibility of manipulative use of race realities and perceptions.

Our qualitative findings support several interpretations. Intentional race discrimination does not appear to play a major role in accounting for racial disparities in processing. Although some officials whom we interviewed believed that some justice officials were motivated by prejudicial attitudes, few recounted specific instances of racially motivated actions. Without question, there are some justice officials who hold and act upon racially prejudicial attitudes. As long as race bias exists in the general culture, it would be surprising indeed if it did not operate through individuals in the juvenile justice system as well. However, we are not inclined to conclude that the disparities we observed are largely attributable to intentional race discrimination.

Instead, we see much evidence of institutional racism. This is evident both in criteria for diversion and pre-trial release that focus on family support and cooperation, and in efforts to provide the economically disadvantaged with resources at state expense that the more affluent can purchase on their own. Obtaining these resources exacts a price in terms of adjudications of delinquency and sentences to confinement. . . .

In closing, we wish to emphasize the tentative nature of our conclusions. Though randomly selected, our interview sample was small. Moreover, the sample was not stratified to include representative numbers of intake officials and judges from both delinquency and dependency courts. Further research is needed to explore the alternative interpretations offered here for the quantitative findings. Interviews with large samples of individuals drawn from both the dependency and delinquency systems would be helpful. In addition, participant observation and other field studies may provide clearer insights into informal agency policies and practices, and organizational climates that provide the context within which race effects may be most fully understood.

B. JUVENILE INSTITUTIONS AND ALTERNATIVES

The articles in Chapter 5 B provide important insights into the processes of juvenile corrections. The Supreme Court in *Gault* belatedly recognized the longstanding contradictions between rehabilitative rhetoric and punitive reality; conditions of confinement motivated the Court to insist on minimal procedural safeguards for juveniles. Contemporary evaluations of juvenile institutions reveal a continuing gap between rehabilitative rhetoric and punitive reality. "Juvenile Corrections," the excerpt from Howard Snyder and Melissa Sickmund, *Juvenile Offenders and Victims*, provides current data on the various types of juvenile correctional facilities and the offense, age, and racial characteristics of their residents. They summarize data on conditions of confinement, types of offenses for which juvenile courts commit youths to institutions, their length of stay, and the like. Again, these data on conditions of confinement suggest the organizational variability of the juvenile justice process. They also report that racial minority juveniles now constitute the majority of youths held in public correctional facilities. Barry C. Feld, "Comparative Analysis of Organizational Structure and Inmate Subcultures," analyzes the relationships between a juvenile institution's "program" and the correctional experiences of confined youths. Feld summarizes some characteristics of "custodial" and "treatment" programs and concludes that violent and oppositional inmate subcultures result from staff security arrangements; the more guards impose authoritarian controls to facilitate security, the higher the levels of covert inmate violence within the subculture. What are the implications of Snyder and Sickmund's descriptions of recent trends toward greater reliance on perimeter fences, locked internal security, and institutional overcrowding for the implementation of the various correctional models that Feld describes?

Peter Greenwood and Susan Turner, "Evaluation of the Paint Creek Youth Center," describe one type of correctional alternative to traditional juvenile institutions. As early as the 1960s, states experimented with community-based corrections in group homes and half-way houses as an alterative to institutional confinement for juveniles. In the early 1970s, the Mass-achusetts Department of Youth Services closed its training schools for delin-quents, returned most committed youths to their families or placed them in community-based facilities and purchased services locally. Greenwood and Turner's analyses of a small, "open" treatment program suggests that such an intervention provide a "cost-effective" alternative to traditional juvenile institutions without jeopardizing public safety.

Juvenile Corrections

HOWARD SNYDER AND MELISSA SICKMUND

JUVENILES IN CORRECTIONAL FACILITIES

Juvenile corrections is comprised of many different components. Some juvenile correctional facilities look much like adult prisons. Others seem much like "home." Unlike adult corrections, private facilities continue to play a substantial role in the long-term custody of juveniles. In fact, although they do not hold as many juveniles, there are many more privately operated juvenile facilities than publicly operated facilities.

This chapter describes the population of juveniles in custody and the facilities that hold them. The long-term custody population is described in terms of demographics, offense, average length of stay, and facility type. This information is based on OJJDP's Children in Custody Census of Juvenile Detention, Correctional, and Shelter Facilities. Information on the characteristics of the facilities themselves (from OJJDP's *Conditions of Confinement* report) is also presented. A somewhat different look at juvenile corrections is provided by OJJDP's *Juveniles Taken Into Custody* report, which presents information on juveniles admitted to State juvenile correctional systems. . . .

JUVENILE CORRECTIONAL FACILITIES ARE CLASSIFIED IN DIFFERENT WAYS

Information on residents of long-term custody facilities is drawn from OJJDP's *Children in Custody* census of juvenile facilities. This census of facilities has been conducted since 1971. Facilities are asked to complete census questionnaires every other year. Private facilities were included in the census for the first time in 1974; however, their response rate has never

Excerpted from Snyder, Howard N. and Sickmund, Melissa. (1995) *Juvenile Offenders and Victims: A National Report*, pp. 163–178. Washington, DC: Office of Juvenile Justice and Delinquency Prevention.

reached the 100% level. Private facility trends are not presented because it is not known what impact response rate variations have had on the data.

The *Children in Custody* census classifies facilities in several different ways. Facilities are identified as *publicly* or *privately* operated. The census also collects information on each facility's primary purpose and categorizes them as *long-term* or *short-term* facilities. Typically, short-term facilities hold juveniles awaiting adjudication, disposition, or placement, and long-term facilities hold juveniles who have been adjudicated and committed to custody. Data are collected on each facility's environment (security and access to the community) and they are categorized as *institutional* or *open* facilities. The census also asks each respondent to identify the facility as either a detention center; shelter; reception or diagnostic center; training school; ranch, camp, or farm; or as a halfway house or group home. Long-term institutional facilities include training schools and some facilities in the ranch/camp/farm group. Long-term open facilities consist of ranches, camps, farms, halfway houses, and group homes.

Some facilities serve more than one purpose. For example, a training school may also have a detention unit, or a detention center may house a long-term treatment unit for adjudicated offenders. While the census groups the facility according to its primary purpose, population counts are reported separately for committed, detained, and voluntarily admitted juveniles.

MOST JUVENILES IN LONG-TERM FACILITIES WERE COMMITTED THERE

Juveniles may be *committed* to a facility as part of a court-ordered disposition, they may be detained prior to adjudication or after adjudication while awaiting disposition or placement, and a small proportion of juveniles are *voluntarily admitted* (by themselves, or referred by their parents, school officials, or a diversion program). Most admissions to long-term public facilities are commitment admissions.

THE AVERAGE LENGTH OF STAY FOR YOUTH COMMITTED TO LONG-TERM FACILITIES WAS ABOUT 6 MONTHS

Overall, juveniles released from long-term public facilities during 1990 remained in custody 5 months on average. The average length of stay, however, varied substantially by facility type and admission status. Committed juveniles remained in custody longer than detained juveniles or those who were voluntarily admitted. Juveniles held in detention units in otherwise long-term facilities stayed longer than juveniles detained in detention centers (21 vs. 15 days).

The average length of stay was longer in institutional than in open facilities. This resulted from the difference in stays for committed juveniles and the greater proportion of voluntary admissions in open facilities.

The average length of stay for long-term private facilities in 1990 was

Releases From Public Long-Term Facilities

Admission status	1990 releases	Average length of stay
Total	93,352*	157 days
Committed	78,880	182
Detained	11,563	21
Voluntary	2,909	22
Institutional facilities	62,659*	171
Committed	53,843	196
Detained	8,728	21
Voluntary	88	28
Open facilities	30,693*	129
Committed	25,037	153
Detained	2,835	22
Voluntary	2,821	22

*Length of stay was not reported for an additional 102 institutional and 152 open releases.
Source: OJJDP. (1993). Children in custody census 1990/1991 [machine-readable data file].

slightly longer than for public facilities—186 days for institutional facilities, 173 days for open facilities, and 175 for the overall average.

MOST JUVENILES IN PUBLIC CUSTODY ARE IN INSTITUTIONAL FACILITIES

Three-quarters of the more than 36,000 juveniles held in public long-term facilities in 1991 were held in institutional facilities—primarily training schools. Compared with the population in long-term public facilities, those in private long-term facilities were more apt to be held in open than in institutional facilities.

Of the roughly 34,000 juveniles held in privately operated long-term facilities, 80% were held in facilities with open environments. Most of these were in halfway houses. The majority of youth in private institutional facilities were in training schools.

MANY JUVENILES IN PRIVATE LONG-TERM FACILITIES ARE NOT HELD FOR ANY LAW VIOLATION

Private long-term institutional facilities held greater proportions of status offenders and nonoffenders than did their public counterparts.

• Status offenders were 12% of private and 1% of public institutional facility residents; nonoffenders were 37% of private and <1% of public institutional residents.

Juveniles Held For Person Offenses and Property Crimes Made Up Equal Proportions of the Public Long-Term Institutional Facility Population

| Most serious offense | Percent of juveniles in public long-term facilities on February 15, 1991 | | | | | |
| | Institutional facilities | | | Open facilities | | |
	Total	Committed	Detained	Total	Committed	Detained
Delinquency	100%	100%	100%	100%	100%	100%
Person	39	39	32	25	25	21
Violent	24	25	18	13	13	6
Other	15	15	14	12	12	16
Property	38	39	32	50	50	56
Serious	24	24	26	32	32	24
Other	14	14	6	18	18	32
Alcohol	1	1	1	2	2	1
Drugs	11	11	16	11	11	2
Trafficking	6	5	10	6	6	0
Other	6	6	6	5	5	2
Public order	4	4	2	5	5	3
Tech. violation	6	5	16	7	7	10
Other delinq.	2	0	1	0	0	7
Status offense	100%	100%	100%	100%	100%	100%
Running away	22	21	43	28	27	42
Truancy	21	21	0	22	23	11
Incorrigibility	31	31	14	27	27	32
Curfew	8	8	0	2	2	0
Liquor	5	5	0	8	8	5
Valid court order violation	11	10	43	12	12	5
Other status offense	3	3	0	2	2	5

- Virtually 100% of the 27,093 juveniles held in public long-term institutional facilities on February 15, 1991, were held for law violations—98% for delinquency offenses and 1% for status offenses. Nonoffenders made up less than half of 1% of the population.

- Compared with long-term institutional facilities, long-term open facilities held a greater proportion of status offenders (6%) and nonoffenders (6%). The overwhelming majority of residents, though, were held for delinquency offenses (91%).

- In both institutional and open long-term facilities, only about 1 in 10 delinquents were female. Females made up a larger share of status offenders, especially in open facilities. About 3 in 10 status offenders were female in institutional facilities, compared with 4 in 10 in open facilities. Only among runaways in open facilities did females outnumber males.

Source: OJJDP. (1993). Children in custody census 1990/91 *[machine-readable data file].*

- About 4 in 10 nonoffenders were voluntarily admitted to the facility.

- Most voluntarily admitted juveniles were referred to the facility by school officials or by their parents. Others were part of a diversion program. Very few juveniles were self-admitted.

- 51% of private long-term institutional facility residents were held for delinquency offenses.

- 40% of delinquents were held for property offenses.
- 35% were held for person offenses.
- 12% were held for drug offenses.

Private long-term open facilities held a greater proportion of nonoffenders (48%) than did their public facility counterparts (6%). As with institutional facilities, about 4 in 10 nonoffenders were juveniles voluntarily admitted to the facility—and about half of these were referred by school officials, another third were referred by their parents. Some juveniles were part of a diversion program. Relatively few were self-admitted.

- 38% of residents were held for delinquency offenses.
- 49% of delinquents were held for property offenses.
- 21% were held for person offenses.
- 14% were held for drug offenses.

MINORITIES WERE MORE THAN TWO-THIRDS OF ALL RESIDENTS IN PUBLIC LONG-TERM FACILITIES

Race/ethnicity	Percent of total juvenile residents
Institutional facility residents	100%
White (non-Hispanic)	31
Minorities	69
White Hispanic	17
Black	49
Amer. Indian/Alaska Native	1
Asian/Pacific Islander	2
Open facility residents	100%
White (non-Hispanic)	44
Minorities	56
White Hispanic	15
Black	37
Amer. Indian/Alaska Native	3
Asian/Pacific Islander	1

Source: OJJDP. (1993). Children in custody census 1990/91 [machine-readable data files].

PRIVATE LONG-TERM FACILITIES ALSO HOUSE A DISPROPORTIONATE NUMBER OF MINORITIES

The custody population in private long-term institutional facilities had a smaller proportion of minorities (51%) than did their publicly operated counterparts (69%). The same was true for private long-term open facilities. Mi-

Both Institutional and Open Long-Term Public Facilities Saw Increases in Their Minority Populations

Race/ethnicity	Number on February 15, 1991	Percent change 1983–1991
Institutional facilities		
Total juvenile residents	27,093	10%
White (non-Hispanic)	8,377	−23
Total minorities	18,716	37
White Hispanic	4,589	58
Black	13,224	28
Amer. Indian/Alaska Native	379	−6
Asian/Pacific Islander	524	495

- The number of minorities held in public long-term institutional facilities increased 37% from 1983–1991; in open facilities the increase was 31%.

Race/ethnicity	Number on February 15, 1991	Percent change 1983–1991
Open facilities		
Total juvenile residents	9,185	2%
White (non-Hispanic)	4,000	−20
Total minorities	5,185	31
White Hispanic	1,407	88
Black	3,408	14
Amer. Indian/Alaska Native	243	44
Asian/Pacific Islander	127	149

- From 1983–1991, the number of non-Hispanic white juveniles held in public long-term facilities dropped—23% in institutional facilities and 20% in open facilities.

Source: OJJDP. (1985, 1993). Children in custody census 1982/83 and 1990/91 [machine-readable data files].

norities made up 41% of juveniles held in private long-term open facilities, compared with 56% of those in public long-term open facilities.

THE PUBLIC LONG-TERM CUSTODY POPULATION INCREASED 8% FROM 1983 TO 1991

The overall increase in the number of juveniles in public long-term facilities on a given day resulted primarily from increases in the number of juveniles held in institutional facilities.

STATE "UPPER AGE" VARIATIONS INFLUENCE CUSTODY RATES

Although State custody rate statistics control for upper age of juvenile court jurisdiction, comparisons made among States with different upper ages are problematic. While 16- and 17-year-olds constitute approximately 25% of the population ages 10–17, they account for more than 40% of youth arrests, delinquency court cases, and juveniles in custody. If all other factors were equal, one would expect higher juvenile custody rates in States where older youth are under juvenile court jurisdiction. In addition to upper age differences, custody rates are influenced by differences in age limits of extended jurisdiction. Some States may keep a youth in custody for several years beyond the upper age of juvenile court jurisdiction; others cannot. Demographic variations should also be considered when making State comparisons. Urbanicity and economics of an area are thought to be related to crime and custody rates.

VARIATIONS IN THE USE OF PRIVATE FACILITIES ALSO AFFECT CUSTODY RATES

In 1991 privately operated facilities accounted for nearly two-thirds of all juvenile custody facilities and held nearly 40% of the juveniles in custody on any given day.

It is important to realize that juvenile courts often send juveniles to private facilities located in other States. For example, Pennsylvania's private facilities hold many juveniles committed by courts in other States. Out-of-State residents are counted according to the location of the facility rather than the jurisdiction(s) ordering the placement. Thus, private data do not support State comparisons—States can only be compared on public facility custody rates. . . .

THE MAJORITY OF JUVENILES HELD IN LONG-TERM FACILITIES ARE HOUSED IN CROWDED FACILITIES

Crowding and Living Space Standards

The broadest assessment of the adequacy of living space is through occupancy rates—population as a percent of reported design capacity. Practi-

Nationwide, There Were 109 Juveniles Held in Public Training Schools for Every 100,000 Juveniles in the Population on February 15, 1991

	Number of juveniles on February 15, 1991	Custody rate
U.S. Total	28,535	109
Upper age 17		
Alabama	403	83
Alaska	193	277
Arizona	526	126
Arkansas	243	85
California	6,351	197
Colorado	304	82
Delaware	95	137
District of Columbia	150	326
Florida	151	12
Hawaii	62	52
Idaho	107	73
Indiana	779	119
Iowa	289	89
Kansas	469	163
Kentucky	330	75
Maine	249	185
Maryland	353	73
Minnesota	381	76
Mississippi	322	94
Missouri	400	200
Montana		

	Number of juveniles on February 15, 1991	Custody rate
Upper age 17 (continued)		
Nebraska	248	131
Nevada	296	228
New Hampshire	86	75
New Jersey	659	85
New Mexico	342	174
North Dakota	70	92
Ohio	2,359	192
Oklahoma	178	48
Oregon	439	134
Pennsylvania	611	50
Rhode Island	150	157
South Dakota	129	146
Tennessee	406	74
Utah	66	23
Vermont	0	0
Virginia	624	96
Washington	483	87
West Virginia	110	51
Wisconsin	684	120
Wyoming	113	182

	Number of juveniles on February 15, 1991	Custody rate
Upper age 16		
Georgia	686	103
Illinois	1,267	113
Louisiana	649	136
Massachusetts	38	08
Michigan	729	78
Missouri	400	78
South Carolina	613	170
Texas	1,439	78
Upper age 15		
Connecticut	210	89
New York	1,800	131
North Carolina	694	130

Note: The custody rate is the number of juveniles in training schools on February 15, 1991, per 100,000 juveniles ages 10 through the upper age of juvenile court jurisdiction in each State.
Source: OJJDP. (1993). Children in custody census 1990/91 [machine-readable data file].

tioners note that as a facility's occupancy approaches 100%, operational functioning may become impaired.

While there are no established occupancy rate standards, there are standards relating to the adequacy of living space. The 1989 American Correctional Association accreditation standards for juvenile facilities required that juveniles confined in one-person sleeping rooms have 70 square feet of floor space and sleeping rooms housing three or more juveniles have 50 square feet per juvenile. The American Correctional Association standards also required that living units not exceed 25 juveniles.

In 1991 only 23% of juveniles in training schools and 31% of those in ranches were held in facilities that were not crowded by any of these measures. Twenty-nine percent of those in training schools and 6% of those in ranches were held in facilities that were crowded by each of these measures.

A Large Proportion of Training School Residents Are Housed in Rooms That Are Too Small

In 1991 more training school residents slept in single rooms (36%) than in double rooms (23%), rooms for 3–10 (12%), or in dormitories with 11 or more residents (28%). Training school sleeping rooms ranged in size from 30 to 110 or more square feet per juvenile. Overall, 35% of juveniles in training schools slept in undersized rooms. Of those in undersized rooms, most were in double rooms or dorms (35% for each), 24% were in single rooms, and 5% were in rooms sleeping 3–10 residents.

The pattern was similar in ranches, although ranch residents were most likely to be housed in dorms (42%). Overall, 23% of ranch residents slept in undersized rooms. As in training schools, most ranch residents in undersized rooms were in double rooms (44%) or dorms (32%), while 22% were in rooms sleeping 3–10 residents, and just 2% were in single rooms. In both types of facilities, most of these undersized rooms could meet the square footage standards if they housed fewer juveniles.

The Number of Juveniles in Living Units Varied Considerably

In 1991, 54% of juveniles held in training schools and 40% of those in ranches were in facilities where at least some of the living units housed more than 25 residents. Among facilities with living units exceeding the 25 person standard, the size of the largest units varied considerably. For both training schools and ranches, 15% of facilities had 36 or more residents in their largest units. Among training schools, only 1% of facilities had units with more than 80 residents; for ranches the figure was 5%.

Perimeter Security Has Increased

In juvenile facilities the use of fences, walls, and surveillance equipment is increasingly common, although they do not tend to have the elaborate se-

62% of Residents of Public Long-Term Institutional Facilities Were in Facilities Operating Above Their Design Capacity on February 15, 1991

Public long-term institutional facilities with a design capacity of—	Facilities		Residents	
	Total	Percent operating above design capacity	Total	Percent held in facilities operating above capacity
Fewer than 111 residents	137	35%	5,705	38%
111–200 residents	50	54	7,210	56
201–350 residents	26	58	6,711	58
More than 350 residents	14	79	9,126	85
All public long-term institutional facilities	227	44	28,752	62

- In 1991, 44% of long-term institutional facilities housed more residents than they were constructed to hold—the 1983 figure was 32%.

- The larger a facility's design capacity, the more likely it was to house more residents than it was constructed to hold.

- Facilities designed to house fewer than 111 residents accounted for the largest number of over-capacity facilities.

- In 1991 over-capacity facilities designed for fewer than 111 residents made up 21% of long-term institutional facilities, but held 8% of long-term institutional facility residents.

- In 1991 over-capacity facilities designed for more than 350 residents were 5% of all long-term institutional facilities, but held 27% of long-term institutional facility residents.

Note: Data are for February 15, 1991. Design capacity is the number of residents a facility is constructed to hold without double-bunking in single rooms and without housing residents in areas not designed as sleeping quarters.
Source: OJJDP. (1985 and 1993). Children in custody census of public juvenile detention, correctional, and shelter facilities 1982/83 and 1990/91 [machine-readable data file].

curity hardware often found in adult jails. In 1991, 44% of juveniles in training schools were held in facilities with a perimeter wall or fence—in 1987 the figure was 38%. In 1991, 50% of juveniles in training schools were in facilities with surveillance equipment—the 1987 figure was 39%. Few juveniles were in ranches with perimeter walls or fences (13%), although the use of surveillance cameras has increased (6% of ranch residents in 1987—36% in 1991).

Most juveniles in training schools in 1991 were in facilities with perimeter checks by staff (84%). Relatively few ranch residents were in facilities with staff perimeter checks (60%).

Locked Sleeping Rooms and Living Units Provide Both Internal and Perimeter Security

Training schools are more apt to be locked than ranches, but even within facility type there was variation in the use of locks.

Juvenile Facilities Tend To Rely on Staffing Rather Than on Hardware for Security

National standards for juvenile facilities express a preference for relying on staff, rather than on hardware, to provide security. The guiding principle is to house juveniles in the "least restrictive placement alternative." Staff security measures include periodically taking counts of the youth in custody, using classification and separation procedures, and maintaining an adequate ratio of security staff to juveniles.

Most long-term juvenile facilities use staff to provide security, but relatively few take all the recommended staff security measures (regarding counts, classification and separation, and staffing ratios). Only 8% of juveniles in training schools and 14% of those in ranches in 1991 were in facilities that met none of the staff security criteria; while 16% of juveniles in training schools and 2% of juveniles in ranches were in facilities that met all criteria.

Most training schools have formal resident counts. More than 8 in 10 juveniles in training schools in 1991 were in facilities with three or more counts each day. Larger facilities were more likely to have formal counts than were smaller facilities.

Juveniles in ranches are more likely to be in facilities that do not conduct three or more counts a day. Less secure ranches tend to rely on informal, rather than formal, head counts to ensure that juveniles have not escaped.

Many training schools and some ranches also use classification and separation as part of their security procedures. Facilities use classification and separation procedures to make even very large facilities seem small. By making the living unit the architectural and organizational focal point, the population is broken down into smaller, more manageable groups. Nearly 6 in 10 juveniles in training schools in 1991 were in facilities that used classification and separation procedures, compared with 3 in 10 juveniles in ranches. Larger facilities were more likely to have established classification procedures than were smaller facilities.

Substandard security staffing ratios were fairly widespread in 1991. Just under one-third of training school residents were in facilities with at least 1 security staff member for every 10.6 juveniles. In comparison, only 16% of ranch residents were in facilities meeting this staffing criterion.

IN A TYPICAL MONTH THERE MAY BE 450 TRAINING SCHOOL ESCAPES

Nationwide, training schools reported 454 successful escapes and 478 unsuccessful escape attempts during a typical month in 1991. This would translate into nearly 5,500 escapes and more than 5,700 unsuccessful attempts per year. Ranches reported 226 escapes and 150 attempts during a 1-month period. Their yearly estimate would be 2,700 escapes and 1,800 unsuccessful attempts.

The rates of attempted escapes and the rate of successful escapes were virtually the same for facilities that met the "three or more counts per day" criterion and for those that did not. These rates were also comparable for facilities with perimeter walls or fences and for facilities without them.

THE USE OF SEARCHES VARIES ACROSS FACILITIES

The use of frisk searches is more common than the use of strip searches or room searches. Nationwide, training schools reported an average of 25 frisk searches, 6 room searches, and 1 strip search on any given day for every 100 juveniles. Some facilities, however, reported that no searches were conducted. The highest search rates reported by any training schools were 15–30 times the average search rates.

MOST TRAINING SCHOOLS PERMIT THE USE OF ISOLATION, AT LEAST FOR SHORT PERIODS OF TIME

Eighty percent of juveniles in training schools were held in facilities that permit isolation. Facilities that did not use any isolation lasting between 1 hour and 1 day held 24% of training school residents. Facilities holding 34% of juveniles allowed isolation for up to 24 hours. Facilities holding 4% of juveniles placed no time limits on isolation.

For every 100 juveniles, training schools reported the equivalent of 1.5 isolation incidents lasting 1 hour or longer each day. Isolations lasting 1–24 hours occurred at a daily rate of 1 per 100 juveniles. The rate of isolations lasting more than 24 hours was 1 every third day per 100 juveniles.

Most Ranches Do Not Permit the Use of Isolation

Seventy-eight percent of juveniles in ranches were held in facilities that permit isolation. All ranches that used isolation had policies that placed time limits on isolation.

RANCHES ARE LEAST LIKELY FACILITIES TO USE MECHANICAL RESTRAINTS

Ranches holding just over a third (37%) of ranch residents and training schools holding nearly three-quarters of training school residents reported some use of mechanical restraints during 1990. More juveniles were held in facilities that reported using handcuffs than were held in facilities using other types of restraints such as anklets, security belts, or straight jackets.

In training schools that permit the use of restraints, 36% of training school residents were in facilities that placed no time limits on the use of mechanical restraints. Although the use of restraints was relatively uncommon in ranches, 58% of ranch residents were held in facilities without policies that placed time limits on the use of mechanical restraints.

TRAINING SCHOOLS AND RANCHES USE PHYSICAL RESTRAINT MORE OFTEN THAN MECHANICAL RESTRAINTS

Nationwide, training schools reported using mechanical restraints at an average rate that for a 100-bed facility would translate into 47 incidents during the year. In comparison, physical restraint (tackling or holds) was used at an average rate that for a 100-bed facility would be the equivalent of nearly 3 incidents per week. The use of physical restraints varied considerably, however. While 18% of training schools reported no use of physical restraints during the month, 10% had rates above 7 per 100 beds per week. The highest rate reported for physical restraints was 27 per 100 beds per week.

Nationwide, ranches reported using mechanical restraints at an average rate that for a 100-bed facility would translate into 16 incidents during the year. In comparison, physical restraint (tackling or holds) was used at an average rate that for a 100-bed facility would be the equivalent of nearly 95 incidents per year. . . .

VARIATIONS IN *JUVENILES TAKEN INTO CUSTODY* DATA ON JUVENILES ADMITTED TO STATE JUVENILE CORRECTIONS SYSTEMS STEM FROM MANY FACTORS

The Juveniles Taken Into Custody program collects individual-level data on State juvenile corrections system admissions and releases. Data are reported by a nonprobability sample of State departments of juvenile corrections. While many more juveniles are admitted to locally and privately operated facilities each year, those admitted to State custody are perhaps the most troubled and troubling youth in the Juvenile justice system.

Differences in the use of State custody reflect not only variations in the juvenile and offender populations, but also State juvenile justice system variations. Factors that influence the *Juveniles Taken Into Custody* data include the upper age of juvenile jurisdiction, the balance of State versus local and private juvenile custody options and uses, and the likelihood of juveniles being tried as adults in criminal court.

MOST ADMISSIONS TO STATE JUVENILE CORRECTIONAL CUSTODY ARE NEW COMMITMENTS

Of juveniles admitted to State juvenile correctional systems in 1992 for whom the type of admission was known, 7 in 10 were new commitments— with no previous admissions to State custody for the current offense. Among new commitments where the juvenile's probation status was known, about half had been under probation supervision prior to their commitment.

Admissions of juveniles previously released from State custody made up about one-quarter of admissions. Of these, most were parole violators whose parole was revoked either because of a new offense or a technical violation. Others were recommitted after being previously discharged or released to conditional supervision other than parole or aftercare or were returned from some other non-State supervision.

Few admissions involved the return of an escaped juvenile who had been removed from the facility roster (less than 1% overall). The remaining 4% of admissions were types other than those described above.

MOST YOUTH IN STATE JUVENILE CORRECTIONAL CUSTODY ARE RELEASED TO PAROLE OR AFTERCARE

Of those youth released from State juvenile correctional custody in 1992 with a known type of release, 69% were released to parole or aftercare and remained under State jurisdiction. An additional 8% received some other type of conditional release, often involving court or local probation agency supervision. Outright discharge was less common; 15% were discharged with no further supervision. An additional 1% received other unconditional releases. Fewer than 1% of releases involved certification as an adult or trans-er to adult jurisdiction. Only 2% were released because they reached adult age ("aged out"). The remaining 5% involved situations such as transfers to other jurisdictions, escapes, and deaths.

Most reporting States reflected the overall pattern—release to parole or aftercare was the most common release type. There was, however, some variation among States. The proportion of releases to parole or aftercare ranged from 100% to less than 20%. In 5 of the 34 reporting States, the most common type of release was discharge without further supervision.

THERE WERE LARGE STATE VARIATIONS IN THE AVERAGE LENGTHS OF STAY IN STATE JUVENILE CORRECTIONAL SYSTEM CUSTODY

Average Length of Stay in State Juvenile Custody for Juveniles Released in 1992

Reporting states	Average days in custody
Alaska	445
California	523
Delaware	160
Georgia	279
Illinois	308
Indiana	167
Iowa	138
Kentucky	229
Louisiana	359
Maryland	156
Massachusetts	92
Mississippi	95
Missouri	201
Nebraska	92
New Hampshire	180
New York	310
North Dakota	113
Ohio	231
Oregon	254
South Carolina	86
Tennessee	140
Texas	189
Utah	126
Virginia	218
Wisconsin	233

Note: New Jersey was unable to provide accurate length of stay data. Vermont had too few releases to obtain a reliable percentage. Oklahoma did not report a full year's data. Minnesota did not report admission dates. Source: Austin, J., et al. (1994). Juveniles taken into custody research program: Fiscal year 1993 annual report.

AVERAGE LENGTHS OF STAY VARY
BY OFFENDER CHARACTERISTICS

In the 29 States reporting length of stay information, person offenders, males, and minorities had a longer average length of stay than other offenders:

- Person offenders—353 days.
- Drug offenders—248 days.
- Property offenders—217 days.
- Weapons offenders—187 days.
- Public order offenders—150 days.
- Status offenders—133 days.
- Males—250 days.
- Females—201 days.
- Hispanics—333 days.
- "Other" races—256 days.
- Blacks—252 days.
- Whites—204 days.

STATES VARIED IN PROPORTION OF JUVENILES WHO ESCAPED

In the 15 States reporting information on escapes, 95% of the youth released from State juvenile correctional custody in 1992 had never escaped. While two States reported no escapes, one State reported an 18% escape rate. About half of escapees were on escape status for a month or more (48%), 42% were returned within 2 weeks, and 10% were returned in 2–4 weeks.

STATE POLICIES HAVE AN IMPACT
ON AVERAGE LENGTHS OF STAY

Some of the variation in lengths of stay can be attributed to differences in States' juvenile correctional policies. For example, the average length of stay in South Carolina was shorter than in other States. South Carolina holds large numbers of juveniles in reception and diagnostic centers for short periods of evaluation (20–40 days) and then discharges or releases them to probation. In fact, 69% of releases in South Carolina were releases from reception and diagnostic centers.

Average lengths of stay were also relatively shorter in Massachusetts and Utah because these States transfer substantial numbers of juveniles to privately operated facilities during their time under State correctional jurisdiction, and such periods of private custody were not included in the lengths of stay calculations.

California's relatively long average length of stay reflects the fact that county-operated facilities generally gain custody of less serious offenders, while the State receives custody of more serious offenders—and can hold them longer than most other States—until age 25.

A Comparative Analysis of Organizational Structure and Inmate Subcultures in Institutions for Juvenile Offenders

BARRY C. FELD

The penological debate over the origins, processes, and characteristics of inmate subcultures in correctional facilities has attributed the qualities of subcultures either to features of the formal organization or to preimprisonment characteristics of the incarcerated offenders. . . .

The two competing explanations of the inmate social system are commonly referred to as the "indigenous origins" model and the "direct importation" model. The former provides a functionalist explanation that relates the values and roles of the subculture to the inmates' responses to problems of adjustment posed by institutional deprivations and conditions of confinement. . . . An alternative interpretation attributes the normative order of adult prisons to the identities, roles, and values held by the inmates before incarceration. Accordingly, inmates' personal characteristics shape the subculture, and in a population of incarcerated offenders an oppositional, criminal value system predominates. Differences in social characteristics such as sex, race, or criminal involvement before incarceration influence both as subculture's qualities and any individual inmate's adaptations to it. . . .

INMATE VIOLENCE IN INSTITUTIONS

The prevalence of inmate violence and its significance for stratification, role differentiation, and subcultural processes represent a recurring theme. However, the relationships between organizational variables, inmate violence, and other characteristics of the subculture have not been adequately explored.

From Barry C. Feld, in *Crime & Delinquency*, Vol. 27, pp. 336–363 (July 1981), copyright © 1981 by Barry C. Feld. Reprinted by permission of Sage Publications, Inc.

Physical aggression, verbal abuse, or psychological intimidation can be used to create or reestablish relationships of domination and submission within the subculture. Many maxims of the inmate code are attempts to regulate violence and exploitation among inmates, and many of the "argot" roles differentiate inmates on the basis of their use of or response to aggression. For individual inmates, many of the "pains of imprisonment"—material deprivations, sexual isolation, and threats to status, self-esteem, and personal security—cited in functionalist explanations of subcultures can be alleviated by the use of violence. While imprisonment imposes deprivations, violence and exploitation provide at least some inmates with a potential solution, albeit at the expense of other inmates.

The prevalence of inmate violence also reflects characteristics of the incarcerated. Many adult and juvenile inmates are drawn from social backgrounds or cultures that emphasize toughness, manliness, and the protection of one's own physical integrity. Preincarceration experiences equip in different ways inmates from diverse social, economic, criminal, racial, or sexual backgrounds to participate in the violent subcultures within some institutions. Thus, a predisposition to violence among the inmate subculture also reflects influences of cultural importation which organizational features may aggravate or mitigate.

... [A] comparison of organizations would permit a fuller exploration of the relationships between formal organizational structure and the ensuing inmate culture, as well as of the influence of preprison characteristics on the adaptations of inmates in diverse settings. Controlling for the effects of preincarceration characteristics on inmates perceptions and adaptations, this study presents a comparative analysis of the ways in which variations in organizational goals and intervention strategies in institutions for juvenile offenders produce differences in the informal inmate social system.

Organizational features affect the inmate subculture and the prevalence of inmate violence both by creating incentives for inmates to resort to violence and by providing inmates with opportunities to use violence. Organizational variations in the nature and extent of deprivations may motivate inmates in different ways to exploit others. Various organizational control strategies differ in the degree to which they provide an environment conducive to the use of violence to relieve these deprivations. The deprivations and control strategies also influence many other aspects of the subculture. This comparative analysis examines the variations in organizational goals, staff intervention strategies, and social control practices that influence the levels of violence and the structure of the inmate social system.

CORRECTIONAL TYPOLOGY

There are several descriptions of the organizational variations in juvenile and adult correctional facilities that can be used as tools to classify systematically and compare the relationships between organizational structure and inmate subculture. A common classification distinguishes juvenile correctional organizations on the basis of their custody or treatment goals, distinguishing differences in goals on the basis of the relative emphases staff place on custody and containment, and on vocational and academic education versus clinical or group treatment. The intervention strategies used to achieve either custodial or therapeutic goals range from group-oriented practices to those more attuned to individuals' characteristics. Group-oriented strategies reflect efforts to change or control an inmate through the group of which he is a member, while individualized methods of intervention focus more directly on the person, without comparable manipulation of the social environment.

Organizational goals—custody or treatment—and strategies of change—group or individual—may vary independently; thus, four different types of correctional organizations may be distinguished on the basis of both their correctional goals and the means used to attain those goals (see Figure 1).

Every juvenile correctional institution confronts the same necessity to explain both what its clients' problems are and how the clients should be rehabilitated. The answers to the questions of cause and cure in turn determine the organizational goals and the intervention strategies and social control practices required to achieve them. The typology in Figure 1 illustrates four different kinds of correctional solutions to the problems of juvenile offenders. It also suggests several interrelated organizational variables: a staff ideology defining inmates and their needs, organizational goals serving those needs, intervention strategies implemented through programs and social control practices, and the structure of relationships between inmates and staff.

A degree of internal consistency among these organizational variables is necessary. Methods of intervention and social control practices must be complementary, since efforts to ensure compliance that alienate the inmate

	Organizational Goals	
Organizational Means	Custody	Treatment
Group-Oriented Intervention Strategy	Group Custody Custodial Obedience/Conformity Protective custody	Group Treatment Group treatment Treatment Therapeutic community
Individual-Oriented Intervention Strategy	Individual Custody Educational Reeducation/Development Protective custody	Individual Treatment Psychotherapeutic Treatment

Figure 1. Correctional Typology

are incompatible with change strategies requiring commitment on the part of that inmate. Compliance strategies and programs will vary with the correctional goals and inmate changes sought and determine the kinds of relationships staff develop with inmates. Amitai Etzioni's compliance framework provides a basis for a comparative organizational analysis of staff control strategies and inmates' responses in coercive and normative-coercive settings. The primary correctional social control strategies are (1) the threat or use of physical coercion, (2) the threat or use of transfer to less desirable units or isolation cells, (3) the use of a privilege system, and (4) collaboration between inmates and staff, which may be either informal or formal.

METHODS

The data for this study were collected in ten cottage units located in four juvenile institutions administered by the Massachusetts Department of Youth Services before the closing of the training schools. A process of institutional decentralization initiated to transform the various cottage settings into small, therapeutic communities provided considerable autonomy and independence for each individual unit. Clinical, vocational, academic, and cottage personnel either formed staff teams or were assigned to cottages to develop coordinated treatment programs. Decentralization resulted in a number of diverse "mini-institutions" in which staff pursued a variety of goals using different intervention strategies.

Since inmate assignments to the various cottages were not randomized, the ten cottages studied were selected to maximize the comparability of inmate populations and the variety of treatment strategies used. The ten cottages studied included seven units for males, two for females, and one co-educational facility, located in four different state institutions. Cottage populations were matched on the basis of age, race, past criminal histories (both official and self-reported), present commitment offense, age at initial contact and number of prior juvenile court appearances, and prior commitments to institutions. . . . The cottages sampled produced comparable inmate groups. Although cottage assignments were not randomized, there was no systematic effort by administrators to match inmate "needs" with particular treatment programs, and the primary determinants were the availability of bed space and the need to maintain a population balance among the various cottages.

In addition to the matching of populations, statistical controls for the effects of background characteristics within each cottage were used to establish cottage comparability. Controls for each background variable were used to determine whether a particular characteristic was systematically associated with differences within each cottage population and whether the differences among cottages were a product of these population differences. In addition to tests for relationships between background variables and attiudes, sign tests were used to allow for interaction effects between inmates' characteristics and cottage treatment strategies. Despite some variations in the respective cottage populations, techniques support the conclusion that the substantial differences between cottages were not a function of variations in the inmate populations and are properly attributed to the cottages' social structures. In institutions with young populations (averaging approximately sixteen years of age), who are presumably less committed to criminal careers than imprisoned adults and who are incarcerated for an average of four months, it is not surprising that background characteristics or preimprisonment experiences are subordinate to the more immediate, organizational imperatives.

Data were collected in each of the ten cottages by a team of five trained researchers who spent about six weeks in each unit administering quesionnaires and interview schedules to both staff members and residents. Between 90 and 100 percent of the staff and residents in each cottage completed hour-long closed-ended questionnaires and equally extensive open-ended structured interviews. Most of the researchers' time was spent in participant observation and unstructured interviews, with field notes transcribed onto standardized forms to simplify analysis, coding, and comparison of observations from different settings.

FINDINGS

Organizational Structure

Although the administrators of the Massachusetts Department of Youth Services told the institutional staff to "do good things for kids," they did not specify what the staff members should do or how they should do it. The process of institutional decentralization allowed staff to pursue a variety of goals using diverse treatment strategies within the autonomous cottages. In structuring programs for how their clients should be handled and changed, staff were guided by their own assumptions about the causes of and cures for delinquent behavior. Although there was some diversity among staff within the respective cottages, recruitment, self-selection, and cottage assignments resulted in relatively homogeneous correctional ideologies among cottage personnel; the focus of this study is on the substantial differences among the various units in programs and goals that emerged and the effects of these differences on the respective inmate cultures.

Cottage Programs and Social Control Strategies

Maximum Security (Group Custody)   Cottage Nine was a unit used for juveniles who had run away from the institution and for youths who had committed other disciplinary infractions. About half of all residents escaped from the institution at some time during their stay; there were no significant differences between those who absconded and those who did not. There was no vocational training, academic education, or clinical program in the maximum-security setting. Intervention consisted of punishment and deprivation, with periods of enforced idleness interrupted only for meals, routine clean-up, and cottage maintenance. All the cottage activities took place in a highly controlled, structured environment, and virtually all activities occurred in a group setting. Staff attempted to coerce inmate conformity and obedience, and punished recalcitrance or resistance. As a result, a typical three- to four-week stay in Cottage Nine before return to an open cottage was an unpleasant experience which residents had little choice but to endure.

Staff used physical coercion and isolation cells—"the Tombs"—to enforce obedience, conformity, and respect. These techniques were feasible since there was no program in which staff needed to obtain active inmate participation, and the staff's physical domination made coercion practicable. Staff members used their limited repertoire of controls to counter major forms of deviance such as riots and fights, as well as inmate provocation, disrespect, or recalcitrance. They also used mass lock-ups and other forms of group punishment. Other control techniques were virtually absent, since there were no amenities or privileges that might be lost, and strategies designed to ensure group control precluded the development of individualized relationships necessary for collaborative controls. The use of coercive tactics alienated inmates, who minimized contacts with staff. Personnel ignored considerable inmate misbehavior that did not challenge their authority, and did not encourage inmates to report deviance that occurred outside the presence of staff members.

Industrial Training School (Individual Custody) Despite considerable program diversity, each of the individual custody settings—Cottage 8, Elms, Westview, and the Lancaster Industrial School for Girls—used vocational training as the primary strategy of change. Most of the trades programs consisted of either institutional maintenance or services for residents—a cafeteria program, laundry program, institutional upkeep, painting, landscaping and groundskeeping, and the like. There were limited academic and clinical programs in some of the cottages. However, individual counseling sessions were not scheduled regularly, and inmates initiated contact with clinical staff primarily to secure a weekend furlough or early parole.

Compared with those in the maximum-security unit, residents of the training school cottages enjoyed greater physical freedom within the institution, which rendered staff control more difficult. Inmate cooperation in the work programs was also problematic. Staff used a privilege system to induce conformity, coupling this with the threat of transfer to more punitive, maximum-security settings. The privilege system was a security-graded progression, with inmates at different levels accorded different privileges or governed by different restrictions. Passage from one level to another reflected the amount of time served and an inmate's general behavior and conformity. Because of the relatively limited privileges available, staff members exercised considerable discretion in the rules they enforced, against whom, and under what circumstances. The staff also collaborated informally with inmate leaders to maintain order, manipulating the privilege system to confer additional status and rewards on the elite. Informal collaboration between staff members and the inmate elite is a common training school control strategy because of the availability of privileges, the discretionary bases upon which rewards are manipulated, and the problems of maintaining order posed by program individualization, the need to secure cooperation, and increased inmate freedom.

Individual Treatment The individual treatment program used all types of clinical treatment, including both individual counseling and individual therapy in a group setting. The cottage program was free and open with few restrictions. Staff minimized deprivations and maximized amenities to encourage inmate commitment and involvement in the clinical process. Staff eschewed universal rules, responding to each inmate on the basis of individualized therapeutic considerations.

Staff relied almost exclusively on a rich privilege system to secure the cooperation and participation of inmates. Although the threat of transfer to a less desirable setting was a possibility, the penalty was never invoked. There was virtually no physical coercion or informal collaboration used to obtain conformity or obedience. In response to inmate deviance, additional clinical sessions were prescribed to reinforce the privilege system—not as sanctions, but to provide additional supports for the recalcitrant resident.

Group Treatment All of the group treatment cottages used a therapeutic community treatment model, which was supplemented with either vocational or academic educational programs. The therapeutic community treatment model used both daily staff–inmate community meetings and group therapy sessions. A daily log provided the agenda for cottage community discussions, with staff and residents encouraged to record incidents that required the community's attention. At these meetings, staff integrated observations of residents on work, school, or cottage living. They then divided the cottage populations into smaller treatment groups and used a type of guided group interaction to deal with interpersonal problems or to resolve issues raised during the community meetings.

Formal collaboration between staff and inmates was the primary means of social control. Staff used the group problem-solving process to define and enforce cottage norms and to mobilize group pressures to deal with specific instances of deviance. Rules and consequences were elaborated in a privilege system that was jointly enforced; each inmate's privileges and freedoms were more dependent upon performance and participation and were less a function of the length of time served than was the case in the more custodial settings. The gradations of privileges and freedom and the responsibilities associated with each level were consistently and energetically enforced.

The strength of the formal collaboration process was the pressure staff placed upon residents to motivate other inmates to change. The concept of "responsibility" was crucial, and residents were responsible both for their own progress and behavior and for that of others. This principle of third-party responsibility provided a therapeutic rationale that significantly transformed subcultural norms governing informing and greatly increased the amount of information received by staff about the inmate group.

The Relationship between Staff Correctional Ideology and Cottage Program Characteristics   The differences in correctional programs and control strategies stemmed from various assumptions staff made about appropriate ways to treat inmates. Since staff members were allowed to form their own cottage teams, there was substantial interpersonal and ideological compatibility within units. For purposes of explaining the diversity in the cottage programs and subcultures, the more important differences were among the different units.

One component of a correctional ideology is the emphasis placed by staff on inmates' obedience, respect for authority, and submission to external controls. Custodial staff were much more concerned with obedience and respect than were treatment personnel, and subscribed more extensively to the use of external controls to achieve inmate conformity.

Cottage staff members also differed in their views of deviance. Personnel in the treatment-oriented cottages attributed delinquency to emotional or psychological problems, while custody staff rejected psycho-pathology or emotional dysfunction, emphasizing as a cause of delinquency such factors as a youth's exercise of free will, which could be deterred by punishment. Because the custody staff rejected psychological interpretations, they found delinquent or bizarre inmate behavior considerably more difficult to understand than did treatment staff. Staff members also disagreed over whether delinquents were capable of establishing "normal" relationships, with those emphasizing custody far more likely than treatment personnel to regard the inmates in their cottages as "hard-core delinquents" who were dangerous and untrustworthy.

A correctional ideology both rationalizes deviance and its control and describes the end result sought—the "changed" inmate. Institutional behavior provides the staff with an indicator of an inmate's "rehabilitation" and readiness to return to the community. Custody staff strongly preferred inmates who followed orders, kept to themselves, and stayed out of trouble, which reflected their greater emphasis on external conformity rather than internalized controls. Their more negative perceptions of inmates and apprehension about collusion also led the custody staff members to disrupt informal inmate associations and encourage self-isolation, while treatment personnel encouraged inmate involvement with other inmates.

These alternative analyses of delinquency led staffs to pursue different correctional goals. When personnel were asked to choose among various correctional goals for incarcerated delinquents, significantly more of the custody-oriented staff members subscribed to custodial institutional objectives isolation, respect and discipline, and training and educating—than did treatment personnel. Allocation of institutional resources provides another indicator of organizational goals; in juvenile institutions, personnel are the primary resource. Organizations pursuing custodial goals assign personnel to control and containment, or vocational and educational functions; treatment-oriented organizations, in contrast, assign more staff members to clinical and treatment functions. The greatest proportion or personnel in the custodial cottages served as guards, work supervisors, and academic instructors, while the treatment-oriented cottages assigned a larger percentage of the staff to treatment roles, with a corresponding reduction in purely supervisory personnel.

The Inmate Subcultures

An inmate subculture develops within the confines of a correctional institution, and its norms and values reflect the focal concerns of institutional life and the inmate population. Inmate roles and subculture stratification reflect conformity to or deviation from these norms, and newly entering inmates are socialized into this system and adapt to the expectations of their fellow inmates. The informal social system often mediates the effectiveness of the formal organization, aiding or thwarting staff members in the pursuit of their goals.

A feature of correctional organization that influences the character of the inmate social systems is the extent to which staff members successfully control inmate violence and exploitation. Institutional characteristics influence the prevalence of inmate aggression by varying the levels of deprivation, a condition that gives some inmates an incentive to direct predatory behavior at others, and by providing the opportunities under which such exploitation may be carried out successfully. Inmate violence is directly related to the quality of relations between inmates and staff and to the information available to personnel about the workings of the subculture. Thus, controlling violence is a sine qua non of effective correctional programming and administration.

There was a clear relationship between the type of formal organization and the informal inmate culture. In the punitive, group custody setting, inmates experienced the greatest deprivation and were the most alienated from other inmates and staff members. Inmate alienation prevented the development of effective staff controls and allowed aggressive inmates to exploit their fellows through diverse forms of violent behavior. In the training school settings, the staff members used a privilege system coupled with informal cooptation of the inmate elite to bring potentially aggressive inmates under some degree of control. This reduced the effectiveness of inmate violence and exploitation, although aggression remained the dominant mode of interaction within the subculture. In the treatment-oriented cottages, especially in the group treatment programs, formal collaboration between inmates and staff members reduced the level of inmate violence and provided a therapeutic rationale for informing that made the workings of the subculture more visible to staff. The greater visibility, combined with significantly reduced deprivation, lowered the necessity for and effectiveness of inmate aggression and exploitation and allowed for the emergence of a more positive inmate culture.

Inmate Perceptions of Staff and Inmates   Problems of institutional living influence inmates' motives for interaction and the types of solutions they can develop. Just as correctional personnel structure their relationships with inmates, residents attempt to structure and control their relationships with staff and other inmates to resolve the problems of the informal organization. The types of relationships and collective solutions available depend upon the inmates' perceptions of the program, staff, and other inmates. Inmate cooperation with staff augers for a more open, visible and manageable social system. If staff cannot obtain inmate cooperation through either formal or informal collaboration, then a more closed, subterranean, and violent social system emerges.

Cottage Purposes   The cottage goals and programs define the organizational context to which inmates must adapt. . . . When asked about cottage purposes and staff expectations, residents of the custody-oriented cottages described the cottages as places for punishment, while inmates in the treatment-oriented settings regarded the cottages as places for rehabilitation and for gaining self-awareness. As a further indicator of organizational purposes and adaptive constraints, inmates were asked whether staff encouraged them to conform or to gain insight into their own motivation and behavior. Responding to staff expectations, inmates in the custody-oriented settings were more than twice as likely to view the staff as demanding obedience and conformity as were those in the treatment cottages, while the latter were almost three times as likely as the residents of custody-oriented settings to describe staff expectations in terms of treatment and self-understanding.

A corollary of the differences in custodianship and punitiveness was the "pain of imprisonment" that inmates described. While some of the problems inmates confront are inherent in incarceration—loss of liberty, separation from family and friends, increased dependency and submission to authority, and the like—other pains of confinement, such as material deprivations, are attributable to characteristics of a particular setting. By virtually every measure, the inmates in the custody-oriented cottages reported far more extensive and severe problems associated with their confinement—boredom, living with other residents, and material deprivations than did the inmates

ı the treatment cottages. These reported differences in institutional ameni-
ies resulted from staff actions, since treatment personnel tried to minimize
he unpleasant, alienating aspects of incarceration to a greater extent than
id custody-oriented staff.

Inmate Perceptions of Staff   Inmates' views of staff paralleled staff mem-
ers' perceptions of inmates. In those settings where staff had negative
iews of inmates, describing them as dangerous, unreliable, abnormal, or in-
orrigible, the inmates held correspondingly negative views of staff, re-
arding them as untrustworthy, unhelpful, or indifferent. In those settings
vhere the staff expressed more favorable views of inmates, residents shared
nore positive views of the staff. Virtually every inmate in the maximum-
ecurity setting and over half the inmates in the individual custody settings,
ıs contrasted with only about one-fifth of those in the treatment settings,
egarded staff as neither concerned nor helpful. Inmates readily equated
ıunitive programs with unconcerned staff and therapeutic programs with
ommitted staff. Likewise residents of the custody-oriented cottages initi-
ıted fewer contacts with personnel and talked with them less about personal
ıroblems than did those in the treatment settings.

Inmate Perceptions of Other Inmates   Characteristics of the inmate social
ıystem also reflect the extent to which inmates can cooperate with one an-
ıther to ease the hardship of adjusting to the institution. The residents of
he custody-oriented cottages reported substantially lower levels of trust
ınd concern on the part of other inmates than did those in the treatment-
ıriented settings. Residents of the treatment cottages also reported greater
ınmate solidarity than did their custody cottage counterparts. Since preda-
ory behavior and subcultural violence were more prevalent in the custody-
ıriented settings, the differences in inmate perceptions also reflect the ex-
ent to which inmates were exploited and victimized by others.

Inmate Adaptations   Differences among the programs in staff expectations
onstitute an additional organizational constraint on inmates' adaptations.
Custodial staff emphasized inmate conformity and obedience, whereas treat-
nent staff emphasized gaining insight and solving personal problems. In re-
ıponse, inmates in the custody-oriented settings chose either overt confor-
nity and covert deviance or obedience and conformity as adaptive strategies,
vhile those in the treatment-oriented settings chose self-understanding.
Similarly, adaptations reflecting elements of prisonization—prompt obedi-
ınce, conformity, and self-isolation—were chosen by twice as many residents
ıf custody-oriented settings as those in treatment programs, closely paral-
eling the staff expectations.

Social Structure of the Inmate Subculture   Inmates interact more fre-
ıuently and intensely with residents of their own cottage than they do with
hose in other settings, and a set of norms and roles based upon those norms
;overn their interactions with other inmates and staff. Differences in staff

intervention practices are strongly related to variations in inmates' perceptions of other inmates, staff, and institutional adaptation, and to corresponding differences in inmate norms, subculture roles, and interaction patterns.

The inmates' and staff's responses to violence and aggression are among the most important determinants of subculture processes. In the absence of effective controls, violence and aggression underlie most interactions within the inmate subculture. Direct action, toughness, and defense of personal integrity are focal concerns of many delinquent inmates, and even a few aggressive inmates can immediately make the control of violence a major concern within the institution. Moreover, the prevalence of violence is closely related to other subcultural norms, particularly those related to informing.

Inmate norms governing interactions with staff and the acceptability of informing personnel of other inmates' activities have been frequently described. Informing and subcultural violence are closely linked, since uncontrolled violence can deter informing, while informing, if properly encouraged by staff, can reduce it. The regulation of the flow of information between inmates and staff thus emerges as a critical determinant of inmate roles and subculture structure.

Inmates' views of staff and inmates and their adaptations to the institution influence the amount of information staff members receive about the inmate social system, which in turn conditions the staff members' ability to control subcultural violence. Residents of the treatment cottages held relatively favorable views of other inmates and staff. Because of the greater availability of privileges and amenities, they had less incentive to engage in covert deviance to relieve deprivations and thus had less to hide. Almost three times as many inmates in the treatment settings as in the custody-oriented settings approved of informing. In fact, a virtual majority of residents of the former approved of informing.

As indicated previously, the treatment inmates' support for informing stemmed, in part, from the staff members' redefinition of informing as "helping" or "being responsible for others" as part of the treatment program. Formal collaboration reinforced the therapeutic rationale for informing and gave inmates greater protection from intimidation by increasing the visibility of informal pressures by other inmates. By legitimating and fostering informing, staff members received an enormous amount of information about the hidden processes of the subculture, which better enabled them to control inmate violence.

Participant observation and structured interviews provided an insight into "strong-arming" and "bogarting"—the subterranean violence among residents. "You have to fight" was a norm in the custody-oriented cottages, and the levels of verbal abuse and physical violence were considerably higher there than in the treatment-oriented settings. Inmates emphasized toughness, resisting exploitation or provocation, and maintaining one's position in the subculture through physical means. Physical and verbal testing and scuffles were daily occurrences, although actual fights were less frequent. The inmate did not have to be a successful fighter, but a willingness to fight to protect himself, his position, and his property was essential. Fighting and defending against exploitation were as important for female inmates as for males in comparable custodial cottages.

An inmate's readiness and ability to defend personal integrity and property were tested very early during confinement as new residents were subtly or overtly challenged for whatever material goods they possessed. As mentioned above, the greater deprivation in the custody-oriented settings made exploitation a profitable strategy for the more aggressive inmates. Residents who fought back could insulate themselves from chronic exploitation, while failure to do so left them and their possessions vulnerable.

There was significantly less exploitation in the treatment-oriented cottages than in the custody-oriented cottages. The field observers recorded fewer incidents of fights, physical confrontations, or expropriation of property. All the observers commented on the virtual absence here of "ranking"—verbal abuse—as compared with the custody cottages. There was less normative support for fighting, and when it did occur most of the inmates condemned it in the community meetings.

The differences in subcultural violence resulted from the steps staff took to control it. In the custody cottages, inmates retaliated with violence to punish those who informed to staff and to discourage other inmates from doing so. Given their limited social control repertoire, custody staff did not encourage inmates to inform, since it only forced them to confront violent inmates directly. When staff members learned of inmate violence or victimization, they seldom took steps to prevent its recurrence. More frequently, they reinforced the values of the violent subculture by encouraging the resident to fight back and defend himself. In view of the unsympathetic and unsupportive staff response to complaints and the retaliatory inmate violence that followed, inmates had little incentive to cooperate with staff. Custody staff were isolated from the workings of the subculture, and unable to combat the violence that stifled the flow of information. In the treatment-oriented cottages, formal collaboration and inmate support for informing provided channels of communication and a mechanism for coping with incidents of violence.

While inmate approval of informing afforded greater control over inmate violence, there were differences in other subcultural norms as well. Responses to a series of hypothetical stories concerning common incidents in correctional institutions demonstrated a further contrast in the norms that prevailed in the various cottages. About two-thirds of the inmates in the treatment-oriented settings, as compared with less than half of those in the custody-oriented settings, supported "positive" inmate behavior—cooperation with staff, refusal to aid escapes, and the like.

Different inmate roles and subculture stratification accompanied the differences in cottage norms. In the more violent custodial cottages, the roles of superior and inferior were allocated on the basis of an inmate's ability to "out-fight, out-think, or out-talk" fellow inmates. Since most inmates were neither complete successes nor complete failures in outfighting, out-thinking, or out-talking their peers, the distribution of roles resulted in a stratification system with a few aggressive leaders at the top, a few "punks"—chronic victims—at the bottom, and most of the inmates occupying a more intermediate status, neither "one-up" nor "one-down." In the treatment-oriented settings, inmate roles and stratification were not as tied to physical or verbal prowess.

The differences in cottage norms and inmate relations were reflected in the characteristics of the inmate leadership as well. A majority of inmates in the custody-oriented cottages, as contrasted with about one-quarter of residents of the treatment cottages, described the leaders as filling a negative and violent role in cottage life. Both observation and interviews revealed that leaders were those inmates who "strong-armed" and exploited lower-status inmates. There was greater normative support for negative inmate behavior in these cottages, and the leaders reflected and perpetuated the dominant values of the subculture.

Norms governing violence and informing constrained inmate leaders in treatment-oriented cottages. Formal collaboration between inmates and staff reduced the leaders' ability to maintain covert physical control over the inmate group, and they played a more positive and supportive role in the institution. Formal collaboration increased their visibility and required that they at least appear to adopt a cooperative attitude in their relations with staff, which enabled other inmates to establish more positive relationships with inmates and staff.

At the bottom of the custody cottages' social structure were the "punks," inmates who were bullied and exploited and who acquiesced in the role of victim. Since the first rule of survival in the violent subculture was to defend oneself, inmates who were unable or unwilling to fight were at the mercy of those who would do so. Punks were chronically victimized, both psychologically and physically, and were the victims of merciless taunting and pummeling. In the custodial settings, the strong norm against informing prevented either the victims or other inmates from revealing what occurred. The inability of staff to control the violence prevented inmates from revealing their victimization and left them at the mercy of their exploiters.

Homosexual rape was the ultimate act of physical aggression by tough cottage leaders against punks. More than exploitative sexual satisfaction, rape entailed conquest and domination of the victim by the aggressor. Every incident of homosexual assault discovered during this study could be analyzed in terms of leader–punk role relationships; such assaults occurred only in the violent custody-oriented cottages.

In the treatment-oriented settings, punks did not suffer as much physical or verbal abuse. Although other inmates regarded them as weak, immature, and lacking self-respect, formal collaboration provided a substantial heck on the extent of their victimization. At least by contrast with those n the custody-oriented settings, low-status inmates in the treatment cottages enjoyed a comparatively benign incarceration experience.

DISCUSSION AND CONCLUSIONS

Organizational structure has a major effect on the informal inmate social system. The cottage programs varied in both the levels of deprivation and the effectiveness of staff controls and confronted the inmates with markedly different organizations to which to adapt. The respective cottage cultures reflected these differences in inmates' perceptions of cottage purposes and goals, in their adaptations to the institution, in their views of staff and other inmates, and in their norms, values, and interaction patterns.

Punishment and isolation were the reasons given by the inmates in maximum security for their incarceration. They suffered the greatest deprivation within the institution, which gave them the greatest incentive to improve their circumstances through violent exploitation and covert deviance. Staff sought inmate obedience and conformity and used physical control to obtain compliance and suppress challenges to their authority. Inmates were alienated by the staff's repressive controls, and the absence of programs prevented the development of individualized relationships, perpetuating the negative stereotypes of one another held by inmates and staff. Motivated by their poor opinion of inmates, staff attempted to disrupt informal groups. The inmates' isolation hindered them from cooperating with one another in the institutional adjustment or in resisting exploitation, while predatory violence reinforced inmates' negative views of one another. Inmates adapted by isolating themselves, avoiding other inmates and appearing to obey staff. In developing covert deviant solutions to relieve their material deprivation, particularly in exploiting weaker inmates for their possessions, tough inmates reinforced their own dominant status and provided themselves with a measure of safety and security. They discouraged inmate contact that would reveal their own deviant and violent behavior and physically punished inmates who informed to discourage the communication of information that would improve staff control. And the dominance of aggressive inmates reinforced staff efforts to isolate inmates within the culture by making inmates distrustful and fearful of one another. The inmates' ability to use violence determined their various roles within the group, and prevented them from engaging in positive forms of social behavior. The failure of staff to support informing or to control violence forced the inmates to seek accommodation with the primary source of power, the aggressive inmate leaders. This, in turn, reinforced their alienation from one another, precluded collective resistance to aggression, and left each individual inmate at the mercy of those who were more aggressive.

Subculture characteristics in the training school cottages were similar to those in maximum security, although organizational differences reduced the extremes of staff–inmate alienation and antagonism. Program individualization engendered more contacts between staff and inmates that tempered somewhat their negative perceptions of one another. The use of vocational programs required staff to obtain the active cooperation of inmates in productive work. Staff induced at least minimal cooperation and participation in work programs through privileges and rewards that reduced the levels of institutional deprivation. The necessity to obtain voluntary compliance limited the utility of punitive forms of social control, and a privilege system provided staff with a more flexible means of responding to inmates than did the use of force and isolation cells. The forms of adaptation among inmates reflected staff members' primary emphasis on obedience and conformity. Staff informally collaborated with and coopted the potentially violent inmate elite, and thus obtained some control over aggression within the subculture. By coopting the inmate leaders through informal collaboration, staff enlisted their aid in maintaining order within the subculture. In the course of protecting their privileged status, the leaders informally maintained control for staff, suppressed some forms of anti-institutional activities, and reduced the levels of violence within the inmate group. The privileges available reduced the levels of deprivation, and covert inmate deviance declined accordingly. With less to hide, there was less need among the inmates to restrict contact with staff. Although inmates disapproved of informing, this was not as ruthlessly suppressed as was the case in maximum security. The lesser degree of deprivation and violent exploitation reduced the inmates' isolation and alienation from one another.

The differences in organizational goals and intervention strategies in the treatment-oriented cottages had a significant effect on the inmates' incarceration experience. Staff both elevated treatment expectations over custodial considerations and successfully communicated their expectations to inmates. Rehabilitation, gaining insight, and solving personal problems were seen as the purposes of incarceration, and these goals required change rather than simply conformity. Staff emphasized more rewarding experiences and privileges, and residents of the treatment settings suffered less punishment, deprivation, or alienation than did their custody-cottage counterparts. The reduced material deprivation also lowered inmates incentive to engage in deviant activities within the institution.

In both the individual and group treatment settings, positive contact between staff and inmates was considerable, occurring in individual counseling and through formal collaboration, resulting in markedly more favorable inmate perceptions of staff than in the other settings. Formal collaboration allowed inmates and staff to make decisions collectively about cottage life and provided them with a common context in which to meet. Formal collaboration fostered greater equality among staff members, between staff and inmates, and among inmates, and reduced inmates' alienation from staff and encouraged more favorable views of fellow inmates.

Formal collaboration coupled with individual and group treatment increased the visibility of the inmate subculture and provided staff and innates with a mechanism for controlling inmate violence. Staff provided a re-habilitation-based rationale for informing, enabling the norm governing this behavior to become more positive than was the case in the custody cottages. Equally important, staff members defined the program itself in such a way as to convince the inmates that personnel were committed to treatment rather than punishment. The increased communication of information enabled staff to control inmate violence, which reinforced this communication. The reduced deprivation, increased freedom, and support provided by formal collaboration for controlling inmate violence combined to foster more positive, less exploitative inmate relationships.

Evaluation of the Paint Creek Youth Center: A Residential Program for Serious Delinquents

PETER W. GREENWOOD
SUSAN TURNER

There are several sources of suggestions and ideas for improving correctional programs for serious juvenile offenders, especially when the current treatment consists of lengthy stays in traditional training schools. For almost two decades critics of these schools have been pointing out their defects and arguing for various management reforms and noninstitutional alternatives. Although there have been several attempts to evaluate programs incorporating some of these suggestions, none of the research designs was adequate to provide compelling evidence regarding the programs' effectiveness in reducing delinquency.

During more recent years, several researchers have used meta-analyses to identify characteristics of correctional programs that appear associated with reduced recidivism. In a meta-analysis covering 80 recent corrections' evaluations, Andrews et al. found that appropriate interventions reduced recidivism by as much as 50%; the indicators of appropriateness included focusing the interventions on high-risk groups; targeting dynamic risk factors directly related to criminal behavior; and using cognitive/behavioral and social learning methods, such as modeling, graduated practice, and role playing. A meta-analysis of over 400 juvenile correctional interventions also found that behavioral, skill-oriented, and multi-modal methods produced the largest effects and that these methods produced larger effects in community rather than residential settings.

Excerpted from *Criminology*, Vol. 31, pp. 263–279 (1993). Reprinted by permission of The American Society of Criminology.

Further guidance regarding the design of programs for chronic delinquents has been provided by recent longitudinal studies and the development of interactional theories, which suggest that such programs must be comprehensive in their ability to deal with each youth's multifaceted needs and individually tailored to suit each youth's capabilities and strengths.

Although not explicitly designed to test any single intervention theory or technique, the Paint Creek Youth Center (PCYC) was designed and developed by a team of correctional professionals who were familiar with recent findings in the evaluation and clinical literature and had successfully designed and implemented innovative correctional programs in the past. As such, it embodies many of the concepts suggested by the evaluation and theoretical literature as being critical to success.

As the evaluators of PCYC, RAND staff designed and operated the random assignment procedures by which youths were placed in either PCYC or one of several training schools operated by the Ohio Department of Youth Services; monitored the implementation and evolution of the program; coded official records; and administered surveys to program staff and youths. The objectives of the evaluation were to determine whether youths assigned to PCYC actually received significantly different programming and treatment from that received by the controls; whether those differences were perceptible to the youths; and whether they resulted in differences in postrelease behavior. We begin with a comparison of the characteristics of the experimental and control programs. We turn next to the design of the evaluation, its results, and implications for future research and practice.

EXPERIMENTAL AND CONTROL PROGRAM DESIGNS

Paint Creek Youth Center (PCYC), located in southern Ohio, was developed as an experimental program in 1984 by New Life Youth Services, Inc. under a grant from the Office of Juvenile Justice and Delinquency Prevention. The explicit goal of the program was to provide a comprehensive array of high-quality programming tailored to the individual requirements of youths convicted of serious felonies. The program draws on a combination of treatment philosophies, including Vorrath and Brentro's positive peer culture, Glasser's reality therapy, and Yochelson and Samenow's criminal thinking errors.

Program activities are divided into distinct phases, beginning with a three-day orientation period and ending with a closely supervised transition period, during which youths return to live in their community. Successive phases provide increased privileges and responsibilities. Movement through each phase is contingent upon well-defined behavioral goals. During the last phases of the residential program, which is located in southern Ohio, youths are permitted to work part-time in a variety of on-site enterprises such as farming, woodworking, and auto repair.

Some of the programming and management techniques that distinguish ᵓCYC from the Ohio training schools in which control youths were placed and most other large institutional programs as well) are

- Small size: provides beds for only 30–35 youths, rather than several hundred.
- Absence of locked doors, fences, and other methods for physically retraining youths: security is provided by close staff supervision and the Positive Peer Culture (Vorrath and Brentro, 1974), a set of techniques and philosophy that entail holding the youths responsible for each other's behavior.
- Problem Oriented Record System (PORS): a highly formalized system for assessing and tracking behavioral deficits (e.g., problem controlling anger, laziness, drug problem) and assets (e.g., popular with peers, good athlete) and which provides the ongoing mechanism for case management and individualizing treatment.
- Clear incentives (e.g., extra privileges) for positive behavior and appropriate punishments (e.g., time-outs, restrictions on participation, demotion) for negative behavior: used to reinforce prosocial behavior.
- Cognitive/behavioral training methods: used several times a week to deal with such issues as anger management, life skills, substance abuse, and victim awareness.
- Daily group sessions: can involve instruction, role playing, or discussion of a particular youth's problems.
- Family group therapy: all families are encouraged and assisted (primarily with transportation) in attending twice monthly (on Sundays) family group therapy sessions, in which families join the youths in their regular groups.
- Intensive community reintegration and aftercare: community workers visit the youth and family during the residential component and have frequent contact following release.

Most juveniles from southern parts of Ohio who are convicted of serious felonies are placed in one of two Department of Youth Services (DYS) institutions—the Training Institute for Central Ohio (TICO) or Riverview. TICO is a maximum-security institution for older and more sophisticated youths; it has a capacity of about 190. Riverview, which is locked but not fenced, is used to house younger delinquents. Both institutions are located on the outskirts of Columbus. TICO appears antiquated and rundown, and much of its furniture is broken or severely abused. Riverview is newer, more modern in design, and is in much better shape.

Both institutions place a heavy emphasis on remedial education and vocational training. Most youths reside in 2-person rooms, grouped into wings of about 40 youths each. In both facilities, youths are locked in their rooms at night, and for disciplinary purposes during the day. Both institutions rely on outside volunteers (individuals, churches, Alcoholics Anonymous, and so on) to provide much of their therapy. Group and individual counseling are provided at the staffs' discretion.

Our interviews with program staff revealed that, compared with control youths in TICO and Riverview, PCYC youths were much more likely to have a job while in custody, have their family come in for counseling, receive drug and alcohol counseling, and receive home furloughs. Interviews with the youths suggest that those at PCYC were more likely to see their program in a positive light. Seventy-four percent of the PCYC youths said they saw their aftercare caseworkers at least twice a week, compared with 19% of the controls. Fifty-two percent said they saw their caseworker more than six times a week.

A survey of the experimental and control program staffs revealed several significant differences that have been hypothesized as contributing to program effectiveness. The PCYC staff were more favorable toward their program director, and the program itself, and were generally happier with their jobs than staff at TICO and Riverview. The PCYC staff also felt closer to the youths and thought that the causes of delinquency were less likely to be external (result of abuse, lack of opportunities, bad homes) than did institutional staff. The PCYC and institutional staff did not differ significantly in their perceptions of their roles. Staff at PCYC were generally younger, more likely to be white, and somewhat more likely to be female, than staff at TICO and Riverview.

Completion Rate and Average Length of Stay

The agreement with the judges who controlled release dates was that youths assigned to the experimental program would stay in the residential phase for at least one year, unless they were removed for disciplinary reasons. Seventeen of the first 75 youths (23%) were so removed, after spending an average of 145 days at PCYC (or about 39% of the usual full stay), and spent the remainder of their term in one of the regular training schools. Of those experimental youths who completed their one-year term, a significant fraction (27%) did not successfully move through all three phases of the residential program; 9% were in Phase 1 and 18% were in Phase 2 at the time they were discharged.

The youths who completed the PCYC program spent an average of 376 days in the residential phases of the program, or about 27% longer than the controls, who averaged 295 days in their training school placements. If we include the "early removals" described above, the average length of stay for all experimental youths was 360 days: 327 in PCYC and 33 in training schools.

Cost of Program Placement

The average daily costs for maintaining controls in TICO or Riverview was roughly $88.60 per day (1988 dollars). The daily costs for PCYC were $76.56 without including aftercare and $81.74 with aftercare included. In order to estimate the costs of placement for each experimental and control youth, we multiplied the daily costs by the average number of days in each program. The resulting estimates were $26,137 for each control youth and $29,653 for each experimental youth.

METHODS

Random Assignment and Data Collection Procedures

Eligible youths were randomly assigned to experimental (PCYC) or control (regular training schools) conditions. In order to be eligible, youths had to be male, over 15 years of age, committed to the Ohio DYS for a class 1 or 2 felony from 1 of 17 counties in the southwest part of the state, and certified eligible for assignment to PCYC by the committing court. Random assignment of study youths started in February 1986. By April 1988, 75 experimental and 75 control youth constituted our study sample.

Sources of Data

Background data on the youths (including self-reported delinquency and drug use) were obtained from personal interviews with the youths approximately six months after entry into their study placement and by coding information from DYS files. In the interview youths were asked to recall their involvement in 29 behaviors, ranging from status offenses to attacking persons. The 29 measures were a modification of the 47 standard items used by Elliott et al. in the National Youth Survey.

Process information was obtained by one-time interviews with a sample of all staff at PCYC and the two DYS institutions; exit interviews conducted with assigned caseworkers or counselors at the time each youth left a program; and items from the initial youth interview. Follow-up information was obtained by interviewing each youth one year after he was released from the program and by reviewing juvenile and adult court records.

Data were available for the vast majority of all 150 youths on all data collection instruments: 149 background files; 148 initial youth interviews; and 146 exit interviews with caseworkers. At the end of the data collection period, one youth was still in placement and one was still "absent without leave." Thus, the outcome analyses focused on 148 of the 150 youths. Of these 148 youths, one-year official record data were collected for all, and one-year follow-up interviews were conducted with 124 of the 148 youths (84%).

A comparison between those interviewed and those who were not revealed no significant differences in the percentage of interviews for experimentals, contrasted with controls, or in terms of race, age, conviction offense, county of conviction, prior convictions and prior probations, prior state-level placements, and family history variables (e.g., arrest, drug addiction, prior incarceration). It did appear that noninterviewed youths were significantly more likely to have prior placements and live in less stable family situations than interviewed youths, which suggests noninterviewed youths were somewhat higher risk youths.

Comparison of Experimental and Control Group Characteristics

... [T]he PCYC experimental and control groups and a sample of the overall DYS population [were compared] on a number of background variables usually found related to recidivism. There are no significant differences between the experimental and controls on any of these variables, which indicates that the random assignment procedure successfully assigned equivalent groups to the two conditions. However, a higher percentage of the experimental youths were on probation at the time of their most recent arrest, and they averaged more prior convictions and placements. In terms of self-reported delinquency, experimental and control youths were similar in terms of the percentage of youths committing offenses, with the exception of misdemeanor assault; 97% of experimentals, contrasted with 81% of controls, reported committing a misdemeanor assault during the previous year they were home.

Comparison of Study Youths and Incoming DYS Population

Since the eligibility criteria for PCYC specified males convicted of felony 1 or 2 offenses in 1 of 17 counties in the southwest part of Ohio, we would expect the study sample to differ from the general DYS population. Information on 20% of the youths admitted to the TDYS during the study time period (February 1986 through the spring of 1988) was coded from departmental logs. The majority of admissions were white males who were just under 16 years of age and convicted of lower felony level theft offenses. In contrast to this general population, the study youths were somewhat older and a slightly higher percentage of them were white. All study youths were convicted of felony 1 or 2 offenses; only a third of the general DYS population were convicted of this level of offense. In addition, study youths were about twice as likely to be convicted of a violent offense as the general DYS population. Overall then, the study youths appear, as they were designed to be, a more serious and older class of offender than those in the general DYS population.

RESULTS

Earlier in this paper we presented evidence to show that the program at PCYC was considerably different from that provided in the training schools and in ways that the intervention literature suggests ought to be associated with increased effectiveness. Our analysis in this section focuses on the crim-nal conduct of youths in our samples, following their release from custody, is reflected in their arrest records and their own self-reports of delinquency and drug use.

Official-Record Outcome Measures

We begin with two methods of analyzing post-release failure based on official court records—recidivism and survival analysis. The *recidivism rate* is simply the fraction of a sample that has experienced at least one failure event (arrest) in a specified time period. *Survival analysis* looks at the rate at which failures occur within specified time intervals and is especially of interest when there is reason to believe that the intervention may at least postpone recidivism, even if it is not reduced in the long run.

... By all measures, the experimental youths appeared to perform better, although none of the differences in rearrest or reincarceration rates is statistically significant. As expected, youths who were removed from PCYC for disciplinary reasons performed much worse than those who completed the program.

Although there was no significant difference in recidivism rates between the experimental and control groups, there are good reasons to expect that the intensive aftercare provided for experimental youths would at least postpone the return to crime. In order to determine if that was so, we conducted survival analyses on the length of time until first arrest. ... The survival curves for experimental and control youths ... are consistent with the recidivism analysis. Although a smaller fraction of experimentals have failed at all points on the curve, the differences are not statistically significant. ...

Self-Reported Recidivism

As part of the one-year follow-up interview, all youths were asked a series of questions about their involvement in seven types of criminal behavior. These measures were chosen as the most serious self-reported delinquency measures generally used by Elliott et al. The items were as follows:

- steal or try to steal a motor vehicle, such as a car or motorcycle
- steal or try to steal something worth more than $50
- attack someone with the idea of seriously hurting or killing him or her
- get involved in gang fights
- have or try to have sexual relations with someone against their will
- use force or strong-arm methods to get money or things from other people
- break or try to break into a building or vehicle to steal something or just to look around.

Overall, 75% of the experimental youths reported committing at last one of these offenses during the follow-up period, contrasted with 62% of controls (a nonsignificant difference). The primary differences between the two groups were that more of the experimentals reported assaults (33% vs. 23%) while more of the controls reported burglaries (38% vs. 28%), thefts (42% vs. 30%), and auto thefts (18% vs. 9%). Neither group reported any forcible sex.

In responding to the seven items, the youths were asked to indicate the frequency with which they engaged in each act during the one-year period after release from placement. The rates for all seven offenses were summed to produce an overall self-reported offense rate during the follow-up period. Results revealed similar rates for experimental and control youths—15.2 offenses per year for the experimentals and 14.4 for the controls.

In summary, the officially recorded and self-reported measures point in different directions, although none of the differences between treatment groups is statistically significant. One of the reasons for the different patterns for self-reported delinquency versus official records is that the samples are somewhat different. The official-record data cover 148 youths; the self-reported data are from the subset of 124 youths who were interviewed. In order to investigate the effect of this difference, we recomputed standard official-record recidivism rates using arrests for only those 124 offenders for whom we also had self-reported data. This analysis revealed that the interviewed youths appear to have slightly more official record arrests: 54.7% of interviewed experimental youths had been arrested compared with 61.7% of the controls. This reduces the almost 11% difference in recidivism rates to 7%, based on the interviewed youths. Thus, these data are consistent with an explanation that some of the discrepancies between self-report and official-record data may be due to the difference in samples.

Another hypothesis is that the two measures reflect different types of offending. The self-reported offenses are a limited subset of all possible criminal behavior, while arrests include everything.

A third hypothesis is that the experimental intervention might make some youths more sensitive or forthcoming in reporting all offenses, or just some types. In comparing self-reports and arrests at the individual level we found that more than 90% of the arrestees in both groups reported some delinquent acts. However, among the approximately 18% in both groups who were arrested for safety offenses (robbery, assault, rape, homicide, burglary), only 69% of the control group reported a safety crime, compared with 92% of the experimentals, a finding that is consistent with the "increased honesty/sensitivity" hypothesis, but inconclusive due to the small sample. Another piece of evidence in support of the "increased honesty" hypothesis is the fact that more of the experimental youths reported committing assaults during the year prior to their placement.

Drug Use

Drug use is a crime in itself and also predictive of involvement in other criminal behavior. There is some reason to believe that youths may be more accurate in reporting drug use than in reporting other forms of criminal behavior, because it involves less social stigma. More of the control youths self-reported use of all types of drugs, . . . and although some of the differences appear quite large, none was statistically significant. Not surprisingly, within the experimental group, the "completers" reported less drug use than the "early removals." Although there was no significant difference between the experimentals and controls in the percentage who reported selling drugs, among the experimentals, three times as many of the early removals, compared with the "completers," self-reported selling drugs (57% vs. 20%), a significant difference.

DISCUSSION

There are at least two possible interpretations of these findings. One is that there were no significant differences in outcomes between the two programs and that the type of youths studied here do just as well in either one. The other is that PCYC may have had some modest positive effects on postrelease behavior and arrests. In either case, these results will not be good news for those who expected the experimental program to produce dramatically lower recidivism rates. For whatever reasons, despite the serious efforts that went into designing and implementing the experimental program, the experimental youths do not appear to have behaved substantially better when they returned to the community.

It does not appear that the failure to produce lower recidivism rates can be blamed on the design of the experimental program, which contained most of the features suggested by current theories or recent evaluations as being associated with increased effectiveness. It may be that the experimental program was not as effective as it could have been with the first group of youths; procedures were still being developed and acceptable staffing arrangements worked out. The PCYC could also have included more cognitive/behavioral efforts in the aftercare component, although without additional funding that would have detracted from the residential phases of the program.

We have previously shown that a higher percentage of the PCYC staff were white females than at the training schools. Since many of the youths were black males who did not have strong father figures in their lives, it could be that the lack of more appropriate role models (preferably black males) detracted from the effectiveness of the PCYC program. Or, it could just be that the antisocial patterns of behavior of the youths are so ingrained, or attractive, or reinforced by their social environment, that a one-year effort does not affect their willingness or ability to change.

Some may argue that the results of this experiment have little relevance to current debates about the effectiveness of rehabilitation because the experimental intervention was not designed to test a specific theoretical approach. We can only point out that delinquency theories in their current form provide little but the broadest kind of guidance regarding program design. The PCYC program is like many well-respected programs designed to deal with other types of behavioral problems in that it draws on an eclectic mix of theories and approaches in attempting to develop an individual plan that responds to the needs of each youth. . . .

For researchers who are interested in testing other interventions with similar types of offenders, it should be clear that larger sample sizes are needed to measure the modest 10% to 20% impacts that even the best designed programs are likely to achieve and that more detailed self-reported information may be needed to clarify discrepancies between self-reports and official reports of offending.

It also appears that more attention should be devoted to maintaining gains in prosocial behavior after youths return to their community. It may be that the forms of surveillance and assistance provided by PCYC are not enough. It may be necessary to create some kind of peer support group, on the order of that provided by 12-Step programs like Alcoholics Anonymous, which the youths would be required to attend. A program for drug-involved adult offenders in Oakland has demonstrated that behavioral contracts can be used to increase participation rates in such groups.

We think that this evaluation has several other implications for correctional practice. For the defenders of traditional training schools, it suggests that even overcrowded ones in systems plagued by antiquated facilities, low morale, and frequent turnovers in management are not as ineffective or harmful as many would argue, at least not in terms of the outcomes we were able to measure here. This conclusion is particularly hard to digest for those who observed the positive and forthright behavior of most PCYC youths in comparison with those in TICO. One possible explanation for why this behavior apparently failed to carry over to postrelease behavior is something like that offered to explain the negative impacts of the Cambridge-Somerville Project: that the intervention raised unrealistic expectations that were not met in the world outside the program. It may be that the somewhat chaotic and calloused environment of TICO does just as good a job of preparing youths for the outside world as the Positive Peer Culture of PCYC, because that atmosphere is closer to the one the youths will actually face when they return to the community. During the first year after their release, about 23% of these youths experienced the death of a family member, another 24% experienced the death of a friend, and 24% were fired or laid off.

For the proponents of small, open programs like PCYC, this evaluation should lend support to the argument that such programs can be run as cost-effectively as training schools and with no undue risk to the public, and that such programs will be perceived as superior to training schools by many judges, academicians and outside observers, regardless of their actual impact. The Ohio Department of Youth Services not only continues to support PCYC, but it is also starting a similar program in the northern part of the state.

C. WHAT WORKS?—REHABILITATION AS A JUSTIFICATION FOR THE JUVENILE COURT

The articles in Chapter 5 C confront the question of "what works" and presents some evidence on the efficacy of treatment as a justification for a separate juvenile justice system. The juvenile court "treatment model" assumes that antecedent social or psychological factors cause delinquent behavior, that courts base individualized sentences on clinical assessments of treatment needs, that correctional staff can apply appropriate interventions to alleviate the sources of criminality and reduce recidivism, and that they can determine when youths successfully complete treatment and release them. Recall from Chapter 1, Mack, "The Juvenile Court," the Progressives expressed considerable optimism that delinquents' youthfulness and greater malleability would enable them to respond more readily to treatment. A comprehensive assessment of rehabilitation research conducted by the National Academy of Sciences questioned both the efficacy of juvenile justice interventions and the assumption that youths manifest greater treatment responsiveness.

It may be implicitly assumed by many that age is an important element in classification because it is, or should be, easier to rehabilitate youthful offenders. *That seems a dubious prospect at best.* By any measure currently available, rates of involvement in criminal activity subsequent to adjudication are at least as high for juveniles as for adults with similar offense histories. It could be argued that given the same circumstances it might be more difficult to rehabilitate juveniles than adults because their very youth is indicative that they have no prolonged periods of satisfactory behavior patterns to which they might be restored by proper treatment. In fact, however, very little is known about differential treatment or potential for rehabilitation of juveniles and adults. Lee Sechrest, Susan O. White and Elizabeth D. Brown, eds. *The Rehabilitation of Criminal Offenders* 50–51 (1979).

Robert Martinson's generally negative observation that "With few and isolated exceptions, the rehabilitative efforts that have been reported so far have had no appreciable effect on recidivism," challenged the fundamental premise of therapeutic dispositions and the juvenile court. ["What Works? Questions and Answers About Prison Reform," 35 *Public Interest* 25 (1974).] More recent evaluations of the ability of juvenile correctional intervention to lower recidivism rates counsel skepticism about the availability of programs that consistently or systematically rehabilitate adult or serious juvenile offenders.

The two articles in Chapter 5 C provide conflicting assessments of the effectiveness of treatment in juvenile courts. John Whitehead and Steven Lab, "A Meta-analysis of Juvenile Correctional Treatment," conduct a meta-analysis, or a study of studies. By coding each evaluation study on a number of variables (e.g., characteristics of the research design, subjects studied, type of treatment applied, and outcome measures), and combining and reanalyzing the studies, they attempt to identify the effectiveness of various types of juvenile correctional interventions. Whitehead and Lab's study draws pessimistic conclusions about the efficacy of juvenile correctional rehabilitation. By contrast, Ted Palmer, "The Effectiveness of Intervention," reviews a number of recent meta-analyses and draws more favorable conclusions about the effectiveness of rehabilitative interventions on selected subgroups of juvenile offenders.

These conflicting studies of studies indicate that juvenile courts' and institutions' claims to rehabilitate young offenders remain unproven and suggest some of the reasons why. Many evaluations of treatment effectiveness lack methodological rigor. Many treatment programs lack a theoretical rationale or consistent intervention strategies based upon that rationale. Some evaluation studies fail to assess whether the program staff actually implemented the prescribed treatment with integrity. Thus, the inability to demonstrate consistent positive treatment effects may reflect either methodological flaws, poorly conceived or implemented programs, an inability accurately to match subjects with programs, or the absence of viable methods successfully to treat serious or chronic young offenders.

Even if some "model" programs do reduce somewhat recidivism rates, what is the likelihood that public officials actually will provide such treatment services for most delinquents when they confront fiscal constraints, budget deficits, and competition from other, more politically potent interest groups? Rather, organizational imperatives to achieve "economies of scale" may mandate confining ever larger numbers of youths in institutions and thereby preclude the possibility of matching offenders with appropriate treatment programs. Even if "treatment" programs do produce some marginal improvements in the lives of some young offenders, are those benefits sufficient to justify the inevitable racial disparities that result from the exercise of individualized sentencing discretion? Finally, if states do not appropriate significant resources and correctional administrators do not provide effective services in responsive environments, then do any practical differences exist between treatment and punishment?

A Meta-Analysis of Juvenile Correctional Treatment

JOHN T. WHITEHEAD
STEVEN P. LAB

Debate over the effectiveness of correctional treatment has been raging for over a decade. The negative position that "nothing works" is probably the viewpoint most prominent in the public mind; it relies heavily on the findings of Bailey, Robison and Smith, Martinson, Lipton, Martinson, and Wilks, Wright and Dixon, Sechrest, White, and Brown, and others. The opposite view stresses that various programs have a positive effect on select clients under specific conditions. Related to this view is the hope that more recent interventions will have treatment integrity. That is, more recent interventions will pay greater attention to ensuring that treatments are actually implemented as intended. The interventions should be more effective than many of the older efforts that often failed to check on treatment integrity. Still another view argues that the rehabilitation philosophy should be retained because it is the only guarantee for humane correctional environments when the effectiveness of treatment programs is so much in question. The present study represents an attempt to contribute to the question of the effectiveness of juvenile correctional treatment by reviewing the most recent evidence and by using the latest methodological technique—meta-analysis—to analyze the evidence.

LITERATURE REVIEW

A review of the literature indicates that there are three basic ways to assess the evidence on the effectiveness of correctional interventions. The first, the so-called ballot-box or voting method, has been the traditional way to summarize the results of individual evaluation studies. The researcher collects as many evaluations of intervention efforts that meet certain basic criteria (e.g., use of a comparison group or pre–post measures) as possible and

Excerpted from John T. Whitehead, in *Journal of Research in Crime & Delinquency*, Vol. 26, pp. 276–295 (August 1989), copyright © 1989 by John T. Whitehead. Reprinted by permission of Sage Publications, Inc.

then simply totals up the findings of successes, failures, and no difference. A second approach, hereafter termed the analytical method, involves going beyond simple tabulation to appraise critically the theory, methodology, and implementation of the various interventions in order to extrapolate common principles or the best substantiated findings. A variation on this method is to select exemplary interventions of various types and rely on the outcomes of such exemplary projects as critical tests. The third and most contemporary approach is meta-analysis. Meta-analysis extends the ballot-box approach by calculating a common statistic (e.g., effect size) that summarizes the individual statistics of each intervention into an overall measure of effectiveness.

Four researchers offer two of the most recent examples of the ballot-box or voting technique. Concerning diversion, Gensheimer et al. find that, based on 44 research designs from 1967 to 1983, "the data suggest that diversion intervention had no effect on outcome measures." While diversion efforts as a whole had no effect, behavioral approaches (for example, token economy, modeling, and behavioral contracting) used outside the residential setting may have a positive impact. Indeed, Mayer et al., reviewing 39 research reports published between 1971 and 1982, conclude that there is "a high degree of effectiveness for behavioral interventions for the recidivism, behavior, and attitudinal outcomes, as well as the collapsed overall results." The major problem with such a ballot-box approach is that it reduces each individual study to a dichotomy: Each individual study is rated as either a success or a failure. Thus much of the complexity in the original findings is ignored.

Geismar and Wood typify the analytical approach in their analysis of studies of family treatment of delinquency. They find no effect for nonbehavioral family therapy: "*Nonfocused* family interventions, that is, those that address themselves vaguely to encouraging communication in general or expression of feelings, are totally ineffective in the treatment of adolescent delinquency." On the other hand, they find that although behavioral family interventions have "*also not been demonstrated to be totally effective, the evidence so far is tilting the scale in their favor*" (emphasis in the original). Another review that used the analytical method produces similar, although even more cautious, conclusions about all types of interventions (not just family interventions) with delinquents. Specifically, Graziano and Mooney, reviewing both traditional and behavioral delinquency interventions, conclude, as Geismar and Wood do about family therapies, that "while nonbehavioral programming has been virtually without demonstrable success—with even some suggestions of unintended negative effects—the behavioral research since the early sixties is a good deal more promising." These researchers emphasize, however, that much of the positive impact of behavioral interventions is often intraprogram whereas "only rarely and only very recently has data been presented to show that delinquent behavior was reduced over a relatively long term through behavioral programming."

As mentioned, Lundman has analyzed delinquency interventions by selecting some of the best interventions. For example, he includes the Provo study that was grounded in delinquency theory and utilized random assignment to place subjects into experimental and control groups. Based on his analyses of such exemplary interventions, Lundman concludes that delinquency prevention (for example, area projects) does not work, diversion is at least as effective as further penetration into the juvenile justice system, probation is effective for moderately delinquent offenders, confrontation programs (for example Scared Straight) have at best mixed benefits, and community treatment of many but not all offenders is equally effective as institutionalization. A major problem with Lundman's variation of the analytic approach is that the selection of the exemplary projects is debatable. Not everyone would agree, for example, that his selection of the California Treatment Project as the ideal probation and parole program is without problems. Most probation and parole programs do not involve the I-level classification system that was such an important part of the California Treatment Project.

There have been at least three meta-analyses of delinquency interventions. Based on a review of 111 studies published between 1960 and 1983, Garrett reports a positive change (overall effect size) of .37 standard deviations and concludes that "yes, treatment of adjudicated delinquents in residential settings does work." This assessment, however, includes only modest effects on recidivism. Garrett also finds that "the better designed studies showed a lower effect size (average effect size of .24) compared to the less rigorous studies (average effect size of .65)." Ignoring the rigor of the study design, interventions primarily based on behavioral theory (either operant or respondent) show the greatest effect size (.63) compared to other types of interventions such as those based on psychodynamic approaches to behavior and attitude change (effect size of .17). Taking study rigor into account reveals that the more rigorous behavior theory studies have a much lower average effect size (.30) than the less rigorous behavior studies (.86). Design quality makes almost no difference in the effect size for psychodynamic interventions. Finally, Garrett finds some promise for two very specific types of interventions—cognitive-behavioral and Outward Bound programs—which yielded average effect sizes of .58 and .38, respectively.

In addition to the ballot-box or voting method analyses cited above, Gensheimer and her colleagues also use meta-analysis to examine diversion interventions. The results confirm the ballot-box conclusion "that diversion interventions produce no effect with youths." Interestingly, this negative conclusion does not influence Gensheimer and her colleagues to call for the abandonment of diversion. Rather, since they find no strong negative impacts of diversion versus "the well-established literature on the detrimental effects of traditional approaches to treating juvenile offenders," they, like Lundman, argue for continued use of diversion but add that there should be attention to improving such efforts. Since most of the diversion programs in their study offered nonspecific services, referred clients to other agencies offering unspecified services, or the original evaluation did not state what type of intervention was used (for example, behavioral or psychodrama), Gensheimer and her colleagues do not offer a recommendation as to the superior efficacy of behavioral or psychodynamic methods of intervention in diversion.

Likewise, Mayer et al. report essentially positive results in their meta-analysis of behavioral interventions (token economies, modeling, behavioral contracting, positive reinforcement, or contingency management) to delinquency. "Overall, it appears that the treatments were moderately effective, although this conclusion must be moderated by the fact that the effect size variances were large and the confidence intervals broad." More specifically, they find a mean effect size of .50 on recidivism in studies that used experimental and control groups and they uncover only one specific type of behavior treatment—token economies—which correlates significantly with effect size (correlation = about .35). Token economies, however, correlate significantly with effect size only in the weaker studies (pre–post design) rather than the more rigorous studies (experiment–control group design). This highlights the general problem that "methodologically, this literature continues to display serious shortcomings." One problem with their research is that they rely on *Psychological Abstracts* and ignore any criminal justice or sociological reference sources, thus limiting the completeness of their study.

Interestingly, the three approaches to summarizing individual evaluation studies into some sort of overall conclusion about the effectiveness of delinquency come to the same conclusion: Many efforts do not work although behavioral interventions are offering promise of effectiveness. Parenthetically, if the finding that behavioral interventions are effective is accurate, it may be at least partially attributable to the greater program integrity of behavioral interventions. That is, behavioral interventions generally include very specific objectives and frequent monitoring of behaviors. These aspects of behavioral efforts do not ensure program integrity, but they do contribute to it. Another factor in the findings of effectiveness is the concern over outcome measures besides recidivism. Many of the positive outcomes fall within the realm of in-program behavior, educational attainment, improved self-concept or other similar measures. Although these may be admirable, they do not address the primary concern of most evaluations, that being recidivism.

The current study summarizes the state of the evidence concerning juvenile correctional treatment and recidivism through the use of meta-analysis. Meta-analysis is a technique that reanalyzes data found in original research reports and arrives at a common measure for all of the studies. For example, the researcher may compute chi-square statistics for all of the target studies. By so doing, the researcher is able to compare the results across the studies. In the absence of such computations, the researcher would be attempting to compare chi-square statistics to regression figures, gamma, or any number of other diverse measures. Meta-analysis, therefore, simply allows the direct comparison of study results.

DATA AND METHODOLOGY

This study focuses on evaluations of juvenile correctional treatment appearing in professional journals from 1975 to 1984 inclusive. Evaluations appearing as government reports, books, dissertations, or theses were not included in the analysis. Unlike other reviews that rely on only one source for data, the current researchers identified the target studies through an extensive search of *Abstracts on Criminology and Penology, Criminal Justice Abstracts, Psychological Abstracts, Sociological, Abstracts,* and the National Criminal Justice Reference Service Index. References for each study were subsequently used to identify other evaluations of juvenile correctional treatment. Studies were chosen for inclusion in the analysis if they dealt with some form of juvenile correctional treatment, included a control group, and provided data in a form that allowed us to meta-analyze the results.

Juvenile correctional treatment was broadly defined as any intervention aimed at reducing subsequent recidivism by the juvenile, whether that activity be the initial deviant act or further offending by an adjudicated delinquent. Interventions whose primary focus was punishment, such as imprisonment or corporal punishment, were not considered as treatment. Additionally, treatments designed specifically to address drug/alcohol usage were eliminated. Treatments that were included ranged from police cautioning to restitution to residential treatment. Recidivism served as the primary outcome measure in the analysis. The specific measure of recidivism took a variety of forms, all of which reflected some type of subsequent contact with the juvenile justice system due to delinquent/criminal behavior.

The initial search of the abstracts yielded over 500 documents of which roughly 200 were professional journal articles. After a thorough reading of the articles, we eliminated all but 50 of the studies. Studies were excluded primarily due to the lack of adequate data. Other reasons for elimination were the absence of a control group, a focus on adult behavior, a duplication of results in more than one journal, or the lack of a clear treatment method.

The present endeavor computed two common statistics for all studies. The first measure, chi-square, is a measure of association that also presents a significance level for the results. The major drawback to the exclusive use of a chi-square, however, is the fact that evaluations based on large sample sizes have a tendency to artificially reach a level of significance. This would bias any results in favor of treatment that are evaluated using large study samples. Due to this inadequacy in chi-square, an additional measure of association, phi, was used. Phi was chosen due to its correction for sample size and its ease of computation and comparison across studies. Phi ranges in size from zero to one with values approaching unity signifying a strong relationship between the variables. While both chi-square and phi are reported in the following results, the major emphasis is on the reported phi coefficients.

RESULTS

Comparison of Treatment Types

The study results can be compared across a number of dimensions. The 50 studies included here cover a range of correctional treatments. It is prudent, therefore, to compare similar treatments to one another. The studies were initially divided into five categories of treatment programs. The first category, nonsystem diversion programs, covers interventions that completely end a youth's contact with the formal justice system through either the termination of any intervention or the referral to a nonsystem-related agency. System diversion, the second type of intervention, represents diversion programs that operate as an extension of the formal justice system. The third type of treatment includes any community corrections-oriented approach such as probation or parole. Institutional or residential treatment programs serve as a fourth intervention category, while novel/specialty interventions such as Scared Straight and Outward Bound make up the final treatment category....

DISCUSSION

The current meta-analysis set out to identify which, if any, juvenile correctional treatments have a positive impact on subsequent recidivism. Through the computation of phi and chi-square statistics for each identified study, it was possible to compare the results of 50 published evaluations appearing between 1975 and 1984 inclusive. The results are far from encouraging for advocates of correctional intervention. On the whole, few programs exhibit high phi coefficients. Additionally, the examination of studies according to different subgroupings of treatment, subjects, methodology, or time periods fails to improve the outlook for treatment. Inspection of chi-square coefficients proves to add little to the analysis due to its heavy association with the disparate study sample sizes.

System diversion appears to be the most promising type of correctional treatment. Almost half of these interventions (7 of 15) are associated with a phi of .20 or greater and all of these are in the positive direction. This means that the more effective programs are able to reduce the recidivism among experimental clients significantly. Nonsystem diversion, community corrections, residential corrections, and novel programs all fail to display ny strong propensity for lowering recidivism. In fact, many of the programs ppear to exacerbate recidivism as shown by the number of negative phi values. This tendency for system diversion programs to reduce recidivism contradicts the labeling perspective that claims that system contact and intervention tend to "label" or stigmatize youth as delinquent and cause them o commit further deviant acts. It would appear that system involvement as the greatest potential for reducing recidivism.

One possible explanation for the surprising results from system diversion may involve both labeling theory and deterrence. Diversion relies on the dea of eliminating the stigmatizing effect of system contact. System diversion, although run as an arm of an official agency, may be able to mitigate he deleterious effects of contact with normal processing. At the same time, he connection of a diversion program with the formal system, even if just in ame, may bring with it a degree of deterrent value that is not associated with nonsystem diversion. The reduction in recidivism, therefore, could result from both the reduction of stigma and the impact of deterrence. Our data lo not allow us to test this possibility and we leave it for future inquiry.

Claims that behavioral interventions are the most promising do not receive support in this analysis. A comparison of results for behavioral and nonbehavioral interventions reveals contradictory findings. Although behavioral programs display a greater percentage of phi coefficients exceeding .20, they also show a much greater number of negative phi values. Thus, although the programs have an impact on recidivism, they make the level of recidivism go up after intervention. The promise of behavioral interventions may rest in the various other outcome measures (i.e., educational attainment) found throughout the research.

Examination of evaluations in terms of group assignment reveals some lifferences in the studies. Studies utilizing random and nonrandom assignment exhibit similar proportions of phi coefficients exceeding .20. This would suggest that the rigor of group assignment has little impact on the outcome of the study. Inspection of the sign of the phi values, however, shows a much larger percentage of negative phi values associated with studies using random assignment of subjects of study groups. It appears that more rigorous studies tend to portray correctional treatment as less effective than those programs and evaluations that choose their clients in some other fashion.

Inspection of the results in a chronological fashion reveals a trend toward less effective treatments in recent years. Counter to the claims that treatment programs are (or should) be improving in recent years, the results show that a greater proportion of evaluations provide positive results in the late 1970s than those conducted in the early 1980s. We examined the possibility that this finding might be due to greater methodological rigor in the more recent studies, but our measure of rigor, random assignment, does not support such a contention. Random assignment, however, is only one measure of study quality. Thus we feel that this issue needs fuller examination, as do other explanations of our findings on chronology.

The results of this meta-analysis differ little from other reviews of the literature. The results clearly support the contentions of Bailey, Martinson, Lipton, Martinson, and Wilks, Greenberg, Wright and Dixon, and Sechrest, White, and Brown that correctional treatment has little effect on recidivism. More recent studies that have used ballot-box, analytic, and meta-analytic techniques also report similar findings when looking at specific types of interventions or using slightly different approaches. The greatest difference between our results and those of other researchers has been in the area of behavioral interventions. As noted earlier, where other researchers find positive support for behavioral techniques, this analysis uncovers contradictory evidence. . . .

The Effectiveness of Intervention: Recent Trends and Current Issues

TED PALMER

The effectiveness of rehabilitation first became a major issue in the mid-1970s when Martinson and others seriously challenged it. This challenge lessened somewhat in the early 1980s as evidence of positive outcomes in the form of public protection as measured by recidivism was slowly but increasingly recognized. Yet, even as of 1983–1984, an unsettled atmosphere existed regarding effectiveness. Neither the global optimism of the 1960s nor the extreme pessimism of the middle and later 1970s seemed justified, and more moderate camps—the "skeptic" and "sanguine"—replaced them.

Within the skeptical camp, some individuals believed it was clear that few rehabilitation programs worked. They reached this conclusion on the basis of what they considered a sufficient body of adequately conducted research. Moreover, these skeptics held that those programs that did work probably reduced recidivism only by small amounts. These individuals felt that rehabilitation, while not a total failure, therefore held little promise and merited only a minor role in correctional programs.

Other individuals believed that very little could be asserted with confidence about the success of rehabilitation. They suggested that because of minor or major flaws in almost all studies, poor implementation of programs, or both, we do not know if any particular approaches work. These skeptics concluded that rehabilitation had not received a "fair trial." They suggested that although some approaches may perhaps work for some offenders, we

Excerpted from Ted Palmer, in *Crime & Delinquency*, Vol. 37, pp. 330–346 (July 1991), copyright © 1991 by Ted Palmer. Reprinted by permission of Sage Publications, Inc.

re in the dark about them because research findings are neither ironclad for any one study nor entirely consistent across studies. As a result, these latter skeptics believed that although rehabilitation might well have promise, no specific approaches could yet be recommended, at least widely.

Members of the more sanguine camp believed that many programs and approaches have been shown, with reasonable scientific assurance, to work for specific subgroups of offenders. Some persons, who might be called the Basic Treatment Amenability Group, claimed that "amenable" offenders respond positively to many approaches under a wide range of conditions; thus they are generally treatable. On the other hand, most "nonamenables" were thought to be largely unresponsive to any rehabilitation efforts.

Other proponents, who might be called the Differential Intervention Group (or, more colloquially, the "different strokes for different folks" camp), offered the somewhat different view that treatment affects offenders in a positive, neutral, or negative way, depending on the specific approach and external conditions to which they are exposed.

COMMON GROUND

Despite their differences, sanguines and skeptics shared some common ground. In particular, many of them largely agreed on at least three points regarding serious or repeat offenders. These were youths and adults who had received increasing attention since 1975, they were not uncommon among correctional—especially incarcerated—populations; some had committed violent offenses, and many were open to change and only moderately committed to illegal behavior:

1. To be effective with these individuals, intervention should be broadly based. More specifically, it should involve a multiple modality approach, for example, simultaneous or successive combinations of such program components as vocational or academic training, individual or group counseling, recreation, cultural enrichment, or other services or activities.

2. Intervention should often be more intensive, for instance, contacts should be frequent.

3. Differential intervention should be used, involving program and offender matching. A program's full range of resources should not automatically be applied to every type of offender subgroup. Instead, only some components or combinations should be used, at least at any one time, with any particular offender type. Intervention strategies should be adapted to the main needs and interests of each subgroup comprising the overall sample.

Together, these core elements of general agreement suggested that, for programs to substantially influence other-than-minor offenders or relatively "good risks," they should be better adapted to the life circumstances and personal as well as interpersonal features of those individuals.

DEVELOPMENTS SINCE 1984–1985

This core of similar views became apparent to many correctional practitioners and researchers by 1984–1985. It helped initiate a quiet, osmoticlike process that, by the late 1980s, resulted in a tacit, de facto consensus regarding certain aspects of correctional intervention, one that was also accepted by various policymakers and academicians. This broadly held but still unsteady consensus was basically quite simple: First, in contrast to the clearly pessimistic outlook and the actively rejecting attitudes of the 1975–1981 period, some forms of intervention *could* probably reduce recidivism and could promote public safety; thus rehabilitation/habilitation might be possible after all. Second, most standard forms and typical variants of intervention, such as types of individual or group counseling, were no longer thought to be intrinsically demeaning or necessarily onerous. Finally, when included in an intervention package that contained clear external controls and accountability, and that involved unpleasant consequences for infractions and illegal behavior, some forms of intervention, such as community-based approaches, were now considered less risky to the public, when used with selected offenders. This consensus received support from a collection of meta-analyses and literature reviews that began about 1984. However, rather than being quiet and osmotic, their contributions were more active and visible. Selected meta-analyses are reviewed below.

This consensus was significant. For instance, by the late 1980s programs and research that involved rehabilitation or treatment were less often considered either anachronisms or exercises in naåvetÇ and futility. In addition, correctional programs were less often described as repressive tools of a ruling-class conspiracy, made up of members of an upper-class "establishment"— which allegedly used various interventions, and incarceration per se, to curb crime in general and to control socially disadvantaged groups in order to maintain its social advantages. Nor was intervention as often considered brainwashing and intrinsically antithetical to various justice system reforms. . . .

In short, the sharp edges of the 1970s and 1980s had softened, and the tacit or implied consensus had helped reduce various scientific, philosophical, and political objections to program development and research. When combined with the core elements that helped produce it, the consensus had another outcome as well. (The core elements were multiple modality programming, increased intensity of contact, and greater attention to offender needs and characteristics.) For instance, those elements, supported by the growing consensus, gave new impetus to many research and development efforts directed at intervention. (To be sure, institutional crowding and societywide fiscal constraints had been more influential in reducing political impediments.)

More specifically, increased intensity of contact and multiple modality programming became central features of various intensive supervision and treatment efforts, particularly intensive or enhanced probation programs for juvenile recidivists and similar parole programs for relatively serious adults. Of course, other factors also contributed to the support for such programs, particularly those emphasizing external controls. Increased intensity of supervision was also related to the demands of some authorities and citizens for "stronger," more punitive approaches.

As impediments to intervention decreased during the mid-1980s, momentum for program development and research increased, at first slowly and then more rapidly. By 1987 multiple modality programming and offender-needs perspectives became incorporated in needs-assessment endeavors, in which attempts were made to identify offender needs and to determine appropriate strategies for meeting those needs. Needs-assessment efforts were also related to risk-assessment activities. (Needs-assessments are usually designed to determine if areas such as employment, education, substance abuse assistance, and personal conflicts resolution require attention. In contrast, risk-assessment centers on an individual's likelihood of recidivating, as indicated by such factors as age at first offense, number of offenses, and type of offense.)

All in all, by the late 1980s the program-development efforts that existed during 1965–1975 but which had then declined for several years had, to a large extent, returned. Many practitioners and researchers were again proceeding with the practical task of discovering useful intervention methods and strategies and of developing and evaluating possibly improved approaches. Despite their continued differences, many skeptics, sanguines, and others were moving in similar directions and were supporting similar goals. In short, the search for effective intervention had been relegitimized.

Nevertheless, uncertainty still exists regarding the effectiveness and utility of intervention. For instance, despite the changes described above and despite increased efforts, the consensus is far from universal, is only tacit, and covers only some offenders. In addition, important issues and differences remain. These issues are scientific, philosophical and practical. Some of them are quite basic, focusing on such questions as what constitutes acceptable evidence of program effectiveness as well as on who should receive certain interventions.

REVIEW OF META-ANALYSES

Before we further examine the current status of intervention, two major meta-analyses of the 1980s should be reviewed. . . .

In meta-analyses, any collection of individual programs is said to comprise a "type-of-treatment" if they resemble each other on specified, salient, or dominant features—for example, family counseling or group counseling.

In most meta-analyses and literature reviews, multicomponent programs such as those involving vocational training as well as recreation are routinely analyzed and reported in terms of their seemingly dominant component.

Lipsey recently described his meta-analysis of about 400 published and unpublished experimental studies of juvenile delinquents (mostly through age 18) in institutional and noninstitutional programs. Of these many studies, 86% were conducted during 1970–1988. Based on a range of behavioral outcome measures (one per study), but most often arrests or police contacts and other justice system contacts, 64% of the results favored the treatment group. In 30% of the cases the control group received the greater benefits, and in 6% of the cases the results favored neither group. (*Favored* was defined as "in the direction of"—whether statistically significant or not. Type of treatment was the factor most strongly related to program impact. Within the type-of-treatment factor, multimodal and behavioral approaches were most often effective, probation and parole enhancements had no positive impact, nor did broadly labeled approaches such as counseling and skill-oriented programs; and deterrence or shock approaches were associated with poorer outcomes for experimental than control cases. (From this point on, experimental cases will be designated as Es and control cases as Cs.)

Offender characteristics, such as first-timers versus repeaters, amenability, and interpersonal maturity level, were also important. Moreover, the results suggested the strong possibility that the most fully implemented programs outperformed the rest. Lipsey's analysis is the broadest and most systematic to date. . . .

OVERVIEW OF FINDINGS FROM META-ANALYSES AND LITERATURE REVIEWS

Taken together, the meta-analyses and literature reviews of the 1980s indicated the following:

1. When individual programs have been grouped together and analyzed as a single, undifferentiated type (e.g., "counseling"), many of them seemed unsuccessful in terms of recidivism reduction. Specifically, when judged by standard to fairly strict criteria (immediately below), these approaches showed neither statistically superior performance ($p < .05$) for Es versus Cs nor Es fairly consistently outperforming Cs (either by any amount or using $p < .05$), for instance, in at least two thirds of the programs that comprised any given grouping, such as counseling.

Lack of success in terms of those criteria was found for each of the following approaches: *confrontation* (deterrence or shock); *diversion* (at least "non-system" and perhaps other-than-behavior-based); *group therapy or counseling; individual therapy or counseling; physical challenge; probation or parole enhancements.*

2. Despite the results described above for programs grouped together, Es outperformed Cs in many or most individual programs. Specifically, using any recidivism reduction ($p < .05$ or not), Es led Cs in about 65% of all programs while Cs were ahead in about 30%; and, using a $p < .05$ criterion they outperformed Cs in at least 25%–35% of all programs, while Cs led Es in about 10%.

Thus, if an investigator had categorized all programs but nevertheless reviewed them individually, he or she would have found statistically successful ($p < .05$) individual programs in almost every category, whether diversion, group therapy or counseling, or individual therapy or counseling. That is, successful individual programs would have been found that would not have emerged as "successful" if they had originally been merged into an overall category, such as diversion, and then had been considered only as part of that category.

3. Although many broad approaches (as vs. individual programs) seemed unsuccessful from an *"E-better-than-C"* perspective, some broad strategies and interventions were probably associated with *equal* outcomes. For instance, community-based and institutional programs seemed to yield comparable recidivism rates; and, under various conditions, even diversion's outcomes probably equalled those of further justice system processing.

4. Again at a broad level, the following interventions were usually regarded, on balance, as the most successful approaches: (a) behavioral, (b) cognitive-behavioral (also called social-cognitive), (c) family intervention, and (d) vocational training. Nevertheless, a minority of the meta-analyses and literature reviews did not find some of these approaches—chiefly behavioral and family intervention—successful. This inconsistency probably resulted from a combination of differing success criteria and the following factors:

First, the various individual programs that comprised those approaches were not entirely identical from one analysis or review to the next; for example, the overlap of programs across several analyses or reviews was about 60%–70%, mainly because of the partly different time periods or program settings that were involved in the respective analyses/reviews. Also reflected were the varied inclusion criteria that were used, that is, the differing bases for selecting programs in the first place, regardless of time and setting.

Second, the approaches, particularly behavioral and cognitive-behavioral, were defined somewhat differently in several meta-analyses and literature reviews, thus complicating the assessment of given approaches. Specifically, some of the inconsistent results from one study to the next were due to differing definitions. For example, in some analyses/reviews, behavioral intervention was defined in ways that substantively overlapped with cognitive-behavioral or vocational training in some other analyses/reviews. Similarly, vocational training, as defined in one or more analyses/reviews, included aspects of social skills, as defined in others. Finally, in some analyses/ reviews, family intervention included programs that, in other analyses/ reviews, appeared under behavioral or cognitive-behavioral. This apparently occurred because some behavioral or cognitive-behavioral principles and techniques were considered integral to the family interventions in question.

Thus varying and nonexclusive definitions complicated and rendered somewhat ambiguous the conceptualization and assessment even of various approaches that several meta-analysts and reviewers considered generally successful or at least among the most promising. Such definitional problems highlight the limitations of existing meta-analyses and reviews with respect to understanding the specific nature and impact of given approaches.

5. For positive-outcome studies, recidivism rates of Es averaged 17%–22% lower than those of Cs. About one of every four such studies had rather sizable recidivism reductions, for instance, 25% or more, and roughly one in five was under 10%. Positive-outcome studies were those in which Es outperformed Cs by any amount, whether or not the difference between Es and Cs was statistically significant. When those positive-outcome studies were averaged together with the negative-outcome studies, Es' recidivism rates were still lower than Cs'—10%–12% on average. Since these reductions applied to the overall target sample, they were undoubtedly larger for some offender subgroups than others, at least in many individual studies. Future research should give high priority to determining which subgroups are most and least responsive to the various methods and techniques.

CURRENT STATUS OF EFFECTIVENESS

Together, the several meta-analyses and literature reviews conducted since the mid-1980s helped change or modify many individuals' views about the effectiveness of correctional intervention. More specifically, they left a fairly strong, cumulative impression that several programs or approaches can very likely reduce recidivism under certain conditions, and not just for "treatment amenables" or low-risks. Currently, this impression is more widely and perhaps strongly held than in the early and mid-1980s. Moreover, largely because most meta-analyses indicate that many positive outcomes exist, this impression, or in some cases definite view, is seldom strongly challenged on empirical grounds.

This relative absence of challenge is nevertheless slightly surprising, since it exists despite the fact that the research designs of many individual studies that comprised the meta-analyses and literature reviews were much less than excellent and were in that respect open to valid question. On balance, it appears that many individuals' general impressions about effectiveness were probably shaped by the following combination of factors: First, many positive-outcome studies appeared to have scientifically adequate designs. Second, there was the sheer number of positive-outcome studies (especially across differing meta-analyses and literature reviews), together with the apparent convergence of evidence from various studies, several of which were good to excellent. These factors may have tacitly reassured individuals that most studies do not have to be excellent in order to help one decide if intervention in general "works," or, at least, often works.

At any rate, based largely on the program developments and research efforts that occurred since 1984–1985 in connection with core elements such as multiple modality programming and increased intensity of contact, and even apart from the meta-analyses and literature reviews mentioned above, the following seems clear: Intervention has a widely recognized and generally accepted role with at least serious and repeat offenders. This role involves not just control- or surveillance-centered approaches, but complex psychological and skill-development methods as well. In the 1990s, particular focus should be placed upon the third core element: greater attention to offender needs and characteristics.

Equally important, however, is the following point. Neither meta-analyses nor recent literature reviews indicate that generic *types* of programs have been found that consistently produce *major* recidivism reductions. This absence of even a few clearly powerful yet widely applicable types of programs contributes to intervention's unsettled atmosphere. It may reflect any of several factors, the following being among the obvious, likely, and important ones. First, many positive-outcome programs may not be powerful or flexible enough to produce major reductions for all offenders combined. Some of them may have large effects on one or more types of offenders in the overall sample but may have limited relevance to the remaining types—those which might comprise much of the sample. Second, many programs that are grouped together and considered a "type" may not be very similar once they are closely examined. In addition, inadequate implementation often occurs, even in programs that *are* perhaps potentially powerful and widely applicable. If implementation were better, major reductions could occur more often. Finally, although many nontraditional, positive-outcome studies may be quite good themselves, various standard or traditional programs with which they were scientifically compared may have been quite good as well. This is a reasonable possibility, given the assumption that some standard programs, like some nontraditionals themselves, doubtlessly had a number of particularly competent or unusually talented line or supervisory staff and that such individuals had some effect on implementation and outcome.

All in all, then, by 1989–1990 the emerging picture or perhaps new implicit consensus among many skeptics, sanguines, and others was that "something" apparently works, although no generic method or approach (as vs. individual programs) especially shines. Stated differently, several methods seem promising, but none have been shown to usually produce major reductions when applied broadly to typical composite samples of offenders.

Greater acceptance of positive outcomes has not just resulted from meta-analyses, increased practical experience, and so on. It implicitly reflects the fact that relatively few researchers and academicians require that only excellent or near-perfect designs and analyses be considered when evaluating intervention. In this connection there now seems to be a combination of increased acquiescence and acceptance regarding studies that, on the surface at least, seem to meet long-established standards of scientific adequacy; and it is these studies that comprised a sizable portion of most meta-analyses and literature reviews. To be sure, there were many mediocre, that is, somewhat less than adequate, studies as well. This mixture of some excellent, many adequate, and many borderline and even poor studies leaves various assertions about correctional effectiveness open to valid question. Nevertheless, the large number and percentage of positive outcomes associated with studies that are at least adequate leaves little doubt that many programs work, and not just with one or two subgroups.

CLOSING REMARKS

Knowledge Building

Intervention's continued progress into the mid-1990s and later, at least at other than a snail's pace, is far from assured. This applies, not just to knowledge building, but to the avoidance of a situation in which growth-centered intervention becomes little more than an appendage to either a management-and-control-centered strategy or a punishment- or just-desert-centered strategy, or little more than a vehicle for providing—at most—modest services to perhaps the majority of offenders, and somewhat more to those actively seeking them or in obvious need.

Regarding increased discovery of and knowledge about effective programs, and of how to establish and operate them, achievement of the following goals, at least 1, 4, and 5, would clearly promote progress:

1. Studies should be well designed. For instance, random assignment should be used wherever possible.
2. More studies should be designed as replications or partial replications. Replicated results could give practitioners and policymakers more confidence in particular programs or given approaches.
3. Purposive variations of earlier studies should be conducted. For example, a "variation" could test—with setting or population Y (say, urban males age 17–20)—results from a previously promising program that dealt with X (rural males age 13–16).
4. Wherever possible, each study should describe the offender subgroups that comprise the overall target sample, and separate outcome analyses should be conducted for each subgroup. These "differentiated analyses" would be especially valuable if differing interventions were used with those subgroups.

Intervention processes, for instance, specific techniques, strategies, and program features, should be examined closely and described more fully, so that researchers may obtain clues or strong evidence as to which of those factors substantially contribute to growth-centered intervention. If researchers could identify such "key elements," correctional knowledge and practice would be on firmer grounds and might advance more rapidly than by any other means.

Process or "black-box" descriptions should obviously include much more than names of particular approaches, for example, behavioral or group counseling, and more than brief or perhaps standard accounts of their main features or variants, for instance, contingency contracting or guided group interaction. Although detailed descriptions could be especially useful if provided separately by offender subgroups, they could also contribute without them. In addition, whether or not subgroups are delineated, key elements may be identified without meta-analysis.

Whether or not goals 1 through 5 are achieved, sizable recidivism reductions should become increasingly possible or common insofar as such core elements as multiple modality programming and greater attention to offender needs and characteristics are increasingly used.

Legitimacy

A key issue that carried over from the 1970s to the 1980s involved intervention's legitimacy. Throughout 1975–1981, numerous individuals virtually declared intervention illegitimate, that is, not just ineffective but inappropriate or at least of little use. However, in the 1980s, intervention in general and rehabilitation in particular more or less fought their way back from this alleged near-illegitimacy. They did so mainly via studies, meta-analyses, and literature reviews that, collectively, demonstrated frequent effectiveness, and partly because personal as well as practical assistance was often provided and recognized as such, for instance, in areas of vocational and academic achievement. These findings and contributions increased or reestablished intervention's pragmatic legitimacy.

In addition, by the mid-1980s it was generally apparent that the *Clockwork Orange* stereotype of treatment as inhumane and dehumanizing—therefore morally illegitimate—seldom applied and was not intrinsic to intervention. (Abuses often existed before 1980, as did several questionable approaches. Moreover, these had been caused by neither institutional crowding nor fiscal constraints. Although not entirely absent, they are now much reduced.) Meanwhile, by the late 1980s, it was apparent that neither justice model proponents nor others had provided convincing arguments to the effect that rehabilitation, first, should be considered intrinsically inappropriate as a major correctional goal; second, was in fact unimportant or perhaps even harmful as a correctional activity; and, finally, should be secondary to punishment in any event, whether for short- or long-term goals. These developments helped maintain and, compared to the decade beginning in 1975, increase intervention's moral and philosophical legitimacy.

The Significance of Research

Finally, it should be mentioned that without scientifically sound research to determine independently if, and with whom, programs have worked, interventions that receive even strong testimonials and high acclaim—and that seem morally and philosophically legitimate—will probably fade after several years. This has occurred repeatedly in recent decades, even with programs deemed exemplary but whose research, when present and adequately reported, proved mediocre. In the long run, sound evaluation may be among the surest bases for a program's deserved confidence and survival, not just an appropriate basis for its legitimacy from the standpoint of increased public protection.

Over the decades, and despite its shortcomings, research has greatly contributed to intervention's progress. It should be challenged to continue contributing in the 1990s—in fact, to provide higher-quality information. Given the opportunity and resources, correctional researchers can meet this challenge. They already have the tools, and enough motivation exists.

CHAPTER 6

The Future of the
Juvenile Court

Changes in the cultural conception of children and in strategies of social control during the nineteenth century generated the *idea* of the juvenile court.
As developed in Chapter 1, Progressive reformers combined new theories
of criminality with new ideas about adolescence to construct a social welfare
alternative to criminal courts to respond to youths' criminal and noncriminal misconduct, to assimilate and integrate poor and immigrant children, to
expand social control over young people, and to structure their transition to
adulthood.

While ideological changes in the cultural conception of children and in
strategies of social control at the turn of the last century led "child-saving"
reformers to create the juvenile court, the Supreme Court's decision *In re
Gault* in 1967 began to transform it into a very different institution. As developed in Chapter 3, *Gault* engrafted formal trial procedures onto the Progressive vision of an informal social welfare agency. Although the Supreme
Court did not intend to alter juvenile courts' therapeutic mission, *Gault*'s
emphasis on procedural formality shifted the focus of juvenile courts from
"real needs" to proof of legal guilt in an adversary proceeding. The Court's
attempt to rationalize juvenile courts' procedures and to reconcile rehabilitative rhetoric with punitive reality provided the impetus that changed juvenile courts and their sustaining assumption about adolescence, criminal
responsibility, and social control. By formalizing the connection between
criminal conduct and coercive intervention, the Court explicated a relationship that historically remained implicit and unacknowledged. Moreover, the
empirical and political linkages between race, violence, and crime control
provide a recurring subtext for all of the subsequent juvenile court reforms.

Chapters 4 and 5 review recent legislative, judicial, and administrative changes in the processing of serious young offenders and ordinary

delinquents. "Get tough" waiver policies increasingly relegate serious offenders, disproportionately minority, to harsher penalties in the criminal justice system. Changes in juvenile courts' sentencing laws and practice result in the imposition of more punitive sentences on those youths who remain within the contracted jurisdiction of the juvenile courts. These changes have modified juvenile justice administration and fostered a substantive, as well as procedural, convergence with criminal courts. The convergence between juvenile and criminal courts eliminates many of the conceptual and operational differences in crime control strategies for youths and adults.

If juvenile courts are unable to provide either therapy or justice, then how should the legal system respond to crimes committed by younger offenders? Chapter 6 explores some of the competing policy options: to rehabilitate the juvenile court and return it to a "modified" social welfare mission; to create a "criminal" juvenile court; or to abolish juvenile courts and try all young offenders in criminal courts. Gary Melton, "Taking *Gault* Seriously," examines some of the implications of developmental psychological research for a reconstituted juvenile justice system that elevates the rule of law over individualized clinical discretion. Melton argues that a juvenile court's clientele must perceive it to be a legitimate legal institution in order for it to accomplish its "rehabilitative" goals. The excerpt by Barry Feld, "Criminalizing the American Juvenile Court," provides a succinct statement of the contemporary abolitionist position. Feld argues that the "real" reason that juvenile courts formally intervene when a child is a criminal is penal social control rather than social welfare. He proposes to try all offenders in one criminal court, but advocates procedural and substantive modifications of criminal courts to protect more adequately the interests of younger offenders than does the current juvenile court. Irene Merker Rosenberg, "Leaving Bad Enough Alone, " contends that abolitionists contrast the "reality" of juvenile courts with an "idealized" vision of justice in adult criminal courts. Rather, she argues, as did the Progressive child-savers a century ago, that juvenile courts remain the preferable alternative to a criminal justice system in which youths would simply become part of an undifferentiated offender group processed on an assembly-line basis.

Juvenile courts' increasing inability to respond effectively to youth crime and violence coincides with declining social indicators of the status of youth—increased poverty, welfare dependency, family instability, and school failure—all of which augur further criminality. The problematic status of youth and juvenile courts' inability to control or reduce their offending presents a twofold dilemma: what social policies and crime control strategies are appropriate when the child is a criminal and the criminal is a child? And what social welfare policies beyond the realm of a juvenile court are appropriate to *prevent* the child from becoming a criminal?

Taking *Gault* Seriously: Toward a New Juvenile Court

Gary B. Melton

INTRODUCTION

Non-culpable children faced with the criminal process must be protected, not by the state, but from the state. There is nothing unique in the juvenile process, including the concept of lesser culpability, that excludes it from this conclusion. This, in sum, is the received wisdom of the last twenty-five years of juvenile sociological and jurisprudential study.

More than two decades have passed since the Supreme Court rendered s landmark decision in *In re Gault*. . . .

Gault promised radical change in juvenile justice. Founded on the priniple that rehabilitation should be the hallmark of the law's response to wayrard youth, juvenile courts rarely had recognized the rights that were deied Gerald Gault by the Arizona trial court. In fact, failure to provide the udiments of due process was believed to be consistent with the therapeuic aim of juvenile courts. As a result, and because many juvenile judges had eceived no legal training at all, juvenile justice was essentially lawless. Alhough the Supreme Court stopped short of asserting that the juvenile court ²as a legal innovation that had completely failed, the Court left little doubt hat, as a matter of both law and policy, juvenile justice would have to change adically if it was to survive scrutiny. . . . With the abrogation of the myth hat juvenile court proceedings were on behalf of, rather than against, the espondents, it was reasonable to expect that juvenile procedure after *Gault* nd its progeny would differ little from criminal procedure.

However, the logic of *Gault* never was followed to its conclusion. Alhough it is indisputable that *Gault* led to significant change in juvenile law, ² is also clear that many juvenile courts have failed to implement its man.ate fully. Many juvenile courts persist in the illusion that they are thera·eutic instruments and, accordingly, neglect the due process rights basic to .n adversary system. Still more fundamentally, little attention has been ·iven to the question of whether a separate juvenile court can be justified .t all when juvenile respondents are entitled to most of the procedural rights ·wed criminal defendants.

.xcerpted from *Nebraska Law Review*, Vol. 68, pp. 146–181 (1989). Reprinted by permission.

With more than two decades of post-*Gault* hindsight, this Article is intended to stimulate new discussion of this issue. Perhaps the time has come to follow *Gault* to its logical conclusion and to "put an effective end to what has been the idealistic prospect of an intimate, informal protective proceeding" and "once again to place the juvenile squarely in the routine of the criminal process." Although I will not go quite so far, I will argue that *Gault* and its progeny, when examined in the light of empirical evidence, require a truly new juvenile court that relies on knowledge of psychosocial development in order not to treat juveniles, but to ensure protection of their right to due process.

II. HISTORIC RATIONALES FOR THE JUVENILE COURT

In consideration of the social utility of the juvenile court and its present and future mission and form, a useful starting point is analysis of the validity of the historic rationales for a separate juvenile court. Social historians now doubt that the founding of the juvenile court is largely or even wholly explained by the stated motives of the turn-of-the-century child savers. However, examination of the ostensible rationales is most likely to provide an answer to the question of whether any coherent justification exists for a separate juvenile court.

Judge Julian Mack's oft-cited contemporary discussion of the nature and goals of the early juvenile court provides a snapshot of the idealized court:

> [The juvenile judge] must be a student of and deeply interested in the problems of philanthropy and child life, as well as a lover of children. He must be able to understand the boys' point of view and ideas of justice; he must be willing and patient enough to search out the underlying causes of the trouble and to formulate the plan by which, through the cooperation, ofttimes, of many agencies, the cure may be effected. . . .
>
> The problem for determination by the judge is not, Has this boy or girl committed a specific wrong, but What is he, how has he become what he is, and what had best be done in his interest and in the interest of the state to save him from a downward career. It is apparent at once that the ordinary legal evidence in a criminal court is not the sort of evidence to be heard in such a proceeding. . . .

A. Juveniles Are Not Responsible

1. The Legal Framework At its deepest roots, this paternalistic vision of the juvenile court was based on the moral premise that youth do not deserve punishment for their violations of law. Rather, in Judge Mack's words, offenders should be "protected" by the state, acting as would "a wise and merciful father" when he learns that his child has erred. To pursue that course, the court must concern itself not with the question of whether a given disposition is a juvenile's just desert, but instead whether the dispositional plan is responsive to his needs. . . .

It is easy to approach Judge Mack's assertion cynically and to focus solely on the adequacy of the juvenile court in delivering the promised rehabilitation. Although the failings of the court in that regard now are well known, it is important to consider the validity of the underlying assumption that it is unjust to brand a juvenile as a criminal. Even if the juvenile court has not matched the rehabilitative ideal, a special system of justice may be defensible if retribution cannot be morally applied to a juvenile.

Indeed, such a line of argument may require merely a showing that youthfulness is a mitigating, even if not an excusing, factor. For example, in a "modest defense" of the juvenile court, my colleague Martin Gardner has contended that the court can be justified by the discrepancy in level of stigma that may exist between *delinquent* and *criminal.* If, as he argues, most juvenile offenders are sufficiently mature that they are culpable for their conduct but sufficiently immature that they do not deserve the same level of punishment as adult offenders, then an intermediate level of punishment is just. Given that labeling by the community as a criminal is a part of the punishment meted out by the criminal justice system, a label with less stigma would be appropriate for juvenile offenders. Therefore, Professor Gardner favors retention of the juvenile court even though he accepts a retributive response to most juvenile crime. Consistent with the general principle that punishment should be proportionate to the offense, he would reduce both the sentence (disposition) and the opprobrium imposed on juveniles convicted of a crime, relative to the sanctions to which adult offenders are subject. Although the first object of his partial responsibility theory could be accommodated in the criminal justice system, the latter may require that a special status be maintained for juvenile offenders. . . .

In short, the desirability of a juvenile court is not perfectly related to the question of the criminal responsibility of juvenile offenders. Nonetheless, it is undeniable that some relationship exists between the modal level of responsibility of juvenile offenders and the age-graded applicability of the usual strictures of criminal law. If most juvenile offenders are not worthy of punishment but the state has a compelling interest, as it undeniably does, in the prevention of continuing antisocial behavior, then a nonretributive justice system is needed to respond to the problem of juvenile delinquency. Therefore, before conclusions are reached about the wisdom of a separate system of juvenile justice, careful consideration is needed of the level of responsibility that may be justly expected of most juveniles.

2. The Psychological Evidence

A. CHANGING VIEWS OF CHILDREN'S COMPETENCE   Such questions are especially acute because of a large body of recent psycholegal scholarship that indicates juveniles, especially adolescents, commonly are more competent decisionmakers than the law historically has presumed. Piagetian theory implied that adolescents, at least by age fourteen, would not differ from adults on average in their ability to comprehend and weigh risks and benefits of personal decisions. That general proposition now has been supported by numerous laboratory and field studies of decisionmaking by youth in various legally relevant contexts.

In fact, if research contradicts the Piagetian hypotheses at all, it generally is in the direction of competence of even younger minors to make personal decisions. For example, some studies have shown elementary-school-age children able to identify material risks of psycho-therapy. Other research has indicated that children in the intermediate grades make adult-like decisions about routine therapeutic and educational matters, even if they are not as competent as adolescents and adults in comprehending and weighing the risks and benefits of the various alternatives. Stated somewhat differently, children can imitate adult models in making decisions for themselves, even when they are not prepared cognitively to explain the merits of those decisions.

Although such studies of actual decisionmaking are most germane to legal concerns, it should be noted that changes in psychologists' perceptions of children's general competence also have occurred among basic developmental psychologists. Recent research has shown children to be capable of sociocentric moral reasoning and behavior at earlier ages than most developmental psychologists (at least those with a cognitive-developmental bent) had believed possible. Although the attribution of subjective responsibility has proven to be one of the most strikingly developmental aspects of moral judgment, researchers who have adjusted their methods to account for young children's poor verbal and free-recall skills have found even preschoolers to apply perceptions of intentionality of behavior to their moral judgments. Observations of empathy and sympathetic distress among children in day care centers are also illustrative of the sociomoral competence of young children, sometimes including toddlers. Indeed, preschoolers refer to others' needs as the basis for their own naturally occurring prosocial behavior.

Similarly, comprehension of physical causality occurs much earlier than children are able to articulate their understanding of causality and, therefore, earlier than Piaget believed was possible. "Adult like" causal reasoning is well established by age four or five and sometimes observable even among two- and three-year-old children. Thus, concepts of agency and intentionality are within the repertoire even of young children.

Although such bodies of research cast doubt on the historic presumption of irresponsibility among juveniles, it is important not to oversell their significance. The capacity to perceive and evaluate the intentionality of behavior does not translate directly into the capacity to form criminal intent. Moreover, some of the research by Piagetian critics that shows children capable of higher-level reasoning than cognitive-developmental theorists typ-cally assumed requires unusual conditions. That children may be able to demonstrate higher-level reasoning when the task is presented nonverbally or the demands on memory are minimized probably has little relevance to the law's view of children's maturity.

Similarly, research on juveniles' competence in decisionmaking is not completely apposite to questions of their responsibility. On the one hand, the cognitive requirements for compliance with the criminal law probably are generally less advanced than the information processing skills needed to make rational decisions about one's physical and economic welfare. On the other hand, the threshold for personal responsibility should be higher than the threshold for exercise of self-determination. Thus, in considering questions of responsibility, we should be sensitive to developmental trends in judgment that we may find irrelevant to the question of whether interests in liberty are to be recognized and protected in nonpunitive situations. I shall consider these points in turn.

B. THE LOW EXPECTATIONS OF THE CRIMINAL LAW   As Stephen Morse has argued in his discussions of the relationship between mental disability and personal responsibility, the expectations of moral behavior that are established in the criminal law generally are quite low. The foundation for this conclusion is especially clear when one considers the lack of obvious legal significance of infantile moral reasoning. The lowest level of moral development often is said to be an evaluation of the morality of conduct in terms of its personal consequences. Although few would seek a society in which citizens refrained from *mala in se* only because of the threat of punishment, such a perspective is deeply embedded in the deterrent purpose of the criminal law. . . .

Our intuition is confirmed to some extent by the fact that most elementary-school-age children and even some preschool children are capable of reaching the same conclusion. Consideration of intent, including hedonistic or exploitive motives, does not require high levels of cognitive development or educational achievement. For that matter, actual conformity to the primary behavioral norms of the community requires even less sociomoral development. Even young children are not inclined to adopt physically dangerous means of responding to slights by their peers. Similarly, the lack of a substantial relationship between age and honesty demonstrates that children understand the rules of an orderly society at a very young age and are capable of responding accordingly, whatever their motive for doing so. From an early age, children can imitate normative social behavior.

C. THE LACK OF CONGRUENCE BETWEEN COMPETENCE AND RESPONSIBILITY   Although the preceding discussion shows that the social expectations embedded in the criminal law generally do not rest on advanced developmental levels, the fact that juveniles appear more competent decisionmakers than the law historically has presumed does not imply that youth generally should be held fully accountable by the state for their misdeeds. I reach that conclusion even though I have argued elsewhere that the new research and theory on minors' competence should be used to establish lower age thresholds for legal recognition of the validity of their decisions.

The age thresholds for recognition of autonomy and privacy, cessation of special age-based entitlements, and establishment of criminal responsibility need not be, indeed should not be, the same. Respect for personhood demands that we err on the side of promotion of autonomy. Therefore, the presumption should be in favor of self-determination and those special entitlements that assist youth in developing the capacity for full exercise of autonomy, but doubt about criminal (or quasicriminal) responsibility should be resolved in the direction of nonresponsibility.

Advocating a "jurisprudence of semi-autonomy" that treats adolescence "as a learner's permit," Franklin Zimring has reached the same conclusion. He has argued convincingly that it is unfair to hold adolescents accountable for their behavior at the same level that we hold adults. When the state systematically has denied adolescents experience in decisionmaking, it is unreasonable for society to expect the same quality of decisionmaking from adolescents that it expects from adults, even if adolescents typically have the same capacity to assess and weigh the risks and benefits of various alternatives. . . .

B. Juveniles Are Especially Amenable to Treatment

Even if juveniles can reasonably be presumed to be responsible for their behavior, a separate system of justice may be a wise policy if juveniles are especially amenable to treatment. The founders of the juvenile court certainly assumed such amenability. Using a social construct that continues to creep into public policy, the early child savers presumed juvenile offenders to be particularly malleable and, therefore, predictably responsive to treatment to prevent their future antisocial conduct. Juvenile crime was perceived as posing relatively little threat to society, and juveniles were believed to be essentially innocent in a Rousseauian sense. If youth were placed in a benign, "natural" setting away from the temptations of the modern city, they could be expected to be restored to their state of innocence and then to be "civilized" appropriately. . . .

Unfortunately, the . . . "treatment" available through the juvenile justice system often remains little more than brutal punishment. Class action suits in the 1970s and 1980s have illuminated inhumane conditions in numerous juvenile correctional facilities and in many adult jails where juveniles also are held. In fact, substantial change is only beginning to occur in many communities where the threat of personal liability now looms for state and local officials who fail to comply with the Juvenile Justice and Delinquency Prevention Act's mandate to remove juveniles from adult jails. . . .

The problem with the implementation of the rehabilitative ideal, though, is not simply a matter of perversion of the juvenile court's purported pur-

)ose. Even when the court's therapeutic purpose has been taken seriously, ts efficacy has not been demonstrated. As a panel of the National Academy)f Sciences concluded, the assertion that "nothing works" in juvenile (and ıdult) corrections still has not been persuasively refuted. The most well-validated treatment for delinquent behavior remains getting older!

It may be argued that this dismal picture reflects inadequate resources, poorly conceptualized treatment programs, and failure to protect program integrity in evaluation studies, rather than intrinsic ineffectiveness of treatment. To a large extent, I agree. Some of the most highly touted negative evaluation studies have focused on programs so poorly developed and staffed that no one reasonably could have expected them to work. Most serious juvenile offenders have a multiplicity of significant, persistent problems— educational delays, family disorganization, a lack of community support, economic poverty, poor social skills, and aberrant social perceptions and expectancies. Some small experimental programs that have incorporated an intensive, integrated response to such problems have shown success. Recent studies of youth who have spontaneously ended delinquent careers also have provided new directions for experimentation in services for delinquents.

Even if treatment is potentially effective for some delinquents, though, the argument that the juvenile court's failure really is just a matter of inadequate investment or careless conceptualization misses the point. First, even if juvenile justice programs are potentially effective in preventing further crime, at least by some youth, rehabilitation programs are not differentially effective for juvenile delinquents to a degree that justifies a separate justice system. Although the claim by some that adolescence is too late for significant change is simply wrong, the historic view that youth is a time of great malleability was equally naive. Most juvenile offenders do not recidivate, no matter what intervention is provided. Insofar as rehabilitation is the goal, it is hard to justify any court involvement for such youth. Among those juveniles who are repeat offenders, there is little reason to expect special amenability to treatment, relative to adult offenders.

Second, it must be remembered that the court's primary purpose is to administer justice. Even an effective rehabilitation system fails in the end if it undermines due process. The traditional quid pro quo theory of juvenile law denigrates the fundamental interests lost in the name of treatment. The legal system should be supported in its preservation of the reality and appearance of justice, no matter what the consequences are for treatment. The fact that the "treatment" often has been ineffective or even harmful simply compounds the insult to the integrity of juvenile respondents and their families.

C. Formal, Adversary Procedures Are Not Conducive to Rehabilitation

The notion that criminal procedure is ill-suited to resolution of matters pertaining to children, youth, and families is deeply embedded in the traditions of the juvenile court. Indeed, in the pre-*Gault* years, it was easy for juveniles to be committed to a training school without ever realizing that they had been in court. . . .

Even today, juvenile courtrooms often more closely correspond to the conference rooms of child guidance centers than the courtrooms in which other matters are heard. The notion persists among professionals and the general public that formal adversary procedures are inconsistent with the psychological well-being of children and youth, a belief that has been given credence by the Supreme Court.

In keeping with the historic, still prevalent belief in the innocence and vulnerability of youth, the intuition of many adults is that children and youth develop most fully when they are shielded from conflict—hence, from adversariness. That view is overly simple. Although chronic exposure to *uncontrollable* conflict may impair children's development, the opportunity to *resolve* conflict actually may enhance psychological growth, especially in older children and youth who may experience a sense of accomplishment. Experience in decisionmaking also may foster a greater appreciation of diverse points of view and, therefore, may stimulate legal and moral socialization. Regardless, the reality is that juveniles accused of delinquent or status offenses already are in a state of conflict with the state and specific adverse parties, often including their parents. Otherwise, there would be no reason for court involvement. The question is not whether to foster conflict in juvenile court, but how to resolve the conflict already present most fairly.

In that regard, psychological research and theory support the *Gault* assumption that the "fundamental requirements of due process" are also the requisites for a psychologically satisfying resolution of the juvenile's predicament: "[T]he appearance as well as the actuality of fairness, impartiality and orderliness—in short, the essentials of due process—may be a more impressive and more therapeutic attitude so far as the juvenile is concerned." . . . Thus, even if the Constitution did not demand recognition of the due process rights of juvenile respondents, preservation of adversary process in juvenile court would be consonant with the state's interests and therefore justifiable on utilitarian grounds.

D. Summary: A Bankrupt Legal Theory

A review of the assumptions underlying the juvenile court shows it to be a bankrupt legal institution. The theories that have guided juvenile law through the twentieth century are without foundation. Adolescents are neither so irresponsible nor so responsive to treatment as to justify a separate juvenile court. Even if the Constitution permits an incomplete application of adversary procedures to juvenile court, neither common sense nor psychological research supports the premise that a nonadversary approach to delinquency adjudications would foster more effective treatment.

In short, the juvenile court cannot rest on its historic rationales. If *Gault* itself did not result in an outright abolition of the juvenile court, its logic ap-

ears to push toward that end. As the Supreme Court recognized, the tra-
itional juvenile court was inconsistent with constitutional mandates for due
rotection of the liberty interests of juvenile respondents. Post- *Gault* de-
elopments give no reason to believe that public policy is consistent with
aaintenance of the residue of the historic juvenile court, because the philo-
ophical and empirical foundations for the court have been shattered.

Nonetheless, I do believe that a juvenile court is desirable, but only if
t is a truly new juvenile court fully consistent with the spirit of *Gault*. I ad-
ocate a juvenile court that has more, rather than fewer, procedural pro-
ections available than in criminal courts. Such a new court would be based
n acceptance of the *Gault* respect for the personhood of juveniles, combined
vith a psychological understanding of children's and adolescents' compre-
ension of fundamental legal rights and their (lack of) access to procedures
ecessary to vindicate those rights.

II. WHY DUE PROCESS REQUIRES A NEW JUVENILE COURT

A. The Developmental Psychology of Procedure

. The Salience of Freedom In constructing a new juvenile court, the most
undamental point that must be recognized is that liberty and privacy are
mportant to children and youth, just as they are to adults. Attempts to deny
he moral personhood of children must take into account the fact that the
ttributes associated with concern for human dignity are displayed at a quite
oung age. Courts cannot legitimately deny rigorous protection of minors'
iberty on the ground that it is unimportant.

Even very young children find choice to be reinforcing and meaningful.
More directly germane to the circumstances in which juveniles' liberty is
hreatened by the state, even the best residential treatment programs are
xperienced as aversive by the children and youth placed in them. The more
'institutional" and less normalized a placement outside the natural family is,
he more intense the resulting anger and sense of degradation are.

. The Social Psychology of Procedural Justice If maintenance of liberty
nd privacy is important to juveniles, then it should come as no surprise when
hey desire procedures that provide the level of care due in a matter as seri-
us as the potential diminution of such primary goods. In that regard, the
arge body of research and theory on perceived procedural justice should be
nformative. Encompassing scores of studies, such research has produced find-
ngs that have proven robust across settings, populations, and methods. To
ummarize, studies of perceived justice have shown that perceptions of the
airness of procedures for dispute resolution provide much of the foundation
or individuals' overall level of satisfaction with the legal and political systems.
Indeed, perceptions of procedural justice color perceptions of distributive jus-
ice (the fairness of the outcome), especially when the outcome is negative.

Process control—the opportunity for each disputant to have a say and to present one's case as one sees fit—is the strongest element in procedural justice. Consequently, both disputants and observers express greater satisfaction with adversary procedures than inquisitorial ones, even in societies in which the latter predominate in the legal system. Care in ensuring that underdogs are heard enhances the evaluation of authorities and the institutions they represent.

The second most important element in perceived procedural justice is ethical appropriateness—treating the parties with respect for their personal dignity. The legal process is viewed more positively when disputants are treated politely and their rights are protected.

The two remaining factors known to affect perceptions of procedural justice are ones that are well known to legal policymakers: honesty and consistency. People desire to be treated forthrightly; dishonest behavior, especially by those in authority, violates the rudiments of respect for persons and fidelity to social contracts. By the same token, the most basic considerations of equity demand that parties in like circumstances be treated alike. Decisions should be predictable rather than arbitrary, and they should not be based on irrelevant personal or social characteristics. An unreliable legal system administers justice ineffectively.

3. Developmental Factors in Use of Procedural Protections Whether the conclusions of social psychological studies of procedural justice can be generalized to children and youth is an empirical question. Unfortunately, few studies have addressed that question. Nonetheless, the empirical evidence that is available suggests that the same principles underlie adults' and children's responses to the legal system. As already noted, even young children appreciate personal control, and a close corollary would be a desire for a voice in disputes involving them. Even first graders evaluate the fairness of dispute resolution at least in part in terms of the procedures used, and older elementary-school-age children generally understand the basic elements of the adversary process and the reasons for them. Those children who understand the process best are also those who are most likely to perceive it as fair.

Taken together, the various lines of research on procedural justice give ample reason for care in the means by which complaints against juveniles are investigated and adjudicated. Just as for adults, the degree of control that juveniles have in the presentation of their cases and the courtesy with which they are treated by legal authorities are apt to shape their response to the legal system. Consequently, even if not mandated by ethics and the Constitution, the preservation of due process in juvenile court would be important in order to socialize respect for the law as an institution. The appearance of fairness is at least as important in juvenile court as in other legal contexts.

At the same time, though, research suggests that due process for juveniles may be different from that for adults. Evidence from Thomas Grisso's program of research on juveniles' waivers of rights is especially persuasive in that regard. In brief, such studies have shown that juvenile respondents rarely assert their fifth and sixth amendment rights; their parents are typically ineffective advocates or even adversaries; they often do not understand key words in the *Miranda* warning; they often do not comprehend critical phrases in such warnings; and experience in the legal system, by itself, does not alleviate such deficiencies.

Such findings stand in contrast to research on adolescents' decisions in other legally relevant contexts, which almost uniformly has shown youth to be substantially more competent in decisionmaking than the law presumes. The reason for the inconsistency of findings in research on waivers of rights in delinquency proceedings with those in studies of decisionmaking by adolescents in other situations is not entirely clear. Such a discrepancy probably reflects social class differences to some extent. However, the hypothesis that social class accounts for most of the variability is rendered less plausible by the relatively greater displays of competence in some other settings that involve disadvantaged youth in serious decisions.

Particular institutional variables may make adolescents appear to be poor decisionmakers in juvenile court. There is a strong cultural belief that "talking" mitigates children's responsibility for misdeeds, whether minor infractions of home or school rules or serious violations of the law. In a survey of middle-class parents of adolescents, Professor Grisso found that about one-third would advise their children to confess to police, and about one-half of the remainder said that youth should remain silent *temporarily* until things "cool down" so that the story could be related in a calm atmosphere. In actual interrogations, parents of juvenile respondents rarely advised their children to remain silent; in fact, the majority did not give *any* advice or counsel to their children involved in an undeniably difficult situation. The picture of the outcome is consistent: juveniles rarely invoke their constitutional rights, and younger juveniles (those under age 16) almost never do.

Professor Grisso's studies suggest that juveniles' difficulties in applying their rights in delinquency proceedings emanate most directly from a belief that those rights are not rights at all, but instead are privileges revocable by people in authority. This "immature" belief may be the product of true age differences in reasoning, but it also may reflect an accurate perception of reality in many juvenile courts and within many relationships between juvenile respondents and their attorneys. . . .

Whatever the reasons for the apparent incompetence of many youth in the juvenile justice system in exercising their rights, there can be no question of its adverse consequences. Not only do juveniles often waive their rights to silence and counsel during interrogation, they often are not represented by counsel at *any* stage of the proceeding.

B. A Psychological Approach to Due Process

1. Dual-Maximal Doctrine   After *Gault*, it is indisputable that the state's position is adverse to juvenile respondents in delinquency proceedings and that minors' liberty is protected by the Constitution. In such a context, defenders of the juvenile court can offer no coherent justification in response to Irene Merker Rosenberg's plaintive "question why, in view of age and competency differentials, the child is given less [procedural] protection rather than more."

As Professor Rosenberg persuasively argued, the logic of *Gault* implies a "dual-maximal approach" that combines "fundamental fairness" and "functional equivalence" in determining the procedures constitutionally necessary to protect the interests of juvenile respondents. In other words, in recognition of the obligation to provide due process, juveniles accused of delinquent offenses should be provided those rights that are necessary to fundamental fairness, even when such rights exceed those possessed by criminal defendants. At the same time, though, juvenile respondents should have all of the rights available to adult defendants, even those not necessarily a part of fundamental fairness as applied to adults, because juvenile proceedings are functionally equivalent to criminal trials. The dual-maximal approach is desirable because "it applies to children all the guarantees already applicable to adult criminal defendants, while also permitting enhanced protection of children because of their vulnerability and immaturity without making the additional protection automatically available to adults." . . .

3. The Need for Empirical Data   In designing the new juvenile court, the overarching question should be the nature and scope of procedures needed to ensure both that respondents *are* treated fairly and that they *feel* they are being treated fairly. In other words, legal policymakers should explore the procedural forms necessary to make justice *meaningful*, in all senses of that word.

For example, the Supreme Court has refused to extend the right to a jury trial to juveniles. It has done so because of a nostalgic desire to save a court whose time has passed. If *Gault* were to be taken seriously, there should be no question of the applicability of the sixth amendment to juveniles under the doctrine of functional equivalence. Nonetheless, the need to preserve fundamental fairness leaves open the question whether the jury must be reshaped to fulfill its purposes when applied to juveniles. If the sense of equity that the jury embodies is to be preserved for juveniles, then its form may require some alteration, while not negating the right itself. . . .

4. The Role of Counsel   As should be obvious by now, I expect that the range of procedures necessary to fundamental fairness in juvenile court is sufficiently disparate from criminal court to merit the existence of the former. I do not expect, though, that a specialized bench is necessary to such a court. The more lawful the court is, presumably the less need there is for a specialized judiciary. The sorts of decisions that a judge must make in the new juvenile court should be similar to those in criminal courts and, therefore, well within the expertise of general-jurisdiction judges.

On the other hand, there may be a need for a specialized bar in the new juvenile court. By stating this conclusion I do not mean to imply that attorneys for juveniles should depart from the role of zealous advocate. It is exceedingly rare that children appear in delinquency proceedings when they are so young that they cannot reasonably instruct legal counsel, an event that is likely to be even more uncommon when the defense of infancy is restored. . . .

Attorneys' ethical duty to represent their clients' interests as defined by the client does not mean, of course, that they should abandon any counseling role. Indeed, effective representation requires substantial investment of time and effort in educating clients about their rights and the options available to the court and the clients themselves. When significant misunderstanding or ignorance about such matters is present, as it often is with juvenile clients, that investment should increase proportionately.

Effective representation of juveniles does not imply simply an increased allotment of time to counseling. The nature of the counseling also may be qualitatively different. Attorneys representing juveniles should be knowledgeable about the nature of common gaps or errors in juveniles' information about the legal process; the kinds of interventions that are necessary to persuade juveniles that their rights are indeed entitlements; the range of dispositional alternatives (especially those that are relatively unrestrictive) available to the court; and the formal and informal procedural innovations that are useful in promoting juveniles' active involvement in their defense and in ensuring that they are treated fairly and perceive that they have been so treated. . . .

V. CONCLUSIONS

Despite the fact that the juvenile court is a relatively recent development in Anglo-American jurisprudence, it has seemed firmly established as a stable legal institution. It has remained so even though its underlying assumptions have been discredited, many of its unique features were eliminated by *Gault* and its progeny, and the court's remaining special aspects have been the object of criticism from both the left and the right.

The time has come to take seriously the message of *Gault* and to institute procedures designed to facilitate justice for juveniles accused of delinquent behavior. Mental health professionals long have been misused in juvenile court to sustain the illusion of a therapeutic institution operating in youth's behalf. Perhaps through critical examination of the court's assumptions and the perceived justice of its procedures (current and potential), psychologists and other behavioral scientists can begin to be used in the service of a more just institution affecting children and youth. For example, psychologists can assist in developing and applying the knowledge necessary to teach youth how to use their rights. Similarly, they can evaluate procedures to determine those that enable youth really to have their say and to feel that they were treated fairly.

At the same time, withdrawal of reliance on the juvenile court is likely to make the child mental health and social service systems more protective of the privacy and autonomy of child clients and thus more humane and just. Not only have juvenile courts misused mental health professionals; mental health professionals also have misused juvenile courts as a coercive "therapeutic" instrument. With a truly new juvenile court, the integrity of both the justice system and the human service system is likely to prosper.

In reaching such conclusions, I am mindful of the difficulty of the task. As Professor Feld noted, "[t]he juvenile court has demonstrated a remarkable ability to deflect, co-opt, and absorb ameliorative reform virtually without institutional change." Nonetheless, the interests at stake are fundamental. More than twenty years after *Gault*, it is certainly time to consider carefully its implications and to design, evaluate, and implement procedures consistent with meaningful justice for youth.

Criminalizing the American Juvenile Court

BARRY C. FELD

For more than two decades since *Gault*, juvenile courts have defected, co-opted, ignored, or accommodated constitutional and legislative reforms with minimal institutional change. Despite its transformation from a welfare agency into a criminal court, the juvenile court remains essentially unreformed. Public and political concerns about drugs and youth crime encourage the repression rather than the rehabilitation of young offenders. With fiscal constraints, budget deficits, and competition from other interest groups, there is little likelihood that treatment services for delinquents will expand. Coupling the emergence of punitive policies with a societal unwillingness to provide for the welfare of children in general, much less for those who commit crimes, there is scant reason to believe that the juvenile court, as originally conceived, can be revived.

The recent changes in procedures, jurisdiction, and sentencing policies reflect ambivalence about the role and purpose of juvenile courts and the social control of children. As juvenile courts converge procedurally and sub-

Excerpted from *Crime and Justice: An Annual Review* 17, pp. 197–267 (1993). © 1993 by The University of Chicago. All rights reserved.

tantively with criminal courts, is there any reason to maintain a separate court whose only remaining distinctions are procedures under which no adult would agree to be tried? While most commentators acknowledge the emergence of a punitive juvenile court, they recoil at the prospect of its outright abolition, emphasizing that children are different and that distinctions between "delinquents" and "criminals" should be maintained. Most conclude, however, that the juvenile court sorely needs a new rationale, perhaps one that melds punishment with reduced culpability and procedural justice.

There are three plausible responses to a juvenile court that punishes in the name of treatment and simultaneously denies young offenders elementary procedural justice: restructure juvenile courts to fit their original therapeutic purpose, embrace punishment as an acceptable and appropriate part of delinquency proceedings but coupled with criminal procedural safeguards, or abolish juvenile court jurisdiction over criminal conduct and try young offenders in criminal courts with certain modifications of substantive and procedural criminal law.

A. RETURN TO AN INFORMAL, "REHABILITATIVE"JUVENILE COURT

Some proponents of an informal, therapeutic juvenile court contend that the "experiment" cannot be declared a failure since it has never been implemented effectively. From their inception, juvenile courts and correctional facilities have had more in common with penal facilities than with welfare agencies, hospitals, or clinics. By the 1960s and the *Gault* decision, the failures of implementation were readily apparent. Any proposal to reinvigorate the juvenile court as an informal, therapeutic welfare agency must first explain why the resources and personnel that have not been made available previously will now become available.

Even if a coterie of clinicians suddenly descended on a juvenile court, it would be a dubious policy to recreate the juvenile court as originally conceived. The central critique of individualized justice is that juvenile courts are substantively and procedurally lawless. Despite the existence of statutes and procedural rules, juvenile courts operate effectively unconstrained by the rule of law. To the extent that judges make dispositions based on individualized assessments of an offender's "best interests" or "real needs," judicial discretion is formally unrestricted. If there are neither practical scientific nor clinical bases by which judges can classify for treatment, then the exercise of "sound discretion" is simply a euphemism for idiosyncratic judicial subjectivity. If intervention were consistently benign and effective, perhaps differential processing would be tolerable. But juveniles committed to institutions or whose liberty is restrained regard the experience as a sanction rather than as beneficial. At the least, similarly situated offenders will be handled differently based on extraneous personal characteristics for which they are not responsible. At the worst, if juvenile courts effectively punish, then discretionary sentences based on individualized assessments introduce unequal and discriminatory sanctions on invidious bases.

The critique of the juvenile court does not rest on the premise that "nothing works" or ever can work. Indeed, some demonstration model programs may produce positive changes in some offenders under some conditions. And some treatment programs may be more effective than the evaluation studies indicate. However, after a century of unfulfilled promises, a continuing societal unwillingness to commit scarce resources to rehabilitative efforts, and intervention strategies of dubious or marginal efficacy, the possibility of an effective treatment program is too fragile a reed on which to construct an entire separate adjudicative apparatus. We should exercise caution in delegating coercive powers to penal therapists to use on a subjective, nonscientific basis.

Procedural informality is the concomitant of substantive discretion. The traditional juvenile courts' procedures are predicated on the assumption of benevolence. If clinical decision making is not constrained substantively, then it cannot be limited procedurally, either, since every case is unique. A primary role of lawyers is to manipulate legal rules for their clients' advantage; a discretionary court without objective laws or formal procedures is unfavorable terrain. The limited presence and role of counsel in many juvenile courts may reflect judicial adherence to a treatment model that no longer exists, if it ever did. But the absence of lawyers reduces the ability of the legal process to invoke existing laws to make courts conform to their legal mandates. The closed, informal, and confidential nature of delinquency proceedings reduces visibility and accountability and precludes external checks on coercive intervention.

The fundamental shortcoming of the traditional juvenile court is not a failure of implementation but a failure of conception. The original juvenile court was conceived of as a social service agency in a judicial setting, a fusion of welfare and coercion. But providing for child welfare is ultimately a societal responsibility rather than a judicial one. It is unrealistic to expect juvenile courts, or any other legal institutions, to resolve all of the social ills afflicting young people or to have a significant impact on youth crime. Despite claims of being a child-centered nation, we care less about other people's children than we do our own, especially when they are children of other colors or cultures. Without a societal commitment to a social welfare system that adequately meets the minimum family, health, housing, nutrition, and educational needs of all young people on a voluntary basis, the juvenile court provides a mechanism for involuntary control, however ineffective it may be in delivering services or rehabilitating offenders. Historical analyses of juvenile justice suggest that when social services and social control are combined in one setting, social welfare considerations quickly are subordinated to custodial ones.

In part, the juvenile court's subordination of individual welfare to custody and control stems from its fundamentally penal focus. Rather than iden-

:ifying the characteristics of children for which they are not responsible and that could improve their life circumstances—their lack of decent education, their lack of adequate housing, their unmet health needs, their deteriorated family and social circumstances—juvenile court law focuses on a violation of criminal law that is their fault and for which they are responsible. As long as juvenile courts emphasize the characteristics of children least likely to elicit sympathy and ignore the social conditions most likely to engender a desire to nurture and help, the law reinforces retributive rather than rehabilitative impulses. So long as juvenile courts operate in a societal context that does not provide adequate social services for children in general, intervention in the lives of those who commit crimes inevitably will be for purposes of social control rather than social welfare.

B. DUE PROCESS AND PUNISHMENT IN JUVENILE COURT

Articulating the purposes of juvenile courts requires more than invoking treatment versus punishment formulae since in operation there are no practical or operational differences between the two. Acknowledging that juvenile courts punish imposes an obligation to provide all criminal procedural safeguards since "the condition of being a boy does not justify a kangaroo court" (*In re Gault*). While procedural parity with adults may realize the *McKeiver* Court's fear of ending the juvenile court experiment, to fail to do so perpetuates injustice. Treating similarly situated juveniles dissimilarly, punishing them in the name of treatment, and denying them basic safeguards fosters a sense of injustice that thwarts any reform efforts.

Articulating alternative rationales for handling young offenders requires reconciling the two contradictory impulses provoked by recognizing that the child is a criminal and the criminal is a child. If the traditional juvenile court provides neither therapy nor justice and cannot be rehabilitated, then the policy alternatives for responding to young offenders are either to make juvenile courts more like criminal courts or to make criminal courts more like juvenile courts. In reconsidering basic premises, issues of substance and procedure must be addressed whether young offenders ultimately are tried in a separate juvenile court or in a criminal court. Issues of substantive justice include developing and implementing a doctrinal rationale—diminished responsibility or reduced capacity—for sentencing young offenders differently, and more leniently, than older defendants. Issues of procedural justice include providing youths with all of the procedural safeguards adults receive and additional protections that recognize their immaturity.

Many recent commentators conclude that "the assumptions underlying the juvenile court shows it to be a bankrupt legal institution" and that it is increasingly penal in character. Rather than proposing to abolish the juvenile court, they propose to transform the juvenile court into an explicitly penal one, albeit one that limits punishment based on reduced culpability and provides enhanced procedural justice. Springer, for example, argues that "no longer will the juvenile court be seen as a quasi-judicial court-clinic but, rather, as a real court, administering real justice in its traditional retributive and distributive meanings. . . . Juveniles should have to pay for their crimes; but . . . society has a duty to its young delinquents to help them to gain moral and civic equilibrium."

The paradigm of the new juvenile court is that propounded by the American Bar Association—Institute of Judicial Administration's Juvenile Justice Standards Project. The twenty-six volumes of Juvenile Justice Standards recommend the repeal of jurisdiction over status offenders, the use of proportional and determinate sentences to sanction delinquent offenders, the use of restrictive offense criteria to regularize pretrial detention and judicial transfer decisions, and the provision of all criminal procedural safeguards, including nonwaivable counsel and jury trials. Under the Juvenile Justice Standards, "the rehabilitative model of juvenile justice is rejected and the principles of criminal law and procedure become the cornerstones of a new relationship between the child and the state."

While proponents of the "criminal juvenile court" advocate fusing reduced culpability sentencing with greater procedural justice, they often fail to explain why these principles must be implemented within a separate juvenile court rather than in a criminal court. The Juvenile Justice Standards assert that "removal of the treatment rationale does not destroy the rationale for a separate system or for utilization of an ameliorative approach; it does, however, require a different rationale." Unfortunately, even though the standards propose a virtual replication of adult criminal procedure, they do not provide any rationale for doing so in a separate juvenile system.

Other commentators have suggested some possible rationales. Rubin, for example, speculates that, since some specialized juvenile procedures and dispositional facilities would be needed, it is more practical and less risky to retain specialized juvenile divisions of general trial courts rather than to abolish juvenile courts entirely. Given institutional and bureaucratic inertia, however, it may be that only a clean break with the personnel and practices of the past could permit the implementation of the procedures and policies he endorses.

Proponents of a criminal juvenile court point to the deficiencies of criminal courts—overcriminalization, ineffective defense representation and excessive caseloads, poor administration, insufficient sentencing alternatives— to justify retaining a separate juvenile court. Unfortunately, these are characteristics of juvenile courts as well. While certain elements of the criminal justice system, such as bail, might pose additional problems if applied without modification to juveniles, those are not compelling justifications for retaining a complete and separate judicial system. Rather, such arguments suggest a comparison of the relative quality of juvenile and criminal justice in each state to determine in which system young people are more likely to be treated justly and fairly.

The only real substantive difference between the "criminal juvenile court" and adult courts is that the Juvenile Justice Standards call for shorter sentences than criminal courts would impose. Particularly for serious young offenders, the quality and quantity of punishment imposed in juvenile court is less than that in criminal courts. Maintaining a separate court may be the only way to achieve uniformly shorter sentences and insulate youths from criminal courts' "get tough" sentencing policies.

If there is a relationship between procedural formality and substantive severity, could a "criminal juvenile court" continue to afford leniency? As juvenile courts move in the direction of greater formality—lawyers insisting on adherence to the rule of law; openness, visibility, and accountability; proportional and determinate sentencing guidelines—will not the convergence between juvenile and criminal courts increase their repressiveness and further erode sentencing differences? Can juvenile courts only be lenient because their substantive and procedural discretion is exercised behind closed doors? Would the imposition of the rule of law prevent them from affording leniency to most youths? These issues are not even recognized, much less answered, by the Juvenile Justice Standards.

2. YOUNG OFFENDERS IN CRIMINAL COURT

If the child is a criminal and the primary purpose of formal intervention is social control, then young offenders could be tried in criminal courts alongside their adult counterparts. Before returning young offenders to criminal courts, however, there are preliminary issues of substance and procedure that a legislature should address. Issues of substantive justice include developing a rationale for sentencing young offenders differently, and more leniently, than older defendants. Issues of procedural justice include affording youths alternative safeguards *in addition* to full procedural parity with adult defendants. Taken in combination, legislation can avoid the worst of both worlds, provide more than the protections accorded to adults, and do justice in sentencing.

. Substantive Justice—Juveniles' Criminal Responsibility The primary virtue of the contemporary juvenile court is that serious young offenders typically receive shorter sentences than do adult offenders for comparable crimes. As a policy goal, young offenders should survive the mistakes of adolescence with their life chances intact. This goal is threatened if youths sentenced in criminal courts received the same severe sentences frequently inflicted on eighteen-year-old "adults." And, of course, the contemporary juvenile court's seeming virtue of shorter sentences for serious offenders is offset by the far more numerous minor offenders who receive longer "rehabilitative" sentences as juveniles than they would if they were simply punished as adults.

Shorter sentences for young people do not require that they be tried in separate juvenile courts. Both juvenile and adult courts are supposed to separate the adjudication of guilt or innocence from sentencing, with discretion confined largely to the sentencing phase. Adult courts are capable of dispensing lenient sentences to youthful offenders when appropriate, although explicit and formal recognition of youthfulness as a mitigating factor is desirable.

There are a variety of doctrinal and policy justifications for sentencing young people less severely than their adult counterparts. The original juvenile court assumed that children were immature and irresponsible. These assumptions about young people's lack of criminal capacity built on the common law's infancy mens rea defense, which presumed that children less than seven years old lacked criminal capacity, those between seven and fourteen years rebuttably lacked criminal capacity, while those fourteen years of age and older were fully responsible. Juvenile court legislation simply extended upward by a few years the general presumption of youthful criminal incapacity.

Common-law infancy and other diminished responsibility doctrines reflect developmental differences that render youths less culpable or criminally responsible and provide a conceptual basis for shorter sentences for juveniles than for their adult counterparts. When sentencing within a framework of deserved punishment, it would be fundamentally unjust to impose the same penalty on a juvenile as on an adult. Deserved punishment emphasizes censure, condemnation, and blame. Penalties proportionate to the seriousness of the crime reflect the connection between the nature of the conduct and its blameworthiness.

Because commensurate punishment proportions sanctions to the seriousness of the offense, it shifts the analytical focus to the meaning of seriousness. The seriousness of an offense is the product of two components— harm and culpability. Evaluations of harm focus on the degree of injury inflicted, risk created, or value taken. The perpetrator's age is of little consequence when assessing the harmfulness of a criminal act. Assessments of seriousness also include the quality of the actor's choice to engage in the conduct that produced the harm. It is with respect to the culpability of choices—the blameworthiness of acting in a particular harm-producing way—that the issue of youthfulness becomes especially troublesome.

Psychological research indicates that young people move through developmental stages of cognitive functioning with respect to legal reasoning, internalization of social and legal expectations, and ethical decision making. The developmental sequence and changes in cognitive processes are strikingly parallel to the imputations of responsibility associated with the common-law infancy defense and suggest that by mid-adolescence individuals acquire most of the legal and moral values and reasoning capacity that will guide their behavior through later life.

Even a youth fourteen years of age or older who knows "right from wrong" and abstractly possesses the requisite criminal mens rea is still not s blameworthy and deserving of comparable punishment as an adult of-fender. Relative to adults, youths are less able to form moral judgments, ess capable of controlling their impulses, and less aware of the consequences f their acts: "Adolescents, particularly in the early and middle teen years, re more vulnerable, more impulsive, and less self-disciplined than adults. Crimes committed by youths may be just as harmful to victims as those com-mitted by older persons, but they deserve less punishment because adoles-ents have less capacity to control their conduct and to think in long-range erms than adults." Because juveniles' criminal choices are less blamewor-hy than adults and their responsibility is diminished, they "deserve" less unishment than an adult for the same criminal harm.

The crimes of children are seldom their fault alone. The family, school, nd community are responsible for socializing young people, and society hares at least some of the blame for their offenses. Moreover, to the extent hat the ability to make responsible choices is learned behavior, the depen-dent status of youth systematically deprives them of opportunities to learn o be responsible. Finally, children live their lives, as they commit their rime, in groups. Young people are more susceptible to peer group influ-ences than their older counterparts, which lessens, but does not excuse, their riminal liability.

The Supreme Court in *Thompson v. Oklahoma* (1988), analyzed the crim-nal responsibility of young offenders and provided additional support for shorter sentences for reduced culpability even for youths older than the ommon-law infancy threshold of age fourteen. In vacating Thompson's cap-tal sentence, the plurality concluded that "a young person is not capable of acting with the degree of culpability that can justify the ultimate penalty." A plurality of the Supreme Court subsequently upheld the death penalty for youths who were sixteen or seventeen at the time of their offenses (*Stan-ford v. Kentucky* [1989]). While recognizing that juveniles as a class may be ess culpable than adults, the Court in *Stanford* decided on the narrow grounds that there was no clear national consensus that such executions vi-olated "evolving standards of decency" encompassed in the Eighth Amend-ment's prohibition against "cruel and unusual" punishment.

The Court in *Thompson* reaffirmed earlier decisions holding that youth-fulness was a mitigating factor at sentencing and concluded that juveniles are less blameworthy for their crimes than are their adult counterparts. Since deserved punishment must reflect individual culpability and "there is also broad agreement on the proposition that adolescents as a class are less mature and responsible than adults," even though Thompson was responsi-ble for his crime, simply because of his age he could not be punished as se-verely as an adult:

> Our history is replete with laws and judicial recognition that minors, espe-cially in their earlier years, generally are less mature and responsible than adults. Particularly "during the formative years of childhood and adoles-

cence, minors often lack the experience, perspective, and judgment" expected of adults. . . . The Court has already endorsed the proposition that
less culpability should attach to a crime committed by a juvenile than to a
comparable crime committed by an adult. . . . Inexperience, less education,
and less intelligence make the teenager less able to evaluate the consequences of his or her conduct while at the same time he or she is much more
apt to be motivated by mere emotion or peer pressure than is an adult. The
reasons why juveniles are not trusted with the privileges and responsibilities of an adult also explain why their irresponsible conduct is not as morally
reprehensible as that of an adult.

The Court cited other instances—serving on a jury, voting, marrying, driving, and drinking—in which states act paternalistically and impose disabilities on youths because of their presumptive incapacity, lack of experience, and judgment. The Court emphasized that it would be both inconsistent
and a cruel irony suddenly to find juveniles as culpable as adult defendants
for purposes of capital punishment.

Quite apart from differences in culpability, there are other reasons why
juveniles deserve less severe punishment than adults for comparable crimes.
Penalties—whether adult punishment or juvenile "treatment"—are measured in units of time—days, months, or years. However, the ways that
youths and adults subjectively and objectively conceive of and experience
similar lengths of time differ. The developmental progression in thinking
about and experiencing time—future time perspective and present duration—follows a sequence similar to the development of criminal responsibility. Without a mature appreciation of future time, juveniles are less able to
understand the consequences of their acts. Because a juvenile's "objective"
sense of time duration is not comparable to an adult's, objectively equivalent sentences are experienced subjectively as unequal. While a three-month
sentence may be lenient for an adult offender, it is the equivalent of an entire summer vacation for a youth, a very long period of time. Because juveniles are more dependent on their parents, removal from home is a more severe punishment than it would be for adults. Thus, sentencing adults and
juveniles to similar terms for similar offenses would be unjust.

Shorter sentences for reduced responsibility is a more modest rationale
for treating young people differently than the rehabilitative justifications
advanced by the Progressive child savers. Adult courts could impose shorter
sentences for reduced culpability on a discretionary basis, although it would
be preferable for a legislature explicitly to provide youths with categorical
fractional reductions of adult sentences. This could take the form of a formal "youth discount" at sentencing. For example, a fourteen-year-old might
receive 33 percent of the adult penalty, a sixteen-year-old 66 percent, and
an eighteen-year-old the full penalty. A proposal for explicit fractional reductions in youth sentences can only be made against the backdrop of realistic, humane, and determinate adult sentencing practices in which "real-
time" sentences can be determined. Several of the "serious juvenile offender"

r "designated felony" sentencing statutes provide terms for serious young ffenders that are considerably shorter than sentences for their adult counerparts. For youths below the age of fourteen, the common-law infancy nens rea defense would acquire new vitality for proportionally shorter senences or even noncriminal dispositions.

A graduated age/culpability sentencing scheme could avoid some of the nconsistency and injustice associated with the binary either/or juvenile ver-,us adult sentencing played out in judicial waiver proceedings. Depending n whether transfer is ordered, the sentences that youths receive can differ y orders of magnitude. Because of the differences in consequences, trans-er hearings consume a disproportionate amount of juvenile court time and nergy. Abolishing juvenile courts would eliminate the need for transfer earings, save considerable resources which are ultimately expended to no urpose, eliminate the punishment gap that occurs when youths make the ransition between systems, and assure similar consequences to similar of-enders.

Trying young people in criminal courts with full procedural safeguards vould not especially diminish judges' expertise about appropriate disposiions for young people. The Progressives envisioned a specialized juvenile ourt judge who possessed the wisdom of a kadi. Increasingly, however, dis-rict court judges handle juvenile matters as part of their general docket or otate through juvenile court on short-term assignments without acquiring ny particular juvenile dispositional expertise. Even in specialized juvenile ourts, the information necessary for appropriate dispositions resides with he court services personnel who advise the judge on sentences, rather than vith the court itself. Even if criminally convicted, court services personnel dvise the judge as to the appropriate sentence, and, within the time limits lefined by the offense, young offenders could be transferred to a family court r social services agency if a welfare disposition is appropriate.

Even a punitive sentence does not require incarcerating juveniles in dult jails and prisons. The existing detention facilities, training schools, and nstitutions provide the option of age-segregated dispositional facilities. Moreover, insisting explicitly on humane conditions of confinement could do t least as much to improve the lives of incarcerated youths as has the "right o treatment" or the "rehabilitative ideal." A recognition that most young offenders will return to society imposes an obligation to provide the re-sources for self-improvement on a voluntary basis.

2. *Procedural Justice* Since *Gault*, many of the formal procedural attrib-utes of criminal courts are routine aspects of juvenile justice administration as well. The same laws apply to arresting adults and taking juveniles into custody, to searches, and to pretrial identification procedures. Juveniles charged with felony offenses now are routinely subjected to similar finger-printing and booking procedures. The greater procedural formality and ad-versary nature of the juvenile court reflects the merger of the court's ther-

apeutic mission and its social control functions. The many instances in which states choose to treat juvenile offenders procedurally like adult criminal defendants, even when formal equality redounds to their disadvantage, is one aspect of this process.

Differentials in age and competency suggest that youths should receive more protections than adults, rather than less. The rationales to sentence juveniles differently than adults also justify providing them with *all* of the procedural safeguards adults receive *and* additional protections that recognize their immaturity. This dual-maximal strategy would provide enhanced protection for children explicitly because of their vulnerability and immaturity.

One example where this dual-maximal procedural strategy would produce different results is waivers of Fifth and Sixth Amendment constitutional rights. Although the Supreme Court in *Gault* noted that the appointment of counsel is the prerequisite to procedural justice, *Gault*'s promise of counsel remains unrealized because many judges find that youths waived their rights in a "knowing, intelligent, and voluntary" manner under the "totality of the circumstances." A system of justice that recognizes the disabilities of youths would prohibit waivers of the right to counsel or the privilege against self-incrimination without prior consultation with counsel. The right to counsel would attach as soon as a juvenile is taken into custody and would be self-invoking; it would not require a juvenile affirmatively to request counsel as is the case for adults. The presence and availability of counsel throughout the process would assure that juveniles' rights are respected and implemented. This is the policy that the Juvenile Justice Standards propose, albeit in a juvenile court setting.

Full procedural parity in criminal courts, coupled with alternative legislative safeguards for children, can provide the same or greater protections than does the current juvenile court. Expunging criminal records and eliminating collateral civil disabilities following the successful completion of a sentence could afford equivalent relief for an isolated youthful folly as does the juvenile court's confidentiality.

Abolishing the juvenile court would force a long overdue and critical reassessment of the entire social construct of "childhood." As long as young people are regarded as fundamentally different from adults, it becomes too easy to rationalize and justify a procedurally inferior justice system. The gap between the quality of justice afforded juveniles and adults can be conveniently rationalized on the grounds that "after all, they are only children," and children are entitled only to custody, not liberty. So long as the view prevails that juvenile court intervention is "benign" coercion and that in any event children should not expect more, youths will continue to receive "the worst of both worlds."

But issues of procedure and substance, while important, focus too narrowly on the legal domain. The ideology of therapeutic justice and its discretionary apparatus persist because the social control is directed at chilren. Despite humanitarian claims of being a child-centered nation, our cultural and legal conceptions of children support institutional arrangements that deny the personhood of young people. A new purpose for the juvenile court cannot be formulated successfully without critically reassessing the meaning of "childhood" and creating social institutions to assure the welfare of the next generation.

Leaving Bad Enough Alone: A Response to the Juvenile Court Abolitionists

IRENE MERKER ROSENBERG

Throughout my legal career, I have been an unabashed reformer and a fervent advocate of children's rights, decrying the diminished constitutional protection and inadequate treatment afforded minors accused of crime in juvenile court. Now, however, I find myself in the awkward and uncomfortable position of arguing to preserve the status quo—albeit with improvements—in the world of juvenile court injustice. Although this gives me considerable pause, it does not change my mind: I do not believe that it would be wise to abolish the delinquency jurisdiction and try children as criminals in the adult court, as recently urged by several commentators, most notably Professor Barry Feld.

I am writing because the question of abolition has gone beyond mere academic discussion. Professor Feld's proposal to eliminate the delinquency jurisdiction was the focus of a session of the Criminal Justice Section of the American Bar Association at the Association's 1992 annual meeting. Debate under the auspices of such a large, mainstream, practice-oriented organization suggests that the abolitionist proposal is being viewed as a serious option. Moreover, liberal advocacy of criminal court as a solution to the lack of constitutional safeguards within the juvenile justice system may mesh with rumblings on the right that it is imperative to stop juvenile court coddling of young criminals and instead to impose harsh punishment. What better place to do so than the adult criminal court? The abolitionist proposal may thus attract strange but powerful bedfellows, which could result in its political acceptance. I am concerned therefore that the well-intentioned abolitionists may be in danger of achieving their goal, providing grist for the

Excerpted from "Leaving Bad Enough Alone: A Response to the Juvenile Court Abolitionists" by Irene Merker Rosenberg in *Wisconsin Law Review*, pp. 163–185 (1993). Copyright 1993 by The Board of Regents of the University of Wisconsin System. Reprinted by permission of Wisconsin Law Review.

adage that one should be careful about what one prays for, because the prayer may be granted. . . .

Before deciding whether to abandon the juvenile courts, two basic questions must be addressed: (1) is the disparity in procedural and constitutional protection between the adult and juvenile courts significant enough to justify opting out of the juvenile justice system; and (2) if children are tried in the criminal courts, will their immaturity and vulnerability be taken into account adequately in assessing culpability and determining sentences? In my view, the answers to these questions are no and no.

First, the abolitionists claim that there is a significant disparity between the constitutional and procedural rights afforded adults charged with crime and children charged with delinquency. In my opinion, these differences are not as substantial as they appear to be, or at least not substantial enough to be a basis for giving up on the juvenile justice system. The conceded inequality in safeguards should not blind us to the incremental changes over the years that have benefitted children. The *Gault* line of cases does give alleged delinquents significant constitutional protection. Indeed, in cases such as *In re Winship* and *Breed v. Jones*, applying the reasonable doubt standard and the double jeopardy requirement to delinquency adjudicatory proceedings, the Supreme Court treated delinquency and adult criminal trials as functionally equivalent for purposes of the implicated constitutional guarantees. . . .

To be sure, in *Schall v. Martin*, which upheld a vague preventive detention law for alleged delinquents, the Court made much of the differences between children and adults, and used these distinctions as a basis for giving children less constitutional protection. The *Schall* holding clearly allowed the state substantial leeway in detaining minors accused of crime and reinvigorated a constricted due process methodology for ascertaining the rights of alleged delinquents. Yet, in the end *Schall* was simply a prelude to the Court's decision in *United States v. Salerno*, rejecting substantive due process and Eighth Amendment challenges to the federal preventive detention statute governing adults. Thus, notwithstanding *Schall's* emphatic pronouncement that children are entitled to custody rather than liberty, *Salerno*, which relies on *Schall*, puts adults in roughly the same position as far as preventive detention is concerned.

The major setback for juveniles was denial of the right to a jury trial in *McKeiver v. Pennsylvania*. As Professor Ainsworth has noted, in the insular world of the juvenile courts, a jury is necessary to protect children from oppression by the government and to assure more accurate and impartial fact-finding. I do not, however, view the loss of even this right as catastrophic. After all, there are relatively few jury trials in the adult criminal court. Instead, the right to trial by jury is primarily a chip to be used in the poker game of plea bargaining—a game of far greater seriousness in the adult courts, where the sentencing stakes, at least for serious offenses, are much higher. Nonetheless, denial of the jury trial to juveniles as a matter f federal constitutional law is significant. One way of dealing with the problem is state law reform. In fact, a number of states already grant juveniles such a right as a matter of state law, and the "New Federalism" is an opportunity for advocates to push for jury trials in juvenile courts. . . .

In determining whether to abandon the juvenile courts because of the disparity in protection, it is also necessary to make a realistic assessment of the constitutional safeguards available in the criminal courts. The Burger and Rehnquist Courts have, after all, taken their toll. Much of *Miranda* has been eviscerated, and the Fourth Amendment and the exclusionary rule are being severely constricted. If children are tried in the criminal courts, they will receive only this diluted constitutional protection, and since minors are less likely to invoke their rights and more likely to waive them, effectively they will still receive less protection than adults. While it is true that the latest Supreme Court decisions give juveniles little more than the right to fundamental fairness, that also is just about all the Justices are now affording to adult defendants. Even the revered Sixth Amendment right to counsel, deemed essential for safeguarding all the other guarantees in the Bill of Rights, is very much under attack.

In addition, this low level of constitutional protection granted to adults is available only theoretically. Nationwide, approximately 90% of defendants plead guilty. A series of Supreme Court decisions establishes that if a defendant does plead guilty, almost all antecedent constitutional violations are waived. So even if children were tried in the criminal courts where they would be entitled to the same guarantees as adults, it is just as likely, if not more so, that they would join the vast majority of their older counterparts who waive such protection to secure the purported benefit of a reduced sentence. In any event, do we really want the child's fate to be determined on an ad hoc basis by individual prosecutors and defense attorneys pursuant to plea bargaining, rather than by a juvenile court judge who has at least some obligation to act in the youth's best interest?

It seems to me that underlying the views of the abolitionists, at least unconsciously, is a somewhat idealized or romanticized vision of adult courts in which the criminal guarantees of the Bill of Rights are meaningfully enforced. Yes, there is a right to trial by jury that is missing in the juvenile court unless supplied by state law. Yes, there is a right to counsel that, as Professor Feld has pointed out, is too often denied in practice in juvenile court. And I surely would not denigrate either of these important safeguards. At the same time, however, the reality of adult criminal proceedings is crowded courtrooms in which justice is dispensed through waivers and pleas negotiated by defense attorneys who are often less than zealous and well-prepared advocates, and in which racism is at least as much a fact of life as in juvenile court. For the most part, the typical criminal court in urban areas is a harsh, tough, mean institution cranking out pleas, with few pauses for individualized attention. It is no place for an adult defendant to be, much less a child. Given such an environment in the criminal courts, will children really perceive the criminal justice process as fairer than the juvenile courts, as Professor Ainsworth has suggested?

Initially, perhaps there would be a burst of concern for the kiddie defendants. But once the glow wore off, and that would not take long, it would be back to business as usual: treadmill processing for adults both over and under the age of eighteen. Let us face it: As bad as the juvenile courts are, the adult criminal courts are worse. Adding a new class of defendants to an already overburdened system can only exacerbate the situation, all to the detriment of children.

That brings me to the second question. Professor Feld and other abolitionists believe that if children are tried in criminal court, rationales will be developed to give them special protection in ascertaining guilt and punishment. While I agree that is what children should get, I am not so sure that is what they will get. This looks a lot like having your cake and eating it too, a difficult request to be making in these hard-nosed, law-and-order times. On the one hand, the abolitionists are asking that children be treated as adults in order to secure equal constitutional guarantees, and on the other, they are asking that children be treated as children in order to protect their unique disabilities. While it is true that taking competency differentials of juveniles into account is simply a means of attaining parity with adults, skeptical legislators may consider these demands internally inconsistent. Thus, although Professor Ainsworth argues that, according to social science research, "the adult-child distinction is a false dichotomy that can no longer support disparate justice systems," she also asserts that after abolition youth will continue to be viewed as a mitigating factor in adult court sentencing. But assuming such a "false dichotomy," puzzled legislators and judges might be pardoned for asking why youth should then be a basis for more lenient punishment.

If states are unwilling to give minors enhanced constitutional and procedural protection when they are within the supposedly benevolent confines of the juvenile court, why would they do so in the criminal court? Bringing children within the criminal jurisdiction is an assertion by the state that minors do not deserve specialized treatment. While it is true that the state will no longer have the bogus rehabilitation argument as a basis for diminishing constitutional protection, the state may argue that because it has elected to treat children and adults the same, there is no reason to give youngsters enhanced safeguards. . . .

Nor in my opinion do the capital sentencing cases involving teenagers, on which Barry Feld relies, lend strong constitutional support for shorter sentences for young people. In *Thompson v. Oklahoma*, the Supreme Court did reverse a fifteen-year-old's death sentence for murder, but the decision was very circumscribed. The opinion stressed that all states had laws designating the maximum age for juvenile court jurisdiction at no less than sixteen, viewing this fact as evidence that fifteen-year-olds are not mature enough to assume adult responsibilities. In addition, only a plurality held

at executing those who were fifteen at the time they committed a capital
fense violated the Eighth Amendment. Casting the fifth vote, Justice
'Connor concurred in the judgment on the narrow grounds that a large ma-
rity of the states prohibited capital punishment for fifteen-year-olds, that
) legislature had made a considered judgment that fifteen-year-olds should
e subject to the death penalty, and that Oklahoma had not made an explicit
olicy choice that such juveniles be executed. She went on to note that,
granting the plurality's other premise—that adolescents are generally less
lameworthy than adults who commit similar crimes—it does not necessar-
y follow that all 15-year-olds are incapable of the moral culpability that
ould justify the imposition of capital punishment."

The very next year, the Supreme Court upheld executions of sixteen
nd seventeen-year-olds, observing that at common law the rebuttable pre-
imption of infancy theoretically would have permitted capital punishment
) be imposed on anyone over the age of seven. The Court concluded that a
aajority of the states authorize capital punishment for sixteen-year-olds,
nd that consequently there was no national consensus that executing such
dolescents was inhumane. . . .

At bottom, Professor Feld seems to believe that, even if the nation's
ighest court shows no mercy, state legislatures will be less Draconian. I
link his position is problematic. If states are willing to deprive children of
onstitutional protection and keep them in appalling facilities that provide
either care nor rehabilitation, why should we assume that they will do any
etter if juveniles are treated as adults? In this regard, my Texas may be
tore representative of the country than Barry Feld's progressive Min-
esota. Five years ago, seeking a middle-ground alternative to treating mi-
ors either as delinquents within the juvenile court jurisdiction or as adults
aived over to criminal court, Texas passed a determinate sentencing law
ubjecting children ten to sixteen years of age to sentences of up to forty
ears in prison if they are charged with committing one of six designated
lonies. The children are tried in juvenile court and if convicted can be sen-
nced to the Texas Youth Council until age eighteen, at which time a hear-
g is held in juvenile court to decide if they will be retained within the
venile correctional system for their minority or sent to the Texas De-
artment of Corrections to complete their determinate sentences. The leg-
lature was careful to give such children almost all the same guarantees as
dult defendants, including the equivalent of a grand jury indictment. Thus
r, all challenges based on federal and state law have failed.

If the legislature is willing to authorize forty-year sentences for ten-
ear-olds within the juvenile court system, what will it do to them if they
re tried at the outset in the criminal court? At least within the present
amework, there is the possibility the child will remain within the jurisdic-
ion of the juvenile authorities and perhaps be released on parole. If the orig-
1al proceeding were held in criminal court, however, there would be no such
ption. Barry Feld sees the Texas law and others like it, which impose pun-

ishment based on the nature of the particular offense committed rather than the needs of the child, as evidence that the juvenile courts are virtually as punitive as criminal courts and therefore should be abandoned. I see such laws as an omen that there is surely worse to come if children are thrown into the adult jurisdiction.

If children are tried as adults, and convicted, they presumably will be subject to the jurisdiction of adult correctional authorities rather than youth services agencies, which are at least to some extent child-oriented. Sometimes I think we forget how terrible the prison facilities for adult criminals in this country are. As Justice Brennan has noted, "individual prisons or entire prison systems in at least 24 states have been declared unconstitutional under the Eighth and Fourteenth Amendments, with litigation underway in many others." In Texas, lawsuits were filed against both the Texas Department of Corrections and the Texas Youth Council. Both cases were heard in federal district court before Judge William Wayne Justice, and orders prohibiting various practices were entered. It is not too much of an exaggeration to say that Judge Justice was in charge of both the Texas adult and juvenile correction systems for the past two decades. His stark findings of fact in these proceedings have captured very effectively the horrors of both systems. Recently Judge Justice delivered a talk at the University of Houston Law Center on the origins of the Department of Corrections suit. I asked him which facilities were worse, the ones for children or those for adults. Without a moment's hesitation, he said that the adult facilities were worse.

Abandoning the juvenile court is an admission that its humane purposes were misguided or unattainable. I do not believe that. We should stay and fight—fight for a reordering of societal resources, one that will protect and nourish children. For example, Mark Soler of the Youth Law Center in San Francisco, has argued that the juvenile court must be re-imagined so as to focus on the child's dispositional needs, making the court serve a coordinating function that assures the provision of a wide range of services that benefit the child. Other commentators stress the need for enhanced constitutional and procedural protection in the adjudicative stage of the proceedings. These differing goals are not inconsistent. We can and should seek both procedural and dispositional reform in the juvenile courts.

Despite all their failings, of which there are many, the juvenile courts do afford benefits that are unlikely to be replicated in the criminal courts, such as the institutionalized intake diversionary system, anonymity, diminished stigma, shorter sentences, and recognition of rehabilitation as a viable goal. We should build on these strengths rather than abandon ship.

It is important to take into account both the chimerical quality of enhanced constitutional safeguards in the criminal courts and the significant benefits afforded to minors even by the existing juvenile justice system, before relegating children to criminal courts and prisons with no guarantee that their immaturity will be adequately considered or their vulnerability meaningfully protected.

Printed in the United States
121646LV00001B/32/A